AF600322

EX-
SOVIETS
IN
ISRAEL

EX-SOVIETS IN ISRAEL

FROM PERSONAL NARRATIVES TO A GROUP PORTRAIT

Larisa Fialkova and
Maria N. Yelenevskaya

WAYNE STATE UNIVERSITY PRESS
Detroit

11 10 09 08 07 5 4 3 2 1

Library of Congress Cataloging-in-Publication Data

Fialkova, L. L.
Ex-Soviets in Israel : from personal narratives to a group portrait / Larisa Fialkova and Maria N. Yelenevskaya.
p. cm. — (Ralph Patai series in Jewish folklore and anthropology)
Includes bibliographical references and index.
ISBN-13: 978-0-8143-3169-9 (hardcover : alk. paper)
ISBN-10: 0-8143-3169-6 (hardcover : alk. paper)
1. Jews, Soviet—Israel—Folklore. 2. Immigrants—Soviet Union—Folklore.
3. Jews, Soviet—Israel—Interviews. 4. Jews, Soviet—Israel—Identity. 5. Jews, Soviet—Cultural assimilation—Israel. 6. Israel—Ethnic relations.
I. Yelenevskaya, Maria N. II. Title.
GR98F525 2007
398.2089240947—dc22
2007001694

∞ The paper used in this publication meets the minimum requirements of the American National Standard for Information Sciences—

Designed by Elizabeth Pilon
Typeset by Maya Rhodes
Composed in Trump Medieval and Formata Condensed

Science is always autobiographical.

Jan Blommaert and Jef Verschueren

CONTENTS

PREFACE

Our interest in the study of the folk culture of the Soviet immigrants to Israel had begun before we first met at a conference where each of us presented a paper on the cultural aspects of immigration. Encouraged by the audience's interest in the evolution of folk culture in a period of transition, we embarked on a study of the personal narratives of Soviet immigrants to Israel. Intuition told us that we had found an exciting research topic. But the depth of the gold mine that we had tapped into dawned on us only later. Our attempt to create a collective portrait of former Soviet citizens in Israel made us look into their cultural heritage and trace its influence on the emergence of the new cultural tradition. Ethnography and folklore of the Soviet Jews remain under-researched. The sweeping changes in the former Soviet Union (FSU) in the 1990s and the mass exodus of the Soviet Jews make it urgent to document ethnographic and folkloric materials linked to the life of Jews in the USSR. Equally interesting is the study of modifications in the "traditional" culture of Soviet Jews when transplanted into a new society. Our purpose was to write an engaging book about the influence of culture on individuals and about the recreation of culture by individuals. If the reader finishes this book with empathy for immigrant life and a desire to read more about the contemporary folk culture of the former "Soviets," our work will not have been in vain.

Much of the material presented in this book has appeared in a preliminary form in ten articles and sixteen conference presentations. The gradual extension of the analyzed corpus (we continued interviewing people and monitoring media until the very last stage of the project) required a major overhaul of all the subject matter presented previously. It has been extensively revised and rearranged to suit a more general argument. In addition, we took into account criticism and suggestions by anonymous reviewers. All the articles based on the materials of this project appear in the bibliography.

ACKNOWLEDGMENTS

We are grateful to the University of Haifa and the Technion-Israel Institute of Technology for awarding us a one-year grant promoting joint research by the academic staff of these two institutions and to the Research Authority of the University of Haifa for encouraging grant awarded to Larisa Fialkova. We wish to thank our research assistants, Ludmila Turovsky and Irina Reznikova, for their meticulous preparation of two-thirds of the transcripts of the interview audio recordings. We are indebted to Edna Heichal, former academic coordinator of the Dov Noy Israeli Folktale Archives (IFA) at the University of Haifa for clarifications on Jewish folklore and Israeli cultural matters. We thank Murray Rosovsky for his editorial assistance. We have greatly benefited from comments and insights of colleagues who listened to our conference presentations and read our articles, in particular, Prof. Dan Ben-Amos, Prof. Haya Bar-Itzhak, Prof. Svetlana Tolstaya, Dr. Olga Belova, Prof. Larissa Naiditch, Judy Levy, and Stella Rozhinskaya. We also owe many thanks to Stella Rozhinskaya for the patience with which she helped us harness our rebellious computers. We are grateful to University of Haifa students Hanna Shmulian, Svetlana Berenshtein, Marina El-Kayam, Christina Barzahian, Alina Sanina, Laura Abramov, and Hanny Manheim, who conducted twenty-two interviews and placed them at our disposal for analysis. We are deeply indebted to all our informants, who generously shared their memories and stories with us and without whose participation in the project this book would not have seen light. Finally our thanks go to our family members Isanna Likhtenshtein, Lev Fialkov, Lilia Dashevskaya, János Makowsky, and Zenaida Turaeva. In the five years we were occupied with the project they all showed loyal support and acted as sympathetic listeners and competent consultants.

A NOTE ON TRANSLITERATION AND TRANSLATION

Throughout the book we have used the U.S. Library of Congress transliteration system for Russian proper and geographic names. Translation of all the excerpts from the interviews is our own. Though some passages sound awkward, we made a decision not to edit them so as to retain the specific features of oral narration and each storyteller's individual style. We also preserved instances of code-switching, and we italicized Hebrew and English insertions in the excerpts from the interviews.

Introduction

This book is a study of personal-experience stories in which Israelis from the former Soviet Union (FSU) relate their immigration experiences. It was conceived as a culture study that focuses on people and their thoughts, memories, and feelings, rather than on artifacts such as magazines, films, or academic books (Billig 1997, 205), though the latter are used as additional sources. Culture studies are multidisciplinary, and this book draws on literature in the fields of folklore, anthropology, linguistics, social psychology, sociology, political science, and geography. We are concerned with both the general problems of migration and the issues relevant specifically to the Israeli experience.

The closing years of the USSR and the first post-Soviet decade saw an unprecedented rise in emigration. Although different immigrant policies in various countries dictate different integration strategies to newcomers, the Soviet past continues to influence the worldview of individuals and behavioral patterns of immigrant groups, whether ethnic Russians, Ukrainians, Jews, Germans, or Greeks. Depending on the immigrants' ethnicity, receiving societies divide former Soviets into repatriates and immigrants.[1] Repatriates are expected to integrate rapidly and easily thanks to common ethnic and cultural roots. Various studies, however, prove these expectations wrong. The Israeli sociologists Shuval and Leshem (1998) compared migrations of dispersed Jews and Germans to Israel and Germany. They concluded that while in both countries the immigrants were ethnically identical to the host population, their basic Jewish or German identities were overlaid with other ethnic identities associated with the cultures and countries where they had lived before emigrating (14). Moreover, psychologists, sociologists, and educators find that while FSU immigrants are considerably different from newcomers from other countries, they display the same patterns of adaptation and acculturation and suffer from similar social problems wherever they settle.[2] In Israel the FSU immigration of the 1990s has had a profound impact on society and accounts for an explosion of literature devoted to the former Soviets. Like their colleagues in other countries, Israeli social scientists find the term *immigrants* more fitting than *repatriates* in reference to the Soviet Jews of the last wave.

The previous wave of immigration from the USSR was relatively short: the peak lasted from 1971 to 1973. This was a period when Soviet Jews could choose to immigrate to the United States, Canada, or Israel, and it is widely believed that only the most ideologically motivated and Zionist-oriented opted for Israel. In the 1970s the decision to leave the country was a critical point in the lives of Soviets, one that could jeopardize the whole family, including those who stayed behind. Many applicants were refused exit visas. Moreover, some applicants lost their jobs and were imprisoned if they were reported as participating in political activities. The decision to emigrate was risky and required courage. Israeli sociologists consider the integration of the wave of the 1970s to have been fairly smooth and successful. Even if not all members of this group aspired to political, business, or academic careers, they managed to find their niche as professionals: engineers, teachers, and doctors (Kimmerling 2001, 140–41; Reznitskaia 2004). But some Russian-speaking social scientists and journalists do not agree with this essentially positive assessment. They claim that a large proportion of the immigrants of the 1970s failed to attain the level of Hebrew proficiency necessary to embark on a new career. Many intellectuals left Israel, while others remained on the periphery of Israeli society (Isakova 2004).

The new mass immigration from the FSU in the 1990s became a test for immigrants of the 1970s. Some of them resented the latest newcomers as competitors and criticized them for their continued loyalty to the culture of their country of origin; others were happy to welcome compatriots with a shared past. Moreover, for many the new wave of immigration signified a reunion with family or old friends from whom they had been separated for more than two decades. The immigrants of the 1990s were themselves divided in their attitudes toward the old-timers: some found new friendships; others were jealous of the benefits the state had given to them in the 1970s. Today, fifteen years after the beginning of the last immigration wave, it is obvious that the two groups are more similar than it might seem. More obscure than their successors, the immigrants of the 1970s established the institutional and cultural infrastructure that was expanded and enriched in the 1990s. Furthermore, children of the immigrants of the 1970s, who had often been ashamed of their links to Russia, suddenly discovered the benefits of speaking Russian and being familiar with the culture of their parents and grandparents. This proved a boon for maintaining personal as well as professional networks (Remennick 2004).

Unlike their predecessors in the 1970s, FSU immigrants of the 1990s can maintain contact with their relatives and friends who stayed behind, and the tourist traffic in both directions is heavy. Electronic technologies give immigrants access to the media in Russia, and the establishment of diplomatic relations between Israel and the countries of the FSU has encouraged trade and cultural and scientific exchange. Immigrants develop multiple identities as the interactions of home and host societies become more intense. As a result, FSU immigrants today are considered to be part of the transnational migration flow (Markowitz 1995; Fialkova 2005c; Fialkova and Yelenevskaya 2005; Yelenevskaya 2005; Remennick 2002c).

Mass migration processes of the 1990s have also sparked the interest of the Russian scientific community in their former compatriots. This is not surprising: in the last decade alone, some 8 or 9 million migrants from the FSU settled in the United States, Canada, Europe, and Israel (Khrustaleva 2001b, 27). While even in the recent past emigrants from the FSU were regarded as separate ethnic groups, today there is a tendency to study them first of all as Rossiiskaia diaspora[3] (Iontsev et al. 2001; Lebedeva 1997; Levin 2001a, 2001b; Makhovskaia et al. 2001; Savoskul 2001; Tishkov 2001a, 2003). Since members of immigrant communities dispersed throughout the world remain psychologically and culturally Russian, the government and the public came to realize that they should not be dismissed as valuable human resources for Russia.

Many immigrant scientists integrated by the host countries' academia also focus on the FSU immigrants of the last decade. They study immigrant communities from within and function as a mediating link between the receiving society and newcomers (see e.g., papers by Russian-speaking Israelis Dymerskaya-Tsigelman, Epstein, Feldman, Kheimets, Naiditch, Remennick, Rotenberg, Zilberg, etc.). Their studies usually go beyond investigations of the in-group because they inevitably touch upon the peculiarities of the society and culture of the old and new countries. Despite common interests, Western social scientists seldom have access to burgeoning Russian literature on immigration; likewise, their Russian colleagues are only now beginning to discover Western immigration studies. Although the Cold War is over, there is still little interaction between the two communities, and immigrant researchers, including the authors of this book, try to bridge this gap.

Receiving new immigrants has been part and parcel of Israeli life since the foundation of the state. Though the country has accumulated valuable experience in dealing with immigrants from every corner of the world, adjustment and adaptation of individuals and immigrant groups remains the focus of the Israeli scientific community and the general public. In the spring of 2000 the Israeli mass media covered the arrival of the one millionth immigrant from the FSU. While the Israeli Ministry of Immigrant Absorption cites a more modest number—835,410 FSU immigrants between 1989 and 1999—this remains the biggest immigration wave from a single country in Israel's history. Integration of Soviet Jews triggered the Israeli scientific community's interest and became the subject of studies in sociology, psychology, anthropology, education, and linguistics.

To a large extent, an immigrant group's success in integration depends on the attitude of the receiving society. Mass immigration of Soviet Jews to Israel had been long expected and desired not only for ideological and sentimental reasons but for instrumental reasons. Politicians hoped that the new wave would serve to preserve the Jewish majority over the fast-growing Arab population, thus helping to maintain power in the settlements and strengthen security. Kimmerling (2001) quotes the slogan invented to persuade Israeli taxpayers to make sacrifices for the sake of the newcomers: "From immigrant to immigrant, our strength is rising" (139–40).[4] Sure enough, in the late 1980s and the very early 1990s veteran Israelis gave a warm welcome and a helping hand to the newcomers (see Yelenevskaya and Fialkova 2005, 156–58). But the enthusiasm dissipated fairly quickly when it became clear that 1990s immigrants were highly competitive on the job market (see the demographic profile of the subjects in chapter 1) and aspired to occupy a socioeconomic position at least as high as it had been in their country of origin. The intellectual elite of Israeli society, however, refused to accept Russian-speaking intellectuals as equals, which some researchers believe contributed to the formation of an almost autonomous cultural enclave (see, e.g., Al-Haj 2004, 109–10). The abundance of non-Jews among émigrés of the 1990s is a never-ending topic, and negative stereotypes of "the Russians," emphasizing their otherness, are widely used in informal and formal discourse. Among the pejorative labels given to the immigrants are pork-eaters, sausage aliya, AIDS-carriers, alcoholics, Mafiosi, prostitutes, parasites, and even Bolsheviks (Prilutskii 2003). A wide repertoire of "anti-Russian" jokes reinforces these stereotypes (see Golden 2003, 161–62). Particularly humiliating for the immigrant group is the claim that prostitution is one of the most widespread professions among "Russian" women (see Fialkova 2005a; Golden 2003; Lemish 2000).

Materials found in the mass media intensify distrust of "Russians" among the general public. Media stereotyping of immigrants is so pervasive that it was put on the agenda of the Knesset Committee for Aliya and Absorption. The committee was presented with a report on the coverage of the life of Russian-speaking Israelis on the two most popular TV channels. During the nineteen weeks of monitoring, only 60 out of 3,000 news items dealt with "Russians," including news replays. Most of those items dwelled on politicians of "Russian" origin, criminals, and couples unable to marry in Israel because of Halachic (Jewish law) problems. On the other hand, the report testified to an abundance of "Russian" images in comedy and satirical programs (Kogan 2004; Yelenevskaya and Fialkova 2005, 142).

Stereotypes are often internalized by laypeople, and also by politicians, whose decisions influence immigrants in various aspects of life. In the mid-1990s the then minister of labor and social security, Ora Namir, publicly complained about the high percentage of elderly and sick, as well as criminals and prostitutes, among the emigrants from the FSU. Another scandal erupted in the media in 2004, when the chairperson of the Knesset Committee for Aliya and Absorption, Colette Avital, pushed for new legislation that would test whether potential immigrants were prone to drinking and using drugs. Russian-speaking Knesset members protested against this initiative, and it was voted down (Mirskii 2004). These and other incidents only harm relations between the veterans and the immigrants.

The authors of this book initiated systematic study of the folklore of the former Soviets. The only other attempt to discover the mythology of the former Soviet Jews in Israel was made by Jeter and Gerasimova (1998), who in 1992 pioneered the topic and conducted informal interviews with immigrants of the last wave. The researchers' goal was to find the images and mythology that had inspired their subjects to immigrate to Israel. To their surprise, the stories they recorded did not reveal any associations with the Bible or Jewish folklore. Could their failure have been caused by a misconception? After all, they looked only for traditional forms of folklore, specifically Jewish legends about the Promised Land.[5] Our material shows that the mythology of the Soviet Jews in Israel is in the making and presents a collage of different cultural and folk traditions—Slavic, Soviet, Jewish, and Muslim. This seeming eclecticism is not accidental, as immigrant cultures are cultures in transition. Their characteristic feature is not stability but fluidity, a constant recombination of old and newly created cultural expressions.

The importance of myths in every society, including the postmodern secular and technocratic cultures, cannot be overestimated. As Pearce and Kang (1987) point out, myth asks four questions: Who am I? Who are we? What is the nature of the world we live in? What is the nature of the answers to these questions? These questions correspond to the academic topics of psychology, natural science, and epistemology (31). Mythology has not lost relevance for the study of contemporary cultures. Lévi-Strauss (1963) argues that there are no qualitative differences between the working processes of the so-called primitive mind and scientific thought: their logic is the same, while the difference lies in the nature of the things to which the intellectual process is applied (230). Ricoeur (1967) emphasizes the role of myth in encouraging gnosis and as an antidote to distress (165, 167–68). This latter characteristic of mythmaking is particularly important for the study of immigrant narratives because immigration experiences are inseparable from stress, anxiety, and insecurity.

Soviet immigrants of the 1990s make up approximately one-sixth of Israel's total population and have changed its cultural scene. While strikingly uniform in its political, economic, and social systems, the former USSR boasted a diversity of geographical zones, cultural traditions, and languages. Jews resided in big industrial cities, in mountainous areas of the Caucasus, in Central Asia, and even in settlements on the tundra and in the Far East. They lived side by side with Christians of different denominations and with Muslims. They spoke various languages and dialects, although Russian was the mother tongue of most. As a result of urbanization, the policy of massive secularization, and the propaganda of international brotherhood (which began in the early Soviet period), intermarriage became commonplace. Naturally, close contacts with other ethnicities and cultures had an impact on the identity of several generations of Soviet Jews coming from different areas; consequently, the patterns of their adaptation to life in Israel differ depending on their previous experience. These differences emerge from the in-depth interviews with the immigrants that form the basis of this book.

Personal Narrative as a Multi-genre Discourse

Life-history research is becoming increasingly popular among sociologists, psychologists, anthropologists, and folklorists. First, according to Niedermüller (1988), it has become the most important instrument of the phenomenology of everyday life and culture, which are objectivized in the form of a narrative (463). Second, individual life stories help us understand general social processes. Their meaning is based on both the individual experience and the ideology of the social group (see, e.g., Atkinson 1998, 70; Bertaux 1981, 44; Brown 1990, 260–61). Finally, the democratization of the social sciences makes researchers focus on an individual as an active participant of research, rather than its passive object whose voice does not reach the audience (R. Miller 2000, 5; Fine et al. 2000, 120; Christians 2000, 138).

In folkloristics the evolution from the general to the individual began in the 1920s. When the systematic collection of folklore started in the second half of the eighteenth century the emphasis was on texts; narrators were perceived as mere transmitters of the tradition. Folklorists recorded their brief biographic sketches without analyzing the complex interactions between concepts of folk culture and local customs and personal values and beliefs. Only in 1925 did the Russian folklorist Azadovskii make a Siberian narrator the primary "heroine" of the Verkholensk[6] tales (see Azadovskii 1974). Von Sydow took the next step in 1934 when he introduced the term *memorates* to denote the genre of personal-experience stories (see Sydow 1977). His work launched the study of both the personal narrative (short, single-episodic tales built on real events and transformed by people's fantasy) and the life history (multi-episodic family tales).

Yet, as late as in the 1970s folklorists still could not agree on whether the personal narrative was an appropriate object of folkloristics and whether it represented an autonomous genre, a subgenre, or a system of genres (see Dégh and Vázsonyi 1974; Honko 1964; Stahl 1977a, 1977b). Nevertheless, personal narratives are so widespread in modern culture that folklorists could not afford to ignore them. Stahl (1989) undertook a comprehensive description of the personal narrative. She defines it as "prose narrative relating a personal experience; it is usually told in the first person, and its content is non-traditional." Stahl singles out two primary features of the genre: the relative stability of these stories in the narrator's repertoire and the overlapping of the roles of the primary character and the storyteller in one personality (12–13, 20, 23). In the 1990s, folklorists developed Stahl's ideas by analyzing the role of the self and the interaction of the self with others. Thus Brown (1990) shows that the act of narration itself is part of the process of self-creation and self-interpretation (258–59). Wilson (2000) contends that even though "I" is the primary "hero," almost all personal-experience stories are populated by other characters as well, and the self is linked to a community of others (8). Narratives function as a changeable form of mediation between the individual and culture. Folklorists' interviews contain stories elicited in dyadic or group interaction that may be part of a person's stable repertoire about certain events or people and yet appear as spontaneous and told for the first time. Moreover, one story often triggers others that may move suddenly from the very personal to societal issues (Bard 1992, 68–69). The latter observation is particularly important for the material analyzed in this book, where folkloric and sociological issues are hard to disentangle.

Most of the life stories we recorded contained both once-only narratives and stories that are part of the tellers' stable repertoire. The latter are narratives proper, complete and structured stories as analyzed by Labov and Waletzky (1966) and Labov (1972). Although all our informants knew they were being recorded, and in most cases their audience was limited to one person, the interviewer, some of the narratives have all the features of folklore performance. The narrators supplemented verbal information with body language, used prosody to render emotions, and created dramatic immediacy by tense shifts, switching between the past and the historic present (Wolfson 1981). The composition of these stories, the harmony of the verbal and nonverbal elements of performance, and the almost complete absence of false starts suggest that these stories were part of the narrators' repertoire. In some cases this assumption was confirmed by the storytellers themselves or by family members and friends. Moreover, as we will show later, some of these stories are already reproduced by other narrators with various modifications.

It would be difficult to imagine an informal conversation or a folkloric interview as a neat sequence of discrete and easily separated narratives. People tend to relate events as incomplete and unresolved (Ochs and Capps 2001, 7). Personal narratives are descriptions of memorable events and attempts to reconstruct and make sense of experiences. They serve as instances justifying the teller's opinions and interpretations. So, these stories do not become understandable without other connective talk (Ukkonen 2000, 144). Besides narratives proper, the interviews that we conducted contain monologue reflections and dialogic exchange with the interviewer and/or other participants. They incorporate traditional and contemporary folklore genres—for example, jokes, proverbs, and sadistic verses—recited to support an argument or clarify the storyteller's position, or as a means of mobilizing cultural knowledge shared with the interlocutor. In addition, our subjects recycled narratives drawn from the mass media. Some of the clichés derived from the media are reproduced as signs of various situations and function like proverbs. These are instances of *secondary folklorization* (a term introduced by the Russian folklorist Shtyrkov[7] [1999, 27]).

The type of discourse in the interviews largely depended on the topic. While such issues as the image of the other, lucky coincidences, and living with two languages proved to be rich sources of stories, deliberations about time and space and reflections on life in the East and the West seldom formed complete, well-structured narratives but appeared in the form of reflections (Fialkova and Yelenevskaya 2001b, 2001c; Yelenevskaya and Fialkova 2000, 2002). Language is reflexive by nature, and speech is permeated by reflexive activity as speakers report utterances, index and describe aspects of speech events, and guide listeners to the proper interpretation of their utterances (Lucy 1993, 11). In postmodern societies, in which information and knowledge rank among the most important commodities, the enhanced role of reflexivity is manifest in the constant reshaping of social practices on the basis of knowledge about those practices (Fairclough 1999, 74). Such reshaping of practices and roles is characteristic of immigrants' lives and consequently of their stories.

Fluidity of genres is a topic of both linguistic and folkloric research. Bausinger (1987), for example, shows links between surrealist jokes and animal tales, film and fairy tales, and legends and modern stories about terrible occurrences. Immigrants' personal narratives also demonstrate an affinity with the narrative forms of traditional folklore such as fairy tales, legends, and historical legends (Elbaz 1987, 287).

Immigrants' Folklore: An Integral Part of Modern Folklore

Literature on immigrants' folklore can be divided into general theoretical studies and investigations of the folklore of specific immigrant groups. Authors developing general theory (Dorson 1964; Kirshenblatt-Gimblett 1978, 1983; Smidchens 1990) are concerned with the degree of stability of the old country's folklore and the hybridity of the immigrants' culture, influenced by the host society's language and folklore. They are interested in transformations that occur in immigrant folklore over time: the transition from immigrant to ethnic folklore, intergenerational transmission, and language shifts in folkloric performances. An important question raised in these studies is how changes in immigrants' mentality and identity are reflected in the group folklore. In the information age the question of immigrant media's influence on the folklore repertoire and beliefs is another topic of folkloristics. Finally, there are issues of data collection, which are closely related to the interaction of material and symbolic culture, as well as to the themes pervading the folklore of immigration.

In Israel the attitude toward the preservation of folklore of the Diaspora has undergone significant changes over time. In the formative years of the state, "melting pot" policies went hand in hand with neglect of the cultural heritage of the "old countries." Dov Noy, founder of the Israel Folktales Archives (IFA), had to overcome opposition to his efforts to collect newcomers' folklore. Consolidation of the state resulted in more flexible attitudes toward the heritage of the Diaspora and paved the way to more pluralistic social policies. Israeli folklorists are making their own contribution to the development of tolerance and multiculturalism, and today the study of Jewish immigrants from different countries (Yemen, Tunisia, Morocco, Poland, Ethiopia, etc.) is one of the major directions of folklore research in Israel (Bar-Itzhak 1992, 1998; Noy 1984a, 1984b; Rosen 1999; Schely-Newman 1995; Salamon 1997–98). The IFA has accumulated an extensive collection of migrants' stories in Hebrew, Yiddish, Arabic, and other languages. This collection expanded through the recent addition of approximately five hundred stories in Russian, most of which were recorded from the FSU immigrants of the 1990s. Stories from our sample also appear in the IFA. When we quote them we mention their registration numbers.

The media and context of immigration stories vary. They can often be heard at public meetings of immigrants of different waves (Golden 2002) and in informal settings. According to our observations, they have become an indispensable part of festivities such as birthday parties, anniversaries, weddings, and the like. Moreover, these stories form a distinctive genre in the immigrants' media and discussion forums on the Internet. Oldtimers share their experience with newcomers in order to encourage them or to warn them against the pitfalls of life in the new country. Accordingly, these stories mostly circulate within the immigrant community and remain inaccessible to members of the host society. Kvideland (1990) points out that as a social activity, storytelling is based on a given worldview (22). It is the researcher's goal to bring this worldview to light through analysis and to study various functions of storytelling, such as reflections on one's place in a complex society.

Stories of immigrant experiences constitute an important part of migrants' biographies. These experiences long remain vivid, and reflections about them involve a wide range of emotions. As Rasmussen (1974) observes, memory is a creative act of consciousness and selects meaningful experiences. In every act of consciousness, the reality of a past and its meanings provide interpretive schemes for understanding the present and laying the foundation for future experiences (10). What interests us in this study is how the culture of the "old country," including its folklore, helps immigrants find their bearings in their new reality.

In mapping multifaceted studies devoted to FSU immigrants, we see our work as related to the books by Feldman (*Russian Israel* [2003], in Russian), Al-Haj (*Immigration and Ethnic Formation in a Deeply Divided Society* [2004], in English), and Komarova (*Russian Boston* [2002], in Russian). Both Feldman and Al-Haj study immigrants of the 1990s from the sociological perspective. Feldman relies exclusively on quantitative methods, while Al-Haj combines surveys with the study of five focus groups. Three of the groups were composed of Haifa University students (immigrants, veteran Jews, and Arabs), the fourth group consisted of participants from the general FSU immigrant population, and the fifth group comprised recent immigrants who arrived in Israel in the framework of the SELAH program (Hebrew acronym for "Students before Parents"). While surveys of the immigrants were conducted in their homes, polls of the veteran Jewish Israelis and Arabs were done over the telephone. Discussions with focus groups were held at the university. The striking difference between these two studies is the bias in the choice of bibliographic sources. Feldman's theoretical background is shaped predominantly by sources published in Russian. In contrast, Al-Haj uses Russian literature minimally; moreover, his emphasis is on general literature on interethnic relations and immigration. Unfortunately, numerous studies devoted to FSU immigrants of the last decade are almost unnoticed by this author. The third researcher, Komarova, is interested in Russian-speaking immigrants to the United States, irrespective of their tenure in the host society. She makes a point of letting the reader hear the voices of her informants. Passages from unstructured interviews conducted in various settings are grouped according to the topics discussed and form the bulk of the book. The purpose of the author's concise commentaries is to introduce the Russian reader to the realities of American life. None of these authors, however, show interest in the cultural roots of their subjects or in the influence of contemporary folk culture on the worldview of the immigrants.

Showing the cultural antecedents of the FSU immigrants is our major task, and by doing this we hope to fill the gap left by our colleagues. Primarily relying on qualitative methods—in particular, content, genre, and discourse analyses of personal narratives, as well as on participant observation—we systematically compare our results with the studies based on statistical data. The bibliography testifies to the interdisciplinary nature of our study: it includes works on folklore, anthropology, linguistics, psychology, sociology, history, social geography, and comparative literature. The bulk of the sources are in English, Russian, and Hebrew; in addition we refer to works in Ukrainian, Polish, French, and German.

The contents of the book are grouped in seven chapters. The first chapter discusses research strategies, explains the three types of sources used as material for the study, and analyzes the demographic profile of the immigrants interviewed for the project. The second chapter looks into the fragments of the Jewish tradition that survived despite the assimilation policy practiced in the USSR and analyzes various aspects of the subjects' self-identification. In the third chapter we show how traditional folk perception of the other affects immigrants' interaction with members of the receiving society. Chapter 4 is devoted to the transformation of immigrants' perception of time and space and investigates how their symbolism affects integration processes. In chapter 5 we show the mobilization of the mythology of fate and lucky coincidences as a means of fighting immigration stress. Chapter 6 presents folk linguistics: laypeople's view of the languages spoken in Israel, their status, and various roles in the life of the immigrant community. Chapter 7 analyzes the evolution of folklore genres and images of the country of origin under new conditions.

1

Fieldwork and Methods

Material for Analysis

Material for the book was drawn from face-to-face interviews with immigrants to Israel from the FSU conducted from 1999 to 2002. The total sample was made up of 123 interviews with 143 subjects who immigrated to Israel between 1989 and 1999. For various reasons 6 prospective interviewees refused to participate in the project. All the informants belong to the same immigration wave, but at the time of the interview their tenure in Israel ranged from ten years to less than two months (7 subjects). Importantly, 5 of our informants re-emigrated to Canada and the United States, 2 others returned to Russia, and 1 went back to Ukraine. The interviews (more than 80 hours of recordings) are transcribed in full. In several cases family members and friends preferred group interviews to individual ones, and this accounts for the discrepancy in the numbers. The context of the interviews varied: some were held in the homes of the interviewers or interviewees, others in offices, and still others in public places such as parks and beaches. In most cases we made preliminary arrangements, fixing the time and place of the interview, but there were also several cases of spontaneous storytelling, which were recorded on the spot. The average interview was 45 minutes; 6 of the interviews were short and were just one or two stories about memorable events of the teller's life. The rest were life-story interviews, some as long as 90–120 minutes. Four subjects (Gaiane A., 77; Elvira D., 34; Dana L., 23; and Noubar Aslanyan, 58) wished to add information after the first interview session and volunteered for a second interview.

Five interviews were conducted in Hebrew (4 of these were recorded by Hebrew-speaking students, and the fifth was with a fourteen-year-old who was not fluent in Russian). The rest of the interviews were in Russian, the mother tongue of both the interviewees and the authors.[1] One of the interviews conducted by a student, Christine Barzahian, contained interesting information but was difficult to transcribe because the subject's Hebrew was not perfect and he frequently mixed it with Russian and Armenian, which we were unable to understand. Fortunately, he willingly agreed to another session, this time in Russian, his second language. The second attempt was a group interview—both his wife and his son joined the conversation. Thus we have three cassettes (one in Hebrew and two in Russian, for a total of 4.5 hours of recording), and some of the stories appear twice. The difference in the interviewee's eloquence in Russian and in Hebrew does not conceal the stability of the narrator's repertoire. This is the only interview in the sample in which the interviewees are identified by their real names. The Aslanyans are performing musicians and are comfortable with recognition. We asked Noubar whether we could use his real name. This is what followed:

NOUBAR ASLANYAN: I am not afraid.

INTERVIEWER: Do you want us to give you these pages for review to check whether something annoys you or whether you disagree with what we will have written?

NOUBAR ASLANYAN: Well, I think you will write only what you have here [*points to the cassette player recording the conversation*].

INTERVIEWER: We won't write anything else, just for you not to . . .

NOUBAR ASLANYAN: I have a membership card of the Soviet Composers' Union. And there is an entry for a pseudonym on it. This line is empty on my card; it's blank. If Shostakovich doesn't have a pseudonym, why do I need one?[2]

Note that Noubar said, "I am not afraid" with defiance, and in this he is different from many ex-Soviets. For most of our subjects anonymity was a matter of concern nourished by the Soviet experience of trying to express "correct ideas" rather than sincere views (see examples of self-censorship on pages 32–33). We are happy to give the real name of a person who dedicates much time and effort to the promotion of interethnic cultural relations in Israel. It was Noubar Aslanyan who organized a charity concert in memory of teenage FSU immigrants killed in a terrorist attack in Tel Aviv in June 2000 (see chapter 3).

All the other interviewees are quoted under assumed names; however, the demographic data are unaltered. Because we did not use any agencies or community centers to find our interviewees—who were dispersed throughout Israel and had come from forty-nine cities and towns of the FSU—they can hardly be identified by the stories unless their relatives and friends recognize their standard repertoire. All the subjects were informed that the interviews would be audio-recorded and used for research and quoted in publications, and oral consent was obtained from everyone. According to the AAA Code of Ethics, informed consent does not necessarily imply or require a particular written or signed document. It is the quality of the consent, not the form that is relevant (www.aaanet.org/committees/ethics/ethcode.htm). We renamed our subjects systematically: people bearing the same name received the same pseudonym. We also tried to reflect the ethnic nature of names: Jewish names were replaced by Jewish pseudonyms, Russian by other Russian names, and so on. We agree with Feagin (2002) that pseudonyms preserving ethnicity and other essential features, such as common or rare names, enhance the readability of a text (33). Whenever a narrator mentions third persons we rename them too, using the same system.

Because mass media have become an important means of folklore transmission in the information age (Dégh 1994, 25) we systematically made use of the Russian-language press in Israel and Internet discussion forums. Immigrant media help the community relive experiences of pre-immigration life. Their role is not declining; rather, they have evolved into an influential institution accepted by the Israeli establishment (see, e.g., Caspi et al. 2002; Yelenevskaya 2000; Zilberg 1995). Our subjects often quoted from and alluded to the media. In addition, the themes consistently emerging in the interviews are the same as those discussed in the media and in Internet forums, whose participants are Russian-speaking immigrants from Israel, Germany, the United States, and so on. Internet portals Israland and Souz

(Russian for "Union") give links to other Russian Israeli sites and contain online bulletin boards. They post the names of the best Russian businesses and clubs, have discussion forums and chat rooms, and include numerous pages with jokes, narratives, and online games. Like other immigrant sites, they have become important sources of sharing and exchanging useful information about the newcomers' new country, with content on law, immigration services, job hunting, language courses, and other services. Sharing this type of information in the mother tongue and with people of similar background is extremely important for immigrants. Moreover the forums have become an arena for heated political and social discussions. As an illustration of the popularity of these sites, in June 2004, Souz had 36 forums, the most popular being "Israel and Us." It contained 2,723 discussion threads with 67,236 messages.

Finally, we kept a diary of our ethnographic observations, including our commentaries on the interviewees' speech and extralinguistic behavior. Some of these commentaries are on the cassettes, recorded immediately after the interviews. We also wrote down stories that could not be recorded and made notes of newly coined idioms reflecting immigrants' experiences in Israel. The goal of gathering different types of data—interviews, observations, documents, and photographs—is to obtain a comprehensive view of the research topic and to cross-validate research data (Patton 1987, 105).

Demographic Features of the Interviewees

The subjects were found in a "snowball" fashion. Some of them introduced us to relatives and friends who were willing to participate in the project. Most of the interviews were conducted with immigrants residing in the enclaves of Haifa, Upper Nazareth, Ashkelon, and Beer Sheva. The rest live in eleven other towns and a kibbutz, and none of these are beyond the Green Line (demarcation of the 1949 Armistice Agreement). Among the interviewees are 100 females (f.) and 43 males (m.), including 6 children and adolescents of both sexes. The prevalence of women is not surprising, for this community as a whole has an excess of females: about 45.6 percent male and 54.4 percent female.[3] In the FSU immigrant community there are many one-parent families,

The mother tongue of most newcomers from Ukraine is Russian, and few of them speak Ukrainian in everyday life. The Ukrainian sign *Lviv* (Lvov) at the entrance of this little store is a true rarity.

most of which are headed by single mothers (Leshem and Sicron 1998, xiii). Besides being more plentiful, women also showed more willingness to participate in the study. The following figure illustrates the age composition of the sample:

Age	16–30	31–45	46–60	61–80
Number	46 (31 f. / 15 m.)	15 (9 f. / 6 m.)	40 (31 f. / 9 m.)	36 (24 f. /12 m.)

Although we did not intend to create a statistically representative sample, the group as a whole reflects essential demographic features of the 1990s immigrant wave from the FSU. First, all the subjects were city dwellers, and most had lived in metropolitan regions such as Moscow (21), St. Petersburg (17), Kiev (14), and so on. As noted, the geographic array of the hometowns of our interviewees is widespread: they came from forty-nine towns of the FSU. Most of the subjects (119) lived in the European part of the FSU, the rest (24) in the Asian and Caucasian republics. Our sample also mirrors the geography of origin of the immigrant wave of the 1990s in that the overwhelming majority came from Russia and Ukraine (Leshem and Sicron 1998, xii–xiii; Al-Haj and Leshem 2000, 8). Second, a high proportion (92) of interviewees held academic degrees, including Ph.D.'s (12). According to recent Israeli sociological research, about 60 percent of the FSU immigrant labor force worked in academic professions, which considerably exceeds the corresponding percentage for veteran Israelis (30 percent) (Leshem and Lissak 1999, 144). The educational level of the informants is relevant to this study and accounts for the inclination to reflexivity displayed by many subjects, as well as their frequent allusions to Russian and Soviet art, literature, and history. To illustrate the ethnic composition of the sample we divided our subjects into four main categories:

- Group 1: both parents of the subject are Jewish (87)
- Group 2: the subject's mother is Jewish; the father is not (18)
- Group 3: the subject's father is Jewish; the mother is not (6)
- Group 4: subjects are non-Jewish spouses of Jewish immigrants (17)

We do not have exact data on the ethnicity of 15 subjects. Eleven of them are registered as Jews, so they belong to group 1 or group 2, and in 4 cases the issue of ethnicity did not emerge during the interview.

Such a division, which deviates from the Halachic categorization of the Jews (children of Jewish mothers), requires an explanation. According to Halacha, there is no difference between our groups 1 and 2 (Jews) on the one hand, or between groups 3 and 4 (non-Jews) on the other. According to Israel's Law of Return, however, immigrants belonging to group 3 are eligible to immigrate on their own. Consequently many immigrants were confronted with a paradoxical situation: urged to return to their "historic homeland" by the emissaries of the Jewish Agency, members of group 3 were labeled "non-Jews" in the Jewish religious national state (Kimmerling 2001, 143). This often leads to complications in various civil procedures, in the first place marriage and burial. In addition, they become targets of prejudiced discourse about the alien, non-Jewish nature of the 1990s immigration wave. The immigrants included in group 4 are entitled to immigration and citizenship only as family members of the immigrants of the first three groups. To be fair, members of groups 3 and 4 receive Israeli citizenship immediately upon arrival. Complications arise if the non-Jewish spouse arrives in Israel later.

In the Soviet Union the difference between group 1 and groups 2 and 3 was relevant and is reflected in the terms *halves* or *half-bloods,* denoting children of mixed marriages. They could choose their mother's or father's ethnicity when they received their internal passport at age sixteen. Always prepared for deterioration in the political situation and new surges of anti-Semitism, most parents instructed their children to register as non-Jews. Referring to the data of Russian sociological research, Dymerskaya-Tsigelman (2000) maintains that 90–95 percent of the "halves" chose the ethnicity of their non-Jewish parent when they filled in the fifth paragraph[4] of their internal passport (39).

Non-Jews figured among immigrants of the previous wave as well, but their numbers were negligible and the legitimacy of their living in Israel was not a cause of contention. The dramatic increase in these numbers in the 1990s not only caused an outburst of anti-immigrant articles in the press but made Israeli sociologists and demographers revisit definitions of Jewishness. Some tend to restrict the group by the Halachic prescriptions (Al-Haj and Leshem 2000, 25); others extend it by introducing the notion of an "enlarged" Jewish population that includes descendants of intermarriages and non-Jewish spouses and in-laws (Brym 1997, 178; DellaPergola 1998, 52; Feldman 2003, 55–64).

We have made a point of discussing the issue of immigrants' ethnicity because it affected a person's status in both countries, as well as people's self-identification. Individuals may change their identification according to the circumstances. In the case of our informants this applies first and foremost to members of groups 2 and 3 but does not depend on which of their parents is Jewish (see discussion of this in DellaPergola 1998, 53; Nosenko 2000). The fluidity of immigrants' identity will later emerge in excerpts from the interviews and their analyses.

Fieldwork Strategies

Interviews are ubiquitous in social sciences and various institutional practices. Based on the degree of structure involved, research interviews can be classified as structured, semistructured, and unstructured (Fontana and Frey 2000, 645). The question of validity and reliability is a serious concern for interview-based studies. Positivists support the pretested, standardized questions of structured interviews as a way of increasing reliability. Interactionists, on the other hand, assume that people's cultural worlds are too complex to be captured by standardized, survey-research-style interviews (Silverman 1993, 106). According to our observations, standardized questions may prompt answers that the subjects would not choose themselves and thus conceal their genuine position.

We chose the unstructured format as the most appropriate for research on personal narratives. Patton (1987) points out that informal conversational interviews are particularly useful when the researcher can stay in the situation for some period of time so that he or she is not dependent upon a single interview to collect all the information needed. Because both of us are immigrants, we stayed in the research situation throughout the project. Although Patton is a proponent of informal conversational interviews, he admits that this method of data collection requires a great amount of time and depends upon the conversational skills of the interviewer (110–11). Different stages of our project, from conducting interviews to making transcripts and classifying data, confirm that the method of informal conversational interviewing is very time-consuming, although highly rewarding on both the professional and social levels. To our profound satisfaction the students participating in the project shared this opinion and found their fieldwork experiences extremely fruitful.

One important benefit of an open-ended, in-depth interview is its collaborative nature. Critiques of the researchers' authoritative voice and the analyses of power relations in interviewing have made social scientists reconsider their fieldwork strategies and view interviewees as research participants and collaborators rather than passive subjects. This re-evaluation of the role of the interviewee stemmed from the growing interest of anthropology, ethnography, and folkloristics in the study of literate society in general and of elite groups in particular—for example, scientists, managers, artists, and so on. Sociologists and anthropologists have undertaken a growing number of immigration studies devoted to the integration of teachers, scientists, and physicians (see, e.g., Epstein and Kheimets 2000a, 2000b; Remennick 2002b; Feder-Bubis 1997). As Angrosino and de Pérez (2000) remark, ethnographers can no longer claim to be the sole arbiters of knowledge about the societies and cultures they study, because their analyses can be read and contested by those for whom they presume to speak (675). The interviewee and the interviewer both participate actively in the process of negotiating meaning, and data collection blends with the initial stage of the interpretive process.

As we pointed out at the beginning of this section, the interview-based research and the understanding of culture in all its complex forms are inseparable from the study of communication. This is why the concepts and models developed by communication theorists have been transferred and applied to culture studies. Jakobson (1960) proposed one of the better known communication models in "Linguistics and Poetics" (353):

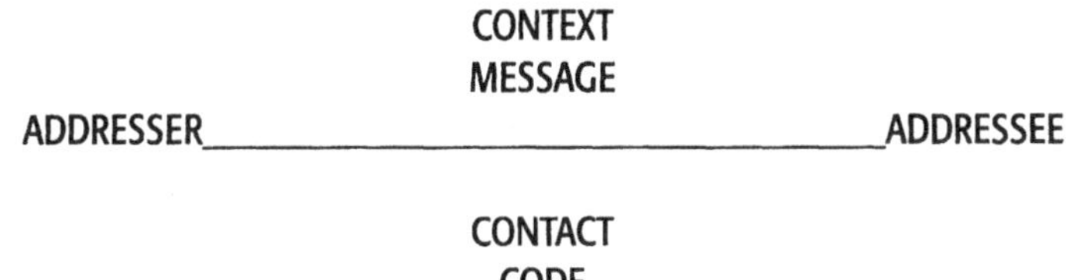

The prominent Soviet semiotician Lotman warned researchers against simplifications in the application of this model to culture studies. He regarded autocommunication, or *internal speech* (a term introduced by Vygotskii), as an independent communication model. In the process of external communication, or the "I-he" system, a text is introduced, encoded in the code's system, transmitted, and decoded. Given that communication seldom occurs without any interference, we frequently observe a decrease in information. In the process of internal communication, or the "I-I" communication, given a text that is encoded in a certain system, another code is introduced, and the text is transformed. As a result of the interaction with the new code an increase in information occurs. While in external communication the code constitutes the constant and the text is the variable, in internal communication the code constitutes the variable and the texts differ at entrance and exit (Lotman 1992a, 76–89; 1977). The communication scheme in this case looks more complicated:

CONTEXT CONTEXTUAL DISPLACEMENT

I⟶MESSAGE 1⟶ –MESSAGE 2⟶I

CODE 1 MESSAGE 1

Lotman discusses the two communication systems in application to fiction, while we are concerned with intercultural investigations of personal narratives. In-depth interviews are akin to diaries, which belong to the internal "I-I" communication. In telling the interviewer the story of his or her immigration, an informant tries to make sense of the past, to rethink and to reinterpret it in light of the experience acquired in the new country. No wonder many of the interviewees expressed gratitude for the opportunity to sort out the experiences of an eventful and difficult period in their lives. On the other hand, an interview is an external "I-he" communication (in the case of this study, "I-she," as all the interviewers are women). Considering that each of the two types of communication includes its own constants and variables, in our interviews the number of variables increases: the informants try to make sense of their past for themselves (namely, a new code is introduced), and at the same time the message is transmitted to another person, the interviewer. The constants are the language of communication, Russian or Hebrew, and the background knowledge about the realities of the FSU, Israel, and the life of the immigrant community.

Because language is inherently ambiguous, we must always leap to conclusions about what the speaker means. We draw inferences on two main sources: the language used and our knowledge of the world. Furthermore, an essential element of this knowledge is our expectation of what is normally said in such circumstances (Scollon and Scollon 1995, 10). Background knowledge is essential for formulating interview questions and for understanding and interpreting answers.

Our interview questions were not standardized. Some subjects were reticent and needed encouragement, which came in the form of probing questions; others took the lead and needed little guidance. According to Bertaux (1981), a good interviewee is a good storyteller who takes control of the interview situation and talks freely (39). The core of our interviews consisted of the following seven topics: subjects' reasons for immigration; first impressions of Israel; contacts with veteran Israelis (Jews and Arabs); work and/or study experience in Israel; leisure activities before and after immigration; habits and customs before and after immigration; and language-use issues. The categories evolved as a result of two rounds of content analysis. First we analyzed the subject matter of five interviews conducted by the MA student Hanna Shmulian and kept in the IFA. The initial categories were then tested in the first twenty interviews, which we conducted ourselves. After this we expanded and reclassified the categories. Subject-matter categories applied to biographic studies enable researchers to determine themes salient for the interviewed individual (Carney 1972, 172–74). The topics covered in our interviews partially coincide with the field guide outline proposed by Linda Dégh in her unpublished "Fieldwork Guide for Collecting Ethnic Culture and Folklore" and quoted by Kirshenblatt-Gimblett (1983, 41). In addition to the listed topics, some other themes came up, sometimes unexpectedly for us, and when we saw that they were important for our subjects we tried to pursue them in the subsequent interviews. One example is interviewees' reflections about the place of Israel on the East-West axis (see chapter 4). Informal conversational interviews allow fieldworkers to be responsive to individual differences and situational changes. Questions can be fine-tuned to establish in-depth communication and take advantage of the situation to increase the concreteness and immediacy of the interview questions and responses (Patton 1987, 110; Punch 1998, 176). Besides analyzing the collected data for recurring motifs, we looked for images, associations, and assumptions of cause-and-effect relationships explaining the interviewees' position (Taylor and Wetherell 1999, 40). Like folktales, personal narratives repeat particular structural lines and rely on a stock of conventional details (Ries 1997, 24–25). These recurrent elements deserve special attention because they signal key categories and mental patterns characteristic of the investigated group.

We made use of several strategies to demonstrate our involvement and to encourage shy speakers.

- We expressed our interest in the stories by verbal and nonverbal means (see Goffmannova 2000 and Miller 1997) and did not refrain from praising their stories as "interesting," "thrilling," and "exciting" or expressing surprise by exclamations of incredulity, which signaled to the narrator that the dramatic effect had been achieved.
- When a storyteller hesitated, searching for an appropriate word, we tried to help. Because some of our interviewees showed signs of language attrition, such instances were not infrequent.
- In spite of our leadership role in the conversation, being responsible for the success of an interaction, we tried to use facilitative and supportive devices such as tags, echo, interjecting comments, and hedges. All of these are not just typical of female conversation style (see Coates 1996, 152–73; Holmes 2001, 284–16; Malz and Borker 1982, 209–11) but are specifically used to avoid playing the role of an expert.
- If we were not sure that we had grasped what the interviewees wanted to say, we paraphrased their statements and asked whether our interpretation conflicted with the meaning intended by the narrator. Sometimes the storyteller made corrections or gave a more precise explanation of his or her position.

In most cases we refrained from arguing with the interviewees, especially when political issues emerged. Instead we asked for the clarification of opinion, and even this was sometimes understood as a sign of disagreement and provoked further arguments or the interviewee's retreat from the previously stated position. On several occasions we noticed that the interviewees vigilantly observed our reaction to their words and even modified their behavior in response to a pause in the conversation, a clarifying question, or a change in the expression of the face and eyes. We tried to record such instances in field notes and later used them in analyses.

When our interviewees deviated from the themes related to immigration we did not stop them, relying on what Goldstein (1964) called the "vacuum cleaner approach" (133–38). As a result we recorded flashbacks of childhood and youth experiences, such as Holocaust stories and "voluntary" labor in the virgin lands of Kazakhstan in the 1960s. Although such stories were not analyzed in the framework of this project, they are of considerable interest and will be used in other research contexts. We chose the vacuum-cleaner approach at the expense of more focused interviewing techniques (Patton 1987, 130; Rosen 1999, 183) to foster the objectivity of the fieldwork, to show respect for the informants, and to avoid missing interesting material. We started the project without preliminary theoretic assumptions. Like Atkinson (1998), we believe that preliminary theoretic assumptions can do damage in qualitative research in general and in the study of personal narratives in particular. He suggests that theory should develop on the basis of fieldwork, not be imposed on it (66). This approach has been successfully applied in immigrant studies by Bekerman (2000, 110).

Folk Groups and Researchers' Roles

The term *folklore group* is related to the discussion on the changing notion of folk in the urbanized world. Dundes applies the term *folk* to "*any group of people whatsoever* who share at least one common factor," be it an occupation, language, or religion. What is important is that the group has their own traditions (Dundes 1965, 2). Brunvand emphasizes the criterion of distinctive folk speech, and both he and Stahl elaborate on the fluidity of folklore groups: the individual usually participates in and transmits their lore among several groups (Brunvand 1968, 21–22; Stahl 1989, 24).

Because both authors and five of the student fieldworkers are FSU immigrants of the 1990s, we are members of the folk group of Russian-speaking Israelis. Some of the students' interviewees were young people and thus shared the distinctive speech patterns and lore of the young Russian-speaking immigrants. One

Hebrew-speaking MA student, Hanny Manheim, is a schoolteacher and chose to interview immigrant teachers. Though an outsider to the group of former Soviets, she shared professional lore with her informants. Of special interest is the story of Christine Barzahian's interviews. Originally, she did not intend to work with former Soviets. Her seminar project was dedicated to Armenians in Israel. Out of the four interviews she conducted, two were with second- and third-generation immigrants, descendants of the Armenian genocide refugees of 1915. One is of mixed Arab-Armenian origin; the other lives and works in an Arab village. The other two subjects happened to be new immigrants from post-Soviet Armenia, both from mixed Armenian-Jewish families. Although Christine is a third-generation descendant of an Armenian refugee, she realized she was an outsider for all her subjects, as she could not speak Armenian and her familiarity with Armenian culture was superficial. Despite common ethnic roots, Christine was not a member of her interviewees' folk groups.

The more folklore groups the interviewer and the interviewee share, the more they rely on allusions and lingo familiar to both. Among the subjects there were eight Mountain Jews;[5] four of them were interviewed by Laura Abramov, three by Larisa Fialkova, and one by Alina Sanina. Narratives related to the traditions of the group were perceived and interpreted differently by Laura, the insider, and by Larisa, the outsider (the interview conducted by Alina did not deal with the culture of the group at all). Contemporary ethnographic and folkloristic research increasingly emphasizes "membership roles" as opposed to roles grounded in pure observation. Georges and Jones (1980) point out that the greater the significance of differences that fieldworkers conceive to exist between themselves and their chosen subjects, the greater the potential for conflict and ambivalence and the greater the potential number of clarifications and compromises (66). Moreover, it is much easier for an outsider than an insider to ask questions about the culture of the other because so many things appear to be novel. On the other hand, in the absence of comprehensive knowledge of the culture the interpretation of the answers is harder for the outsider. Membership roles contribute to the communicative success of interview-based research, which largely depends on the common apperception basis (Golanova

1996, 431). Depending on the degree of their involvement with the studied group, researchers can be divided into three groups: "peripheral member" researchers, who believe they can develop a desirable insider's perspective without participating in the core activities of the group; "active member" researchers, who become involved with the central activity of the group but who do not necessarily commit themselves to members' values and goals; and "complete member" researchers, who study scenes where they are already members or who become converted to genuine membership in the course of research (Adler and Adler 1994, 380; Angrosino and de Pérez 2000, 677).

As we indicated earlier, all three research roles were performed by different fieldworkers involved in this project. There is still another role that can be enacted by investigators applying observational techniques, that of a self-observer, which is practiced in sociology and in folklore. This role is close to the "members" and augments researchers' observations of others with observations of their own thoughts and feelings (Adler and Adler 1994, 385–86; Fialkova 2001; Wilson 1986, 231). At the start of the present project we decided not to interview each other or any of the students taking the course Folklore and Immigration for fear that familiarity with professional literature might influence the narrators. But we did record several stories that are part of our own storytelling repertoire. All of them are devoted to our immigration experiences, and we used to tell them before we became interested in the subject of immigration professionally. Although we are not afraid of making them public knowledge, we decided that as narrators we are no different from our informants. While in the IFA these stories appear under our real names, here we use pseudonyms.

The question of researchers' positionality is treated differently in different academic cultures. Russian social scientists, for example, do not always find it necessary to state it. First, declarations of one's position may alienate potential readers who belong to a different social group or have a different political orientation. Second, it is assumed that unlike an essayist whose goal it is to shape the reader's views by using various strategies of persuasion, a researcher aims to achieve objectivity in interpreting material under study and tries not to be led by ethnic and social allegiances. Statements of one's position are considered less reliable than the biases reflected in the analyses. By contrast, Western social scientists believe that for the reader to form an opinion about the researcher, it is essential to know the author's background and political standing. Because this book targets Western readers we act in accordance with the latter convention.

We both emigrated from big industrial cities of the Soviet Union in the early 1990s, having decided to leave for personal reasons. We come from secular Ashkenazi families and have a strong affinity for Russian culture. In our own behavior and attitudes we often observe traits typical of Soviet personalities and are not ashamed of it. In the years spent in Israel we have made good friends with veteran Israelis from different ethnic communities. We also maintain close relationships with friends and relatives, Jews and non-Jews, in the FSU. In addition, we are regularly in touch with friends who immigrated to the United States, Germany, Canada, and so on, as well as with colleagues we have met at conferences. Having worked at Israeli universities for almost fifteen years, we constantly deal with members of different ethnic and religious groups. Although we are not affiliated with any political parties, we support the left-wing sector of Israeli society.

When talking to even "complete member" researchers, the subjects often perceived the context of the interviews as ambivalent. On the one hand, the interviewer was associated with an Israeli institution, which prompted some of them to be cautious (about the inherent features of power relations in interviews, see Christians 2000, 141–42; Feagin 2002, 25–26; Ryazanova 1996, 155–60). On the other hand, when the subjects realized that their interlocutors had gone through similar immigrant experiences, they relaxed. The common past was an important factor for breaking barriers and transforming the interview into an informal and friendly conversation. Ex-Soviets are known to be more open with insiders because in the recent past sincerity with strangers could lead to repression (see Goodwin et al. 1999).

Social anthropological, and folkloric investigations are a serious test of a researcher's objectivity. While carrying out fieldwork in his or her own group, a researcher's bias may stem from shared ideologies, social goals, and stereotypes of the group. In spite of our honest efforts to be unbiased, as we analyzed the transcripts we realized that sometimes we had reproduced the stereotypes typical of the analyzed group. In addition, insiders may overestimate their knowledge of their own group, or describe only what they like to see in it (Smidchens 1990, 135). Conversely, when entering a group of strangers a researcher may interpret cultures on the basis of his or her own values and attitudes, which are remote from or even incompatible with those of the studied group. In the context of Israeli society the type of subjectivity might vary depending on whether the researcher is secular or religious, Jewish or Arab, Zionist or post-Zionist. Unfortunately, no research context safeguards against bias. Ideally, an investigator aims to minimize his or her dependence on group attitudes. Those studying their own group would benefit from the analytical method known as estrangement and formulated in 1929 by the Soviet theoretician of literature Shklovskii (1983). He considered it a central technique of literature and art and argued that repeated encounters with a phenomenon lead to automatic perception. Only when we view and describe the phenomenon as if it were first seen do we de-automate our perception (15).

We occasionally shared our own stories with the interviewees to create a reciprocal relationship, which is an essential feature of life-story interviews (Honko 2001, 7; Miller 2000, 103). Researchers who are members of the investigated group, who share the language and cultural codes with the subjects, have access to a wealth of information unavailable to outsiders (Smidchens 1990, 135). We understood cultural allusions and shared many of our subjects' concerns and emotions, which contributed to the atmosphere of trust.

Ethics in Personal Narrative Research

The ethical problems of qualitative research are repeatedly debated in the Western scientific community but are relatively new to Russian anthropology and folkloristics. In a pioneering work, Panchenko (2001) points out that all fieldwork is exploitation and results in the usurping of symbolic values (9). Personal narrative research reflects the interest of the humanities in the individual and his or her private world. Public access to the informants' private thoughts and feelings raises ethical issues concerning the folklorists' responsibility to their subjects and their rights. This brings us back to the problem of anonymity of personal narrative research mentioned in the first section of this chapter. A key issue of the anthropological and folkloristic codes of ethics is protection of informants, including their right to remain anonymous (AAA Code of Ethics). Some authors have published works on personal narratives that give the narrators' real names (see, e.g., Razumova 2001, a study on the contemporary Russian family, and Keramida 1999, a case study of Pontiac Greeks). Sometimes interviewees want their names to be published, especially if they sponsor the research project (see, e.g., Rosen 1999, a book on Carpatho-Russian Jews). Our interviewees, including those who didn't suffer from shyness, were often concerned as to whether their candor might affect their well-being in the new country. Like many other former Soviets, they had retained a fear of omnipotent and prosecuting authorities and would open up only after they were assured that their names would not be published.[6] At the same time, after the interview many said that they had enjoyed the conversation, as it gave them a chance to sort out their experiences and relive some of the memorable episodes. Some of the interviewees we later met socially expressed interest in the progress of the project and hoped that the materials would be published not only in English but in Russian as well.

Some of our subjects were convinced that having the same background and similar immigrant experiences meant that we should share their opinions on the topics discussed. As stated, we were resolved not to show disagreement with or surprise at the opinions expressed, and we did not disclose our own. Rabinowitz (1997) discussed a similar situation when he studied Jewish-Arab relations in Nazareth and Upper Nazereth. His Jewish subjects viewed him, a young Jewish male, as a person who was supposed to share the idea of Judaizing the Galilee. Those who knew about his project saw or could see him as a renegade, because his sympathy toward Arabs caused an ideological mismatch (21–22, 105–8). Our informants perceived us as members of the same in-group; however, the knowledge that we were investigating Soviet immigrants put us in a special position as mediators between the immigrant community and Israeli institutions. Consequently relations of solidarity and power were mixed. Some of the prospective subjects refused to talk, as they did not want to be recorded; others asked to switch the tape recorder off when private issues came up in the conversation or when they perceived their own views as politically incorrect. One interviewee (Isaak Sh., 70+), a former lecturer in Marxism who was eager to have his jokes recorded, became suspicious when we asked about his own experiences. He insisted on checking the recording before approving its use for research. Apparently, the result satisfied him, as he exclaimed, "Ha, you could broadcast it on Reka[7] right away!" Another informant (Natalia Z., 61) was anxious to read the article with her story as soon as it was published in order to check whether she was recognizable. We observed instances of self-censorship in other interviews as well.

The task of protecting the research subjects is particularly sensitive when informants report conduct violating a society's legal or moral rules (see, e.g., Fialkova and Yelenevskaya 2006a; Miller 2000, 83). Our sample contains several narratives about deception, bribery, and document forging. Luckily, there were no accounts of serious crimes involving treason or endangering other people's lives or property. One characteristic of Russian and some other FSU cultures is the distance separating the notions of law and of morals. For the Russians, justice is more important than truth (Lebedeva 1999, 128–38). The law is seen as an instrument, often immoral at that, used by the state against an individual. So juggling it for the sake of an individual is considered to be both moral and appropriate. Ries, who studied contemporary Russian speech genres, identifies a genre of male mischief stories (1997, 65–82). These can be divided into two groups: stories aimed at depicting the narrator's boldness, courage, and wit, examples of what is known in Russia as "hussar behavior," and trickster stories. In our opinion mischief stories are popular among males and females alike, though dominant themes differ in their narratives: while males brag about drinking, womanizing, and fighting adventures, females tell stories about seduction and the taming of husbands and mothers-in-law. In addition, both sexes excel in telling stories about outwitting "the system" and circumventing the law. Immigration produced new types of mischief stories, such as narratives about faking documents, deceiving customs, and emigrating without obtaining close relatives' consent—in other words, trickster-type stories. Some single mothers proudly told us how they succeeded in outwitting their former husbands, who did not want to let their children leave permanently and whose right to veto the children's emigration was protected by Soviet law (a similar regulation exists in Israel). The narrators assumed that the fathers wanted to prevent the children from leaving the old country not because they loved them but to humiliate their former spouses and bend them to their will. These women felt themselves victims of the male-biased system. Some of the fathers may have really shown lack of care for their children, but the mothers may have been biased in their stories too. Here is an example:

Yulia Kh., 53

YULIA: As a matter of fact, I decided to leave[8] when Innochka [*Yulia's daughter*] was five. I wanted to leave, I was thinking about it. But my husband would not sign.

INTERVIEWER: The permit?

YULIA: Yeah, he refused to sign the permit.

INTERVIEWER: Were you already divorced then?

YULIA: Oh, I divorced ages ago, a long, long time ago. And I couldn't, well, because of the child, I could not leave, that's how it was. And as I was an experienced teacher, and I was influential. . . . In my classes there were children of a judge, lawyers' children, children of teachers from all the schools. Only in my classes . . . such children were only in my classes. I am a solid teacher. Well . . . and so I had connections and I managed to find a notary who was ready to help me. I came to his office and said, just like this, without concealing anything, "Look, my situation is like this, like this, and like this. If you do it for me, nobody will know about it. I will pay you a lot of money." A thousand rubles . . . at that time it was very big money. It was, well, one can say, it was ten, eight, or nine monthly salaries. He says, "And if you leave, won't he [*the former husband*] create problems?" I say, "There will be no problems. All the problems will be resolved with me. If I leave . . . if I leave . . . this will be the end of it. There will be no problems left." And so he agreed.

By the time of emigration, Yulia's daughter had already come of age, but even adults over eighteen had to obtain their parents' permission to emigrate (a story similar to Yulia's was told by Zena B., 53). No exceptions were made, even for those who had not seen their parents for decades. Two of our interviewees (Ekaterina B., 23, and Anastasia Ts., 48) had to search for their fathers, who lived in other towns and had had no contact with their daughters from the ages of five and three respectively. There are also two entries in our ethnographic diaries with the stories of two immigrants (Ekaterina R., 40, and Rimma A., 50) who had to leave for Israel on tourist visas: Ekaterina couldn't find her father, and Rimma's ex-husband, who had never had any contact with their ten-year-old child, refused to sign the necessary papers.

The second theme—deceiving Soviet customs—is represented by stories about illegally emigrating with art objects, jewelry, and private collections. Every country has its own customs rules, which may seem unnecessarily strict to travelers. Soviet customs rules prohibited emigrants from taking with them foreign currency (more than $150 per person), antiques, diamonds, and even books published before 1945, pre-revolutionary photographs, and so on. Some of these objects had only symbolic value as family relics, so customs restrictions were perceived as merely the last attempt of the Soviet state to suppress its citizens. Success in smuggling them out is the topic of numerous narratives (see Fialkova and Yelenevskaya 2006b).

The most sensitive theme in the mischief stories is deception related to registration of ethnicity in both the Soviet Union and Israel. Some of these stories were recorded; others, especially about registering illegally as Jews in Israel, were told before or after the taped interview session. In Israel, registration by a Soviet Jew of himself or herself as a Russian or a Latvian (see chapter 2) in order to avoid discrimination in the old country is treated much more tolerantly than registration by a Russian or a Latvian of himself or herself as a Jew in Israel.

We agree with Al-Haj and Leshem (2000) that white-collar crimes are regarded by FSU immigrants much more leniently than by Israelis (51–53). Stories about them are of high tellability; that is, they are frequently told and members of the community appreciate them (Ochs and Capps 2001, 33–36). When respondents in Al-Haj and Leshem's sociological survey reported their unwillingness and/or willingness to inform officials about certain white-collar crimes they did not expose themselves. Their answers showed a general attitude but did not imply action. When our informants told us stories about their wrongdoings they made themselves vulnerable, so it is unlikely that theses stories would be told to an outsider. An insider, however, is supposed to know what made the perpetrator act illegally and therefore does not pose a threat. Our personal attitude to mischief stories notwithstanding, we feel obliged to be discrete and not to betray our informants' trust. As stated in the AAA Code of Ethics, researchers' primary ethical obligation is to the people, spaces, and materials they study and to the people with whom they work.

2

Immigration and Evolution of Identity

In chapter 1 we raised the issue of immigrants' self-identification when we discussed the demographic profile of the FSU immigrants. Now we will look into factors that influence the personal and collective identity of the FSU immigrants in more detail. While the concept of identity has long pervaded academic discourse in the social sciences, folklorists have focused on it only fairly recently (Dundes 1965, 1984; Brunvand 1968; Bauman 1971). As noted in chapter 1, Dundes and Brunvand touched upon this subject in their definitions of the folk group. For Dundes (1965), shared identity is the main dimension of a folklore group (2), and for Brunvand (1968), the core concept is shared folklore (21–22). Later, Dundes (1984) elaborated on the issue and pointed out the multiplicity of identities, both personal and social. He drew a line between permanent and temporary identities: involuntary associations such as sex and race cannot be changed, in contrast to such variables as social class. Bauman (1971), on the other hand, noted that folklore was used as a mechanism of interaction across tribal lines, and no image of a homogeneous folk with shared identity and a collective folklore could account adequately for the realities of the situation on the ground. Emphasizing the performance element in folklore, he showed the importance of differentiated identity, meaning identity features of different cultural and linguistic groups. But for verbal performance the shared linguistic code is described as having crucial importance (35).

Part of the material in this chapter has been published in Fialkova and Yelenevskaya 2003 and 2004b.

Oring (1994) developed Dundes' conception of identity as affiliation with certain symbols and their meanings. He defines personal identity as a particular mental disposition and with contents composed of memories, identifications, and repudiations of individuals, ideas, and experiences, which come to constitute a perhaps shifting, but nevertheless discernible, configuration. He specified that what underlies these configurations constitutes and distinguishes a person. Collective identity refers to those aspects of personal identity that are derived from experiences and expressions common to a group (212). Dundes believes that the notion of identity is inseparable from distinguishing the self from others. Oring takes this further by including rejection of individuals and ideas as an integral part of the concept. For Dundes and Oring, as well as some other folklorists, identity is one of the key issues of folklore in general and immigrant folklore in particular (see, e.g., Dégh 1984; Jones 2000). In contrast, Kirshenblatt-Gimblett (1994) questions the use of identity as an organizing concept for the discipline. She fears that preoccupation with identity has a political agenda and may transmute into racism. Similar ideas are found in Ricoeur (1992), who states that when national traits are separated from concrete history and geography they are "solidified and lend themselves to exploitation by the most harmful ideologies of 'national identity'" (123). Our observations confirm Kirshenblatt-Gimblett's and Ricoeur's uneasiness, and we would prefer not to deal with identity issues; but the question of the FSU immigrants' Jewishness is ever present in the public and scholarly discourse in Israel. The relative autonomy of the Russian-speaking community, the problems with Hebrew acquisition, the attachment to the culture of the old country, and even the criminal activity of immigrants are sometimes attributed to a large number of non-Jews among them (see, e.g., Horowitz, Shamai, and Ilatov 2003). Moreover, the problem of identity troubles the immigrants themselves, as attested to by heated discussions in the Russian-language press and in Internet discussion groups. We did not ask our informants to define themselves in terms of group affiliation, as is often done in sociological research. Our way to explore the subjects' identity is to analyze the choice of stories they told about themselves and their past. We examine how they adapt different aspects of their identities (Jewish, Soviet, Russian, Ukrainian, Armenian, etc.[1]) when they reflect on who they are. People may choose to remember or forget aspects of their past and venerate some ancestors while discarding others. The significance of these choices may be striking, particularly for individuals influenced by several cultures (Fenton 1999, 7; Jones 2000, 134). The question "Who am I?" becomes increasingly difficult for immigrants to answer as a result of attributions by both the self and others. Does this then mean that autobiographies characterized by variation and changes of belonging lead to identity diffusion? (See more on this issue in Rosenthal 1997, 22–23.)

The question "Who am I?" emerged in the interviews when immigrants recalled their confrontation with anti-Semitism in the USSR, spoke about elements of the Jewish tradition in their families, explained what triggered their decision to emigrate, and talked about their place in the new society. These four themes often overlapped, as is evident in the excerpts quoted in the next section.

Reasons for Emigration

Our subjects willingly talked about their reasons for emigration. These correlated with the results of the surveys obtained by sociologists in Israel (Leshem and Sicron 1998, xiv; Leshem and Lissak 1999, 141; Al-Haj and Leshem 2000, 11–13; Feldman 2003) and in the FSU when potential emigrants were investigated (Brym and Ryvkina 1994, 78–81; Ryvkina 1996, 186).[2] All these studies conclude that the immigration of the 1990s was motivated more by push factors (a desire to leave the FSU) than by pull factors (an attraction to Israel).[3] While pull factors have a positive nature and are characterized as facilitating or enabling, push factors are associated with constraints and exclusion (Berry 1997, 16). Not surprisingly, then, many of the narratives about the last period of life in the USSR are stories of anxiety.

Using content analysis we singled out nine main categories (because some of the informants gave multiple reasons for emigration, the total number of responses exceeds the number of interviewees): "avalanche" (see explanation in the following paragraph) (38); deterioration of the economic situation (31); anti-Semitism (21); the children decided to emigrate (18); for the sake of the children (9); increase in the level of crime (7); military conflicts in the Caucasus (9); insecure future (6); Chernobyl disaster (5); other reasons (10); no information (24).

Among the twenty-four informants who did not touch upon the subject, thirteen were children and young people aged sixteen and under when they immigrated. The psychologists Mirsky and Prawer (1999) found that in many families, adolescents were not asked whether they wanted to emigrate, and they were not involved in the process of decision making (86). The three primary reasons mentioned by our interviewees were "avalanche," the deterioration of the economy, and anti-Semitism. We use the metaphor "avalanche" to describe the situation in which our informants decided to emigrate because they felt that their social environment was vanishing. Quite a few of them said that they were afraid they would be left in the lurch; they were convinced that a mass exodus could not be accidental. Others admitted that this crucial decision was made at the suggestion of friends or mere acquaintances; still others said they emigrated to keep their friends company. Here are some examples:

Tamara Z., 51

This is what I thought: if Jews are emigrating, there must be some reason for it. Jews are no fools. If other Jews emigrate, so should we.

Piotr G., 43

Piotr: It all started accidentally. We had common friends in N., the town where we lived; we got acquainted at a party. And this woman, it turned out she was the head of the Visa and Registration department. . . . Incidentally, it would be better if you didn't give the name of the town.

Interviewer: Of course, we won't!

Piotr: So she is the head of the Visa and Registration department, and she, sort of, said, "Come on, do it, and I'll help you with the formalities."

Interviewer: Sort of, What are you waiting for?

Piotr: Yes, What are you doing here? She said, "If I could, I would also do it." And this is how it happened, and very fast it was.

> We simply applied and got the papers. It was very simple then. All the papers were prepared very quickly, and we left. The whole thing took no more than two or three months. And we woke up, as if from a dream, only here!

Piotr was not the only interviewee encouraged to emigrate by a non-Jewish friend. Yulia Kh., 53; Ella V., 69; and Emma R., 56 confided to us that they wouldn't have seriously considered emigration without such encouragement. Moreover, in the case of Yulia Kh., that encouraging friend was a KGB official, whose professional duties were to stop "politically immature" citizens from making "reckless" decisions. The other motif of interest in Piotr's story is his reminiscences of the preimmigration period as a semiconscious state, a dream. The literary scholar Vaiskopf (2001) also noticed the significance of this image in immigrants' perceptions (see his article dedicated to the theme of exodus in Russian-language fiction in Israel, "We Were as If in a Dream").

Anastasia Ts., 48

> How did we decide to emigrate? Well, it's a very difficult question. Everyone decided to move. I used to work in an antique bookstore, and every day people came to sell lots of books. And if once in a while there was a non-Jewish face I was surprised. People were moving. And nothing would stop them: neither the complicated emigration procedures nor the things they were leaving behind, whether it was property, apartments, or something else. The people . . . it was like a dam [*a "broken dam" is a metaphor used in Russian to symbolize powerful, uncontrollable movement or events previously long suppressed*]. . . . I think that sort of life [*pause*], LIFE THERE WAS ALWAYS BAD, in the psychological as well as in the physical sense, and it was always very difficult to survive there. . . . And so we left. But now it's next to impossible to explain these reasons clearly.

Many subjects mention various signs of the exodus: telephone books with names crossed out, disappearance of friends, an increasing feeling of loneliness, and so on. For Anastasia the most revealing symptom was the number of books brought to the secondhand bookstore where she worked. Note that she introduces the word combination *a non-Jewish face.* As we will discuss further, it is typical of ex-Soviets to determine members of the in- and out-groups on the basis of physical features.

Virtually all the Soviet Jews faced the question of whether or not to emigrate. As is evident in a newspaper interview with the Russian satirist Shenderovich, this question tormented even those who chose to stay.

> Interviewer: Did the idea of leaving [*the country*] ever appeal to you?
>
> Shenderovich: Well, it's not that it appealed to me, but when at the beginning of the 1990s, half of my telephone book moved to other countries for permanent domicile, I had a strange if not a panicky feeling. . . . Am I stupid? Everybody, but everybody, is leaving! Luckily I stayed. (Trolle 2002, 29)

Our material does not show that the mythology of homecoming to Israel had any palpable impact on the choice of migrants' destination. But this mythology was still strong in Israeli society in the early 1990s. Although the immigrant wave of the 1990s is referred to as the "big aliya," sociologists show that it was more of a migration (in Hebrew, *hagira*) than an aliya. The term *aliya*, "going up," has strong religious and Zionist connotations. The return to Zion has been incorporated into Jewish law as a religious obligation of the individual Jew and has been chosen by secular Zionism as the cornerstone of its political agenda (Wigoder 1989, 748). The metaphoric notion of "going up" has positive connotations and is coherent with the metaphorical structure of the most fundamental concepts in the culture (Lakoff and Johnson 1980, 22). Phraseological units containing the word *aliya*—for example, *aliya le-Regel* (going up for the festival, pilgrimage) and *aliya la-Torah* (going up to the reading of the Pentateuch)—illustrate the validity of this statement for Hebrew speakers (see Wigoder 1989, 47).

The motivation of the immigrants of the 1990s (primarily push factors) sharply contrasts with what is believed to have been the motivation of the immigrants of the 1970s. Yakhot (1973), claims that a sense of Jewishness presupposes the desire to live in Israel (42). Many individuals belonging to different immigration waves were without doubt ideologically motivated. Yet the uniqueness of immigrating to Israel as an ideological homecoming is overestimated, and so are the expectations that immigrants driven by Zionist ideas integrate more smoothly than others. Psychological studies show that immigrants with high motivation, be it "pull" or "push," tend to suffer from intense adaptation problems (Berry 1997, 16, 23). Thirty years later, some immigrants of the 1970s reevaluate their own motives and aspirations. One of the leading Russian-language journalists writes that the aliya of the 1970s was overwhelmingly anti-Soviet and potentially Zionist (Isakova 2003b, 22). In another article Isakova admits that Zionist enthusiasm faded away in the confrontation with Israeli bureaucrats. She believes that defeated expectations partially determined the modest, peripheral role of the 1970s immigrants in Israeli society. Isakova sees two more reasons for this: the lack of self-confidence and the relative small size of that immigration wave. She writes, "One thing is to fight the much-hated Soviet power, the other thing is to fight the people who had created the state, fought for it and treat you as an ungrateful orphan who was let into the house out of charity and who is not ashamed to show ingratitude. . . . For two decades we had to wait for mass support, and it finally came with the arrival of the aliya of the 1990s" (Isakova 2003a, 7). We find a similar conclusion in Kimmerling's sociological study (2001): "In the end, the two waves complemented each other. People of the first wave [of the 1970s], primarily its elite, established the institutional and cultural infrastructure into which the people of the second wave [of the 1990s] were absorbed, indirectly enabling the creation of the 'Russian' cultural and political enclave in Israel" (140). Apparently the distinction between the "ideological" wave of the 1970s and the "economic" wave of the 1990s, often ironically referred to by the immigrants themselves as the "sausage aliya," is not as clear-cut as is believed in Israeli society.

It is not only the Israeli mass media that influences and is influenced by this myth but also the everyday talk of the laymen and the social expectations from immigrants' stories. Many Israelis showed disappointment that the new immigrants of the 1990s did not fit the existing model of aliya. "Proper repatriates," "good *olim,*" would be expected to display their exhilaration at returning home and to show alienation or at least indifference to the old country, its language, culture, and traditions. Naturally, the society hoped the immigrants would undergo fast and total assimilation. But it quickly became clear that the FSU immigrants were unwilling to give up their affinity with the culture of the old country and often evinced indifference to the history and culture of the new one. Such an attitude to the Jewish state betrayed the expectation of Israeli society that the new aliya from the FSU would have a strong Jewish identity; otherwise there would be no reason for migrants to come to Israel (see Beker 1991, 454–56). Only recently have some questioned the mythology of uniqueness. Sociological and psychological studies show that immigration to Israel resembles immigration to any other country, and most newcomers are influenced by the political, social, and economic conditions in the countries of origin, not by any ideological attachment to the country of destination (Mirsky 2005; Shuval and Leshem 1998). The difference between those who wanted to immigrate to Israel and those willing to leave their unfriendly society without any particular wish to become Israelis was crucial when a choice of destinations existed. In 1989 the United States stopped granting automatic refugee status to Soviet Jews who left the USSR with an Israeli visa but "dropped out" and instead immigrated to the United States (DellaPergola 1998, 62).

As noted, our sample gave the same list of reasons for emigration as sociological investigations have yielded, although the distribution of responses is different. In the survey by Al-Haj and Leshem (2000), for example, only 4.4 percent of the respondents said that they had immigrated because "everyone else has done it" (11). According to Feldman's data, 54 percent of the respondents declared "avalanche" as the main reason, and in our sample, 26.5 percent. We attribute the marked difference in the number of subjects who chose this category to different interview types. Although Al-Haj and Leshem's survey was based on face-to-face interviews conducted in Russian, the respondents were offered a multiple-choice questionnaire, and the list of proposed options may have influenced the respondents' replies. Lebedeva (2001) cites the Russian psychologists Freinkman-Khrustaleva and Novikov, who investigated the reasons for emigration among the Jews, Germans, and Russians who emigrated to Germany at the beginning of the 1990s. "Everybody had left and so we left too" was marked as one of the main reasons by 65–72 percent of their informants (149).

Similarly, there are considerable differences in the immigrants' responses concerning the choice of destination. According to Al-Haj and Leshem (2000), "About half of the immigrants (50.2 percent) claim that even had they been totally free in their choice of destination they would still have come to Israel" (13). In our sample only a negligible number of subjects (five) claimed that they had consciously chosen Israel, as they wanted to be "among their own people." Most of our interviewees admitted that they had planned to immigrate to America and eventually landed in Israel only because "America had closed down."

Economic insecurity emerged as a prominent reason for emigration in the sociological surveys we have cited, and this is confirmed by our data. Because there are no discrepancies in various studies regarding this category and it does not elucidate the issue of immigrants' identity we will not dwell on it. The category that interests us most in this respect is anti-Semitism, the third most frequently cited reason in our sample. The remaining categories will not be discussed in detail because few narratives were devoted to them.[4] We observed only one difference between the motives of Jews and non-Jews in the distribution of categories: anti-Semitism. It emerges in the interviews with Halachic Jews and in the interviews with children of mixed marriages registered as non-Jews in Soviet documents. According to the data of the Russian historian Nosenko (2004), children with one Jewish parent, mother *or* father, experience discrimination both in Soviet and post-Soviet periods (217–47). It is important to note that in Al-Haj and Leshem's survey, fear of pogroms, anti-Semitism, and fear of discrimination were regarded as separate categories. However, according to our observations, discrimination was perceived by Soviet Jews as part of the anti-Semitic policy of the USSR, and the threat of pogroms as its most violent manifestation. The following interview excerpts illustrate this point.

Olga G., 72

> All my life I worked as an engineer-translator of technical literature, in a classified institute. . . . And at some point, our "special people" called for me. [Osobisty, *or "special people," is a Soviet newspeak term for KGB officers, employees of "special departments" in big enterprises and in academic institutions.*] Several times I was summoned to report there and they kept

> asking me about my attitude to Israel. I say, "I have no attitude at all." And they say, "Are you loyal to that country [*Israel*]?" I say, "Although I am Jewish, I don't consider it my country. It is completely alien to me, I have nobody abroad." And it was true. "My children are here, and my husband is here, and I have nothing to do with that Zion." And they summoned me for such talks five times. As far as I remember, it went on for two years. I didn't understand what it was all about. It never really reached the Urals, and in particular such "closed" towns as our Zlatoust. [*Apparently she means that few people emigrated from the Urals.*] And as a matter of fact, I wouldn't have left had it not been for a fateful coincidence. . . . Even bad food, you know, and stuff like this, didn't bother me. But once, in 1991, there was a program on the central TV, "The Voice of the People." And a middle-aged man went into that room with microphones and to my extreme surprise he said this, "Comrades Jews! You have ruined our country. You have turned Russia into a country of drunkards. You have captured all the cushy jobs everywhere, everywhere, everywhere." And he lists all these jobs. "And remember," he spoke long, "remember that a day will come, and there won't be enough planes for you!" When I heard that, I immediately remembered fascism and what things were like in those times. And I thought, "Will my children, will we in our old age, will we have to go through everything I have already been through?" And then my husband who was anxious to leave began to pressure me and I agreed. And we started making arrangements for going to Israel. We kept it secret, because there was some sort of a veto in our town on this issue. And finally after this whole ordeal we came here in 1992. We didn't know anybody and we didn't know anything. We came to emptiness.

Olga's story gives an example of the state anti-Semitism. Jews were suspected of disloyalty to the Soviet state and support of Israel even when there was no evidence. Yulia P., 58, for example, was turned down for a job on the mere suspicion that she used to go to the synagogue, which in fact, was wrong. Yulia M., 70; Galit B., 60+; Anastasia F., 43; and some others told stories of discrimination related to their university studies[5] (see these motifs in Azbel 1982). The lack of trust, however, was a familiar background for Soviet Jews, and many people learned to live with it.

Olga does not hesitate to show her complete indifference to Israel. Like four other non-Jewish spouses in the sample, her husband initiated the family's emigration. Some informants openly stated that they had actively opposed immigration to Israel but finally acquiesced because of their family's pressure or because of America's new immigration policy, which had "closed the gate." In Olga's case only an open manifestation of anti-Semitism in the mass media and implied threats broadcast by a central TV channel made her succumb to her husband's insistence on emigration.

The increase of Soviet nationalism in the early 1990s was, according to historians, a defensive response to the fall of communism and a painful transition to a market economy (Brudny 1998, 2). Nationalist intolerance was one of the main push factors not only for Jews but for FSU migrants of the 1990s in general (Iontsev 2001, 337–38; Lebedeva 2001, 150). Anti-Semitism always becomes more violent in periods of crises and social transitions (see, e.g., Cała 1995, 184–219). During perestroika, state-sponsored anti-Semitism was gradually becoming a thing of the past, but Jews were confronted with a new form of community anti-Semitism prevalent in the West but previously unfamiliar to Soviet Jews (Chlenov 1997, 14). The relaxation of censorship, one of the positive outcomes of glasnost, was accompanied by the emergence of various voluntary associations and organizations. Some of them were ultranationalist, such as the Russian National Patriotic Front "Memory" (in Russian, Pamiat'). In addition, numerous private publishing houses sprang up and circulated anti-Semitic propaganda leaflets and periodicals. They incited readers to do away with the so-called Judeo-Masonic conspiracy. These organizations intensified and legitimized popular anti-Semitism by institutionalizing it. Soviet Jews accustomed to covert state-sponsored anti-Semitism perceived the state's silence as implicit approval of these organizations. A number of interviewees mentioned that their decision to emigrate was directly influenced by the increasing influence of Pamiat'.

Laura M., 55

LAURA: [*About her decision to emigrate*] This was a slow process and in some sense, hardly noticeable at all. Is it working?

[*Points to the recorder.*] There were some instances that provoked and accelerated it. There were gatherings in the Rumiantsev Garden, those Pamiat' mobs. They were a curious and scary bunch to watch. Then there were some [*demonstrations*] with yellow banners and with lists of names. Do you remember this?

INTERVIEWER: I remember the meetings but I don't remember there were lists of names.

LAURA: Near the Kazan Cathedral. They had huge banners, and there were real names written on them, Sverdlov, you know, and, well. . . . They dug all of it out and. . . . Now it doesn't . . . but then it was all new, a real novelty. And it was scary. Then we found a flyer in our mailbox. I don't remember its exact contents, but I do remember it said there that on this and that date, be ready! Be prepared! And we would leave the town. We went to the country to my mom's; we went to my mother's.

INTERVIEWER: Was it in 1989? D'you remember when it was?

LAURA: I think it was in 1988. And then, when we received . . . we received the invitation; that is, we . . . oh, yes, this is how it was. . . . Our relatives began to attend some meetings. Either these were meetings with the staff of the [*Israeli*] embassy. . . . There were several meetings in the Kirov Palace [*one of the biggest community centers in Leningrad*]. And so we joined, to keep them company, because we are also Jews, and because we were also interested. . . .

Several times during the interview Laura mentions that her decision to emigrate was in some sense accidental and influenced by various coincidences. In this excerpt, although she shows that the fear of pogroms motivated her decision, she downplays the menace of the mounting anti-Semitism by saying that its new manifestations were so unusual that besides fear they inspired curiosity. Her memories of this period are associated with specific places in her hometown, and several times she appeals to the interviewer, also a Leningrader, to involve her in these reminiscences more actively. When she recalled that demonstrators had carried lists of names, she mentioned the name of a prominent Bolshevik, Yakov Mikhailovich (Moiseevich) Sverdlov. The search for scapegoats in the late 1980s, just as in the late 1940s, was accompanied by the disclosure of Russian pseudonyms of Jewish party leaders and members of the country's scientific and cultural elite. The nationalists wanted to show that Jews were the true perpetrators and bore responsibility for the failures in politics, the economy, and social life (see Oren and Prat 1988, 4:526–27 on the anti-Semitism of the 1940s and 1950s in the USSR).

The next passage is representative of many immigrants who left in the early 1990s. The narrator became fully aware of the threats of the ultranationalists only after warnings from a neighbor, who was not in danger herself. Equally menacing for Ella was the feeling of the "vacuum."

Ella V., 69

> The idea of emigration, this idea first emerged with the, er, panic, which began after the threats by the Leningrad "society Pamiat'" . . . We were told that there would be Jewish pogroms. . . . Er, it was in 1990. . . . And my neighbor, from the apartment next door, also heard it. This simple woman, [*pause*] a Russian, immediately came over and said, "Ella, if something happens, come over to my place at once." And it was simply horrible, because it was such a palpable feeling of fear. I'd never had it before. And until she came, we, er, we sort of. . . . But when she, a simple Russian woman, realized that there was danger for us and took it so seriously, we also considered the problem seriously. And the other thing, er, people started leaving. And I caught myself thinking that I keep crossing out numbers in my telephone book. And months passed by, and . . . we understood that we were left in a vacuum.

The same image previously used by Olga G.—when she said she had no friends and "arrived in emptiness" in Israel—was evoked by Ella when she described her hometown without old friends. Like Ella, many of our interviewees said that in the late 1980s and early 1990s their towns, and the entire country, which they had always considered to be their own, all at once became inhospitable and alien.

Tatiana Zh., 70

> Well, to start with, when the situation in Russia began to change, and not for the better, when Zhirinovsky[6] appeared [*pause*] and we didn't know what was behind him. And when these fascist organizations came into being, the TV sometimes showed their marches. . . . All of it was very unpleasant and worrisome, because, of course, I knew about anti-Semitism but never felt it myself. Because I am half Jewish, and my mum, my mum was Jewish. . . . She tried to do everything for me not to feel that I was Jewish; she did not want these genes to affect me. . . . To be honest, I didn't suffer. Well, I had a chance to do a Ph.D. without any problems, and I got a chair [*Tatiana was head of a university department*] without any trouble, and all of it. . . . But in spite of it all, inside. . . . When I saw how things were, I came to feel very uncomfortable to be here [*in Russia*] [*inaudible*]. For example in a street car . . . I avoided taking a seat, because I was afraid that someone would say, "Stand up, you kike! How dare you sit here?!" . . . These are just trifles, but the big thing, when I felt it was time . . . this was when Zhirinovsky won the elections. Then I really got scared. I was not scared for my own sake. My children didn't want to . . . they didn't want to move; they never raised this question at all. That is, my son, his wife is Russian, and my granddaughter, she is also Russian, because her mother is Russian. And he is not completely Jewish either, because I. . . . But she [*the granddaughter*] looks very Jewish. You know, her hair, her elongated face. . . . Well she looks precisely as a Jew, although she is blond and all that. . . . And I was scared, although she was Russian in her passport. But as they say, they hit you in the mug; they do not hit your passport. And I started acting in order to get out.

Later on Tatiana says that her children did not share her fears. She believed that by immigrating to Israel she was "blazing a trail" for the rest of the family. Her efforts proved to be futile because the children chose to immigrate to the United States. Note that Tatiana was not only registered in her Soviet papers as a non-Jew but her Jewish mother did her best to distance her child from her Jewish roots. While "clean" documents protected her career, they became an obstacle to emigration: it took Tatiana considerable effort to prove to the authorities that she was eligible for emigration. She was driven by fear for her granddaughter, and this fear also illustrates the change in the situation. Formally, the young girl was not Jewish, so she should not be subject to state-sponsored anti-Semitism, but her Jewish genes, which Tatiana's mother had tried to neutralize, played a cruel trick: the girl could become a target of anti-Semitism because of her physical features. To prove that "Jewish looking" Russians were bigger targets for anti-Semites than "Russian looking" Jews, Tatiana alludes to a frequently told joke, which we will discuss in the next section.

Tatiana felt particularly uncomfortable in crowded public places, which implies that she feared that a potential attacker, not the victim of anti-Semitic abuse, would find support in the passersby. Abuse in public places, particularly in public transport and at stores during times of food shortages, was reported by several other interviewees—for example, Vladimir B., 70; Sofia Y., 48; Rimma G., 69; and others. The interviewees spoke about the feeling of anxiety, caused by the ultranationalists' activities, anti-Semitic speeches broadcast on central TV, and anti-Semitic flyers and posters that appeared in towns in the late 1980s and early 1990s. According to Ryvkina's data, anxiety among FSU Jews remained intense into the mid-1990s. Both she and Lebedeva point out that the number of respondents reflecting on anti-Semitic activities considerably exceeded the number of those who had faced them personally (Lebedeva 2001, 150; Ryvkina 1996, 115–37).

The widely publicized, violent anti-Semitism of that period frightened Jews and sped up decisions to emigrate. Moreover, it made people reconsider their past, in which anger and pain caused by prejudiced hatred were suppressed because the Jews, except for dissidents, felt themselves powerless and unable to oppose discrimination actively. Anti-Semitism did not always cause people to emigrate, but readiness to face it was an important part of feeling Jewish.

Feeling Jewish in the USSR

In the Soviet Union, Jews were viewed as an ethnic group with shared genetic characteristics. The systematic destruction of Jewish cultural institutions, persecution of Hebrew teachers, and discrimination against religious believers made several generations of Soviet people, including the Jews themselves, forget the religious culture that defines and unites Jews wherever they live (Garfinkle 1997, 5). Gitelman (1992) points out one of the many ironies of this Soviet practice. The state based on Marx's vision of the disappearance of nations had adopted measures, such as official registration of nationality and the near impossibility of changing it, that ensured the preservation of ethnic identity and consciousness even among those who would have liked to get rid of it. Jews remained identified as Jews in the USSR, not because they wished to be part of the Jewry but because the Soviet state classified and registered them as such. Society similarly regarded them as a distinct entity and sometimes put them in a defensive position, thereby forcing them to acknowledge and defend their identity. In the USSR the distinction of Jewishness, understood as *ethnic identity,* from Judaism, understood as *religion,* made possible the survival of Jewishness despite the near destruction of Judaism (Gitelman 1992, 76). Today, the subversive role of the "fifth paragraph" is discussed by social scientists in Russia. Referring to it as the "ill-famed fifth paragraph," Ryvkina (1996) points out that it was the source of numerous problems in public and private life and prevented complete assimilation (82–86). In the essay "Farewell to the Fifth Paragraph" Tishkov (2001b) says that the practice of registering ethnicity in the internal passport, introduced in 1934, was absurd and subversive as a concept and as a procedure (88).

After immigrating to Israel, Soviet Jews became aware that the concept of Jewishness has aspects that were completely new to them. Many were surprised to find that not all Jews are white-skinned, and that religion and observance of the tradition are important dimensions of being Jewish. This topic leaves few of the FSU immigrants indifferent, because heated discussions about "how Jewish" the immigrants of the 1990s are persist in the media and in laypeople's talk even fifteen years after the beginning of the big wave of immigration. The next two excerpts exemplify the confusion in the immigrants' perceptions.

Zena B., 53

ZENA: I had never seen black Jews, and I didn't even SUSPECT that Ethiopians were Jewish too. And somehow, for a moment it occurred to me that Jews were not a nationality but a re-li . . . a faith . . .

INTERVIEWER: Well, many people think so.

ZENA: I don't understand it. In the Union [*the Soviet Union*], there, in the old times I thought that a Jew is a nationality. And now I simply don't understand. If you take this into consideration. . . . I feel confused and do not understand who I am. It's very difficult, very! And if you take it seriously, I think, it involves a lot of problems. So I try to distance myself from it not to think about it too much. To have one more problem now. . . . I've ENOUGH without it!

This excerpt reveals the interviewee's confusion and bewilderment. It's not only the triple repetition of the words "I don't understand" and the alternation of hesitation and emphasis, indicated in the transcript by the punctuation marks. Her otherwise smooth and eloquent speech turns into a series of unfinished sentences. In oral communication, fragmented sentences, repairs, hesitations, or pauses may signal doubt. Hesitation and modifications may also indicate self-censorship or uneasiness when topics with negative associations are discussed (van Dijk 1989, 119; Wodak et al. 1999, 10). In the preceding excerpt broken sentences reveal the interviewee's face-keeping strategies. The problem bothers Zena even though she is not personally affected. As the daughter of a Jewish mother and a Polish father she was registered in the USSR as a Russian while in Israel she is registered as a Jew. She can afford not to deliberate on the meaning of Jewishness because it does not affect her children's or her own status in Israel (the fathers of her three children are non-Jewish). Moreover, she is reluctant to think about the problem of ethnic identity, fearing that her nonconformist opinions will get her into trouble. Equally, she is afraid to show her dissent with what she believes to be the mainstream opinion about Arabs (see chapter 3). Fear of holding political opinions different from those prescribed by society is the legacy of the Soviet past and is shared by some middle-aged and elderly informants. Like many people brought up in a collectivist culture, Zena values the sense of belonging, yet she sees that it means more than an appropriate entry in the ID. She is afraid to face the dilemma of finding what unites her with her new compatriots. In this regard, Zena represents many immigrants, who tend to focus on everyday problems rather than on metaphysical issues.

Arkadii T., 57

> I thought that Jewishness is just blood. Let's compare, say Christians. Say, he is a Catholic. Say, in England, Poland, Russia, or, say, Africa or Australia. But this African guy, from, say, Mozambique, doesn't become English, French, or a Pole. It's just his faith. Well, with us, as we see, it doesn't really matter where you come from. A black Ethiopian or a Taimanets [*Russified Hebrew for a "Yemeni"*]. . . . The main thing is your faith. . . . Well, after all, why not? If this is what matters . . . then may it be as long as he is, as they say, a true *ben-adam*, a proper human being.

Arkadii claims that he has accepted religion as a major dimension of Jewishness, but in fact his definition of a Jew is based on an idealized image and includes such features as intellect, a sense of responsibility, and a humane character. He is ready to come to terms with the fact that dark-skinned Yemenis and Ethiopians are Jewish if they are "proper human beings." Many immigrants are still grappling with the concept of the Jew even after a decade of living in Israel. In the Soviet Union the concepts of nationality and citizenship were separated, hence Arkadii's inability to understand that an African from a former French colony can be a French citizen. This misconception was also reported by other informants. Anastasia F., 43, for example, recounted an incident in the airport in Paris. An official at the border control corrected the entry form by replacing "Jewish" with "Israeli" in the entry for nationality, despite her protests that an Israeli can be an Arab, a Ukrainian, a Uzbek, and so on. While Anastasia equated nationality with ethnicity, the clerk equated nationality with citizenship.

In some sense the Soviet legal system encouraged Jews to give up their ethnic identity. In the USSR children of mixed marriages could choose their mother's or father's ethnicity when they received their ID at the age of sixteen (see chapter 1). Although most of the "halves" were registered as non-Jews, their self-identification varied. The dilemma of how to register often created an inner conflict, for example in single-parent families when a teenager was forced by circumstances to choose the ethnicity of the father who was not involved in his or her upbringing (see stories about the choice of nationality in Fialkova and Yelenevskaya 2004b, 146–50).

There was seldom talk of Jewishness in the presence of children. Parents deliberately avoided it so as not to "traumatize" the young.

Inna Kh., 52

INNA: At home, the atmosphere was refined, devoid of any national traits. It was devoid of anything special! . . . But I did know, and again because this is what the courtyard is for, I knew that my father had a reputation, he had a reputation of a defender of Jews.

INTERVIEWER: Was such reputation an asset or a drawback?

INNA: I cannot even say this for sure. In principle, the attitude was good.

INTERVIEWER: To your father?

INNA: Yes. And then . . . well, in some sense, I was untainted; I did not understand these things. I grew up in this, what did we call it? In the family of brotherly nations. But again, thanks to the courtyard I understood that it was better to be Byelorussian than Jewish; no one would call you a "kike's snout."

Attempts to bring their children up in the spirit of internationalism were a combination of fading romantic hope for building a society of complete equality and a silent admission that these hopes had failed.[7] Ironically, Inna refers to herself as "untainted" by unnecessary knowledge and calls the atmosphere at home "refined." But the stark truth of de facto inequality emerged in communication with her peers and often was in complete contrast with the ideals and principles preached at home. Another "half," Veronika R., said that she started defiantly telling everyone that she was Jewish at the age of fifteen or sixteen after a school friend told her he would never marry her because she was Jewish (from the ethnographic diaries[8]). Sofia Sh., 31, also recalls that as an adolescent she considered it important to declare her Jewishness, as if it were a handicap. She felt that concealing it could complicate future relations with people. But even while declaring herself Jewish, she did not have affinity with Jews. The family never observed the traditions, except for eating matzoth when Sofia's grandmother sent it from another town. She said, "Like all the normal people [*non-Jews*] we used to tell jokes about Jews." We agree with Nosenko and Sinel'nikov, who conclude that ethnic identity of the "halves" varies depending on the circumstances but is not determined by the sense of belonging to Halachic Jews (Nosenko 2004, 124; Sinel'nikov 2004).

Children whose parents were both Jewish also faced difficulties in identifying themselves as Jewish. Anastasia F., 43, for example, admitted that at the age of twelve she had to force herself to learn to answer the question directly instead of clumsily avoiding the issue and murmuring, "What difference does it make?" Similar feelings were described by Larisa Bogoraz (1973), a dissident who immigrated to Israel in the 1970s. She wrote that only at school had she learned she was Jewish and that in this way she differed from her schoolmates to her disadvantage. She recalled that in 1945–46 she felt more Jewish than ever because of growing anti-Semitism. She declared with demonstrative pride that she was Jewish. But the show of pride was only to boost her own courage: "See, I'm not afraid to admit this shameful fact of my biography" (61–62). For several generations of Soviet Jews these feelings were inseparable from the process of growing up, part of the rite of passage. The acuteness of the inner conflict could bring an adolescent to the brink of nervous breakdown.

Maria S., 25

> My aliyah began long before. . . . It was like this. One day, my mother came into my room, and her eyes were shining with excitement. She said: "Isa wants to go to Israel, and I also want to!" I was terrified. Isa is my mum's friend. I was simply terrified. What's this? Shall we betray our Motherland? I fell into a trance. For a long time I couldn't recover. But later I digested it. I was in the eighth grade then and I was thinking about it all. At the time there was an exhibition of Israeli books in Moscow, and my grandpa went to see it. I was terrified. How can he do it? They will catch him in the act! In fact all my life I was afraid to be unmasked. When I went to school, my parents registered me as non-Jewish. And during all those ten years I

> was terribly scared. In the middle of the night, I would wake up, all sweaty, because I had nightmares that I was unmasked. I was very scared. I did my best not to think about having such a blemished biography. And then I hear such a thing from my own mum! It's not only that she admits that she belongs to the Jewish nation, but she also wants to betray our Motherland. But time passed and I digested it. How can I tell my friends about it [*emigration*]? God forbid! I was terribly afraid that somebody would learn about it. But finally my parents said: "You have to apply for the internal passport. And you know what you have to write there." . . . Trembling with horror, I went to the housing office, or to some other office of this sort. I went to apply for an internal passport. I handed in all those documents, and my hand was trembling. Then some time later I received my internal passport, and in a rather clumsy way the word Jew was written there; it was not calligraphic at all. I looked at it, slammed the passport shut, and put it away quickly. At the end of the tenth grade I had to bring it to school. And on the day I gave it to them—they needed it to write out my matriculation certificate—my fears of being exposed finally came to an end. As soon as the head teacher of my class saw the documentary proof of what she had always suspected, she rushed to tell everyone about it right away. They flunked me in several exams, those which were supervised by our headmistress, who was a terrible anti-Semite.

Maria, her papers possibly faked to make her school life easier, was anxious that her Jewishness would be exposed and that she would become an outcast. Her choice of words to describe her inner state shows the dimensions of the drama: "nightmares," "trembling hand," "terrified," "terribly scared," and so on. Even with the word "Jewish" written in her brand-new passport she could not accept that it applied to her. She perceived Jewishness as shameful and criminal: she was afraid that merely going to the government-sanctioned Israeli exhibition could be punished. Like Shimon K., 18, Maria considered emigration to be treason, which shows the impact of the Soviet propaganda on the minds of minors.

Maria's family considered it important to hide their Jewishness, but as soon as the decision to emigrate was made the values changed, and from a stigma Jewishness turned into a password. Another informant who immigrated as an adolescent ironically referred to a similar change of self-identification in his family:

Victor P., 22

INTERVIEWER: And how did you . . . how did they [*your parents*] explain to you where you were leaving for, why you were leaving . . .

VICTOR: Well, they explained, it's clear, it's . . . I understood right away where we were going. We were going to Israel, er . . . and everything, so to speak, took the right shape. And we immediately became Jewish.[9]

INTERVIEWER: And before that?

VICTOR: And before that we were Russian.

The repressive nature of the Soviet state not only nurtured fear of doing something not allowed or approved of it also inspired people to look for ways of bypassing the law and cheating the system (see chapter 1). It takes two to cheat, and the representatives of authority who were involved helped for a bribe or as an act of friendliness. One of our interviewees, Ella O., 55, confided in us that she had been persuaded by a police official to register as Latvian although both of her parents were Jewish (Fialkova and Yelenevskaya 2004b, 148–49); another informant, Anastasia Ts., 48, told us with amusement that she had managed to obtain three internal passports. In two of them she was registered as Jewish, and in the third one as a Russian. The reader is free to guess which of them she presented to her prospective employers.

We have already seen how the "fifth paragraph" could be manipulated. It was thought easier to conceal one's identity when the father was not Jewish because of his non-Jewish surname and patronymic. Only under certain circumstances—if a person was being considered for a prestigious position or if he or she was traveling on a business trip to the West—did a person have to fill in more detailed applications, which required the mother's maiden name and would thus reveal the person's Jewish roots. These closer screenings often led to a denied promotion or to the cancellation of a trip. If the father was Jewish, his name tagged the child as Jewish for the authorities. In that case the only way to hide the

Jewish roots legally was to give the child the mother's surname.[10] But the ruse did not rid the person of the stigma; it only changed its nature. When a child bore his or her mother's name it could signal one of the two things, illegitimacy or concealed Jewishness. This practice was distained by Jews and non-Jews alike.

The desire to sever all ties with the Jewry triggered numerous jokes and sayings. Many of them were related to physical features, family names, and patronymics. Let us compare two examples. In the first a teacher comes to class and says, "Children, tomorrow we are to host an Arab delegation. Rabinowitz, Haimovitz, and you, Ivanov on your mother's side, stay at home tomorrow." The other example is the jocular phrase "Ivanov, a Jew on his mother's side." The two phrases look almost identical, but refer to two different situations. In the joke, "Ivanov on his mother's side" has a Jewish father so he is not a Halachic Jew (i.e., not a Jew according to Jewish law). Nevertheless, he, too, is subject to anti-Semitic abuse. As a rule, children bore their father's name, although as noted, they could legally choose their mother's family name. But, as emerges from the joke, the mere change of name would not deceive a vigilant anti-Semite. In the second example the father is Russian and the name has not been changed. Paradoxically, having a Jewish father made a person more of a Jew in Soviet terms. Although any person with a Jewish mother is a Halachic Jew, in the Soviet mind the name Ivanov was only for Russians. It was as much of a symbol of Russian-ness as Rabinowitz was of Jewishness; so a Jew bearing the prototypical Russian name Ivanov is a hilarious absurdity. At the same time both phrases could be used by Jews to indicate that these "ethnic marginals" belonged to the in-group and so were not rejected.

Voronel (1973) observes that when a Soviet Jew filled out an internal passport or any other questionnaire and answered a question about nationality, he or she was singled out willy-nilly. While this type of information in the passport of a Russian or a Ukrainian had no practical effect on the person's future, for a Jew—and we should add Gypsies, Germans, Chechens, Tatars, and some others—it was the cornerstone of his or her biography. "In the eyes of the policymakers, of the people around Jews and even in their own eyes, a Jew became a member of a category, not an individual in his/her own right" (30; see also Alexandrova 2002; Bezelianskii 2000). Thus Jewish identity was imposed, not chosen by free will. To get rid of this "birthmark" that hampered their upward mobility, Soviet Jews Russified their family names, assumed literary pseudonyms, or bribed officials to change the entry in the notorious fifth paragraph of their internal passports (Remennick 1998, 242).

Boastfully calling itself "the family of brotherly nations,"[11] the Soviet Union bred interethnic intolerance and xenophobia, which was frequently reflected in the language. It is from the Soviet Union that Russia inherited an underdeveloped culture of interethnic relations, in which citizens of a country are treated not as citizens but as "bioids," species with different blood and facial features (Ryvkina 1996, 137).

As we have already mentioned, Soviet social realities triggered the emergence of the concepts of "half" and "quarter" with respect to ethnicity. In addition, the expression "Jew on her mother's/father's side" was often used in earnest. Our sample provided the following example, recorded from Boris N., 59. He remarked: "My daughter [*pause*] went to university. Her friends seemed a peculiar bunch of people; that is, well, there were all sorts there, Uzbeks and Jews, and you know . . . And then she goes and marries a Jew, well, a Jew on his father's side, yeah, a Jew on his father's side." An ethnic Russian, Boris boasted that all his life he had Jewish friends, who always considered him "one of ours." Yet when describing his daughter's multiethnic environment he referred to its denizens as a "peculiar bunch of people" and people of "all sorts," both phrases having slightly pejorative connotations. The outcome of these friendships—his daughter's marriage to a "Jew on his father's side"—did not fill Boris with enthusiasm because it increased the chances that his daughter, a "Jew on her mother's side," would emigrate, an option that other family members were not considering at that time.

The concept of "halves" outlived the Soviet system and is still widely used in the immigrant community. Recently one of the authors overheard the following conversation between two supermarket workers. One of them explained to her colleague how to make Uzbek dishes such as *plov, shurpa, manty, samsa,* and so on. The latter asked in surprise:

"How do you know all this?"

"Because I am half Muslim;[12] after all, my father comes from Central Asia." (from the ethnographic diaries)

The distorted Soviet concepts of ethnicity, ethnic identity, nationality, and religion persist despite the far more intense exposure to Jewish culture in Israel than in the FSU, and even the knowledge acquired during studies in Israel. Here are some more examples from our sample:

LEONID B., 36: According to my ID, I'm Byelorussian.

EKATERINA R., 24: My father's classmate . . . and incidentally, if you are interested in nationality, he was a Muslim.

Iakov K., 80, speaking to his colleagues on his retirement, said that in the Soviet Union he had never concealed his nationality and added, "I have never been religious, I have never been a Zionist, but I have always been a Jew!" (ethnographic diaries). A Haifa University student submitted a course project in which she interviewed immigrants from the FSU and then analyzed their narratives. On an interviewee personal-data form, she described one of them as "half Jewish, half Christian."

Just as the new meaning of "halves" has gradually spread from the description of Jews to other ethnicities and even religions, another cliché of the Soviet era used in talking about Jews has become a stable element in the xenophobic vocabulary of the post-Soviet period. In the Soviet press and public discourse the word "Jew" was carefully avoided, as if it were pejorative. Instead, Soviet propaganda coined the phrase "persons of the Jewish nationality." In his collection of words and expressions of Soviet newspeak, Sarnov refers to this absurd combination as a euphemism, a manifestation of the Soviet hypocrisy. But all of the replacement for "Jew"—"rootless cosmopolitan" "Zionist," and "person of Jewish nationality"—were political labels and were continuously used to expose the "enemies of the people." Sarnov and Lemon conclude they were no more than calques of the "kike's snout" (Lemon 1998, 46–47; Sarnov 2002, 221–27). In the 1990s, the same euphemism was applied to people from the Caucasus. Whether they were Chechens, Ossetians, or Circassians, they all came to be called "persons of Caucasian nationality" or "persons from the Southern nationalities" (see Krysin 1996 about euphemisms in contemporary Russian speech). These, of course, are mythological constructs. It is typical of an ethnocentric worldview to see various others as a uniform group—for example *"aziaty, chornye, churki, Uzbeki"* (Asians, blacks, lumps, Uzbeks), all referring to people of non-European appearance. Such a usage not only expands the meaning of the words, it makes its connotative components prevail over the denotative. Members of various ethnic minorities are sensitive to the contempt expressed in such labels, and this is reflected in folklore. Aleksandra L., 82, a pensioner from Moscow, told us a joke, essentially a pun: the Russian word *litso* has several meanings, among them "face" and "person." The joke runs as follows: "Advertisement: I would like to exchange the face of a Caucasian national for a kike's snout. Additional payment guaranteed." Since the beginning of the unrest in the Caucasus (ethnic conflicts in Nagornyi Karabakh and Abkhazia, and above all the Chechen war), xenophobic attitudes toward people from the Caucasus have become more marked than toward Jews. The joke implies that the social status of the Jew has greatly improved thanks to the possibility of emigration from Russia.

We have assembled an entire collection of texts containing the original cliché and its paraphrases. These range from academic essays to newspaper articles, published in both Russia and Israel. For example, when analyzing various waves of emigration from Russia, the linguist Zemskaia (2001) writes, "The third wave, to a large extent, consists of dissidents, persons of Jewish nationality, and representatives of various creative and intellectual professions, who had to leave or were expelled from the USSR" (41). The statement seems peculiar not only because a linguist forthrightly uses a cliché that has become notorious for its xenophobic connotations but also because it implicitly includes Jews in the groups opposing Soviet power. Hinting at the special status enjoyed by the residents of Moscow, a journalist of the popular weekly *Argumenty i fakty* (Arguments and Facts) referred to them as "persons of Moscow nationality." In an article on Islamic terrorism the same paper expressed concern about the rapid growth of the Arab population: "Already today, sixty out of every hundred people in the world are 'persons of the Arab-Asian nationality.'"[13] The rising xenophobic tendencies in Russia mostly target nonwhites and are supported by the actions of the authorities. As Lemon (1998) has observed, in the post-Soviet years those called "blacks" and "southerners" have been routinely rounded up and expelled from Moscow for document violations (46).

In a growing number of texts, allusions to the cliché are used to criticize and mock xenophobia. The Russian historian Diatlov (2000) titled a chapter of his book on ethnic relations in Siberia as follows: "Persons of Geographic Nationality: Migrants from the Caucasus in the Socioeconomic Life of Irkutsk." He points out that the gradually evolving notion of a *kavkazets* (Caucasian) now frequently includes people from Central Asia (91). Here, too, the meaning of the word is expanding.

In an article about the various difficulties confronting non-Jews in Israel the Israeli journalist Martynova (2002a) writes that "persons of a 'mistaken nationality' still cannot get married in Israel or invite members of their family to visit them." The most curious example of all is the title of an article by the literary critic Barabash (1999), "'Persons of Basurman Nationality' in the Writing of Gogol' and Schevchenko." *Basurman* is an archaic word used to denote someone alien, a person of a different faith, primarily Muslims. In contemporary speech it is used pejoratively to refer to people from Central Asia, Muslim clergy, and even drug traffickers from Central Asia (Mokienko and Nikitina 2001, 53). Thus the Soviet stereotype can even be applied to the analysis of pre-Soviet literature, where it requires the addressees to make complex transformations, and to the interpretation of historically distant texts within the framework of the same social code (see Hodge and Kress 1988, 162–68). Importantly, the greater the semantic disparity between the attribute and the noun "nationality" in these examples, the more complex the transformations and the more intense the ironic power of the allusion. Honko (1986) points to the importance of such linguistic phenomena as implications, allusion, and ellipses for folkloristic research. They "fill" sentences with meaning via the context; it is impossible to read the meaning only from the wording of the sentences because they act as signals carrying the transformed meaning to the addressee (41).

We have already given examples of the use of allusions and jokes in the interviewees' talk about identity. They are also used to reproduce the stereotypes of Jews. Stereotypes are simplistic descriptions and tend to be exaggerated, overly generalizing, and ideologically charged. Many of them have no clear relationship to social facts (Eriksen 1995, 252–53). In our sample the autostereotypes are bipolar and either idealize Jews or humble them.

Inna F., 26

INTERVIEWER: Inna, you say that in Russia you considered yourself to be Jewish. What does this mean?

INNA: In Kaluga it was prestigious.

INTERVIEWER: Prestigious?

INNA: Yes. Because in our town Jews were university lecturers, chief engineers of all the factories, directors of warehouses, and so on; that is, it was elitist. To meet a Jewish boy and date him was an object of desire and a cause of endless envy on the part of the girls. It was, these were the most interesting boys who studied in the best colleges.

Anastasia N., 61

The only thing which really upsets me here [*in Israel*] is that . . . I had always thought that en masse Jews are very intelligent. Intelligent and sensible, that is, like Prometheus, seeing things ahead of time. And they turned out to be Epimetheus, every one, I think. Well, with few exceptions, just like anywhere else.

Yulia P., 58

We did not receive a particularly hearty welcome, but it was okay and businesslike. It was at the end of December when sunny Israel welcomed us. In three hours we were already in Haifa, and it surprised us by its greenery. I was afraid that an accumulation of Jews is a terrible thing. I imagined them screaming and with hooked noses. But it all turned out to be different.

Mikhail N., 64, and Yulia N., 63

INTERVIEWER: Do you feel psychologically more comfortable here than in Ukraine?

MIKHAIL: Yes, yes, but I cannot say that in the thirty-nine years I worked in the mine, I was ever confronted with anti-Semitism. To go down to the mine, to put on a uniform, to take a flashlight and safety equipment—everyone does it. And everyone is below the rock that can cave in on you any second. So this makes everyone equal.

YULIA: Jews were such a rarity in their mine!

MIKHAIL: There were four Jews in the mine. But they were treated like everybody else.

YULIA: Because they worked like dogs, like everybody else.

MIKHAIL: Well, probably because of this, they were honest decent people, normal.

YULIA: The professor, who operated on him, this kidney surgery, you know . . . [*in Israel*]. And he says . . . when we came to the hospital he examined him, and he says, "Why are you so bored?" [*In conversational Russian "bored" is sometimes used instead of "sad."*] Well, his Russian was not very fluent. "Why are you so bored? What was your occupation?" He [*the husband*] says to him that he'd worked in the mine. And he [*the professor*] says, "A Jew working as a miner? It's impossible!" (IFA 21740)

Both positive and negative autostereotypes tend to be volatile, and they were often reevaluated after immigration. Inna refers to Jews as the elite of her town and unwittingly repeats the anti-Semitic conviction that Jews had captured all the prestigious positions. In the USSR she was proud to be Jewish although she was registered as Russian. In Israel she is also registered as Russian, which from time to time creates difficulties in her life; for example she could not get married in Israel but had to arrange her wedding by proxy in Paraguay. In a way, she was deprived of part of her identity. While Anastasia N.'s image of the Jew was devalued, Yulia P.'s anti-Semitic attitudes gradually faded. Yulia reproduces a typical anti-Semitic stereotype emphasizing the unattractiveness of Jewish physical features. Upon arrival in Israel she was surprised and a little ashamed to find that her image of the Jew had been distorted. We see it as a sad result of the long-term anti-Semitic propaganda in the Soviet Union, which made some Soviet Jews internalize the anti-Semitic stereotypes. Nurtured in the Diaspora, they have not disappeared in Israel completely. One example is the belief that Jews avoid jobs requiring physical strength and danger (see Mikhail's story). Another is self-hatred.

Simona K., 23

> [*About the first impressions in Israel.*] I remember somebody, a guide or something of the sort, he drove us into a room, well, probably he didn't drive us but showed us into a room. . . . And he said, "Look guys, Jews are okay when they are few, they are like manure . . . they fertilize soil when they are few. But when they are many . . . they simply burn it."[14] I remember this very vividly. And I also remember that he was wearing some horrible sandals and shorts. And I looked at him totally bewildered [*laughs*]. What was it?

This excerpt repeats the motif expressed by Yulia P. and recorded in our ethnographic diaries. As an adolescent in the Soviet Union, Simona was ashamed of her Jewish family name, which made her feel different from others. But she was humiliated and shocked by the first joke she heard on Israeli soil from an Israeli official. Note that although she does not remember who the teller was, her memory has retained his "horrible sandals and shorts." Like long hooked noses, which were part of the Jewish stereotype in the USSR, sandals and shorts worn in informal and formal settings have become part of the stereotype of the Israeli among the immigrants (see chapter 3).

Returning to the self-perception of Soviet Jews, it would be an exaggeration to say that their Jewishness was reduced merely to a stamp in their internal passport. Many spoke about some elements of the Jewish tradition that had been preserved in families despite all the obstacles. But the meaning of the tradition had undergone significant changes, often remaining obscure even to those who tried to observe it.

Arkadii T., 57, and Yulia T., 50

INTERVIEWER: Was your family interested in its Jewish roots?

ARKADII: Yes, yes, we . . . we were forced to . . . because beginning with our internal passport, from the fifth paragraph . . . and very often "they wouldn't hit your passport, but would hit you in the mug."

YULIA: No, Arkadii, the question was, whether your family had observed any Jewish traditions.

ARKADII: I believe the Jewish traditions were observed in many families of the intelligentsia. We tried to observe such holidays as Pesakh [*Hebrew for "Passover"*]. . . . We liked it because when we were students, we mostly mixed with Jewish kids. And those who knew at least something would even show off their knowledge of Jewish traditions and the Jewish way of life.

Arkadii's misunderstanding of the interviewer's question is not accidental. He habitually interprets everything Jewish in terms of nationality, rather than as culture and a distinctive way of life. Moreover, unwittingly, he reveals that he perceived his Jewishness as an act of coercion on the part of the state, not as an internalized and consciously chosen identity. Arkadii mentions the notorious fifth paragraph, which has already appeared in excerpts from other interviews. Although it was found on all internal passports, it came to connote Jewishness and was used in such expressions as "he has the fifth paragraph," "he didn't get this job because of the fifth paragraph," and "he/she is an invalid of the fifth group/paragraph."[15] Martynova's definition of non-Jews in Israel as "persons of a mistaken nationality," which we quoted earlier, is a milder version of "invalids of the fifth paragraph," and implies that their situation mirrors that of the Jews in the Soviet Union. The connotative meaning of the fifth paragraph was ultimately fixed in the language after the anti-Semitic practices of the Soviet authorities were derided in a song by the prominent poet and cult figure of the 1960s and 1970s, Vladimir Vysotskii. The song is about two drunkards, a Russian and a Jew, who decide to immigrate to Israel. The Russian is granted permission to emigrate, while the Jew is not, because of the fifth paragraph.

Arkadii implies that Jews, including "halves," were always ready to confront anti-Semitism. He alludes to the Soviet joke built on the antithesis of official documents and physical features; Russian-ness as expressed by the prototypical name Ivanov versus disguised Jewishness.

> "Ivanov, don't go to Lenin Street."
> "What's up?"
> "They beat Jews up there."
> "But what does it have to do with me? It says in my passport that I am Russian."
> "You don't understand. They won't hit your passport; they'll hit your bloody mug."

When Arkadii's wife clarifies the interviewer's question about his interest in his Jewish roots, he does not give a direct answer about his family, but prefers to generalize. It is not clear from his enumeration of the Jewish holidays whether he was familiar just with their names or really knew their history and meaning. The only exception is Passover, which is consistent with what we heard from other subjects: even secular and assimilated Jews knew about that holiday and tried to get or even make their own matzoth.

The other interesting motif in this extract is that Arkadii links the observance of tradition to social class. In claiming that it was the prerogative of the intelligentsia he turns tradition into an elitist practice. Moreover, even meager knowledge of it would elevate someone in the eyes of his or her peers. Judging by the other interviews, Arkadii is wrong in his assumptions about the role of the intelligentsia in the preservation of Jewish tradition.

The Fractured Mosaic: Fragments of the Jewish Tradition

As we have already noted, most of our interviewees admitted ignorance of Jewish culture. Yet we cannot agree with Leshem and Lissak (1999) that "for a large portion of Jews from the former Soviet Union, Jewish identity is a purely technical matter expressed in their passport or through their illegibility to immigrate to Israel under the amendment to the Law of Return" (139). One should not dismiss the feeling of in-group solidarity, which was closely associated with the perception of a common fate and collective memory. This memory was perpetuated by folklore: songs in Yiddish, parables, jokes, and, above all, personal narratives. These narratives recounted stories about pogroms, Nazi atrocities, and Stalinist anti-Semitic campaigns, in particular, his prosecution of "rootless cosmopolitans" and the "Doctors Trial."[16] Besides,

Soviet Jews used to share stories about difficulties at entering universities, getting jobs and promotions, and clandestine news about the life of friends and relatives who had emigrated. In addition, when lists of prizewinners—whether for achievements in sciences, arts, or sports—were published, Jews used to look for Jewish names and compute their percentage of the total. Success and fame of co-ethnics usually triggered joy and pride for "our own." As a rule, the audience and participants in such conversations were either Jews or people whose friendly attitude was not in doubt. The ability to share memories, rage, and laughter was a distinctive feature of the group.

As we have already mentioned in chapter 1, questions about customs and traditions were standard in our interviews. We learned that some informants could speak only about Soviet holidays and customs.

Yulia N., 63

> You know, I was a bad Jew. I grew up in such a family . . . my father was a communist, it was before the war, well, and when I got married, my husband's father was the party secretary of a mine. It was this sort of family, you know what I mean. . . . By the way, I knew about the existence of Pessakh, just from some people. But I learned about Rosh ha-Shana only here, in Israel, and I feel ashamed of it.

Noubar Aslanyan, 58

INTERVIEWER: Were there any holidays, any elements [*of the Jewish tradition*] in your family?

NOUBAR: You know what? I won't lie. Back there we were all good or almost good Armenians. There is a proverb. They say in Armenia: If a dog is placed next to another dog, it will learn how to bite and how to bark.

Yulia N. was hardly ashamed of her fully assimilated life while she lived in the Soviet Union. Note that she attributes it to her father's and her father-in-law's influence. The latter made a career as a party secretary, and it was inconceivable that any religious traditions would be maintained in the family of a party official. While Yulia refers to herself as a "bad Jew," Noubar generalizes and refers to all the Jews of Armenia as "good or almost good Armenians." Both of them imply affinity or lack of affinity with the culture and tradition (compare this with the American Jews, who define a "good Jew" in vaguely moral terms [Heilman 1998, 80]). In fact, in the pre-immigration years Noubar became an active member of the Society for Armenian-Israeli Friendship. Such societies were in vogue and sprang up in Armenia in the early 1990s: "We wanted to do things, but we did not know what Israel was all about. And so we took an encyclopedia. We opened the page for Israel and . . . well you know how much information there was there." Noubar is honest and does not try to embellish his biography. Speaking ironically about his own ignorance, he mentioned that the first thing he did after arriving in Israel was to buy books in Russian about the Jewish tradition and send them to Erevan to his friends from the Society for Armenian-Israeli Friendship. To justify assimilation he alludes to folk wisdom. He approves of the symbiotic relations between Jews and Armenians and proudly refers to a fellow countryman, now an Israeli politician, as a "Jewish son of the Armenian people."

Immigration to Israel activated one other type of stories. New impressions and new information acquired in Israel rejuvenated memories about the "strange behavior" of grandparents, which began to make sense only after our narrators immigrated to the Jewish state.

Laura M., 55

INTERVIEWER: You live in such a beautiful place.

LAURA: Yes, and I have a warm feeling toward the land of Israel.

INTERVIEWER: Laura, did your family observe any Jewish tradition?

LAURA: Not really. My mum made holidays for herself. She baked a matzoth pudding. And she had [*inaudible*], a friend. When she [*mother*] forgot the date of some holiday . . .

INTERVIEWER: She reminded her.

LAURA: Yes. You see, when I was a child we lived in Nikolaev; I lived there with my parents. The synagogue didn't function. But I remember that once we were in the synagogue. I was still very small. And I remember that we were waiting for the star.

> And mum was hungry. She was not allowed to eat, while the kids were fed. So we ran around and ate white bread. And I thought, "Poor, poor mum, we may eat, while she may not!" That's it. This is all I remember. And then there was . . . there was no synagogue in Nikolaev. And so they kept . . . on their own, one was an engineer, another was [*inaudible*], all of them were known to be friends and they sort of . . . they, at least they kept a record of the holidays. Mum made her own matzoth and she did . . . Simhas Toirah and Rosh ha-Shanah and what else? Well, mum was in charge of it. . . .

In Israel, immigrants sometimes complain that Jewish holidays don't have the same atmosphere of elation that they experienced in the USSR on Soviet holidays, such as the New Year, International Women's Day, and May 9, Victory Day. They may be missing familiar public rituals such as decorated fir trees on the streets at the end of December, the scent of spring flowers given to women on the Women's Day, and a military parade on the Victory Day. In contrast, Jewish holidays in the Soviet Union were kept secret from outsiders. Some interviewees expressed surprise that even though Jewish culture was almost entirely suppressed, their relatives managed to keep a record of the important dates. As Gitelman (1992) points out, "there were severe restrictions on the production of ritual items, matzoth being a marginal exception" (77). A more lenient attitude toward matzoth may account for its being the most frequently mentioned element of the Jewish tradition in the narratives. Yet as follows from Laura's story, in some areas matzoth was inaccessible.

The problems of getting matzoth had folkloric interpretations. Our informant Anastasia F., 43, who had never been in the synagogue in her hometown of Kiev, remembers rumors that matzoth was available there only to the veterans of the Great Patriotic War (World War II).[17] Anastasia F. also recalls that she used to send matzoth home from Riga, where she often went on business. She would buy more than ten kilos for her extended family in Kiev and for a cousin in Riga. The cousin, a lecturer at the local university, was afraid to be seen in the synagogue, so he would wait for Anastasia in a neighboring garden to give her a hand with the heavy load.

Note that neither Laura M., in the preceding excerpt, nor other informants quoted use the word *fast* in association with religion but instead resort to its neutral substitutes "was hungry," "did not eat," "would not drink a sip of water." Equally, like the other interviewees, Laura mixes Hebrew and Yiddish words when she talks about Jewish tradition.

Simona K., 23

INTERVIEWER: Did you have any idea about [*Jewish*] holidays?

SIMONA: Not at all. Nor about Yiddish, I don't speak Yiddish.

INTERVIEWER: Did you eat matzoth?

SIMONA: Yes, there was matzoth; I knew about matzoth, but I don't like it, even today I don't.

INTERVIEWER: But you, sort of knew . . .

SIMONA: Yes, yes, I knew what matzoth is, but I didn't know that it should be eaten over Pessakh. It was something Jewish for me: matzoth, gefilte fish, stuffed fish. I didn't know [*the name*] gefilte fish, I only knew it as stuffed fish. My granny used to make it. I knew it was a Jewish dish. Or *farshemak* [*chopped herring mixed with hard-boiled egg and apple*]—it was only here that I learned it's a Jewish dish [*laughs*]. Because I always ate it, mum used to make it . . . that is, we are those assimilated ones who had a vague idea. . . . And now dad says that there, in Lugansk, Jews kept together. I don't remember this; I didn't see that. My friends, almost all my friends were Russian. And my parents' friends were also Russian, and we didn't observe any holidays. [*Simona is not the only informant who confuses observation of tradition with holiday celebration and blends the two in her speech.*] Although they tell me that my granny knew about Yom Kippur and it was impossible, even one sip of water . . .

INTERVIEWER: To pour into her . . .

SIMONA: On that day? No. For me I only learned about it here, and it sounded crazy to me, well, I don't know.

It is typical of our interviewees to associate dishes of the Ashkenazi cuisine, but not necessarily keeping kosher, with the Jewish tradition. Sometimes, dishes eaten on specific holidays were completely dissociated from them. Matzoth, for example, was eaten long after Passover if there was enough left. Only after immigrating to Israel did Veronika R. connect the biscuits that her mother used to bake throughout the year with Purim. Although these Purim pastries did not have the characteristic triangular shape of "Haman's ears," the family called them *shoilakh munes,* Yiddish for the Hebrew *mishlo'ah manot.* According to rabbinic law, Purim festivities include the exchange of food gifts among relatives, friends, and neighbors, known as *mishlo'ah manot.* While the ritual was lost, no gifts were sent, and even the holiday had been forgotten, the name survived but underwent semantic transformation. Another revelation awaited Veronika, a professional translator, when she worked on a text about *kashrut.* She finally understood why whenever her grandmother bought a chicken, she kept it, raw, for hours in a pot filled with water. She would start cooking only when the chicken was white (ethnographic diaries).

Even those who tried to be traditional failed to behave consistently. A case in point is Ekaterina R., who recalled that her grandmother would never serve meat with dairy foods, yet pork chops were among her specialties (ethnographic diaries). Elvira A., 20, a Mountain Jew who defines her family as traditional, said that her grandmother had kept a kosher house. Yet she believed that pork steaks were an essential component of young children's diet. Significantly, when the children ate pork she served them at a small table separating them from the rest of the family. Mixing kosher and nonkosher foods could be accidental, but there are two stories—told by Dana L., 23 (see Fialkova and Yelenevskaya 2003, 16–17), and Sergei S., 42 (interview, recorded in 1996; see Fialkova 1997, 1998a)—in which the informants were perfectly aware of the violations. Here is one of them.

Sergei S., 42

> My mother sometimes brought matzoth from the synagogue. As a rule it took a long time to eat it up, because my family is not religious. So I would take it when I was off hiking. It is very convenient to have on a trip: it's light, easy to pack, and an excellent substitute for bread. So I told my companions, those who didn't know what matzoth was . . . I explained—it was fun

> for me, but I did it with an earnest expression on my face—I used to tell them that these were special biscuits for paratroopers. And they accepted my story at face value. It's a bit of a blasphemy, but a matzoth sandwich with properly salted, thin slices of lard makes an excellent snack.

Both Dana and Sergei obviously enjoyed their stories, although Sergei qualifies his behavior as blasphemy. Playing jokes amuses them for several reasons. First, they feel they possess secret knowledge, which gives them a sense of superiority. Second, although they are not afraid of the consequences of violating the rules of *kashrut;* forbidden fruit is sweet. In addition, Sergei enjoys telling his non-Jewish friends tall tales and tricking them into eating Jewish food.

Because Passover and Orthodox Easter are close to each other, some immigrants tell stories about having festive meals at which matzoth, Easter eggs, *kulich* (a Russian Easter cake), and *paskha* (sweet cream cheese eaten at Russian Orthodox Easter) were served together. In some mixed families, cooking Jewish dishes by non-Jewish wives was a sign of devotion and respect for the spouse's roots. The ultimate manifestation of this was making gefilte fish, considered one of the more complicated recipes of the Ashkenazi cuisine. One of our informants told us about the reversal of roles in her family, where her Ukrainian father undertook the task of preserving the Jewish tradition.

Sofia Y., 48

> Ours was an international family. My mother was Jewish, and my father was Ukrainian. He grew up in a small town, and from early childhood he loved theater. In his hometown there was only one theater and it was Jewish. The performances were in Yiddish. As a child he constantly went to that theater and learned Yiddish, well, at least to such an extent that he could communicate a little. Then he grew up and married my mother. And you know, after that he broke away from almost all the members of his family because they were all anti-Semites, and they were shocked that he had married a Jew. Er, we lived in Leningrad, and my mum's family . . . although grandma and grandpa were both from Ukraine, and I think, my

Sofia Y.'s late grandmother would have never dreamt that the *rushnyki* (Ukrainian for "towels") that she embroidered in Priluki would end up in a town on the Mediterranean. *Photo courtesy of Janos Makowsky.*

> great-grandfather was a rabbi, but no [*Jewish*] traditions were preserved in the family. Neither my mum nor my aunt knew Yiddish, and they were quite indifferent to the Jewish holidays. The only person in our family who spoke Yiddish was my dad. Every year he would find out the dates of Pessakh, would go to the synagogue and buy matzoth. He would come back home and say, "Some Jews you are! If it were not for me, you would not even know the taste of matzoth!"

Earlier in this chapter, we mentioned the widespread opinion among the Soviet Jews that Ukrainians were anti-Semitic. Deliberations on this topic are frequent in informal conversations and in the immigrant press. Vershinin (2003), for example, juxtaposes superficial Russian anti-Semitism with the deep-rooted Ukrainian one (32). We believe such generalizations to be wrong. Our material also refutes such label: we have recorded several stories in which immigrants speak with great warmth about their friendships with Ukrainian neighbors, and about the sharing of culture.

Scarred for the rest of their lives by Stalin's purges, the older generation kept their cultural knowledge to themselves for fear that it could expose the younger generation to problems. As Parkes (1963) justly remarks, "It is possible to conceal one's beliefs but impossible to disguise one's practices" (148).

Inna F., 26

> My family, that is, my mum, my dad, my brother, and I, celebrated both Paskha and Pessakh. So for Pessakh we were at my grandma's. Ourselves, we never arranged anything on Jewish holidays. But on Yom Kippur I never went to school. I don't know how granny managed to find out on what day Yom Kippur was because there was no synagogue in our town after the war, after the Great Patriotic War. Now the building [*the synagogue*] houses the college training culture secretaries [*persons in charge of cultural and educational activities in an organization*]. How funny! So all of this [*Jewish holidays*] was associated with grandma's and grandpa's house. And all the rest of the holidays, Russian and Christian, we celebrated at home.

A synagogue or a church turned into a club, a theater, or even a store was typical of almost any town in the Soviet Union and can be traced to the antireligious campaigns of the 1920s and 1930s. While Inna refers to it as a funny absurdity, older people may have perceived it as an insult. In our material, though, there are no stories reflecting this. As we showed in chapter 1, most of our informants were assimilated and belonged to the educated classes. General education did not make these people curious about the culture of their ancestors. This observation concerning assimilated Soviet Jews is confirmed by sociological data: the level of education is inversely related to involvement in Jewish cultural life. The higher the level of education, the less intense is the involvement (Ryvkina 1996, 54).[18]

Anastasia F., 43

> This story has been always told in our family as an amusing an-

ecdote. My grandfather was a very educated person. He could recite poems by Esenin, Pasternak, Pushkin, Lermontov all night long. But he was absolutely ignorant of the Jewish culture. Once he had a patient from the Kiev synagogue, it was a *gabbai*, or something of the sort. And to express his gratitude he [*the* gabbai] invited grandpa to the synagogue on some holiday. He showed grandpa to a seat for honorable guests and gave him a prayer book. For some time grandpa sat there and then he noticed that an old Jew sitting next to him was casting sidelong glances at him. Then plucking up courage the man addressed grandpa: "Herr Professor, excuse me please, but could you lend me your prayer book. You're holding it upside down anyway."

As we see, most of our interviewees link fragments of the Jewish tradition to the elderly and reveal that its observance hardly affected their own life and education. Among our Ashkenazi informants only one told us that the elderly wanted to and succeeded in passing the tradition on to the young. Well integrated into the Russian culture (see chapter 6), Shimon K.'s family, all of whom had academic degrees, were nevertheless determined to be Jewish not only on their passports.

Shimon K., 18

SHIMON: Our family observed all the traditions, in particular grandpa observed whatever he could observe under the circumstances. We tried to observe whatever we could, and grandpa knew quite a bit. Not that . . . well, I was small then [*inaudible*]. . . .

INTERVIEWER: What holidays did you celebrate?

SHIMON: In fact, all the Jewish holidays. And of course the most important event of the year was Pesakh. We always had seder. And Yom Kippur, yes, we celebrated all of them, and we observed Shabbat too. What we didn't observe was fasting, we didn't always fast. . . . Seder in our family lasted until about five in the morning, because we had the *hagada* in Hebrew, which none of us could understand and . . .

INTERVIEWER: But could you read it?

SHIMON: Grandpa could. Grandma would translate it to us into Russian, so that we would know what it was all about. Because grandpa knew. They could even write in Yiddish, they wrote in *Sovietish Kheimland* [*Yiddish for* Soviet Fatherland, *a Yiddish magazine*], they wrote in their leisure hours, when they didn't have to work. . . . And how did my family preserve the tradition? Until 1986, and it was so fortunate for us, my great-grandmother, that is my grandpa's mother, had lived with us. She studied at school before the revolution, and she knew all about it. She was born in the nineteenth century, in 1899. And she knew all of it. My grandpa's family was religious. His parents preserved [*the tradition*], and they brought grandpa up in this spirit. . . . And this is how he brought up his own children. . . .

INTERVIEWER: But they were not persecuted by the authorities, were they?

SHIMON: Well, they were, to some extent they were. They were fired.

INTERVIEWER: Oh, they were . . .

SHIMON: Grandpa was expelled from the party. . . . I know that in 1986 there was an attempt on his life; that is someone on the street hit his face with brass knuckles, and then they refused to treat him [*in the hospital*]. And naturally, they refused to look into the complaint he lodged. They gave him a sign, but he wouldn't stop. And this is just one example of what could be done. And they had other problems as well. I know that granny's Ph.D. thesis was flunked, although she had a publication in [*names one of the more prestigious Soviet publications in science*].

Even in such a dedicated family, Shimon, then an eight-year-old child, was opposed to emigration because loyalty to "your own country" was among the first things taught to the young children at school. Despite Shimon's parents' interest in Judaism, apparently they did not know either Hebrew or Yiddish, and the whole family depended on the grandparents for interpretation of the religious texts. Note that while other interviewees talk about the threat of physical violence against Jews, Shimon's grandfather suffered from it. Shimon is convinced that the assault was authorized by the authorities and was meant as a warning to stop the family's promotion of the Jewish culture. This may be true, although it might have been just a crime devoid of any political implications. Shimon suspects that refusal to open an investigation betrayed the authorities' involvement in the offense. Yet it could stem from the usual reluctance of the Soviet police bureaucrats to open a case when chances of finding perpetrators were minimal.

Shimon's story refers to the last decades of the USSR. Yulia Kh. recalled a case of coercion against religious Jews that referred to the period of collectivization in the 1930s.

Yulia Kh., 53

> In these years, in the years of collectivization they had to work for collective farms. They were forced to. And a person who never . . . He was a teacher, my grandpa was a teacher . . . He joined [*the collective farm*] so that no one would say that Rabbi So-and-So does not work. So he joined the collective farm. And before that, before he had to join the collective farm, they had expropriated his plantations, his gardens; they had seized everything, all his wealth. He went to work. On Shabbat, he was forced to work. He pleaded, "I'll work on any other day, but please, on Shabbat . . ." "No, how can it be? Sunday is the day off for all. And on Shabbat everyone has to work." So he took off his shoes, grandpa did; he walked barefoot and asked god to forgive him. He was going to work—that's the strength of belief—he was crying, tears ran down his face, "Forgive me! I am going to work on such a holy day. But not on my own free will. I am forced to. It doesn't depend on me." And he went barefoot to work and back. . . . Grandma always told the story that on Shabbat he walked barefoot and asked God to forgive him because it was against his will. Mum recalled that, too.

Even when observing tradition did not involve open conflict with the state, it was difficult in the complete absence of institutional support and the necessary self-discipline and sustained effort.

Yulia Sh., 51

YULIA: [*In Russian "aunt" and "uncle" are commonly used as a form of address, particularly by children instead of a more formal name and patronymic*] [*Aunt Liuba*] was the only true believer I've ever seen in my life. And she observed all the traditions. My mom, when she returned after evacuation . . . my mom had a set of silverware that she had once won [*in a lottery*]. So she gave Aunt Liuba two knives, because she needed a knife that . . .

INTERVIEWER: For milky stuff?

YULIA: Yes, *milheke* [*in Yiddish*] and for meat. And she left one for her own use. She gave one [*knife*] to everyone [*all her friends*] and two to Aunt Liuba because she . . . So Aunt Liuba used to read the Bible. She had it and she read it. And she observed everything although it was next to impossible. Only I know how difficult it was. Now when I see our *khloptsy* [*Ukranian for "fellows"*], just look at him, he is a believer, he is already wearing a *kipa* [*Hebrew for "skull cap"*], he is already observing everything. I ask him, "So what, were you a believer in the Union?"

"Yes."

I say, "It's not true! You couldn't have observed."

I saw what an effort Aunt Liuba made to observe it all. It was very complicated. And she always said . . . I used to know a Baptist who invited everyone to the House of Prayers and said that they had great respect for Jews. But Aunt Liuba always said, "I don't recognize those religions which were invented by people. Only the Jewish religion was invented by God, and all the rest were invented by people." This is what Aunt Liuba used to say.

INTERVIEWER: And so she observed. She managed to observe.

YULIA: Yes, she managed to observe. It's the only person . . . She was our neighbor, and she prayed and she observed. In her whole life, she never tasted sausage. She died already, well this is also. . . . She left for Germany together with her daughter. But before that she had shared her life with my mom in their communal kitchen. And how much they . . . They separated in 1990, yes, we left in 1990. And they had moved into our apartment in 1945. So, it makes it forty-five years.

INTERVIEWER: But how could such a deeply religious person move to Germany?

YULIA: A good question! The children left, her daughter left, and she left together with her daughter, although her own sister was . . . Oh, we had a wonderful corridor [*the metonymy for residents of her communal apartment*]. She brought up her niece. The girl's father was Russian, and her mother was Jewish, Aunt Liuba's sister. And they were in the occupied territory [*Yulia refers to the territories occupied by the Nazis during World War II*]. And people hid them, both the girl and the mother. And just a couple of weeks before liberation, someone surrendered them and they were shot. The mother was shot, and only Alla [*the daughter*] survived. And this family [*Aunt Liuba's*] brought her up. But they left for Germany. And even in Germany, already in Germany, although kosher foodstuffs were available there, she didn't eat sausage.

INTERVIEWER: Was she afraid?

YULIA: She was afraid something would be wrong.

INTERVIEWER: So in her whole life she never tasted sausage.

YULIA: Never!

Unlike her neighbor and friend, Yulia Sh.'s mother remained a staunch atheist until her last day despite her religious upbringing. This did not prevent her from understanding her friend Liuba's need to be properly equipped to keep kosher. Her peculiar type of atheism didn't ban traditional Jewish foods from the family menu. Yulia says, "We knew all the holidays by the pies and dishes which belonged to different holidays. What did each of these holidays signify? Well, we had a superficial idea, just superficial." A similar story of perseverance in keeping kosher was told by Vladimir B., 70, whose parents remained religious throughout their lives. When it was no longer possible to obtain kosher meat in their town his mother turned vegetarian.

Yulia fully admires Aunt Liuba's dedication even though she herself is not at all religious. She sees Liuba's efforts to keep kosher as a religious sacrifice and is skeptical about the young immigrants who turned religious in Israel. Ironically she refers to them as *khloptsy* (Russian and Ukrainian for "young lads"), as if "demoting" them from being Jewish. Yulia suspects this quick transformation may be only skin deep and pragmatic. Indeed, some Jews both in post-Soviet Russia and in Israel became interested in the Jewish culture not so much because of conviction or inherent features of personality but under the influence of favorable social conditions (Ryvkina 1996, 95–96). Fast transformations are in fact not always long lasting, and the force of habit may prevail, as happened with Maria S.

Maria S., 25

> A year before departure we began to celebrate Jewish holidays. And during our first year here [*in Israel*] we kept on. When we came here, I even made friends with a lot of *datishnye* [*Russified Hebrew for "religious"*] people in Jerusalem. I don't remember now at whose expense it was, but our whole family went to celebrate Easter [*apparently she refers to Passover*]. For four days we went on guided tours and it was very interesting. But the longer we live here, the more we ignore Israeli holidays. Now they don't exist for us anymore. We celebrate the Soviet New Year, on the eve of the first of January. And during Israeli holidays we go camping.

Although Maria S. and Galit B. (see the following excerpt) differ in age and life experience, both of them have changed their self-perception and attitude to Jewishness under the influence of external circumstances.

Galit B., 60+

GALIT: And then he [*Galit's son*] said he planned to go to the States, and the attitude to this was more or less okay. . . . And he said, "Mum, if I fail to get to America via Italy, I'll go to Israel." I said, "No, no, no, no!" I didn't understand it; I couldn't imagine it, with all those rumors. I [*pause*] knew that Jews exist; I knew that I was Jewish myself. I knew that there were some holidays, and what sort of holidays they are. I remember my grandpa. I remember Pessakh. And since I was the youngest in the family, so this piece, the remaining piece of matzoth, what is it called?

INTERVIEWER: Yeah, I know what you mean.

GALIT: Well, this, what's it called? I am afraid . . .

INTERVIEWER: *Afikoman.*

GALIT: Well, of course, *afikoman.* When Pessakh comes, I'll recall this [*custom*]. Yes, I always got the *afikoman.* I remember how he [*her grandfather*] [*pause*] prayed. And I remember, er, that we all respected this. Moreover, our apartment, our house was close to the synagogue. That is, I witnessed all the holidays. . . . We lived on the ground floor, and [*pause*] and on Yom Kippur people were well dressed; they walked past us looking beautiful. On Rosh ha-Shana people put on their best clothes. Well, all those holidays when people go to the synagogue, and on Yom Kippur, in particular, the street was simply, er, it was simply er, overcrowded. . . . And this *tsom* [*Hebrew for "fast"*], it was literally in front of our eyes. In the evening mum put a big kettle [*on the table*], and when people returned [*from the synagogue*], she always baked beforehand. And [*pause*] this first moment, to have a cup of tea with cake, this was in our yard. And after that people went home.

In the Soviet Union, Galit distanced herself from Jews, although in contrast to Maria she did not hide her ethnic origin. She made her son take her family name because it sounded less Jewish than her husband's. In Israel she hebraized her own name and became interested in the history of Israel and its language. Unlike Maria, her interest in her newfound roots did not fade away. She returns to her childhood memories of the Jewish holidays and her family's involvement as heirs of the tradition, although it hasn't become part of her life in Israel.

Of the eight Mountain Jews in the sample, six spoke at length about their families' Jewish traditions. Gitelman (1991) observes that the Jewish identity of those who resided in the non-European areas of the FSU was more positive than that of the European Jews, and was based on tradition, religion, and a conscious commitment to protect and preserve ethnic distinctiveness (39). But even those of our Tat informants who identify themselves as religious or traditional deviate in their habits from mainstream Judaism. These deviations range from a more than liberal interpretation of *kashrut* to clothing to the observance of Shabbat. In addition Mountain Jews speak of the Tat language as a distinctive feature of their community (see chapter 6). As in the stories of our assimilated informants, Passover emerges as the most prominent event linking them to the Jewry.

Yulia Kh., 53, and Lilia B., 56

[*About childhood memories of Passover*]

YULIA: It was something extraordinary. First, my mum made new clothes for all of us, some of them were ready made, but she made a lot of them herself: dresses, blouses, and panties. And she had new boots for all the children. Everything was hidden and was ready for Paskha; everybody knew that it was ready for Paskha. Secondly . . .

LILIA: For Paskha all the clothes we put on were new.

YULIA: Yes, yes, everything was renovated. Even if everything in the house was clean, we washed everything again, and repainted and whitewashed before Paskha. All the china which we did not use [*apparently she refers to the Passover set of dishes*], we took it out and cleaned and washed it anew. Everything was done anew, the carpets were laid, the beds were made. The Paskha is today, and on its eve everything is ready and everything sparkles! And today already in the morning there is not a single bread crumb left. If you are hungry, go to the yard. And there is one pot with food ready, and plates prepared to eat today. Everything, all this china, all these dishes . . . So we had breakfast, we were allowed to eat not later than eleven, after that it was prohibited. The stomach had to be emptied. All the dishes, after we finished eating mum washed the dishes and put them away into the shed. That was it. Not a biscuit, not a candy, not a bread crumb was left in the house. . . . In the evening granny reads Torah, so it is seder. This is what Jews from the Caucasus used to do. Granny had a huge lounge, it was huge. And we put mattresses and cushions all over the lounge.

LILIA: Everything was on the floor, everything was put on the floor.

YULIA: Yes, on the floor. . . . So we all sat on the floor, and everyone had a cushion on her side, everything was prepared. Granny begins to read the history of the Jewish people, all the history. She read, and she spoke our language. . . . We thought that it was written in our [*language*]. But then we go and check. No, we only see points and hooks. What is it?

INTERVIEWER: And she was reading . . .

YULIA: And she knew the ancient Jewish language, ancient Jewish Hebrew, she knew it so perfectly, that she simply read it silently, but aloud she said it in our language. She read and wrote Hebrew marvelously.

INTERVIEWER: [*turning to Lilia*] And you, did you celebrate holidays?

LILIA: Sure we did! We never missed Pesakh, or Rosh ha-Shana celebrations, or something . . . Derbent is little Israel.

This excerpt shows the closeness of the culture of Mountain Jews to the Oriental tradition. Carpets, cushions, and mattresses were not only important components of furnishing of a house but were always included in a young girl's dowry and an immigrant's luggage, as they testified to prosperity. Yulia Kh., like other Mountain Jews, mentions that her grandmother could read Hebrew, but she did not teach the children. In the best case the young generation could speak Tat, but the main language of communication was Russian, and stories from the Bible were told in Russian or in Tat.

Eclectic religious beliefs are characteristic of Soviet Jews and non-Jews alike. We would like to cite two more examples from the interviews of our younger informants, both from Muslim republics of the FSU. One of them, Rasul O., 24, a Mountain Jew from Makhachkala, Dagestan, claimed that "as strange as it may sound, the elementary customs of the Torah, of the Jewish Bible, have been transferred to the laws of the Shariah. That's why the people of Dagestan and their laws are a combination of the laws of the mountain people [Jews] and the Shariah, i.e., Islam." Another subject, Ekaterina R. from Tashkent, considers herself Christian. Her mother is Russian and Christian, and her father is Jewish. In Tashkent the family was well-integrated in the Muslim and local Uzbek cultures. Ekaterina remembers that both her grandmothers "purified" the house with prayers—one with Jewish prayers, the other with Christian ones. Ekaterina is in search of an integral religion, and she told us about her encounter with a member of a sect preaching symbiosis of the great religions. She hoped that it might help her remain loyal to the diverse traditions of her family.

Ekaterina R., 24

> Three religions are combined in this movement. The sign of this religion, and this is what she showed me, is Magen David [*Hebrew for the "Star of David"*]. Inside it there is a cross and below is a crescent. Have you heard about it? And a person [*follower of the movement*], according to what she told me, should be a Muslim by education, the basis of the laws is the Torah, and the way is Christian experience.

When studying the personal narratives of Soviet Jews it is important to take into account the ambivalence of their identity. They identify themselves with Jews on the basis of nationality and common fate. In the Soviet era, after World War II in particular, Jewish cultural and educational institutions were systematically destroyed, the teaching of Hebrew was suppressed, and the use of Yiddish was discouraged. Stalin's purges of the late 1940s and early 1950s specifically targeted Jewish intellectuals. As a result the processes of assimilation intensified. Jewish culture mostly remained as fragments of Jewish customs, often mixed with Christian customs, specific jokes, proverbs, and songs in Yiddish. Above all memories of pogroms, the Holocaust, and the limitations imposed on Jews by the Soviet authorities contributed to the perception of a common fate. According to a sociological study conducted in Russia in 1995, ex-Soviet Jews have lost their national culture. But in spite of "acculturation" and the predominantly Russian cultural profile, ex-Soviet Jews not only retain Jewish self-perception, they have an affinity with the Jewry as a national and cultural community (Ryvkina 1996, 58).

In the Jewish tradition, returning to Israel is both a duty and a privilege. Although for the most part Soviet Jews were secular and assimilated, the notion of the Promised Land was not obliterated from the collective consciousness. It was not preserved in traditional forms but in jokes and in secret stories about relatives or friends who had lived in the Soviet Union in misery and found happiness and prosperity in Israel. This intricate maze of cultural traditions, which nurtured former Soviets, is represented in the analyzed narratives. In most cases we fail to find a consistent system of beliefs; rather, we see their eclectic combination. Voronel (1973) argues that a common origin and two thousand years of dispersion have developed characteristic traits and interrelational practices in Jews, creating a psychological community (33). Ryvkina (1996), twenty-three years later, says that in spite of acculturation and assimilation, Russian Jews remain Jewish as regards their history, genealogy, racioethnic features, and psychological affinity to Jewry (58).

Our material does not give statistically valid data, yet it shows immigrant moods and attitudes to the problems of ethnic discrimination. It reveals that our informants' Jewish identity was mobilized not by the observance of the tradition, the knowledge of Hebrew, or attachment to the Jewish culture, but was a form of silent opposition to state and popular anti-Semitism. While those registered in the Soviet documents as non-Jews did not suffer from state anti-Semitism, they were still exposed to popular anti-Semitism and were constantly on alert for it. The policy of anti-Semitism affected the identity of Soviet Jews in that they partially internalized negative anti-Semitic stereotypes.

Self-identification is a complex phenomenon that defies a straightforward definition. It is a process that is never completed (see Hall 1996, 2–3; Rosenthal 1997, 23). Symbolic boundaries are not stable; they vary in different periods of life and they can emerge to divide families. Shifts in social preferences often strengthen some aspects of identification and weaken others. One of our informants, Mariula F., 25, is a Halachic Jew whose father is a Gypsy. She identifies with the culture of her father, while her younger sister is ashamed of it and tries hard to hide her ties to it. She is afraid to find herself again among the minority and wants to shed her otherness.

3

The Image of the Other in Personal Narratives

There is hardly a society without a division of *we* and *they* based on various distinctions, be it race and ethnicity, religion, or social status. The problem of the other has long been studied by philosophers and sociologists in the context of self-identification. This is a process of comparison of the self with the others on the basis of similarities and differences. On the one hand, people tend to choose the familiar and reject the unknown (Rathzel 1995; Riggins 1997); on the other hand, the distant and the unfamiliar have the charm of novelty and exoticism.

In the lexicon of Israeli society, all members of the diverse group of FSU immigrants are dubbed Russim (Russians).[1] Israeli society thus classifies and perceives them mainly in terms of this "Russian-ness." Kimmerling (2001) observes that despite all the differences in FSU immigrants from various republics, they too view themselves as belonging to one distinguishable category—Russian. They shaped themselves into a sub-society, contributing to the centrifugal trend of adding elements and "islands" to Israeli civil society and giving the Israeli state a more "culturally pluralistic character" (137). Referring to the FSU immigrants as Russians is consistent with the popular way of identifying Israeli Jews by their country of origin (Gitelman 1991, 38). The division is not neutral, as each group—"Americans," "Ethiopians," "Moroccans," "Rumanians," and so on—have distinctive images in Israeli society and occupy different positions on the social ladder. Smooha and Kraus (1985) point out the substantial ethnic inequal-

Part of the material in this chapter has been published in Yelenevskaya and Fialkova 2000, 2004a, Fialkova and Yelenevskaya 2001c.

ity present in socioeconomic and demographic background and in status achievements. In their investigation of the Jewish sector of Israeli society, they conclude that ethnic inequality is institutionalized in status attainment, evidenced in the transfer of inequality to the second generation (171). Al-Haj (1998) includes the Arab sector in his study of social stratification and asserts that it is a dual system distributed on two levels, Jews and non-Jews, and within the Jewish population Jews of European and American origin (largely Ashkenazim), and Jews of Asian and African origin (largely Sephardim). Ashkenazi Jews are ranked at the top of the ladder, Arabs at the bottom, and Sephardim are placed in between (212). An additional factor that determines the level of the group's prestige is its tenure in Israel. The status of the FSU immigrants is particularly complex. Like Ethiopian Jews, they are newcomers, which puts them close to the bottom of the ladder. On the other hand, the group is upwardly mobile; it competes actively and successfully for position in the country's middle class (see, e.g., Kimmerling 2001, 137–49). The exodus of the Soviet Jews had been long awaited in Israel to secure the Jewish majority, but the number of non-Jews among the FSU immigrants and their firm opposition to assimilation made this goal elusive. In addition, the demographic composition of the group—which included a high percentage of elderly, disabled, and one-parent families—disappointed Israeli society and is perceived as a burden to taxpayers (Habib et al. 1998; Katz 2000; Remennick 1999), causing resentment among members of the lay public. The ambivalent attitude to the FSU immigrants illustrates the often repeated maxim, Israelis like immigration but they don't like immigrants. Israeli sociologists and anthropologists agree on the explanation of this attitude: it stems from fear of strangers and defense mechanisms that the host develops toward the stranger. The long-term Jewish consensus on the importance of immigration for the nation's existence is, for large sections of the population, merely declarative, as individuals are unwilling to sacrifice their well-being (Leshem 1998, 324). The perceived threat to the in-group through competition over valued resources leads to prejudice and negative intergroup attitudes that are particularly potent among people with below-average incomes, the young (under thirty), those with a partial high school education, and among people of Asian-African extraction, especially the native-born second generation (Bizman and Yinon 2001, 691; Ilatov and Shamai 1998, 284; Leshem 1998, 323; Lewin-Epstein et al. 1997; Resnik et al. 2001, 436–37). In the wake of the huge immigration wave, Israeli Arabs and Sefardi Jews alike shared the fear of a deteriorating economic situation, and further, Israeli Arabs suspected that the arrival of the Soviet Jews would increase the probability of their transfer (Al-Haj 1998, 214, 219). Shuval and Leshem (1998) point to the similarities in the reaction to the returning Diaspora in Israel and Germany. In both countries repatriates are formally accepted by the state. They are given citizenship and full civil rights, receive financial support and work permits, and are entitled to attend free language and training courses. Social acceptance of repatriates is also reflected in the official rhetoric. Yet there is evidence that these groups are perceived by members of the public as aliens (12–15).

The Image of the Other in Slavic Folklore and Russian Literature

Traditional culture in modern discourse is actualized in times of instability of the sociocultural context, which affects everyday life (Bausinger 1987, 21–31; Bogdanov 2001, 22; Dubin 2001, 149). Such is the situation of immigrants and it is characteristic of Israeli life in general because of ongoing political conflict. As we have shown in chapter 2, our interviewees have a strong affinity for Russian and Soviet culture, so tradition in the framework of the present study can be traced to Slavic and Soviet mythology. This mythology keeps the community's existential anxiety under control, as it helps immigrants to interpret the reality of Israel in terms of familiar symbolic systems.

Folklorists studying different cultures have found common traits in the representation of the other. One of these is dehumanization, such as the representation of others as animals. In the folklore of Eastern Europe, other ethnicities are likened to dogs, horses, wolves, birds, and pigs. In Slavic folklore, Jews and Muslims are most frequently linked with the pig, which is particularly humiliating for believers of both faiths, who regard pigs as unclean. Belova (1997) reproduces a Montenegrin folktale that "explains" the origin of different religious groups. A man had a beautiful daughter whom young men from three different families wished to marry. An angel appeared before the perplexed father to advise him: "Marry your daughter into the first family;

give your dog to the second one and a pig to the third." The man obeyed, and the girl's progeny became Orthodox Christians. According to the tale, malicious, doglike Catholics originated from the dog, and the pig was the progenitor of Muslims (26). Belova also cites Slavic folktales that claim blood relations exist between pigs and Jews. According to a widespread Slavic legend, Jews don't eat pork because Christ transformed a Jewish woman into a pig. A tale with the same motif, but slightly different in details, exists in Hungarian folklore (Görög-Karady 1992, 122–23). In Slavic folklore Jews are also identified with other animals, such as horses and wolves, and with birds, for example, magpies and hoopoes (Belova 1996, 112, 114, 115; 1999a, 90).

In literature and in everyday discourse the other is often associated with insects. Hollingsworth analyzed the symbolic features of a hive and an anthill and showed that they embodied the extreme form of dehumanized sociality. He pointed out that insect society had always suggested otherness, which came to be one of the master metaphors in nineteenth-century European literature (Hollingsworth 2001, 152–86). In the Russian folk and literary tradition, bees and ants do not appear as exponents of evil but symbolize industriousness, which is reflected in phraseology and paroemias—for example, "to work like a bee," "an ant is small but builds a mountain," and "an ant always carries a load too heavy for his size, but no one will say thank you to him," and "a bee carries just a small drop and serves God and people." In etiological legends bees are perceived as pure, divine creatures and, according to some folk beliefs, sting only sinners (Gura 1997, 448–49).

The image of the cockroach in Slavic traditional folklore is ambivalent. As heralds of prosperity, black cockroaches were believed to protect the house. In some areas they were not only lovingly kept but even taken to a new house when the family moved. On the other hand, there were various rituals of killing and burying cockroaches. Various nicknames link the cockroach to the ethnic other. In Russian it is often called *prusak* (a homophone of *prussak*, "Prussian"), and in Ukrainian, *prus, shwab, shwed, zhidochok, moskal'* ("Prussian," "Swabian," "Swede," "little kike," and "Russian"). In Russian urban culture cockroaches have negative symbolism similar to that of the hive, as analyzed by Hollingsworth: a collective observed from above, an alien and threatening order. Cockroaches are demonized in the works of the Russian writer Remizov (1978). They proliferate at a frightening rate and overwhelm humans. They possess evil power and symbolize a way of life that is incomprehensible to humans and that endangers their existence (Fialkova 1998b, 73–74). The Russian-Soviet poet and translator Chukovskii (1990) wrote a children's poem titled "Cockroach the Giant" in which the evil insect torments all the animals and feeds on their young. This poem has been a favorite for generations of Russian-speaking children since the mid-1920s. In Tolstoi's tale *Nevzorov's Adventures, or Ibicus* (1963) and in Bulgakov's play *The Flight* (1989), both of which were also written in the 1920s, the game of chance known as "Cockroach Races" symbolizes the frustrated and degrading Russian emigration wave of the 1920s (Gudkova 1989, 554). Bulgakov's play is very popular in the FSU; it has been staged by many theaters and reached its height of popularity among the public after its 1971 screen adaptation, where the scene of the cockroach races is one of the most memorable. In the final scene one of the central characters, General Khludov, sums up his feelings about life away from home: "Foul Czardom! Filthy Czardom! Cockroach races!" and shoots into the crowd gathered at the races (Bulgakov 1989, 295).

Another common feature contributing to the negative image of the other in the folklore of various nations is the association of the other with evil spirits. Trachtenberg (1966) found that the Jew has been associated with the devil in European folklore since the Middle Ages. Goldberg-Mulkiewicz (1970) gives examples from Polish folklore: The devil appearing in tales is sometimes dressed as a German and sometimes as a Jew (152). Belova (1999b) extends this list by adding a Frenchman, a Lithuanian, and an Ethiopian to the devil's various disguises (416). Cała (1995) found a widespread belief in blood relations between foreigners and the devil in Polish folklore: "The Jew, the German and the devil are children of the same mother" (176). In contemporary narratives, the other retains satanic features. In Israel, for example, new societal fears—such as child pornography, rising crime, and a growing concern for children's safety—contribute to the invention of the satanic "folk devil" in the press and in informal discourse spread in several sectors of the society, primarily by the ultra-orthodox. Ironically, the dissemination of satanic cults has been blamed on immigrant youth from the FSU, who are viewed as exponents of alien culture lacking bonds to Judaism or Zionist ethos (Cavaglion and Sela-Shayovitz 2005, 258–59). Indeed, cases of witchcraft and witch hunting among immigrant adolescents have been observed and documented. But the reasons for these incidents are more complex than what journalists suspect. For example, in a case study conducted by the psychologist Tartakovsky in a boarding school that accommodated FSU adolescents who had immigrated to Israel without parents, witch hunting is shown as an attempt to empower members of the group and a reaction to isolation and alienation from members of the receiving society (2001). It is also important to know that witchcraft and narratives with satanic features are well-known components of contemporary Russian school folklore that can target outsiders and undesirable insiders alike.

Importantly, the evidence of the demonic nature of people professing various other faiths is seen in their "blackness" (Belova 1999a, 86). This brings us to the third trait: the other is associated with specific colors.

The heir of this prejudice is the racist attitude toward colored people found in various parts of the world. Psychologists have also studied the interdependence of interethnic attitudes and color-coding customs in various cultures. Allport (1979) remarks that of all physiognomic "handicaps" the reference to color, clearly implied in certain symbols, is the greatest (182). Williams (1966) also notes that "color names such as white and black are regularly used in other contexts as general cultural symbols to convey different connotative meanings such as goodness and badness" (531). In Russian culture, black has strong negative connotations, as reflected in idiomatic expressions such as *videt', predstavliat' chto-libo v chernom tsvete* ("to see, represent something in black," which connotes overly negative perception), *chernaia neblagodarnost'* ("black ingratitude," which is used to describe malice in response to kindness), *chernyi den'* ("a black day," which refers to the time of need and hardships), and *chernyi iumor* ("black humor," with reference to gallows humor). The negative symbolism of black is used in literature, where it signifies poverty, madness, and death. Metaphors of black are varied: Nekrasov's appeal to Death starts with the words "*Chernyi den'! Kak nischii prosit khleba, Smerti, smerti ia proshu u neba*" (A black day! As a pauper begs for bread, I beg the heavens for death) (Nekrasov 1979, 332). In Chekhov's story "Chernyi Monakh" ("The Black Monk"), the ghost of a monk in a black habit is a complex symbol in which romanticism blends together madness and death (Chekhov 1986, 226–57). Esenin develops the theme in the poem "Chernyi chelovek" ("The Black Man"). A multiple repetition of this phrase turns it into an epithet of a malicious ghost (Esenin 1962, 210–14). In the gloomy days of Stalin's purges, covered trucks that carried the arrested people away were called *chernye voronki* and *chernye marusi* ("black ravens" and "black Marias"). The fear and despair that these vehicles aroused in the people are captured in Akhmatova's "Requiem" (1989, 113).

The fourth feature in the perception of the other prominent in Russian culture is the belief that aliens have no soul. Boym (1994), for example, observes that in Dostoevskii's world, Germans, Jews, and Poles are deprived of the soul and this makes a "truly monstrous 'other' of the Russians" (85). Pesmen (2000), who conducted ethnographic research in Siberia in the 1990s, came to the conclusion that nationalism remains stronlgy woven into the meaning of "soul." In Siberia, the soul is still conceived of such that "Russian soul" makes sense, but "Jewish soul," "Turkish soul," "Tatar soul," and "Ukrainian soul" do not (14). The importance of the soul in the Russian conceptual system is reflected in the adjectives *dushevnyi* and *bezdushnyi* ("soulful," denoting kindness and responsiveness, and "soulless," used to describe indifference and cruelty). In contemporary folk beliefs the absence of a soul is conceptualized as the lack of universally accepted moral values such as honor, honesty, and kindness—a deficiency often attributed to other ethnicities.

When talking about various others, immigrants often reproduce folk beliefs and re-create negative stereotypes. The frequency of such instances depends on the personality of a speaker and the type of communication. As a high percentage of our interviewees were aware of conventions of political correctness, their reference to people outside their own group was mostly reserved and self-censored. In addition, our subjects felt restrained by the knowledge that the conversation was being recorded. Our ethnographic diary gives many examples of uninhibited use in informal talk of the folklore images and pejorative folklore-related phraseology.

The trend is even more pronounced in discussion forums on the Internet. Electronic culture, often referred to as "second orality," enables participants to carry out quasi-conversations (Fialkova and Yelenevskaya 2001a, 75–79). Because of anonymity, Internet users do not hesitate to express the most extremist ideas in the spirit of folklore stereotypes. We did not come across demonic motifs in our material, but comparisons with animals—and the antithesis of white and black as applied to European versus Oriental and Ethiopian Jews, Jews versus Arabs, and secular Jews versus religious Jews—were frequent.

In the USSR and in post-Soviet Russia the pejorative metonymies of "blacks," "black asses," and "chocks" refer to the peoples of the Caucasus and Central Asia and are perpetuated by jokes and graffiti. In Israel these insulting nicknames connote the same features: their bearers are seen as cunning and treacherous, dirty, lazy, and ignorant. But now they refer to new groups of others, with which immigrants had had no previous contacts, namely Arabs and non-European Jews. Pejorative reference to Moroccan Jews as "the blacks" was also characteristic of Polish immigrants of the 1950s (Bar-Itzhak, 1998, 201). Orthodox Jews are also scornfully called "the blacks" by predominantly secular FSU immigrants because of the color of the men's clothes.

Strangers among Our Own People

As indicated, even fourteen years after the beginning of the "big wave," the FSU immigrants are perceived as a distinctly different other. A closer look, however, shows a variety of others. When applied to the immigrants from Ukraine, Uzbekistan, Estonia, and so on, the label "Russian" is even more incongruous than when it denotes Jews who used to live in Russia. Gitelman (1991) observed that very little is known about the perceptions and feelings that Soviet people themselves had about the nationalities or about Soviet nationalities policies. (28–29). Knowledge of interethnic feelings and attitudes can be derived from personal narratives, which according to Ricoeur (1992) are never ethically neutral (115).

In the shared consciousness of the FSU immigrants the group is fragmented, and one criterion for affiliation is the area of the FSU where people lived before immigration. Besides the division into Jews/non-Jews, or Europeans/Asians, there is a distinction between central and peripheral regions of the country. The periphery was formed by non-Russian republics, and even the majorities of the non-Russian regions had to maneuver to balance complex relations of power between the national peripheries and the Russian core (Suny 2001, 245). In their study of interethnic preferences in the FSU Hagendoorn and colleagues point out that the resulting ethnic homogenization of the republics and the actual Russification introduced under the ideological banner of "Sovietization" may have reinforced the perception of ethnic hierarchies. Titular nationalities of some republics were referred to as national minorities, *natsmeny*, in the Soviet jargon. Lexicographers Mokienko and Nikitina note that paradoxically this word, which had pejorative connotations, was in use even in the republics where the so-called *natsmeny* were in the majority (about *natsmen*, see Hagendoorn et al. 1998, 486–87; Mokienko and Nikitina 1998, 361). Importantly, in laypersons' talk this stump compound was applied to the residents of Central Asian republics, some areas of the Caucasus, and the extreme north, but never to Slavic and Baltic republics. Another pejorative nickname for the people from the Caucasus and Central Asia was *chuchmek*, which also means "stupid, dumb" (Mokienko and Nikitina 2001, 679). Jews were not included in either category. The fragmentation of the immigrant community retains Soviet ethnic and social hierarchies and is manifest in social networks. Evidence that metropolitan regions of Russia and the Baltic states have preserved their aura of prestige is that in singles ads in the Russian-language press in Israel people look for marriage partners from specific areas of the FSU. Moreover, former Muscovites, Leningraders, and citizens of the Baltic capitals enjoy the reputation of the most prestigious candidates (Yelenevskaya 2001).

The dichotomy of *my own people* and the others has subjective aspects, and the differences between them are often mythologized. Immigrants are particularly concerned with this division because of the changes in their environment, and old allegiances are reconsidered under the influence of new ideologies.

Elvira D., 34

> I have a story about the *ulpan* [*Hebrew, here meaning a "school for intensive Hebrew study"*]. . . . And once, in the interval between classes, when everybody already knew where each one

> of us came from and what nationality we were . . . I NEVER hid who I am, never! And all of a sudden, an *olimka* [*Russified Hebrew for a female "immigrant"*] like me says to me that I am stupid, that I should have arranged for making myself Jewish. I should have done it still there [*in the USSR*] so that my children could be Jewish. I was shocked. I came home in the state of hysteria and I said I wanted to go back [*to Georgia*]. I had run away from there because there was nothing in store for my children there, no future. I came here, and this is what happens to me! And if the same thing happens here, I won't be able to survive. But my husband tried to comfort me, "Don't listen to them!" Well, I even missed several days of classes because I didn't want to be together with those people who had said all those things to me. But then I resumed classes. I simply made up my mind and went back to study. I finished the *ulpan*, I began working. And nobody ever, EVER, said to me, "You are not Jewish." And my children—to be singled out? NEVER! I simply made a conclusion for myself: a local, a local Israeli would never . . . he might make a note for himself, but to say such a thing openly? No, never. I have never come across such a thing. But our compatriots, er, those who came from there, they, er, are very concerned about it, in particular when mothers are not Jewish, they don't want their children. . . .

The pragmatic attitude to ethnicity that Soviet Jews developed as a protective mechanism against discrimination is at work in the new surroundings as well. This narrative mirrors Ella O.'s story about the faking of her internal passport (Fialkova and Yelenevskaya 2004b, 148–50). Obviously, Elvira's fellow student did not mean conversion to Judaism but was surprised that Elvira had not faked her birth certificate. Elvira was humiliated by the idea of the rejection of her roots. She had left her home and parted from her parents and relatives to save her children from the devastation of the war. The suggestion that her origin might be an obstacle to their future in the new country came as a blow. Moreover, it insulted her that the reproach for irresponsibility came from the people she considered members of her in-group, new immigrants like herself and former Soviets. Categorization of self and other as members of the same category makes them stereotypically identical and interchangeable as regards cognitive and affective reactions (Hogg and Abrams 1988, 107). Elvira's emotional reaction would not have been so violent had the criticism come from an out-group member, whom she would not have expected to understand her own worldview. A story similar to Elvira's was told by the Aslanyans. A friend of theirs, who had immigrated to Israel a short time before them and was herself married to an Armenian, urged the Aslanyans to find a Jewish fiancée for their son because "Jews accept only pure Jews." This advice was ignored, and, like Elvira, the Aslanyans have retained unpleasant memories of this episode.

The behavior of old friends and acquaintances in the difficult pre-emigration and first post-immigration periods is a frequent topic in our interviewees' stories. Deep friendship is of great importance in the Russian hierarchy of values and is reflected in Russian literature and language. Various researchers have noted that intensive interpersonal bonds were part and parcel of Russian culture in pre-Soviet times, to a large extent due to the oppressive atmosphere in Czarist Russia. The increase of political and ideological pressure in the Soviet period enhanced the significance of friendship as a protective mechanism against the state (see, e.g., Shlapentokh 1989, 170–77; Smith 1976, 108–10; Wierzbicka 1997, 55–84). FSU immigrants transfer their dislike of formal organizations and formal relationships to their new environment and continue relying on informal personal networks (Remennick 1998, 256). The most important aspect of friendship is reliability, and the Russian saying *drug poznaetsia v bede* (the equivalent of the proverb "A friend in need is a friend indeed") is often quoted in everyday speech. In addition, it's highly important to have a network of close friends who have the same cultural background and can understand one another using the same allusions and can take even the slightest hint. The value of friendship intensifies in periods of crisis. For immigrants, domestication of the new space is linked to the making of new friendships and is particularly important for the young.

Rasul O., 24

RASUL: When I came to Israel, today when I tell my friends this story it sounds absurd, but then it was like this . . . I came to class . . . it was a class for gifted children, in Hebrew it is called *kitat mekhunanim*. And everybody there was Russian. So I came there, and it was my third or fourth month in the country. I was thirteen and I was two years younger than all those who studied there. They were fifteen or sixteen, it was the tenth grade, *iud.* And a guy came up to me and asked, "Are you from the Caucasus?" And he looked like one of us. Dark-skinned and with this sort of nose . . . He was from Baku. His name was Vitia. My friend, today he is one of my closest friends. He asked me, "Are you from the Caucasus?" When I looked at him the first thing that occurred to me was that clear stereotype, as I always imagined people: This was an intelligent, cultured, modest guy from Derbent.

INTERVIEWER: You mean a Jew?

RASUL: Yes, precisely, like me, and this was the stereotype that was engraved in my memory: intelligent, modest, tidy, and noble. So it's a person of high standards. [*inaudible*] And it was my first association. Many years later I found out that if it hadn't been for me . . . First, I learned that he was an Ashkenazi. I was a bit shocked. Well, this did not really matter. After all, he was from the Caucasus. [*inaudible*] Several years after we became friends, I learned that he was not a Mountain Jew. And I was an exception for him. He didn't even know that there were people like me among Mountain Jews. And for a long time he was also shocked too. He recalled his life in Baku near Kubinka. Kubinka is a Baku district where our people used to live. So all that so-called cream of our society was there with all the stereotypes for which people detest us.

Anatolii P., 26

ANATOLII: At school, my only friend, a real friend was Misha. He was from Donetsk. . . . We got acquainted in some way. And he had this Ukrainian accent and there was something . . . And I say "Aquarium" [*a popular Soviet rock group*], and he says, "What is this shit?" Well, but at some point we became very close friends. . . . And er . . . at some point we realized that we could talk about music. . . . And we became friends during that year. We even began to play together. Well, [*pause*] and the next year, we had a [*Hebrew, inaudible*] organized by the army, some sort of a trip organized by the army for schools. . . . Well, and there I meet another Mike. That is, this one was Mishka, and that one was Mike, he was Michael. And he is American. And he is also from the WIZO school. And he was also an *ole hadash* [*Hebrew for "new immigrant"*]. Well, and I don't remember for sure, but I think he was born in Israel and when he was four, his parents took him away, but now he is here again. He is a strange-looking fellow, big and red-haired, and he is so . . . well . . . but all of a sudden we spoke the same language with him, although it was English. And all of a sudden I realized that finally there was someone I could talk to. And it's not only that we spoke the same language, but that he speaks English about things I would like to discuss, and moreover, I would like to discuss them in Russian. . . . And mind you, he is American, and sort of, has a different status, he is from a different layer; that is, for Israelis he is a "white man."

INTERVIEWER: And what about us?

ANATOLII: At that time we were sort of second-rate citizens. It is only now that they are gradually catching on that we are not second-rate; but then Americans were something, well, you know that here everyone hangs on every word Americans say, and it has always been like this.

These two excerpts have several aspects in common. The first is the context of the encounters: Rasul and Anatolii met their future friends at school shortly after arrival in Israel. Second, both of them found friends among new immigrants, not among veteran Israelis. Third, both interviewees exemplify Soviet stereotypes. Skin color features in both excerpts. Rasul used it as the primary indicator of the in-group, and for him dark skin has positive connotations. His friend, on the other hand, categorizes him as an out-group member by the same criterion. Placing his new acquaintance among Mountain Jews, Rasul's new friend determines that his social status is low and he is intellectually inferior. Anatolii, on the other hand, uses the notion of whiteness metaphorically as the marker of social superiority. The phrases "to travel like a white man" and "to live like a white man" are not individual mannerisms but are used as stable phraseological units in Russian.

Another stereotype destroyed by Anatolii's personal experience is the inferiority of a speaker with a Ukrainian accent. Residents of metropolitan Russian areas often ridiculed south Russian and Ukrainian accents as markers of "uneducated speech." After Brezhnev took power these accents came to be associated with the dumbness of the Soviet party bureaucrats (Gusejnov 2004, 61). In the 1980s, the attitude toward accents did not change, and Ries (1997) observes that Gorbachev's provincial accent (south of Russia) made him the target of laughter and mockery (40). (Narratives revealing the symbolic role of language and accent will be discussed in chapter 6.) The previously quoted excerpt demonstrates the antithesis of center–periphery: Donetsk, a big industrial city is, for a Leningrader, a provincial town and its residents are a priori categorized as backward.[2] The indicator of backwardness for an adolescent was ignorance of popular rock groups. Knowledge or ignorance of rock groups is not a random choice in describing a personality. For Soviet youth it signaled Western-oriented interests and a challenge to the official Soviet culture (Shlapentokh 1989, 142). Love of rock music unites Anatolii with his junior schoolmate, and both of them with a newcomer from the United States. Despite being a new immigrant, Mike enjoys a privileged status among his peers solely because he is American. Note the role of language for Anatolii. He is eager to discuss things that interest him in his mother tongue, but because his new acquaintance does not speak Russian, they communicate in English—not in Hebrew. To reveal the feeling of mutual understanding Anatolii uses the metaphor "to speak the same language." Thus he contrasts the foreignness of English and the nearness of the rock music culture. In both excerpts the adolescents were prompt in grasping the social stratification of the two societies, the USSR and Israel.

An important feature of stereotyping others is treating outgroups as homogeneous and thus depersonalizing individuals. We have already given examples of wrong identification of group members stemming from stereotypes. But while Rasul and his friend were misled by stereotypes formed in the FSU, the next excerpt is about stereotypes that have emerged in Israel.

Tamara D., 11

It happened when I and my friend, Yulia, the story is about her, were about six or seven years old, something like this. And we went to the park near our house. We strolled a bit, we didn't

> bother anyone, we just sat on the swings and had some laughs; we sit there and have fun. And facing us there is a fat woman and she pesters, well, you know, she quarrels with everyone. She was in the park with her granddaughter, a girl of two or three. And so she looks at Yulia and says to me, "Why have you made friends with this Moroccan?" Yulka [*the diminutive form of "Yulia"*] was taken aback and in plain Russian asks her, "Excuse me, but what have I done to you?"
>
> "Come, girl, aren't you a Moroccan?"
>
> "No, I am from Leningrad."
>
> "You are lying! It cannot be true . . . you are so dark."
>
> That's all. We stood up and left. (IFA 21739)

As in Rasul's story, Tamara's friend is an Ashkenazi Jew, but her tanned complexion mobilizes the stereotype of the Oriental other. As follows from many interviews and from our ethnographic observations, FSU immigrants regard Moroccan Jews as an unfriendly and inferior group.[3] The place of the other in this narrative remains vacant but is marked nevertheless. The stranger tried to impose social control and to protect a white-skinned and, consequently, "Russian" girl from "bad influence." The girl's polite reply in Russian was not enough to make the woman reconsider and include the girl in the in-group. The girl's statement that she is from Leningrad, which as we have already mentioned is a city of high prestige, increases the woman's incredulity even further. Prejudiced people are vigilant in spotting and recognizing strangers and would rather make a mistake excluding a member of the in-group than including an outsider in their in-group. Although we quoted only a few examples, we chose those that reflect stereotypes found not only in the interviews but also in our ethnographic diary and in the press. According to Tajfel (1981), "Stereotypes can become *social* only when they are 'shared' by large numbers of people within social groups or entities—the sharing implying a process of effective diffusion" (145).

The Receiving Society as a Conglomerate of Jewish Others

Just like the Israeli old timers, immigrants from the FSU make a clear distinction between *us* and *them*. They perceive Israelis alternately as one group united by the Hebrew language and as different ethnic groups. The primary criteria used in discussions of similarities and difference between *us* and *them* are physical features, general education, patterns of behavior, and children's upbringing. Because most of our informants were secular and did not have any religious education, they did not speak about differences in religious tradition. Nor did they compare foods or home design and decoration. We never asked questions about styles of dress, yet our interviewees often spoke about them and criticized Israelis for sloppy clothes. These confirmed the immigrants' conviction that Israelis "lack culture."

Alexander A., 43, and Victoria A., 43

ALEXANDER: [*About the first impressions of Israel*] It was a merry, merry country. My first impression, I am serious about it, was that everybody walked around wearing underpants. And so I also bought myself a pair of underpants for eleven shekels. What was good about them is that you could wear them when you went to the beach. You'd go for a swim, dry in the sun, and then take a bus and go back to town. Then later I used to wear them to the Technion [*Israel Institute of Technology*]. I wore them when I went for an interview [*job interview*]. I wore underpants.

VICTORIA: And it went on like this until he went to Tel Aviv. He goes for an interview and says, "Well, I got off the bus," he says, "wearing my underpants and at *takhana merkazit* [*Hebrew for "central station"*] I somehow felt that in Tel Aviv things are different. I didn't really feel as good wearing my underpants as before. After all, folks didn't walk around wearing underpants in Tel-Aviv. Yes, this is how it was.

ALEXANDER: Yes, underpants were a surprise.

INTERVIEWER: Were they?

ALEXANDER: Yes, and I remember underpants even today. And the rest vanished.

INTERVIEWER: But your first impression was also . . .

ALEXANDER: Underpants.

VICTORIA: No, no, the first thing, when we went to town, we were already in Haifa, we walked in Hadar, we went along Herzl . . . We, what really amazed us, was the multicolored crowd. Because after all, we had lived all our life in Moscow, and the crowd there is homogeneous, that is, its national [*apparently she means ethnic*] composition. And here we came and saw the blacks, the yellow, the brown, and the whites. And wearing all those clothes, and national dress, and Druze clothes, and some colored clothes. And everything, so to speak, moves . . .

ALEXANDER: And the underpants.

Alexander and Victoria were interviewed three years after they had re-immigrated to the United States. Former Muscovites, used to dressing formally, they now live in San Francisco, where they returned to a familiar "urban" style of clothing. Alexander is an ironic person. While some of our informants became aggressive in their descriptions, he makes fun of himself as much as he does veteran Israelis. His wife's joining in the story implies that this narrative has become part of the family repertoire. Here we again come across the center-periphery dichotomy, but this time the role of the lackluster province is assigned to Haifa. Alexander means "shorts" but he deliberately calls them "underpants" to show their inappropriateness for public settings. This word becomes the leitmotiv of the narrative and symbolizes the breaking of the boundaries between private and public space. Naturally, women discuss clothes more frequently than men, but the attitude remains the same and is summarized by Anastasia L., 50: "This is a country of *shlepers* [*Yiddish for "untidy"*] and for *shlepers*."

The second motif emerging in this narrative is Israel's ethnic diversity. Victoria asserts that it was a marked change from her hometown and implies that Moscow, as she remembered it, was predominantly Russian. She is not quite right, because Moscow has always attracted students and workers hoping to get resident rights (*propiska*) from all over the Soviet Union; moreover, in the last three decades many refugees from the Caucasus have moved to Moscow. But few of these people wear traditional dress and do not always stand out in the crowd. Israel's ethnic diversity often emerged in the interviews in connection with Jewish identity (see chapter 2) and was often treated by the subjects emotionally.

Evgenii L., 66

> [*About the image of Israel before immigration*] It was simply great! It was formed on the basis of two sources. The starting point was rejection of many things there [*in the USSR*]. And secondly, here everything was to be diametrically opposite and a priori good. And I must say that the work of the Jewish Agency was excellent in achieving its goal. At least they managed to achieve their goal as far as I was concerned. I saw those happy smiling faces on the posters. I saw pictures ruled and divided into small boxes. And in each box there was a person of a different color. And all of them together made up Israel—smiling, hospitable, and united. And it was so tempting, so unusual, so romantic, and at the same time so idealistic that it couldn't but attract. I am quite serious about it. . . . But the most attractive thing was . . . and I don't know whether it was the work of the Jewish Agency or our psychology, but I imagined Israel as something very friendly in its composition, in its structure. I will never forget my first textbook for beginners. It says there, *"Ruti, ani mi Morocco"* [*Hebrew for "Ruthy, I am from Morocco"*]. And then comes another name, *"Ani mi Tsarfat"* [*Hebrew for "I am from France"*]. And everybody was in the same classroom, and it was as if they were ready to embrace each other. It was some manifestation of the overwhelming unanimity. And it was very attractive for me. And I pondered how wonderful it was to be one of "us" among your own people! (IFA 22138)

Evgenii was among the few who had some idea of the ethnic composition of Israel before immigration. Because one of the main reasons for his leaving Ukraine was growing nationalism, he embraced and idealized the idea of "brotherly" Jewish groups. His hopes for idyllic friendship and mutual understanding did not stand the test of reality and elsewhere in the interview Evgenii admits that his vision was only utopian. Equally disillusioned were Rasul O., 24, and Anatolii M., 33, who had hoped to see "the brotherhood of nationalities" in Israel.

Anatolii M., 33

INTERVIEWER: Can you explain the difference between the Israel you had imagined and the Israel you saw in reality?

ANATOLII: Well, it might have been only an illusion. I thought it was a country from a fairy tale. I thought that all the people were brothers; that is, everyone gets to live in peace, but in reality it is just the opposite.

Anatolii associated Israel with childhood images of a fairy tale (see this motif in chapter 4). But his fairy tale was populated by people who like he himself were white. He openly admitted that his attitude to Orientals and Ethiopians in particular was bad, although he had had no personal contact with them. This is how he explained his intolerance.

ANATOLII: I think God created the man white and he has to be white, so . . .

INTERVIEWER: And who created them [*the blacks*]?

ANATOLII: The Almighty created them [*the whites*] in his own image. It doesn't say there [*in the Bible*] that Adam was black, or that Eve was black. No, he . . . the first humans were white. And this means that Jews are the whites. And all of this is simply Filka's edict [the idiom *Fil'kina gramota* means an obscure, invalid document and is used ironically], nothing else.

The contradiction between the ideals of the fairy tale and the racist denial of the black people's equality does not bother Anatolii. Unlike him, many of our subjects expressing ethnic prejudice felt uneasy and tried to overcome an inner conflict. Adorno (1950) points to the standard form under which the conflict between societal demand for tolerance and personal negative opinion about out-group is expressed. It is the formula "I shouldn't, but . . ." Adorno believes that while a prejudiced person "appears to rebel against the slogans of democracy and equality, for reasons that are strictly personal, he is actually backed by powerful social trends. And yet he will claim, at the same time, that he acts as a sincere and independent person who does not care what others think" (627–28). Describing variants of the same formula, van Dijk (1989) asserts that this denial of a tolerant attitude toward out-groups is a form of positive self-presentation (127).

Inna Kh., 52

INNA: How I loathe this—all the men are like this, and all the women are like that. I would repeat it, that in fact, all the Israelis . . . I admit that they are different. But, unfortunately, I also begin to imagine that there are those Moroccans, and those Ethiopians, because we used to live among them. Dun'ka [*Inna's daughter*] used to be DEAD afraid of them.

INTERVIEWER: Afraid?

INNA: They would throw stones at us. They could run up to me—mere kids—and say, "bitch and whore, bitch and whore," because they'd learned these words from someone.

INTERVIEWER: Was it in N.?

INNA: Yes. From the adults—never and nothing. Everything was among kids. My seventeen-year-old niece, she also . . . she shunned them too, because they, this small fry pestered her. They were all in the same school . . . they had Ethiopians in their class. . . She . . . Dunia, came to hate them terribly, fiercely. She was afraid of them and hated them, because they were like, you know, like black cockroaches, and they simply terrorized [*Russian-speaking children*]. And that's why . . . and the house where we rented an apartment was surrounded. Later when we moved, we hardly saw them at all if we made a detour. And so I understood that there were Moroccans, there were Ethiopians, and somewhere there were those very Ashkenazim, who . . . they were somewhere else, not there.

The excerpt above is the only one in the sample that presents Ethiopian Jews as a threatening force. Inna's image of the cockroaches used to describe her daughter's fellow students is another example confirming the persistence of traditional folklore models in the representation of the other (see this motif in Markowitz 1993, 128). Inna is not the only informant who said that Russian curses were the first words to be learned by the non-Russian-speaking Israelis. Irina I., 25, also complained that she and her little boy were harassed by children on the playground. The children, who she emphasized were from religious families, shouted Russian slurs. While she was convinced that the foul language was used to humiliate her, she was not sure that the children understood the meaning of the words. She may be right. Anastasia F., 43, recollected that when her daughter was seven she came home from school cheerfully reciting "suka-black." Anastasia deciphered the meaning correctly but to be on the safe side asked the girl what she meant. No explanation followed, but the child claimed that "everybody says it." Apparently she misheard the same words—"suka, bliad" (bitch, whore)—addressed to Inna's daughter, Evdokia, and substituted the familiar "black" for the unfamiliar "bliad." The Russian "suka" did not bother her because with the stress on the second syllable it was familiar from Hebrew, translating to "hut."

As noted, in general the attitude of FSU immigrants toward Ethiopian Jews is less hostile than toward Moroccan Jews. One of the possible reasons is that the former are perceived as a socially weak, low-status group that has no chance to compete with FSU immigrants. Our informants seldom spoke about Ethiopian Jews, and when they did they mostly showed surprise that Jews could be black (see Yelenevskaya and Fialkova 2000, 257).

In the previous section we touched on the value of friendship for former Soviets. We continue with this theme and quote several excerpts in which our interviewees reflect on the possibility of making friends outside the in-group.

Rosa Ch., 27

ROSA: I don't have friends among Israelis. But it is not because I sort of want to mix with Russians. It's simply that I [*pause*], I have only a slim chance to meet them [*veteran Israelis*]. If I had, and if I established some interesting relationships, then I would have no problem. I studied together with a girl. She is from Brazil, and we found a common language, a common Jewish language, because we didn't have any other. And for three years we communicated in Hebrew. And from the point of view of improving our Hebrew it wasn't bad for both of us. And [*pause*] although mentalities differ, hers was closer to ours, the Russian [*mentality*] than . . .

INTERVIEWER: How do you define mentality?

ROSA: Well, I don't know. Probably, it is the attitude to life, the type of upbringing, that is [*pause*]. But, you know, we have probably found common ground in such a specifically female domain as clothes. I paid attention to her during the first year of studies. I thought that that girl, she sat alone, and I thought, "Probably, she is not an Israeli. And she is not an Arab, because she is fair." She is absolutely fair. Because Arabs, Christian Arabs in particular, they dress . . . well, you look at them and it is as if they stepped off the cover of some fashion magazine. So. I looked at her and I thought, no, probably not. And she spoke with an accent, and I couldn't place it.

INTERVIEWER: Not with the Russian [*accent*]?

ROSA: Not with the Russian, but neither was it Arabic or English. And I think, "What is this animal of an unknown breed, and what does one eat it with?" [*An idiom connoting puzzlement at the meaning and function of something.*] Later, we started chatting, and it turned out she was from Brazil. Her grandmother was from Byelorussia and in the nineties she lectured on music in Moscow [*Rosa is confused about the dates*] and she [*the grandmother*] speaks Russian fluently.

INTERVIEWER: And does she [*Rosa's friend*] speak Russian?

ROSA: No, she doesn't. And we had fun because of it throughout the three years of communication.[4] She always sat together with us, there were several Russians [*in class*]. "Shame on you! By now, you should speak Russian fluently." Now, again, about stereotypes. There was a course in pedagogics, it was rather boring, like all the philological science. And the teacher used to say, "*Ani medaber beseder? Ani medaber beseder?*" [*Hebrew for "Do I speak clearly?"*] And it was, [*pause*] it is my subjective opinion, [*pause*] he wanted to humiliate us a little bit. There were some other aspects too. And [*pause*] "*Atem aliya mi Russia*" [*Hebrew for "You are immigrants from Russia"*]. And he points to all of us, and to the girl from Brazil too. And so we . . . all the time she . . . [*pause*] we used to say, "We compromise you. It's because of us that you, sort of, have to suffer. "*Tov, atem aliya mi Russia.*" And then it spread to other courses. She sits with us all the time, didn't she suffer!

INTERVIEWER: I've heard recently that kids from a Jewish Moroccan family, who speak French at home, began to talk French to each other at school, so others began to scoff at them for speaking Russian.

ROSA: Once she also found herself in a similar situation. She was in the bank together with her husband. Both are blond. So they were in the bank and spoke Portuguese. . . . They stand there and talk to each other. And all of a sudden, a little old lady says, *"Mi'ad tafsiku ledaber rusit! Ma ze? Ze busha! Im atem lo tafsiku ledaber rusit, atem leolam lo tyd'u ledaber ivrit!"* [*Hebrew for "Stop talking Russian at once! What is this? Shame on you! If you don't stop talking Russian, you will never learn to speak Hebrew!"*] She was fuming with indignation and said that it was such a *khutspa* [*Hebrew for "insolence"*] to speak Russian in a public place. Just horrible. She [*Rosa's friend*] says, "I might be happy to stop talking Russian, but I cannot—I don't know Russian!" [*laughs*]. And she says, "Imagine, Rosa, it is so uncultured! My husband and I . . . Okay, so I don't speak French, but I *lefahot* [*Hebrew for "at least"*] can *lezahot* [*Hebrew for "distinguish"*]! Even if I don't understand I hear the difference, this is Russian, and that is French." "It is," she says, "SIMPLY AWFUL! It is *hoser tarbut!"* [*Hebrew for "lack of culture"*]. (IFA 22144)

Like many other interviewees of her age, Rosa does not have Hebrew-speaking friends. Her explanation that she does not find herself in situations which could lead to friendships with veteran Israelis is strange because at the time of the interview she had studied for four years at an Israeli university. In a sixty-minute interview Rosa emerges as a tolerant, unprejudiced person. Even though she constantly categorizes people in terms of ethnicity, she is not hostile to any ethnic group. Social psychologists writing about stereotypes observe that to cope with a complex social environment people construct a simplified picture of that environment and perceive it in terms of cognitive categories. When social categorization is neutral and not value-loaded, stereotypes do not present much of a problem (Hogg and Abrams 1988, 66–78; Tajfel 1981, 150–54).

Rosa does not divide Israeli society into Jews and Arabs but into Israelis and Arabs, thus ignoring the citizenship of the latter. Russian-speakers form a special category and are never identified with Israelis. Neither does she perceive her new friend from Brazil as an Israeli. This approach is reminiscent of Anatolii P., who did not perceive his friend Mike as an Israeli even though the latter had been born in Israel. Rosa uses physical features, accent in Hebrew, and the style of dress as the primary criteria to categorize her new friend. An immigrant from Byelorussia, Rosa is amused and pleased to find out that her friend also has Byelorussian roots.

In class university students keep together in groups of coethnics. Such a division was noted by several other students interviewees and is confirmed by our own observations as university lecturers. Jocular remarks about "Russians" compromising Rosa's friend and her suffering from it show that in the consciousness of the students these groups do not enjoy equal social status.

The scene in a bank is also a typical situation. As follows from many interviews, any incomprehensible language is automatically thought by veteran Israelis to be Russian. While nobody reprimands English speakers for using their mother tongue in public, FSU immigrants often complain that they are scolded for not using Hebrew when they speak to each other (see chapter 6). In the excerpt quoted above, the woman who tried to make immigrants speak Hebrew unwittingly contributed to immigrants' solidarity and intensified the mental opposition of *us*, immigrants, against *them*, Israelis. Like Anatolii P., Rosa uses the metaphor to "find a common language" and juxtaposes the direct and figurative meanings of the word "language." Rosa's attachment to her mother tongue does not prevent her from intense code-mixing. In the interview she frequently inserted Hebrew words and phrases not only when quoting Hebrew speakers.

Besides the illusory lack of situations that might stimulate friendly relations with veteran Israelis, Rosa, like many other interviewees, mentions the difference in mentality as a factor preventing friendships.

Inna F., 26

INNA: Well, my friends, say, *iedidim* . . . I cannot say that they are friends, rather they are acquaintances. Yes, I feel good, at ease and comfortable with them. But there are some themes which I never discuss with them. And it is not that I wouldn't like to know their opinion, it's just that I know that it is sure to be different from mine.

INTERVIEWER: And what are these themes?

INNA: Say, more philosophical things. For example, I would never talk about the sense of life with Israelis. Because . . . well we have other themes to discuss.

Yeva F., 40

I have a network of acquaintances and a network of friends. Friends for me, if you want a definition, a friend is a person whom I don't have to tell an old joke to the end [*laughs*] or to speak in complete sentences. . . . For me a friend is someone who hints something to me. I understand him and he will also understand whatever I hint to him.[5] And it is not even the question of mutual help. I assist, I help, and I can ask for help people whom I don't include in the network of my friends.

The English word *friend* does not directly correspond to the Russian word *drug*. Wierzbicka (1997), who made a comparative study of patterns of friendship in Russian, Polish, and English cultures, points out that in Russian the categorization of human relations is particularly richly developed, in comparison not only with Western European languages but also with other Slavic languages (57). Depending on the degree of closeness and intensity of the relationship, Russian speakers distinguish *drug*, *priatel'*, and *znakomyi*. The English concept *friend* covers all three. The Russian *drug* tops the hierarchy of friends. Even though *znakomyi* is at its bottom, it denotes closer relations than the English *acquaintance*, which is often given in dictionaries as its equivalent. And *priatel'* has no equivalent in English at all. One other word, *tovarishch* (comrade, mate, colleague), is becoming obsolete because of its associations with the form of address used in the Soviet times before male and female names, for example, comrade Ivanov, comrade Petrova. Those who still use it to describe friendly relations place it in contexts that make it either stronger or weaker than *priatel'* (Wierzbicka 1997, 58).

Neither Inna nor Yeva are prepared to include veteran Israelis in the category *drug*. Both of them admit to this category only people from whom they expect full understanding. Inna identifies privileged topics reserved for close friends and mentions the proverbial Russian debate about the meaning of life as one of them. Yeva says that having a common pool of jokes is important. As we will show in chapter 7, the habit of using only punch lines of popular jokes is a characteristic feature of our interviewees' conversation with in-group members.

Our subjects of different ages told us about their initial enthusiastic attempts at friendship with Israelis. Many recall with warmth and gratitude a veteran Israeli or a whole family that helped the new immigrants in the first stage of life in the new country, be it finding a job, helping with bureaucracy, or voluntarily teaching Hebrew. But each of these interviewees describes these friendships as an exception and not a rule and emphasizes that real friendship ties them only with co-ethnics. The ethnic composition of intimate friendship networks is considered an important criterion of ethnic convergence. The sociologist Benski (1992–93) claims that it is even more revealing than intermarriage patterns because of the multiple relations found in an individual's social life in contrast to the singularity of a marital partner (2). Experiments carried out by social psychologists have shown the effect that personal friendships have on the changing attitudes to out-group members. There is evidence from various countries that friendships across group lines reduce prejudice. In fact, having an out-group friend plus an in-group friend who has an out-group friend ought to reduce inter-group prejudice (Smith 1999, 192–93).

As noted, the shortest way to the heart of an immigrant is to give him or her a helping hand at a moment of trial. And the immigrants' best praise for a veteran Israeli is, "He is just like us."

Simona K., 23

SIMONA: I have a very good friend, a local, a *ta, ta, taimanets,* something associated with Taiman.

INTERVIEWER: A Yemenite?

SIMONA: Yes, from Taiman, a Yemenite.

INTERVIEWER: A Yemenite.

SIMONA: Oh, so a Yemenite. Well the Yemenite has a Rumanian roommate. He mixes only with Russians, he decided that Russians are [*laughs*], I don't know why, he says "Russki [*instead of "Russkie"*] although his Russian is excellent, almost as good as mine, at least he knows all the slang perfectly well.

INTERVIEWER: Has he learned it here?

SIMONA: Yes, he's learned it all here, just by communicating. I, myself, wrote the alphabet for him, and he can read Russian too, and er, he listens to music, literally all our Russian—Makarevich and Rosenbaum [*popular Russian singer-songwriters*[6]]. And, naturally, some Hebrew stuff too, well, I don't know. And because he communicates with us, he got interested in where we had all come from, and he went to Ukraine and stayed with some of his friends there for three and a half months. He stayed in West Ukraine, in the Carpathians, in the mountains.

INTERVIEWER: In what towns?

SIMONA: I am not sure about the names of the towns. From his stories, I guess he stayed in villages. That is, he told me that to wash his face he used, well, you know, there is this thing, you press and water runs. It was . . .

INTERVIEWER: A water fountain.

SIMONA: Yeah, this sort of . . . a street fountain.

INTERVIEWER: Yes, yes, it is a street fountain, a street fountain, a street fountain.

SIMONA: I don't even know what it is called; first you pour water into it, and then you pour it on yourself.

INTERVIEWER: Oh, so it's a washstand.

SIMONA: A washstand.

INTERVIEWER: A handstand.

SIMONA: A handstand.

INTERVIEWER: I know, I know, it's a handstand used in villages, I know.

SIMONA: Down there, there is a finger—you press, and the water runs.

INTERVIEWER: Yes, I know, I know.

SIMONA: And he says it was simply wonderful, freezing cold water, er . . . he found, he told me, he'd found a Jewish cemetery somewhere in the mountains. He says, "I recited kaddish [*here Hebrew for "mourner's prayer"*] over every single one of them, because I don't know for how many centuries they hadn't heard Kaddish." And he said this to me, "Why did you come

> here? Look at what you have there? Why did you come here? I," he says, "I looked and I decided, I understood that that's THE PLACE. I had never felt like that—neither in London nor in Paris, not in Africa, not in South America, not even in Israel! I," he says, "I love Acre, I adore Acre, the most beautiful sunset is here, on the beach of Acre." He says, "I honestly, think so, but there, I," he says, "I felt more comfortable than anywhere in the world. I don't know why, because of the people, or atmosphere, or nature—I just don't know. Most likely, just the atmosphere, the atmosphere and the people." And it's not the first time that I hear this sort of thing, and in fact, honestly, I am proud [*laughs*].

Contrary to the previous interviewees, Simona discards Israelis as potential friends. Elsewhere in the interview she mentions that as an adolescent she and her Russian-speaking friends despised those immigrants who had made friends with Hebrew- and even more so Arabic-speaking Israelis. Now grown up, Simona has not changed her extremist attitudes toward the "locals" even though she understands that they are socially unacceptable: "We preserved the purity of the race, [*laughs*] literally, in a fascist way, you know." Such cases of total rejection of Jewish out-group members are rare in our sample and in studies by other researchers (see Niznik 2003). More commonly our interviewees express attitudes toward out-group members that confirm Adorno's conclusion (1950): "the 'good' out-group members would be those who the subject personally knows, whereas the 'bad' ones would be those at a greater social distance—a distinction obviously related to the differences between assimilated and non-assimilated sectors of the out-group" (623).

The emergence of the Russian youth subculture, which openly rejects everything Israeli and exalts the superiority of their in-group, concerns Israeli society and is discussed in the Hebrew-language media (see, e.g., Shor 2002). The Russian-language press also dwells on the topic, but in the articles devoted to the "Russian" subculture in Israel irony and mild criticism intermingle with pride in the community's success (see, e.g., Solganik 2001).[7] We agree with Gershenson (2003) that Israeli society, accustomed to "colonizing" immigrants, was confronted with a new phenomenon in the 1990s: "Russians" tend to view themselves as colonizers and refuse to be colonized. The reversal of roles, or at least their overlapping, is manifested on various levels. It ranges from everyday habits (loyalties to the Russian language, favorite leisure activities) to aggressive reaction to complaints that "Russians" refuse to assimilate to high culture (see, e.g., Gershenson 2003).

For Simona the key to joining the immigrants' teenage cohort was aptitude in Russian. Note that in the original, introducing the story about her friend, "a Yemenite," she refers to him as *tovarishch.* In the course of a ninety-minute interview, Simona often expressed pride that members of various out-groups praise her old country. According to the investigations carried out by social psychologists in various West European countries, feelings of patriotism and glorification of an in-group are in relation to prejudice against out-groups (Smith 1999, 189).

Admiration of the Russian language and culture do not prevent Simona from feeling Jewish. She loathes any manifestation of anti-Semitism (see chapter 2) and pointedly tells the interviewer that while in Ukraine her Israeli friend visited Jewish graveyards and said kaddish. Another interesting motif in this excerpt is Simona's amusement at her friend's joy at staying in a Ukrainian village devoid of even basic conveniences such as running water.

Despite being an ardent lover of Russian, Simona's speech is an example of language attrition. She could not recall the names of those very objects that symbolized Ukrainian country life for her and had to ask the interviewer for help. After the prompt she used the words *umyval'nichek* and *rukomoinichek* ("washstand" and "handstand") with endearing suffixes signifying nostalgic memories. Her other mistake is an attempt to form an adjective by adding a Russian suffix to a Hebrew proper noun, Taiman, Yemen. She is not only at a loss for the Russian name of this African country but also for the adjective *Rumanian,* trying to use the same suffix by analogy—*yemenets-rumynets* instead of *rumyn.* The suffix *-ets* is neutral and is used in the nouns *gollandets, avstriets, kitaiets,* Russian for "Dutchman," "Austrian," and "Chinese." Simona's misuse of the suffix is an example of intralanguage interference. In other interviews, however, the misuse of ethnonyms *efiopets* instead of *efiop, evreets* instead of *evrei,* and *arabets* or *arabes, arabie* instead of *arab/s* were pejorative. In street conversations and in Internet discussions we have also encountered equally scornful *izrael'tossy, marakosy,* and *amerikosy* for Israelis, Moroccans, and Americans and *palesy* for Palestinians.

As indicated earlier, one of the groups often negatively appraised by the FSU immigrants are Orthodox Jews. Besides being predominantly secular, former Soviets grew up in a country where religion was kept separate from the state and militant antireligious indoctrination was part of education on all levels.

Moisei V., 74

MOISEI: Somehow, they think us to be . . . well, certainly not everybody, I cannot say that, but most of them, and in particular, those orthodox guys, they consider us . . . they don't consider us to be human: "The Russians! You came from a swinish country, you go to swinish stores," as they say. Ella has been to a Russian food store recently. And there was this guy in the street. And suddenly he says, "Why do you . . . you are Jewish, so why do you go to this store?" She says, "How come I don't tell you: Why do you go to the synagogue?" So . . . He says, "I go there to pray." She says, "And I go there to buy food. That's all." She says, "If you don't like it, how can I help you? I can't." She says, "There are many things which I don't like either. For example, I don't like it that you don't work. I don't like it that your children don't serve in the army. I don't like it that you don't do anything, and that you live off us." To make it short, she gave him a . . .

INTERVIEWER: And what about him?

MOISEI: That's it. He had nothing to say to this. He says, "We pray." She: "Why does my son have to go to the army and be a target for bullets while yours stays here?"

"Because," says he, "he prays for it [*Israel*]." She says, "Ha-ha, then I'd rather have my son stay here and pray too, without having to fight. If they don't fight, if they don't serve in the army, if they don't work, who will produce some, well, goods for this country? Who will defend the country if everybody is like this, like you, if everybody joins, so to speak, your Shas party, if everybody converts to your orthodox faith? There will be nobody left here to . . ." He says, "Don't worry, we will win

This deli selling Russian, Ukrainian, Georgian, and other traditional foods is called Home Cuisine, the name frequently used for delicatessens in the USSR.

> by praying." That's all. And he is convinced, he is a fanatic, well, you know what I mean. (IFA 21741)

The theme of dehumanization of the other, typical of traditional folklore and discussed at the beginning of this chapter, emerges in this excerpt. As shown in chapter 2, a nonkosher diet does not prevent immigrants from feeling Jewish. Moisei understands that not keeping kosher marginalizes his co-ethnics but rejects this as a manifestation of intolerance on the part of veteran Israelis. The British political scientist Jones (2001) has made observations similar to ours. He has been studying immigrants to Israel from the FSU since the beginning of the 1990s and has found that they define themselves as Jewish in terms of Jewish values associated with the Ashkenazim, rather than in any overt religious sense. Importantly, it is this secularism and close tie with European culture equated with Christianity that repels Oriental Jews and makes them call immigrants from the FSU *goyim* (pejorative for non-Jews).

Many immigrants would prefer noninterference with their habits, an example of which is colorfully described by Yeva F.: "There is this woman [*a colleague*], and we are very friendly. And she wears a wig. But we do not try to influence each other. She does not prevent me from eating pork at home and I do not tear her wig off." One of the main arguments against ultra-orthodox Jews repeated in the Russian-language media and in everyday talk is that they receive welfare benefits and do not serve in the army. Immigrants see defense of the country as one of the most important civil duties. The fact that some young FSU immigrants serving in the army are rejected as non-Jews, and in some extreme cases are not even entitled to Israeli citizenship, causes fury among members of the community and is frequently discussed in the Russian-language media (Martynova 2002b). As Smith (1999) has shown, emotional reactions against out-groups are often caused by resentment that the latter attain undeserved benefits that are not shared by, or are disproportionate to, those attained by the in-group (187).

The accusations exchanged in the passage from Moisei's interview are typical. It is not accidental that the conversation started outside one of the numerous "Russian" food stores that have become an important part of the immigrant-run consumer industry (Fialkova 1999a). These food stores are nonkosher and most of them are open on Saturday and during holidays. So they are not only disliked as competitors on the food market but are perceived as a violation of the Jewish way of life and another manifestation of the ghettoization tendencies of FSU immigrants (see, e.g., Chen 2002). A different analysis and interpretation of the function of the "Russian" food stores and immigrants' eating habits can be found in Berenstein 2000. She shows that since different foods have symbolic value and are essential ingredients of various traditions and rituals, practices connected to food and images associated with them provide information about the com-

The glutton beaming at the public on the highway Tel-Aviv—Haifa is holding a sausage in his hand, advertising nonkosher foods produced in Israel and imported from the FSU. *Photo courtesy of Janos Makowsky.*

munication system of the immigrant community. Stores selling Russian foods and gatherings around a festive table help immigrants cope with the stress of adapting to a new situation.

As previously shown, immigration makes people question various aspects of identity, and an important component of identity is the name. The semiotic nature of names is well known. When people convert to another religion or join Christian monasteries the event is marked by a name change. Some peoples, including Jews, used to change the name in case of severe illness to protect an individual from evil forces. In different cultures children are named after members of their family. While for Russians it is customary to name in honor of the living people, which is supposed to extend spiritual ties with the child, Jews give names of deceased relatives as if to commemorate their best and loved features. The superstition against naming a child after a living person stems from fear that spirits could choose the wrong person "upon whom to lavish their unwelcome attentions. And angel executing a decree of sickness or death might visit upon the first who answered to the designated name" (Trachtenberg 2004, 79). Another manifestation of the symbolism of names is the use of nicknames among adolescents and criminals; these often make no sense to outsiders but are transparent for members of the in-group.

As a rule, in assimilated Soviet-Jewish families children bore Russian names.[8] Fainberg (2003) observes that traditional Jewish names such as Sarah and Abram, which had been used for millennia, came to sound derogatory. Parents often chose names etymologically or phonetically associated with Jewish names, for example, Boris substituted for Baruch, Misha for Moshe, Rita for Rivka, and so on (28). By rejecting traditional Jewish names people tried to be like everybody else and diminish their otherness.[9] This sort of disguise was a source of self-deprecating jokes ridiculing attempts to conceal Jewish roots. Following is one example:

> Three Jews—Yokhanan, Pinkhas, and Srul'—decided to convert to Christianity. While baptizing them the priest said, "You were Yokhanan, and now thy name is Ivan. These names are similar and, indeed, equivalent. You were Pinkhas and now thy name is Piotr. These names are similar and, indeed, equivalent." Then he turned to Srul'. "You were Srul', and now thy name is Akkakii. These names are not similar, but they mean the same."

Both the Jewish name Srul' and the archaic Russian name Akakii are phonetically similar to Russian words for excrement.

Like other Soviet people, Soviet Jews often gave their children names with political connotations—for example, Stalina, Lenina, Oktiabrina, and in recent years, names of celebrities, like Christina, after the Russian singer Christina Arbakaite. The Christian connotations of the name were ignored. While in the USSR the use of Russian names was part of the assimilation process, in Israel the reverse mechanism was activated. Non-Jewish names mark new immigrants as other, which provokes various reactive strategies. Many, young people in particular, change their names. Like their relatives in the Soviet times, they also make use of associative mechanisms: "Svetlana" is transformed

At the kindergarten center called Svetlana, teachers speak Russian to the children. Like other businesses the Russian name of the owner is used as advertising.

to "Liora" or "Ora" (the root of both the Russian and the Hebrew names means "light"); "Galina" is changed to "Galit," "Galia," or "Gali"; "Elena" to "Ilana"; and so on. From the mythological point of view, transition from one state to another is seen as the "act of complete change of all the proper names" (Lotman and Uspenskii 1992, 70). The newly acquired names don't always replace the old ones completely. The latter remain in use at home and with old friends. We know several young immigrants who gave up their new Hebrew names and returned to their original Russian names. This may be related to the end of the adaptation period; when teenagers feel secure they do not have to resort to mimicry. Returning to an old name may also have the deep symbolic meaning of shedding "Israeliness." A case in point is the internationally known gymnast Svetlana Tokaeva. She immigrated to Israel as a fourteen-year-old in 1991. Like many of her namesakes, soon she became Or and clipped her surname to Tokaev. Under this name she participated in tournaments and achieved results previously unknown in Israel. Recently she was refused funding needed for training for the Olympics in Beijing and decided to re-emigrate to the USA, where she intends to continue her career but as Svetlana Tokaeva (Sergei Bavli, "Or Is Svetlana Again," www.migsport.com/news/scandals/250906_142939_52326.html, 25 September 2006).

In contrast, many immigrants show strong devotion to their original names and sometimes the decision to keep the name evolves into a challenge to society. Sofia Sh., 32, told us of the pressure from fellow kibbutz members when she decided to give her firstborn the Russian name Natalya instead of the proposed Noga or Mor (see Yelenevskaya and Fialkova 2000, 259–61). For Hebrew speakers both of the proposed names are beautiful and poetic: *Noga* means "starlight and Venus" (the stress is on the first syllable, contrary to the Russian word *noga,* "leg," in which the stress is on the second syllable) and *Mor* is "myrrh" (and a homophone of the Russian "wholesale death"). The interference with the mother tongue was so overwhelming that the narrator didn't even care about the Hebrew meanings. She perceived the prospect of giving either of these names to her daughter as irresistibly funny. Like in the joke quoted earlier, the comic effect is created by phonetic similarity and semantic difference.[10] Sofia's story is an illustration of the cultural perception of names. Lotman and Uspenskii (1992) make a connection between name and myth. They assert that in the sphere of proper names we see words and their denotations blend. This is characteristic of mythological perception of reality, which is manifest in the emergence of various taboos on the one hand, and in ritual changes in the proper names on the other (62).

In narratives the individual and the shared perception of the in- and out-groups constantly intertwine. Some of the plots repeat from interview to interview, and one of the more frequent ones is the first shelter people found in Israel. Since FSU immigrants enjoy the status of repatriates, the official propaganda has created the image of prodigal sons welcomed to the hospitable home. A program of integration offered by the kibbutz movement, for example, was called "Your First Home in the Fatherland," and the repatriation itself came to be called "The Return to the Historic Fatherland."[11] This bombastic phrase triggered the emergence of a paraphrase: immigrants refer to the FSU as "The Pre-historic Fatherland." In some sense the Israeli media and propaganda machine are recycling the image of the Promised Land.

Repatriation is associated with the notion of home, and for many of the informants the first refuge on Israeli soil, at least to some extent, determined the success of their further integration. Because of the scarcity of state-subsidized apartments most newcomers had to rent rooms or apartments from private persons. Many interviewees thought that their landlords had mistreated them and perceived themselves as victims of cruel and indifferent others (see Yelenevskaya and Fialkova 2000, 261). In this case the dividing line was not ethnicity but private property. Renting contracts usually preclude tenants from having live-in guests without special arrangements with the landlord. First, many could not read Hebrew and signed agreements without having a clear idea of the rental conditions. Second, former Soviets were not accustomed to respecting private property. Even though in the USSR many of them lived in crowded conditions, receiving a guest was never perceived as a luxury but as a moral imperative. The habit was transferred to Israel, and many families invited their families and friends to stay with them until they could find an appropriate apartment to rent. Moreover, to provide a soft landing for their relatives or friends some new immigrants rented apartments for them in advance but did so in their own names. This is how our interviewee Asia Sh. comments on such a situation.

Asia Sh., 56

> This was all due to our Soviet *mentaliut* [*Hebrew for "mentality"*]. And it didn't matter there [*in the USSR*], that is, if I rented an apartment, I could let my mother, my daughter live there. And here it is forbidden. It's a grave violation!

Stories with this plot give another illustration of the conflict between the law and moral norms (see chapter 1). Although in the

Soviet Union most of the urban dwellers did not own their apartments, they did not feel restrictions imposed by the state ownership in everyday life. It became an issue only in critical situations: death of a family member, complications with the registration of domicile, and exchange of apartments, particularly in the case of inter-city transactions. In Israel the situation was radically different. Tenants felt surveilled and controlled by the owners. Tatiana, D., 27, for example, mentioned that her family's first landlady had a habit of paying them surprise visits to count the number of shoes at the entrance to ensure that the conditions of the contract were not being violated (IFA 21750). When the immigrants' first experiences were negative—when instead of solidarity, they were confronted with indifference to their difficulties and unwillingness to make concessions—they felt unwanted and rejected.

The necessity of living in a rented, temporary home is almost universally perceived by former Soviets as a predicament. By contrast, immigrants from other countries, for example, the United States, don't view renting as deprivation. While Russian culture values attachment to roots and birthplace, Americans glorify mobility and border crossing. For them a rented apartment is a home that doesn't bind one to a place and gives freedom (Moyle 1989). For former Soviet Jews, a rented apartment signifies dependence on others and has no associations with freedom or a real home. (We discuss the symbolic meaning of the home in chapter 4.)

Parallel to stories about "cunning" landlords are immigrants' stories about their co-ethnics' ingratitude and exploitation of veteran Israelis' goodwill.

Anastasia Ts., 48

> I'll tell you . . . So there is this woman, Valentina Efimovna. She comes here and tells me everything. So she was extremely lucky. An Israeli let her a room in her apartment. That woman has a hard life; she needs money for medical treatment. She has a three-room Amidar apartment [*subsidized housing*]. The children have left, and she is living out her days alone there. And she let a room to her. And Valentina Efimovna comes to see me and complains. She curses her; she simply stamps her feet on the poor woman using the worst words imaginable. I say, "Valentina Efimovna, why are you doing this? She is so kind to you!"

> "What do you mean kind? So she makes tea for me and offers me sandwiches. And she gave me some clothes and some furniture. But if she is so kind, why does she make me pay the rent?" And Valentina Efimovna is simply unable to understand that . . . one shouldn't exploit others however miserable you were. Or when I say to her, for instance, "Valentina Efimovna, why should she tolerate you, a mere stranger, in her own house and not charge you? Why?" And then she says, "Then she should not pretend to be kind!" (IFA 22125)

Anastasia was annoyed with her fellow immigrants' self-centeredness, talking about their problems incessantly and not only expecting everyone to turn a sympathetic ear, but to be obliged to help them. Isanna L., 65, told us a similar story about an elderly couple who had been given shelter by a single woman, a complete stranger. She let them stay in her apartment gratis during the peak of immigration in the early 1990s when rental apartments were extremely difficult to find. The couple stayed for over a year and constantly complained about the inconveniences they had to suffer. Our ethnographic diaries contain other stories showing that some immigrants were convinced that Israel and Israelis owed them for the mere fact of their immigration to Israel. This psychology was bred by the principle of forced egalitarianism that thrived in the Soviet Union. Ries (1997) devotes a whole chapter to what she found to be one of the most widespread speech genres of contemporary Russia: litanies and laments. She points to the continuity among traditional Russian laments, the Misery-Misfortune complex, and the contemporary litanies. Like their cultural predecessors, contemporary litanies were inherently about the structures of power in which both "victim" and "villain" seem to be eternally enmeshed (83–125).

We have already seen that immigrants come to Israel with "ready to use" stereotypes about Jews. Members of the Israeli public have their own stereotypes of various immigrant groups, their traits, and behavioral patterns. Labels such as Moroccan "knives," Rumanian "thieves," pedantic and rigid German "yekkes," and Russian "alcoholics," "prostitutes," and "mafiosi" (Golden 2003) are frequently used in lay discourse and in the mass media, and can hardly contribute to mutual understanding among various societal groups (see Yelenevskaya and Fialkova 2000, 262–63).

"Come on, Luba! The Mediterranean festival is going on." A character from the Israeli comedy TV series *This Wonderful Country*, the supermarket cashier Baba Luba (Grandma Liuba) was played by the male actor Tal Fridman and became a public favorite. Dexterous and efficient but constantly reprimanding customers, Luba amused the spectators by her "typically Russian" appearances and accent. In 2004–5 she starred in supermarket advertising campaign and stared at Israelis from billboards, newspaper advertisements, and TV commercials. The image became so pervasive that many Hebrew speakers began to address Russian-speaking cashiers as Luba without realizing that the allusion to the comic character might be offensive.

Negative stereotypes of the "Russians" persist fifteen years after the beginning of the big wave. Stories condemning "Russians" have recurrent plots and have been labeled in the Russian-language press as the "Russian disease" infecting Israeli society. They feature Russian gangsters, women stripping their Israeli partners of their property, criminal businessmen attempting to make political careers, and so on. Caricatures of the "Russians" are used in advertising. Mirskii (2005) cites a poster that hung in all branches of the Discount Bank. It represented two stocky men wearing Russian-style fur caps squeezing a shy scared-looking man, a typical Israeli. The caption over the heads of the trio reads: "The Russians are putting on pressure? Come to the Discount Bank for help!"

Episodes analyzed in this and the previous sections concerned intercultural communication and stereotyping. According to Forgas (1988), "Intercultural communication is a case par excellence when shared situation representations, the basis of all successful communication, are themselves problematic or confused" (187). This is why we often observed conflicts and misunderstandings stemming from false expectations when reality was less rigid and predictable than schemes. Chafe (1990) asks the rhetorical question, Why do we enjoy xenophobia? He believes it is a mechanism of adaptation to the complex world that threatens our accustomed modeling of the world. The result is rejection accompanied by excitement, anger, and aggression. This reaction explains the satisfaction people find in xenophobia (82–83).

Constructing the Image of the Enemy

Relations with Arabs is among the stormiest subject of public discourse in Israel. Among those known for their extremist attitude toward Arabs are FSU immigrants.[12] In this section we will try to trace and explain the antecedents to this attitude. Note that most of our interviews were conducted in 1999–2000, a relatively quiet period before the Al Aqsa Intifada, and thirteen subjects were interviewed at its very beginning.[13] Russian-language newspapers, Internet discussion forums, and our ethnographic diaries suggest that the attitude of FSU immigrants to Palestinians and Israeli Arabs has deteriorated since the beginning of the Intifada. Because our project is not longitudinal, however, the interviews do not show this dynamic. The topic of relations with and attitudes toward Palestinians and Israeli Arabs emerged spontaneously in the interviews. In some cases subjects gave value judgments; in others they told stories of personal encounters. Altogether there are thirty-three narratives and twenty-five opinion statements. Out of thirty-nine interviewees discussing the issue, fifteen introduced the subject themselves and the rest responded to the interviewees' questions. Some people told us more than one story about their encounters with Arabs. Only three narratives were about contacts with Palestinians living beyond the Green Line. According to Rabinowitz (1997), the term "Palestinian citizens of Israel" is more appropriate than "Israeli Arabs" or simply "Arabs" (12–13), but the last is the one used by our subjects. We will also use it, although we are aware of its ambivalence.

In the preceding sections we showed that immigrants' discourse reproduces animal images of the other. Our interviewees do not refer to Arabs as animals, but they use phraseology typical of talk about animals and slaves. Much wider is the use of animal images in the Internet discussion forums. Among the animal names applied when Arab-Israeli relations are discussed, the dog and the rat appear more than others; for example, Palestinians are referred to as "mad dogs" that need to be hunted. The policy of restraint is despised, and Israelis supporting it are likened to "rats hiding in their holes." Internet discussants assume that only veteran Israelis are capable of showing leftist "weakness," so there is an often repeated antithesis of *them,* veteran Israelis, versus *us,* the "Russians." The actions of the Israeli police and the army seem to forum participants to be too soft and are indignantly referred to as nothing but the "trilling of a beak." Almost unanimously, Internet users agree that concessions are dangerous because they show weakness. Negotiations are considered useless, and international public opinion can be ignored: "There is nothing I want to say to them [*Palestinians*] except: SHOO. And if he doesn't understand shoo, then I'll kick him, so that he doesn't come close. . . . Every *lumpen* proletarian on all the continents considers himself 'the bulwark of civilization.' The hell with him—dogs bark, but the caravan goes on" (Glaz, discussion thread "Arabs and Jews: Hostages of Political Games," www.souz.ru, 4 January 2002). We remind the reader that the language of the quoted forums is Russian; we also cite the Russian proverb used in the original text: *sobaka laet-veter nosit.* It has a slightly different imagery: "The dog barks but the wind blows it away."

Many immigrants are convinced that Arabs are unable to understand anything but brute force. They elaborate on this theme to justify cruelty and violence directed against Arabs. In addition, both interviewees and Internet users support their xenophobia by paraphrasing biblical quotations, which have entered Russian speech. A case in point is our informant Anastasia L.'s criticism of Israelis for too "soft" a treatment of the Arabs: "we only turn the other cheek" (cf. "Resist not evil: but whosoever shall smite thee on thy right cheek, turn to him the other also" Matthew 5:39). Another is an Internet user's appeal for revenge after terrorist attacks: "Blood for blood" (a paraphrase of Exodus 21:24: "Eye for eye, tooth for tooth, hand for hand, foot for foot").

Israeli Russian-language newspapers also often dwell on the subject of Arabs' animal-like hatred of Jews and Israel. They regularly reproduce anti-Israeli passages from the press in Arab countries. To illustrate this point one writer, a psychiatrist, notes that for Arabs a Jew is nothing "but a mixture of a pig and a monkey and for an Arab to kill a Jew is no more of a crime than for the reader to kill a cockroach" (Dobrovich 2002, 6). To justify the use of force against Arabs, journalists attempt to show that terrorist attacks deliberately target FSU immigrants (see, e.g., Martynova 2003a) and appeal to the experience of immigrants from the Muslim republics of the FSU, veterans of the military conflict in Nagornyi Karabach, and wars in Afghanistan and Chechnya (Shraiman 2001, 21). The tendency to draw parallels between ethnic conflicts in the FSU and in Israel, between Arabs and Chechens, has been increasing in the years of Intifada (see, e.g., Briman 2001; and Solganik and Goldshtein 2002). Stereotypes formed in pre-immigration life do not disappear but are reinforced by the post-Soviet ethnic conflicts and the rising anti-Muslim moods in Russia. These form a conceptual basis for interpreting events and people's behavior in the "new country."

Besides traditional folklore, immigrants' discourse on Arabs shows the strong influence of Soviet and post-Soviet mythology. According to Dubin (2001), this has three main components: myth about the West, myth about a threat, and myth about a

One of the most popular Soviet posters by Dmitrii Moor appeared in 1920 and urged young males to join the Red Army. It has become one of the most frequently quoted images in advertising in immigrants' enclaves. This one appeals to the Russian speakers of Haifa to join customers of the bookstore Moskva (Moscow).

"special" personality (150). Immigrants have retained all three components, although in a modified form. In the Soviet Union, the attitude to the West was ambivalent (see chapter 4). Although defamation of the capitalist West was one of the major goals of Soviet propaganda, it often achieved the opposite effect. The concept of emigration from the Soviet Union presupposed moving to the West, and even Israel was viewed as such. Israel's Oriental character was a heavy blow for many ex-Soviets and sharpened their rejection of Orientals, be they Buchara and Moroccan Jews or still more Arabs, who are seen as Orientals par excellence. Importantly, the theme of relations with Arabs in the interviews often emerged when our subjects reflected upon the place of Israel on the East-West axis.

The second component of Soviet mythology, myth about a threat, is connected to the category of space and its dimensions. All-important concepts such as truth, heroism, unity, newness, and (pseudo-)sacredness were expressed in terms of size (Kaganskii 2001, 139). The size of the country itself was a source of pride and boasting. Having moved to Israel, ex-Soviets experience fear of a small space. This is manifest in readers' letters to the press fiercely opposing any territorial concessions and in laypersons' talk: "Israel is a small European country, squeezed on all sides by the sea of barbarians. It is like the state of the Crusaders, it is like the first colonies in America" (Burunduk, discussion thread "Arabs and Jews: Hostages of Political Games," www.souz.ru, 2 January 2002). The image of a tiny country, a narrow stretch of land surrounded by a sea of hostile neighbors is a common metaphor and is a symptom of siege mentality (Bar-Tal and Antebi 1992, 251). So too is the slogan, "We have nowhere to retreat, behind us is Afula" [a town in the north of Israel] ("Israel and the Middle East," www.souz.ru, September 2002). This is an allusion to a Soviet school classic, Lermontov's poem "Borodino." The narrator, an anonymous hero of the Napoleonic war of 1812, calls on the soldiers to be prepared to die because behind them is Moscow (Lermontov 1969, 265–66). The symbolic power of Lermontov's lines was reinforced during World War II in the appeal to the soldiers of the Red Army attributed to the commissar of General I. Panfilov's army defending Moscow, Vasilii Klochkov. Today the allusion has become a clichéd way to appeal to patriotism and a call to pool resources to achieve an important goal.

The third component of the Soviet myth was the very special personality of a Soviet citizen, synonymous with the Russian, a hero and a winner. Gomel (2006) observes similarities in the attempts of communist, Zionist, and American ideologists to construct a utopian vision of the "new personality" having many features in common (20–25). Anti-Semites often claimed that it did not apply to Jews, asserting that they were cowards and did not fight in the Great Patriotic War (World War II).[14] Many Soviet Jews perceived Israeli military victories as proof that that claim was slander. The image of Israel as a powerful and ferocious aggres-

The glory of the Soviet system was an important part of mythology and was supported by numerous symbols and paraphernalia used in rituals. Today, red banners, the Soviet emblem, young pioneers' drums, and bugles decorate various stores and public institutions in immigrant enclaves. The comeback of the Soviet symbols is partially ironic and partially nostalgic.

sor, created by the Soviet propaganda, was much more appealing than the old image of downtrodden Jews of the *shtetl.* Although the new stereotype caused apprehension about the surge of anti-Semitism, it also served as illusory compensation for the humiliation of social inequality. These sentiments were reflected in the jokes circulating in the USSR in the 1970s and 1980s. Here is one example from the series.

> A Jew immigrates to Israel and keeps on reading Soviet papers.
> "Why do you ignore the free Israeli press?" they ask him.
> "Because when I read local papers, I am convinced that I came to live in a small country besieged by enemies. I see that everything is a mess, there is no consensus in society, and we are all doomed. When I read the Soviet press, I feel that I belong to a superpower that has established influence over one half of the globe and is threatening the other half." (Shturman and Tiktin 1987, 536)

As mentioned before, Israeli media and the lay public often claim that a high percentage of FSU immigrants are not real Jews because of the multitude of mixed marriages, a negative attitude to the religious, and loyalty to the language and culture of the old country. This is considered one of the reasons "Russians" refuse to assimilate. Such a position was previously associated only with Arabs (Smooha 1988, 206–11). Yet unlike Arabs, Russians are not seen as a hostile minority. Since the beginning of the Intifada, many immigrants, both Jews and non-Jews, have emphasized their special role as defenders of Israel. The continuity of this perception can be read from history: Russia prided itself on the liberation of Europe from the Mongols and Napoleon, and the USSR on saving it from Hitler. Today Israeli "Russians" see themselves as defenders of Israel from the Muslim world. The parallels with World War II are reinforced by the Russian-language press, which widely alludes to the Soviet songs, poetry, and aphorisms of the period when reporting on military operations of the Israeli army in the West Bank and Gaza (see Yelenevskaya 2007).

Ambivalence in the Image of the Arab

Stereotypes of Arabs and Jews have been investigated by psychologists, sociologists, and educators (see, e.g., Bar-Itzhak 1998; Rabinowitz 1997; Smooha 1988; Steinberg and Bar-On 2002; Zemach 1980; etc.). Quantitative as well as qualitative methods have been used. In his doctoral thesis, the folklorist and educator Marcus (1977), for example, applied a combination of the two. Psychologists Mahameed and Gottman (1983) investigated auto- and hetero-stereotypes of Arab and Jewish adolescents studying in the same school in Haifa. Using closed questions they classified the children's attitudes toward self and the other on the basis of twenty-three personality categories. Maoz (2000) studied power relations in inter-group encounters. Her subjects were Arab and Jewish teachers who regularly met to discuss political and professional issues in the framework of a program organized by the Van Leer Institute in Jerusalem (1983–93) and aimed at promoting shared civility and coexistence between the sides. The attitudes of the former Soviets toward Arabs are touched upon by sociologists Al-Haj and Leshem (2000, 39, 66–67), Al-Haj (2004, 171–77) and the ethnologist Kenigstein (1999, 34–36). Contrary to the quantitative research (Mahameed and Gottman; Al-Haj and Leshem), which presents a range of attitudes structured by the categories chosen by researchers, Maoz and Al-Haj give readers access to the actual statements of the participants recorded during discussions and collected by Kenigstein from the participants who answered his open-ended questions in writing. These were made in the context of institutional settings and are part of public discourse. Private discourse is analyzed in the book by the Israeli anthropologist Rabinowitz (1997) and in earlier works by two non-Israeli authors, the American journalist Shipler (1986) and the American political scientist Hasan (1986). Their books contain many personal narratives and provide ample material for comparing attitudes and prejudices as expressed by Arabs, veteran Israelis, and immigrants of the 1970s and earlier waves. Whereas Shipler and Hasan show a wide spectrum of the Israeli society, Rabinowitz conducted his fieldwork in Upper Nazareth in the late 1980s. The time gap of more than a decade separating these studies and ours enables us to see both the general and the specific, the constant and the dynamic, in the image of Arabs as viewed by former Soviets.

In the foregoing sections we have shown that negative stereotypes of other ethnicities perpetuating folk beliefs are irrational and often unrelated to the experience of our contemporaries. In his influential study of the nature of prejudice, Allport (1979) asserts that our minds "seem to make no distinction in category formation: irrational categories are formed as easily as rational" (22). This finds support in prejudiced attitudes toward Arabs evident in our material. Note that none of our interviewees had encountered Arabs before immigration; moreover, many had never met Arabs while in Israel either. The negative stereotype of the Arab in the discourse of FSU immigrants emerged very quickly and stabilized in the conditions of the on-going Arab-Jewish conflict. This stereotype was partially based on previous anti-Oriental attitudes and partially on Israeli anti-Arab discourse reproduced by the Russian-language press, rather than on the basis of historic knowledge or folklore. In this respect, ex-Soviets differ from Jews who immigrated to Israel from Islamic countries such as Morocco, Syria, Iraq, and Yemen. These groups have a long tradition of storytelling devoted to the conflict between Jews and non-Jews, the latter being mostly Arabs. Marcus (1977) analyzed and classified these tales, focusing on those that disclose the polarity between reality and suppressed longings. They shed light on the stereotype of Arabs, both as a community and as individuals, as held by Jews who emigrated from Islamic countries. Marcus shows that compared with Ashkenazi folklore, the majority of the tales from Islamic countries seek not only to show the triumph of the Jew over the non-Jew but also emphasize the element of punishment; and of all the possibilities it is the punishment by death that awaits enemies of the Jews.

The only folklore genre in which Arabs were represented in the USSR was jokes. Their context is Arab-Israeli wars, primarily the Six Day War and the Lebanon war. Many of these jokes emphasize the incompetence, cowardice, and stupidity of Arabs compared with Israelis. Others focus on the Soviet military aid to Arab countries and ridicule the Soviet choice of allies (Shturman and Tiktin 1987, 528–38; Evplov 2000). Yet the image of the Arab appeared only sporadically as the non-Jewish other, as it did for our informants, and was associated with other ethnicities.

Social psychologists differ as to the influence of personal contact on the formation of group stereotypes. According to Adorno (1950), stereotyping is a device that feeds on deep-lying unconscious sources. The distortions that it produces are not to be corrected merely by taking a *real* look. Rather, experience itself is predetermined by stereotyping (617). While some researchers believe that stereotypes are rigid and insensitive to context, others claim that personal experience can change out-group stereotypes (see, e.g., Hogg and Abrams 1988, 87; Oakes et al. 1999, 71–72; Tajfel 1981, 238). Investigations of interethnic relations carried out by Russian scholars showed that peoples living far from one another and having no contact formed a favorable image of one another, whereas negative stereotypes were more likely to emerge among closely interacting peoples (Denisova 2000, 207). Mahameed and Gottman (1983), at the beginning of their project, expected to find that personal contacts would contribute to the weakening of the negative stereotypes of Arabs among their subjects, but their research refuted their hypothesis (95, 97). Our material shows that the lack of contact, and more importantly ignorance, leads to the formation of irrational negative stereotypes.

According to our interviewees, their knowledge about Arabs was limited to the information provided by the Soviet mass media, which invariably presented Israelis as aggressors and showed sympathy to the Arabs. As stated earlier, Soviet propaganda often achieved the result opposite to that desired. This mechanism of inversion transformed Arabs from "friends of the Soviet Union" into enemies who not only threatened Israel but who were also indirectly responsible for the growing anti-Semitism in the Soviet Union. Everybody knew about the Arab-Israel conflict, but few were aware of Israeli Arabs, who make up approximately one-sixth of the country's population. Here are two excerpts from the interviews illustrating these points.

Laura M., 55

INTERVIEWER: And what did you know about Israel? . . .

LAURA: Nothing. In fact, today it is difficult to imagine and understand. It's even amusing. So a manuscript circulated. It was an essay about somebody's trip here, in Israel. And he spoke to Arabs. And when I read this, it made my hair stand on end. How could he have talked to Arabs? That is, the minimum of what was known was that Arabs mean death.

Yulia N., 63

INTERVIEWER: Have you ever had contact with Arabs?

YULIA: Never. I am deadly afraid of them.

INTERVIEWER: But if you don't have any contact with them, why are you afraid of them?

YULIA: They stroll in the park here. I don't know why, but their faces are sort of aggressive. They seem to me to be like this. I don't know.

INTERVIEWER: Have they ever offended you?

YULIA: No, no. I've never so much as exchanged a word with them. I, you know, I . . . In the beginning, I couldn't even recognize them. But now, by their clothes and appearance, I can sometimes recognize an Arab. And they come to our park and walk here. And sometimes I look and it seems to me . . . Or could it be that it is already a prejudice, a borrowed attitude? Their faces look aggressive to me. I might be wrong.

It is relevant to our analysis that Yulia N. is retired and her integration into Israeli society is minimal. She does not speak Hebrew, so her sources of information and personal contact are limited to the Russian-language community. By contrast, Laura works among Hebrew speakers and lives in a town with a large Arab population. Apparently, she has overcome her initial fear and refers to it with self-irony. Yulia was interviewed at the beginning of Intifada, when the anti-Arab mood in the country began to increase. She does not rationalize her negative attitude. In the absence of personal experience she relies on background knowledge and expects manifestations of hostility. In such a situation it is important for her to be able to recognize the "enemy." As noted, physical features serve as the main criterion in classifying others for our interviewees. New immigrants cannot "read" the physiognomic types in the new surroundings, which intensifies their anxiety and insecurity. Yulia is convinced that everyone shares her fears, and the mere fact that the interviewer asks her to clarify the source of her anxiety perplexes her and makes her less assertive. At once she questions her own imagination and is ready to admit that it could be influenced by hearsay.

Immigrants often perceive Israel as a besieged country and are afraid of the danger within and without. Common reference to Israeli Arabs as a "fifth column" labels them as traitors. This label perpetuates the Soviet use of the internationally known expression, which came into use in the 1930s during the Spanish civil war. In various periods, xenophobes in the USSR referred to Jews, Volga Germans, Crimean Tartars, and other minorities as a fifth column. In the era of Stalin's purges, labeling an ethnicity in such a way preceded its transfer to remote regions of Siberia and Central Asia.

In immigrants' stories, encounters with Arabs occur in two distinctive settings: accidental meetings in public places and contacts in everyday life and at work. According to sociological reviews and anthropological data, Israelis in general and "Russians" in particular prefer not to live in mixed neighborhoods, but the "Russians" are more adamant in their desire to keep distant (Al-Haj and Leshem 2000, 39; Smooha 1988, 191–92; Rabinowitz 1997, 8). Yet because of their low socioeconomic status many FSU immigrants are forced to live in those areas. Importantly, while repulsive talk about Moroccan Jews is common among immigrants, political alienation has exclusively anti-Arab implications.

In our sample, stories revealing acute intolerance were recorded in Upper Nazareth and Acre, towns where Arabs and Jews live in close proximity. Upper Nazareth was built in the late 1950s to host immigrants from Poland, and in the early 1960s immigrants from North African countries also settled there. This was part of what Rabinowitz (1997) called the project of "Judaization of Galilee" (6–7). Gradually Arabs from the lower town began to buy apartments and look for jobs in industrial enterprises of the upper town. Such integration was never completely peaceful (Shipler 1986, 278–88; Rabinowitz 1997). In the 1990s the city expanded considerably thanks to the influx of new immigrants from the FSU. To encourage newcomers to settle in Upper Nazareth, as well as in other developing towns, the state offered better conditions for purchasing apartments there than in other areas (Gonen 1998, 252–53). In addition, the socially underprivileged had a better chance of obtaining inexpensive state-owned housing there. Today, the town has changed in its appearance and in its linguistic "landscape." The language that dominates the streets is Russian. Before the beginning of the Al-Aqsa Intifada, FSU immigrants, residents of Upper Nazareth, often went shopping and invited their friends to sightsee in Nazareth. The conflict has now changed the "socioscape" and has separated the two towns, divided by symbolic borders whose trespass, as shown in the interviews, is deemed threatening.[15] FSU immigrants are concerned about what they call "the arabization of our town" (see Yelenevskaya and Fialkova 2004a, 85–86). The right to victimize others as compensation for one's own sufferings is a frequent theme in the immigrants' discourse. This way of thinking was recently parodied by the journalist Eterman (2002), who paraphrased the old Soviet slogan chanted at meetings: "We are not slaves. Slaves are not us." Allusion to the chant links the psychology of a slave and racism, "We are not racists. Racists are not us. Racism is when a Jew is beaten up. When a Jew beats up his neighbor, he is just returning a debt. It is justice re-established" (10). The desire to live in a mono-ethnic environment is another symptom of siege mentality present in the community. Many exclude the possibility of equality between Jews and Arabs in Israel. Jews were so used to their own underprivileged status in the USSR that they are convinced that the opposition of the powerful and the powerless is the rule in a multiethnic society, and Jews have the right to be "masters" in Israel. Immigrants who express such extremist views feel the land belongs to them by virtue of their ethnicity. This idea was formed in the "old country" and was reinforced in Israel (see, e.g., Ryvkina 1996, 160–63; Smooha 1988). The question of what determines the right to territory often arises in ethnic conflicts. The Israeli politician Geula Cohen was quoted as saying: "The fact that a few Arabs lived here doesn't give them any right over Palestine any more than those Jews who lived in Poland had a right over Poland" (Hasan 1986, 267). Equally, anti-Semites have always claimed that there is no place for Jews in Russia, and shouts of "Go to your precious Israel" could be frequently heard in street brawls. Today, it is not unusual to hear former Soviet Jews "sending" Israeli Arabs to go join their brethren in Jordan, Syria, or other Arab countries.

Some of the interviewees spoke at length about separation of the two peoples.

Simona K., 23

SIMONA: I was a social worker in the army. We worked with families where someone had perished. We made arrangements for them, for example, for their other sons serving in the army. We helped them. I saw all that pain in the families, I saw all of it. . . . That is, if I were allowed to choose where to live, in Acre, for example, or in a place where there are no Arabs at all, and only this one thing would be checked—not that one place is better or worse—only whether it is populated by Arabs, then I would choose the place where there are no Arabs at all.

INTERVIEWER: Does it disturb you that they are in Acre near you?

SIMONA: You know, I cannot positively say that they disturb me, but . . . That is, I cannot say that it disturbs me that an Arab lives in the house next door. But when something happens, on the level of a brawl, when someone was stabbed, you know there is crime in Acre . . . Moroccans live there, I don't know. But the first thing that comes to my mind is, "It was done by the Arabs." I don't know, when I see on TV that someone perished, it strikes me again with all the force. (See the continua-

> tion of the narrative in Yelenevskaya and Fialkova 2004a, 87.) (IFA 22152)

Simona often has contact with Arabs: they are her fellow students, her coworkers, and neighbors. Her traumatic army service determined her overall attitude toward Arabs as the source of the tragedies she encountered. She tries to be honest, and elsewhere in the interview says that she has met good people among Arab colleagues. Yet she emphasizes that these are mere exceptions. Such an approach is reminiscent of anti-Semitic attitudes often mocked by the Soviet Jews: "Every anti-Semite has a Jew among his friends, but only his friend is a *good* Jew." Simona has created her own stratification of society into good and bad, and she expects each group to act according to the roles assigned. "Russians" are educated and interesting; veteran Israelis are acceptable if they respect "our" values (for example, if they are interested in Russian culture); Moroccans are likely to be a source of trouble. But the true evil is the Arabs. Any deviation from this schema would make her world more complicated, so she wants Arabs always to be in the wrong.

Before the beginning of the Al-Aqsa Intifada secular Israelis frequented Arab quarters, particularly on weekends when most public places run by Jews, including shops and restaurants, are closed. A boycott of the Arab economy is discussed on the Internet as a means to suffocate the neighbors.

> Holmes: Consider it a party assignment. Explain it to everyone and try to act in this vein yourself. NEVER, even when peace comes, NEVER BUY ANYTHING FROM AN ARAB. Not a ribbon, nor a piece of a rope. It is not even necessary to shower them with contempt. Do not say anything to them so as not to give them reasons for a response. BOYCOTT! (discussion thread "Russian Youth in Israel: An Explosion in the Disco," www.souz.ru, 3 June 2001)

The first sentence of the quotation is a Soviet ideological cliché widely used in everyday speech to formulate important tasks, another example of the recycling of previously internalized categories in new situations.

Nina K., 60+

INTERVIEWER: You live in Nazareth, and here two cultures are next to each other, the Jewish culture and Arab Christian. What is your attitude to our compatriots?

NINA: To our compatriots? You mean our cousins?

INTERVIEWER: Yes, to our compatriots who speak Arabic.

NINA: Those who speak Arabic? Well, what can I tell you? Well, I don't know. It's just . . . I was educated to be an internationalist. If they treated me w— . . . That is, my attitude to them is reasonable. But sometimes, some unpleasant things emerge. Here is my neighbor across the street, and he tells me, "So you don't buy things in my store anymore. And who will protect you when Hamas comes? I won't protect you." Well, or something more or less in this vein. Well now it sounds funny. Of course, sometimes I ponder . . . so I live here. In principle, I wouldn't like my kids to live here.

INTERVIEWER: You wouldn't? And why?

NINA: Well, er, why? I simply don't know what awaits our town. I wonder whether at some point we won't find ourselves cut off [*pause*] from the rest of the country. But I've figured out it won't happen during my lifetime, for the rest of my life. But as to the kids . . . I don't know what will happen to our Natzrat Ilit [*Russified Hebrew for "Upper Nazareth"*]. Because now many Arabs move here, to our town. And, apparently, most of them are Muslims.

Even though Nina is less aggressive than other interviewees from Upper Nazareth, she also delegitimizes her Arab neighbors. It strikes her as odd that they are her compatriots just like all other Israelis. Nina often echoes the interviewer's words, yet when she repeats the word "compatriot," she prefers to give a clarification, and refers to Arabs as "our cousins." This biblical allusion explaining the origin of Arabs (Genesis 16) is often used in Israel with a tinge of irony.

In fact, as recently as the mid-1980s even some veteran Israelis did not know that Arabs could be citizens of Israel (see, e.g., Shipler 1986, 534). Nina recognizes signs of prejudice in her own position, but she justifies her desire to isolate Arabs by her fear for her children's survival. She is particularly concerned about the growing number of Muslims in Nazareth. In general the attitude of our informants to Christian Arabs was better than to Muslims, because Christianity is associated with European culture, and Christian Arabs are believed to be more "civilized" and peaceful. Our subjects who grew up in the Muslim republics of the USSR are an exception. Nina is afraid of being cut off from the rest of the country and living in a town where Jews rather than Arabs would be in the minority (see Rabinowitz 1997, 33). In spite of her fears she is capable of seeing the humorous side of the otherwise gloomy situation. Nina's neighbor, the shopkeeper, suffers from a shortage of customers. He may be right in suspecting that people in the neighborhood deliberately avoid his store. So the shopkeeper cannot think of a better marketing gimmick than hinting to Nina that buying from him may pay off as a protection against terrorists.

But even peaceful encounters with Arabs can be perceived as potentially dangerous.

Igor K., 59

INTERVIEWER: Do you have contact with Arabs?

IGOR: [*laughs*] Here is a story for you. One encounter. My sister came here. My own sister came from America. She teaches English there. And she teaches a group of Arabs. And one guy, Achmet, or what's-his-name, asked her to come up to, to come up to an Arab, when she is in Israel, and shake his hand. I say, "Yula, damn it!" I say. She says, "No, I cannot. I promised Achmet, or what's-his-name. Give me an Arab, so that I could shake his hand." Oh, bugger it! We drove along the road, and all of a sudden she . . . We drove in the direction of Carmiel. There is a side road through Arab fields there. They sell stuff; there are little stores. They sell there . . . So we come to the, er . . . most Arab-looking store. So I go in there. I say, "This one is surely an Arab." And so my Yulka [*Igor uses a diminutive form of the name*] comes in too. And she says all sorts of things in English, like, "I teach Arab students, and Achmet so-and-so asked me to shake your hand." And she extends her hand. The guy froze. He doesn't know what to do. He shouts to someone.

> He . . . I say, "Yulka, let's get out of here. They'll simply kill us, and that's it." Then some guy came out to meet her and shake her hand. I led her away and we left. That's all. I don't have any other contact. And even this one was through my sister. In the institute, I've never had any. (IFA 22056)

This episode shows the impact of secondary socialization. Under the influence of two different receiving societies, the brother and sister have different expectations of Arabs' behavior. Yulia has professional contacts with Arabs and at the time of her visit to Israel could hardly perceive them as dangerous. We don't know whether she only felt obliged to keep the promise she had given to her student or whether she supported the gesture of solidarity that the handshake expressed. Igor, on the other hand, believes his sister's determination is nothing but a whim endangering their lives. But his sense of hospitality makes him risk an unwanted encounter. Humorously, he implies that the owner of the shop was also scared, although the man might have been surprised by the violation of the gender conventions, or simply couldn't understand the woman's explanation in English.

It would be wrong to claim that the immigrant community is unanimous in its attitude toward Arabs. In the Russian-language press as well as our interviews we find empathy for Palestinians and Israeli Arabs and honest attempts to look at the Arab-Israeli conflict in an unbiased way. Three stories in the sample are about Palestinians from across the Green Line working in Israel. In two of them (Vladimir K., 73, and Olga Z., 50), Palestinian workers are described as victims of the political and economic situation. Four other stories were told by women employed in Arab businesses and private homes (see Fialkova and Yelenevskaya 2001c, 157–59; Yelenevskaya and Fialkova 2004a, 88, 90–92).

Before the last wave of immigration from the FSU, street cleaners, cleaning women, home attendants, gas stations attendants, and cashiers were mostly Arabs. The new arrivals from the FSU to a large extent ousted Arab workers. Many perceived success in this competition as a defeat rather than a victory, in particular immigrants with university degrees. But even immigrants hired to do unskilled jobs enjoy higher social status than Palestinians. Vladimir K., for example, referred to the Arab labor market in Ashkelon as a slave market,[16] and his compassion is not limited to words. He helped the Palestinian workers he encountered by giving them used clothes, kitchen utensils, and furniture and found himself a benefactor capable of helping the needy—not a typical role for a new immigrant. Like other interviewees, Vladimir refers to Israeli Arabs as the "fifth column." But contrary to others he ascribes manifestations of disloyalty to the group's unjust treatment and exploitation.

Our subjects met with Arabs as their employees, colleagues, clients, patients, neighbors, and so on. According to our observations, favorable attitudes toward Arabs are often formed when immigrants see that Arabs, either as individuals or as a group, have something in common with them—be it schooling in the USSR and knowledge of Russian, professional and/or social values, or experiences of ethnic discrimination or high competitiveness as a result of discrimination (see, e.g., Kheifets 2005 and Reider 2005). We agree with Steinberg and Bar-On, who regard personal stories and expressions of feelings that evoke empathy as a means of better understanding the other (Steinberg and Bar-On 2002, 211). Thus Anastasia N.'s story about the diligence of Arab medical students outdoing their Jewish peers destroys the negative Israeli stereotype of lazy and inefficient Arabs. This prejudice is reflected in the Hebrew phrase *avoda aravit,* "Arabs' work," which refers either to an unskilled job or to poorly done work (see Shipler 1986, 514). Anastasia did not explicitly refer to Arabs as an underprivileged minority but compared their situation with that of Soviet Jews, who tried to be the best achievers to keep on an equal footing with others.

Several stories about friendly relations with Arabs emphasize that difficulties with Hebrew were not seen as an obstacle but as a unifying factor. The same social status can also be an appealing factor in the perception of Arabs by immigrants. Equally, Arabs who are middle-class professionals are more likely to appeal to our interviewees who hold academic degrees. Thus Olga Z., 50, and Emma R., 56, emphasized that their employers belonged to the intelligentsia—the highest praise one can expect from an educated Russian speaker. Emma, for example, made friends with an Arab family while working as their babysitter. Although she claimed that she was not interested in politics, it is difficult to be completely detached from it in Israel's politicized society. She painfully concluded about the similarity between Jews and Arabs: "I feel sorry for them, because they don't have their own corner on this planet, and neither do we." Even living in the Jewish state, Emma still perceives Jews to be homeless; in her opinion both peoples, Jews and Palestinians, are doomed to be outcasts (see Yelenevskaya and Fialkova 2004a, 92).

Immigrants sometimes clash on the issue of relations with Arabs. And while in the excerpt quoted below the disagreement was between two strangers, sometimes arguments and quarrels arise among close friends and families.

Zena B., 53

> Once I was terribly, but really terribly ashamed. I will tell you this story if . . . I was standing in a queue at *Bituah Leumi* [*social security office*]. There was a woman in front of me and a man behind me, and we had a lively conversation in Russian. It turned out that we were colleagues. The woman in front was a teacher of Russian; I am a teacher and a journalist; and the man behind us—he spoke with a slight accent, and I couldn't place it. I thought he was from the Caucasus [*pause*], but it turned out I was mistaken. He was also a journalist and had studied in Leningrad. And we had a lot in common with him. We were having an interesting and lively chat, until a question rose . . . no, this is wrong wording . . . until we touched upon the Arab question. And when a cultured woman standing in front of me said, "The best Arab is a dead Arab," and the man standing behind said, "But what have I done wrong to you? I am an Arab," I was so ashamed of this woman that I had to apologize and explain to him that not everybody thinks like that. I said, "Believe me, I think differently!"[17] (IFA 22110)

Zena suspected the interviewer would disapprove of her sympathies to Arabs. Her experience in Israel made her think that hostility toward Arabs was the rule among the immigrants, and she hesitated before she dared tell her story. At the beginning of the narrative she treated participants as members of one group: they were united by common language and interests, common professional background, and, above all, by the same predicament. All three were jobless and were standing in line for welfare money. Against this background, the only dissonance was the man's slight accent in Russian. The turning point came when the topic of the conversation changed. The unity was instantly destroyed. Zena felt embarrassed and ashamed. She dissociated herself from her prejudiced compatriot and tried to restore the image of her fellow countrymen in the eyes of her Arab interlocutor. What she found particularly annoying was that the woman belonged to the same social group as the other two. In Zena's view, prejudice is incompatible with membership in the intelligentsia. As indicated in chapter 2, in the Soviet Union Jews were likewise much more tolerant of anti-Semitism when it was expressed by the working class than by members of intelligentsia.

The sentence "The best Arab is a dead Arab" is a paraphrase of the proverbial slur "The only good Indian is a dead Indian" often attributed to General Philip Sheridan from 1868 or 1869. Mieder (1997) analyzes the history of the proverb. He shows that it has become a productive model for insults of various others and gives a list of lexical innovations of the proverb, all of which repeat the structure "The only good X is a dead X" (154).

Like Zena, our next subject feels no hostility toward Arabs. In her interview Rosa spoke with warmth about her Arabic-speaking fellow students. Contrary to most of the subjects, she is fascinated by the exoticism of the Orient, which Arabs and the Muslim culture are an integral part of.

Rosa Ch., 27

> I had been only two days in the country. Well, so I took a cold shower and the window was open. And the consequences were clear and fast. I had to go to the hospital. And it was another *etgar* [*Hebrew for "challenge"*] for me. That is, I knew some Hebrew and tried to speak. And, incidentally, about the attitude of the local population, without dividing it into Israelis and non-Israelis, there was a woman in the room with me. I don't know whether she was an Arab or a Druze.[18] I got to the hospital with a terrible fever, and I was very sick. The first day, when the temperature was very high, I tried to comb my hair, but I didn't have enough strength to hold a comb. And so she came up to me. She didn't speak any Hebrew. While I knew at least some words, she didn't. And she took a comb and combed my hair, and made a braid. And here I was—all yellow, with black rings around my eyes but with a braid. And she was so

> pleased with her job that she stroked my hair and kissed me. And then, you know how they come for visits, a whole *hamulah* [*Arabic for a "clan," a loan word in Hebrew*] shows up. So she hands me a bottle and shows that it hasn't been opened, and nobody has drunk from it. The same was with sweets, or something else, "Take it, nobody has touched it." And that's how it was—we communicated using only body language. (IFA 22146)

As mentioned before, first encounters with members of the receiving society can be a difficult experience for immigrants. When people feel disoriented and insecure, they are particularly sensitive to veterans' behavior toward them, and this may determine immigrants' long-term attitudes not just to individuals but to a whole group. Rosa remembers the time spent in the hospital as a challenge to her ability to make use of her knowledge of Hebrew and even more so to her ability to cope with an unfamiliar environment. As a newcomer Rosa was unable to distinguish between Arabs and Druze, but she had no trouble recognizing the woman's kindness and compassion. Note that she includes Arabs and Druze in the group of "locals" but excludes them from Israelis. Rosa finds it amusing that her rudimentary Hebrew was better than her fellow patient's and that the language of gestures proved to be more reliable. We don't know whether Rosa's interpretation of the woman's signs was correct, but it is worthy of attention. One of the most common ethnic slurs is the claim that people of the disliked ethnicity are dirty. Rosa does not directly refer to her roommate's cleanliness, but the fact that the woman made a point of showing her that the offered food had not been touched was an indicator of both hygiene and sensitivity.

Untold Stories

None of our informants told us love stories whose protagonists were mixed Arab–Russian couples. Reflections about Arab–Russian intermarriage were minimal: Simona K., 23, heartily disapproved of "Russian" girls going out with young Arab men; and Dana L., 23, briefly mentioned that her acquaintance had an Arab boyfriend. Devoid of anti-Arab attitudes in her relations with neighbors and fellow students, she could not conceal her surprise at her friend's choice. The surprise also stemmed from the mood of the boyfriend: "And that Arab said that 'I [*pause*] hate all Jews. But you are Russian for me. And I like you.'" The third and the last story in the sample appears in the ethnographic diary. As an adolescent, the daughter of the narrator rebelled against her parents and their views about which friends were appropriate for a girl from a family of the Leningrad intelligentsia. First, to her parents' dismay, she dated a boy from a *yeshiva*; then she became involved with a Palestinian living beyond the Green Line. She lived with him for about a year, from time to time paying visits to her family. After one of these visits she was stopped from crossing the border. After waiting a year for a reunion she reconciled to separation and returned to school and restored friendships with Jewish-Israeli peers.

Interestingly, love stories with a fixed structure and with a tragic end (a Jewish girl killed by her lover) were highly popular among Polish immigrants. Their social function was similar to those of the sacred legends about the divine punishment of the apostate (Bar-Itzhak 1998, 200–201). The theme of intermarriage was almost nonexistent in the Russian-language press and the Internet forums until recently. The taboo has been broken by publications in the two most popular Russian-language papers, *Vesti* and *Novosti Nedeli,* which interviewed couples and analyzed the social and psychological problems confronting them (Lisnianskaia 2005; Martynova 2005a). Yet according to our observations, veteran Israelis are convinced of the prevalence of Arab–"Russian" intermarriage (see, e.g., Al-Haj 2004, 176–77, 203; Golden 2003, 169–70; Lemish 2000, 342–43). Both facts are meaningful: the scarcity of immigrants' narratives about love affairs points to segregation, and the veterans' narratives emphasize the otherness of the "Russians" by connecting them to Arabs.

The Crucial Division: Arabs and Non-Arabs

The ever-present dichotomy Arab/non-Arab is one of the more prominent aspects of identity in Israeli society, just as skin color remains an essential aspect of American identity (Jessel 1978, 38). Wodak et al. (1999) use the term *multiple identity* to "describe the fact that individuals as well as collective groups such as nations are in many respects hybrids of identity, and thus the idea of a homogeneous 'pure' identity on the individual or collective level is a deceptive fiction and illusion" (16–17). This fluidity of identity is compellingly demonstrated in the immigrant group. Many Soviet Jews felt like they were an undesirable minority in the USSR and have vivid memories of humiliating interpersonal and state-sanctioned anti-Semitism. In describing their immigrant experiences, some of our subjects feel that in Israel they are again underprivileged, but this time as newcomers and as "Russians" who can be exploited and treated unfairly. As a result in most of the interviews we find the opposition *we*, the Russians, versus *they*, the Israelis. But as soon as Arabs are discussed, this division disappears and is replaced by the opposition *we*, the Israelis, versus *they*, the Arabs, where Arabs are perceived as the *eternal other* (a term introduced in Blommaert and Verschueren 1998, 15–20).

In Israel, for the first time in modern history, Jews have become a dominating majority. Yet the fast-growing Arab population makes the Jewish majority vulnerable, and it is a source of constant anxiety among Israelis that the Arab population will outgrow the Jewish sector. Under such conditions, immigration is an important means of maintaining the status quo. Even the assimilated secular Soviet Jews are perceived as desirable additions to the population. Yet as indicated earlier, many in Israeli society are concerned about the number of non-Jews among the FSU immigrants, which they feel jeopardizes the Jewish nature of the state. "Ethnic democracy" (Smooha 1990), formerly aimed mostly against Arabs, is applied to a new target. Israeli media try to divide the "Russian" community into pure and impure, and debates about changes in the Law of Return do not cease in either the Hebrew- or Russian-language Israeli press.

Discussing the effect of the immigration of non-Jews to Israel on its demographic and political processes, Lustick (1999) points to Israel's transformation from a clear division between a Jewish majority and Arab minority into a country "whose 'Jewish' majority is more accurately and meaningfully regarded as 'non-Arab'" (418). Lustick's observation and our data confirm Allport's conclusion (1979) that in-group memberships are not permanently fixed. Depending on one's need for self-enhancement an individual may affirm one category of membership, and for other purposes a slightly larger category (35). In an interview with the Russian-language newspaper *Vesti*, Arnon Sofer, a professor at the University of Haifa, confessed:

> I am ready to embrace all the Russians who come to Israel (I emphasize that I mean Russians, not the Russian-speaking Jews) on condition that they want to accept the history and traditions of our country. Repatriates from the FSU, even if they are not Halachic Jews, or belong to such categories as a 'son/grandson/relative of a Jew,' do not oppose the Jewish nature of the state of Israel. They do not demand that the Jewish symbols, the national anthem, the flag and the emblem, be given up. By contrast Arabs and Bedouins want to change the nature of the state by eliminating its Jewish essence. This is why I know who my allies are if I want to live in the Jewish state. (Martynova 2003b, 9)

The sad conclusion one can make on the basis of such statements is that "Russians" are accepted as "ours" only as long as the Arab-Israeli conflict goes on. As soon as it is over, the nonconformism of the group in every other respect will return them to the category of the unwanted other.

Since the beginning of the Al-Aqsa Intifada, the Russian-language media have taken advantage of the intense Jewish-Arab conflict as a means of legitimizing the non-Jewish immigrants. To give just one example: "And it does not matter so much what blood flows in their veins as long as we know that they are WITH US, but not AGAINST US. But then let's be honest and say to the whole world: Everyone who wants to share the heavy burden of the residents of Israel and stand shoulder to shoulder with us to oppose our enemy—welcome!" (Shraiman 2002, 8). It has become commonplace to refer to Arabs as enemies on the pages of the Russian-language press. Equally often one can hear it in informal talk. The presence of the "enemy" magnifies the role of the Israeli army, and as indicated earlier, when it comes to military service, the non-Jewish immigrants are considered the perfect defenders of the Jewish state. What matters then is that Russians, Ukrainians, and Uzbeks, whether secular, Christian, or Muslim, are non-Arabs. This theme is often discussed in the Internet Russian–Israeli forums, in which many participants are young people who have served or who will serve in the army. Here is an example of an exchange we found on the www.souz.ru discussion forum "Israel and the Middle East."

> The Defender of Israel: [*The choice of nicknames used by the discussants often reveals their position: Arab, Judge, Outsider, and even Adolf Hitlerovich von Brauman*]. I think any person irrespective of nationality or religion can become an Israeli. But let me add that this person shouldn't express dissatisfaction, and what is even more important, he shouldn't insult the nation as a whole . . . otherwise he should be legally responsible. The author of this is a simple *Goy* [*Yiddish pejorative for "gentile"*].
>
> Bugs Life: Absolutely right.
>
> Gishevt: Isn't it a shame for the country to be defended by a non-Jew. Oh-oh-oh! It's a tragedy. Sokhnut [*the Jewish Agency*] brought plenty of non-Jews to the Holy Land, and now they defend it. (discussion thread "Who can be called an Israeli?" www.souz.ru, 13 November 2000)

Gishevt's irony directed against the detractors of the non-Jews cannot conceal his pride that immigrants from the FSU have become defenders of the country. Army service is crucial for becoming an Israeli, and the army is sometimes perceived as equivalent to the country itself (Garfinkle 1997, 113–14; Shipler 1986, 441). The mere fact that most Israeli Arabs do not serve in the army makes them social outcasts and creates the feeling of superiority among immigrants.

An external threat, not mythical in the ongoing conflict, is a powerful unifying factor. Every terrorist attack in which immigrants are wounded or killed—in particular the June 2001 terrorist attack in Tel-Aviv in which all twenty-two victims were Russian-speaking teenagers, Jews and non-Jews—increases Israeli society's perception of the "Russians" as Israelis. At the same time, terrorist attacks sharply aggravate the anti-Arab mood among members of the immigrant community.

Reflections on Readers' Feedback

We are making final revisions to the manuscript six months after the publication of the Russian version of this book. It has already been reviewed in the academic and general press, and two presentations have been held in Israel. The audience at these meetings was composed of FSU immigrants and veteran Israelis, Jews and Arabs. In formal and informal discussions with readers and listeners we found this chapter, about the image of the other, caused the most heated discussions. Different groups were interested in different issues. Arab students attending the presentation at the University of Haifa took it for granted that FSU immigrants were overwhelmingly anti-Arab and wanted to find out whether that mood was imported from the FSU or bred after arrival in Israel. They also asked which factors reduced the "Russians'" hostility, and if affiliation with Christianity was one of them. Furthermore, they wondered if our subjects had any preferences among the peoples of the Middle East or disliked all of them equally. Questions from veteran Jewish Israelis showed that it was hard for them to come to terms with the isolationist behavior of the FSU immigrants of the 1990s and their stubborn refusal to abandon their habits. In addition they were anxious to know about the frequency of mixed Arab-Russian marriages. Finally, questions and comments from FSU immigrants, our colleagues and members of the lay public, confirmed the opposition between *us* and *them* that we demonstrated in this chapter. Interestingly, one of the reviewers of the Russian book, a historian and philologist, agreed that the symbolism of the threat, of the opposition of the East and West, and the special features of the Soviet personality formulated by Dubin (2001) and used in our analyses, indeed influenced the discourse and behavioral patterns of the FSU immigrants. On the other hand the reviewer refused to interpret these as mythology but pointed out that they are based on reality (Cherniak 2005, 15). Primarily identifying with our mapping of the immigrant community, many blamed us for portraying FSU immigrants as racists. At the same time these very people expressed extremist attitudes toward Arabs and were convinced that we underestimated their threat to Israel. Like our informants, they did not distinguish between Palestinians and Arab citizens of Israel but perceived all of them as enemies. Here we reproduce an entry from our ethnographic diary, a discussion with one of the readers of the Russian edition of the book. The conversation was written down from memory, but it was on the same day it took place.

Reader: How could you represent us as such racists? You know me very well and you know that I am not a racist. The questions you asked [*in the interviews*] are incredible! How could you even dream of asking about our attitude to Arabs? Don't you know that most of them support terrorist attacks and dance on the roofs after each attack?

Author: I have heard a lecture at the National Security Study Center and the lecturer said that only two to three percent of Palestinians living beyond the Green Line support terror.

Reader: I wish I could believe it. But just look at those wild raging crowds shown on TV. Why do those who are against [*this*] keep silent?

Author: What if the TV doesn't show them?

Reader: I don't know, I don't know. But your questions . . . It's like asking the survivors of a Byelorussian village burnt down by the Nazis about their attitude to the Germans. What do I have against Arabs? They simply do not let me live. Recently, I caught myself thinking about why I didn't mind sitting next to the blacks on the bus. Because I know for sure that they aren't Arabs and they don't emanate danger. Unfortunately, I cannot distinguish Arabs from others.

Author: Don't you think it makes better sense to compare our questions to the questions one could ask hypothetical survivors of that village about their attitude to the Volga Germans?

Reader: How can you compare them? I used to know quite a few of them. These were decent people. I came to this country to live in peace and quiet. I am sick and tired of being among others.

Author: But they have always lived here.

Reader: What does it have to do with what you wrote? After all, you wrote about us, but not about them!

We would be happy if it turned out that we had been mistaken. Unfortunately this and similar discussions confirmed that our informants' xenophobia was not exceptional. Constantly reproducing extremist ideas about the other, immigrants consider this a legitimate reaction to violence. As noted earlier, the Russian-language media in Israel do not try to prevent the spread of ethnic intolerance. In January 2006, Mossawa, the Advocacy Center for Arab Citizens in Israel, sent a letter to the Israeli government legal adviser demanding that measures be taken against the Russian-language newspaper *Vesti* for publishing a racist poem about Arab citizens of Israel by Gershon Ben-Yacov (http://cursorinfo.co.il/novosti/2006/01/01/massawa_vesti/, 2 January 2006).

4

Symbolic Dimensions of Time and Space

Time and space are among the most overworked categories discussed in various fields related to society--philosophy, sociology, psychology, behavioral geography, literary studies, folkloristics, and linguistics. Scholars in these disciplines are less concerned with the physical characteristics of time and space than with their social perspectives, symbolic dimensions, and cultural differences in their perception (Adamowsky 1999; Arutiunova 1998; Bakhtin 1979a, 1979b; Ricoeur 1984; Turaeva 1979).

In contrast to the topics we discussed in chapters 2 and 3, deliberations about time and space seldom form complete well-structured narratives. In most cases they appear in accounts of the pre-emigration image of Israel, descriptions of the first impressions of the country, and nostalgic reflections. While passages devoted to adaptation to the new environment and familiarization with the new system of social time appear in virtually all the interviews, not all the informants are conscious of how closely attached they are to the process of acculturation.

It is axiomatic for social scientists that time is a social construction (Adam 1990, 42). People use it as a resource to establish a truth, to put events in context, and, important for our study, to present an identity. The discursive presentation of self is inseparable from what Taylor and Wetherell (1999) call "construction of place-in-time as a personal possession" (39). Because time is constituted by social activity, its perception varies across cultures and it changes over time. Growing up in a culture, we internalize

Part of the material in this chapter has been published in Yelenevskaya and Fialkova 2002 and Fialkova and Yelenevskaya 2004a.

a specific system of social time characterized by regularities, cycles, and repetitions. The temporal regularity of our social world has significant cognitive implications. It creates expectations regarding the temporal structure of our environment and helps us to develop a sense of orderliness. Temporal irregularity, on the other hand, contributes to uncertainty and insecurity (Zerubavel 1981, 12).

First and foremost, the novelty of social time for immigrants to Israel is manifested in a different calendar. The Jewish lunisolar calendar, used to determine religious holidays, starts from the Creation and reckons time from 3761 BC. So the year 2000 of the Gregorian calendar corresponds to 5760–5761, as the Jewish New Year begins in fall. Immigrants also have to get used to a different division of the week into weekdays and the weekend on Friday and Saturday being the day of rest instead of Saturday and Sunday. All immigrants, in particular those coming from the north of the FSU, are surprised to learn how early the workday begins. Another surprise awaits newcomers on Tuesdays, when many offices and stores are closed in the afternoon. Changes in institutional time are reflected in the fact that some secular holidays celebrated in the USSR and much loved by the people—for example, New Year, International Women's Day, and the Victory Day—are regular workdays in Israel.[1] In contrast, Jewish religious holidays, which are also state holidays in Israel, are not always meaningful for the former Soviets, as discussed in chapter 2.

Government institutions in Israel make use of both calendars. Official papers often print the date according to both calendars, the Jewish and the Gregorian, and various institutional forms may require the marking of the year and month according to the former. Like other Israeli radio and TV channels, the channels broadcasting in Russian always announce the Jewish date. Yet in everyday life people are quite content with the Gregorian calendar, and none of the interviewees uses the Jewish chronology in reference to time, except for the days of the week. In Hebrew these are either marked alphabetically or numbered: Sunday is *yom aleph* or *yom rishon,* the first day; Monday is *yom bet* or *yom sheni,* the second day, and so on. In contrast, in the Soviet and post-Soviet calendars, the first day of the week is Monday and the last is Sunday. This doesn't prevent immigrants, even those who speak no Hebrew at all, from quickly learning the names of

The concert "Dedicated to the Great Victory," which commemorates the Great Patriotic War of 1941–45, is an important annual event for the Russian-speaking community. The performers are the stars of the Russian pop, rock, and variety shows. This open-air concert is held in the Tel-Aviv park ha-Iarkon and attracts thousands of young spectators.

the days. The reason for fast internalization of this part of the new time system stems from the importance of ordering one's everyday life as a succession of workdays and days of rest. While the difference in the division of monthly and yearly cycles hardly influences the life of urban dwellers, particularly if they are secular, the difference in the weekly cycles is experienced by newcomers from the very first day in Israel. As a result, it is customary among immigrants to name days of the week in Hebrew, this being one of the most pervasive cases of code-mixing. In the mind of an immigrant, the association between Sunday and a day off lingers on, while the first day of the week, whatever it is called, is linked to the beginning of the workweek. The weekly cycle is a purely artificial construct, and by virtue of its conventionality is subject to confusion (Zerubavel 1981, 27). The shift in the system of a weekly cycle increases the possibility of errors in reckoning the order of days.

As regards the similarities between the systems of social time in Israel and in the USSR, two are of particular interest.

Both the establishment of the Soviet republic in 1917 and the creation of the State of Israel in 1948 signified a break in continuity. The foundation date was the crucial point in the history of both countries and was often treated by ideologists as the creation of a new world. The two dates are similar in the sacral meaning ascribed to them by society. Another point is the importance of time in Judaism. As in many religions, time is divided into sacred and profane; moreover, it is sanctified. The past is viewed as the national and universal memory, and certain events of the past have a unique holiness. Observing religious norms on the days that mark these events is extremely important (Kellerman 1989, 76). Heschel (1951), Zerubavel (1981), and Golden (2002) point out that the sanctification of time is particularly prominent in Diaspora Judaism, which lacked territory. In the Soviet Union, religious holidays were ignored and at times prohibited. However, the state holidays that replaced them—for example, October Revolution Day,[2] Soviet Constitution Day, and International Labor Day—were also sanctified. These anniversaries were highly ritualistic and charged with ideological meaning. It is not accidental that they were referred to as the "red-letter days of the calendar." The system imposed their importance upon the people by making teams and individual workers pledge labor achievements in commemoration of the Soviet holidays. Citizens were encouraged and sometimes even forced to participate in festive demonstrations. Naturally, in the last decades of Soviet power, the stage of mass disillusionment with the system, many people did not conceal skepticism and contempt for the glorification of events with which they no longer identified. This, however, did not prevent the population from enjoying the days off and the opportunity to meet friends at a festive dinner.

In our material there are instances of reflections about both time and space, but thoughts about space predominate. We are interested in the construction of cultural space, defined by van Baak (1983) as "any property or manifestation of space that can be anthropologically meaningful and as such receives semiotic value" (37). Our various relations with environment, including space relations, are systematized and made expressible in semiotic codes, thereby receiving an intersubjective and autonomous function of signs that describe and regulate the human's cultural behavior. Immigration is always a spatial change. Human territory is a multidimensional notion, according to Gold (1980) not limited to physiological needs but serving social and personal needs as well. Gold emphasizes the significance of individual and social fixed territories commonly used as a means to satisfy human needs for status and recognition, and as a medium through which one's self-image may be communicated to the outside world (86). As discussed in chapter 3, every immigrant loses one of the most valued personal territories—home. Lotman (1997) notes that the antithesis of *home* and *anti-home* has always been among the most important themes of world folklore. One's *home* is safe and culturally organized. It is the space protected by the deities, while *anti-home* is "the forest home"—an alien, demonic space, a place of temporary death. Finding oneself in such a space is equivalent to the journey to the *other world.* The archaic models of consciousness linked to this opposition are stable and productive in the history of culture (748). The importance of *home* as a refuge from the omnipresent "system" increased after decades of communal life in the USSR, when not only apartments but even rooms were sometimes shared by several families. "My house" may not have been the Briton's "castle," but it was one of the main components of well-being and stability. Hence, many of our informants have bitter memories of the feeling of homelessness that haunted them in the first period of immigrant life.

Our interviewees' perception of space has been influenced by several cultural traditions. One is the Slavic perception of borders, which separate "our world" from the "other world." In Slavic cultures border crossing has negative connotations and is often associated with crime, danger, and death. Numerous rituals performed on the border point to the role of borders in social life and in the metaphysical perception of life and death (Tolstoi 1995, 537–40). Such an attitude toward borders can be traced in Russian folktales in which "not only are people who come into the village from outside suspect; anyone who has left home and traveled, thus crossing boundaries in space, seems to be incapable of returning to the village except as one of the unquiet dead" (Moyle 1989, 89).

In Soviet times, the concept of border crossing was charged with ambivalence. Official ideology associated it with betrayal of motherland and its ideals, while at least some part of the population perceived it as escape from the suffocating political system and poverty, and associated life outside the USSR with freedom and prosperity. The Soviet myth about a threat, discussed in chapter 3, and the siege mentality also involve the notion of borders. The symbolism of the border is associated with a potential threat, assurance of the group's safety, and in a broader sense with the complex of surrounding hostility (Dubin 2001, 154–56; Tolstoi 1995, 537–40). The Soviet-era expression "the border is locked," ridiculed in folklore of the Russians in Israel (Zilberg 1995, 7–8), has recently been revived in the Russian-speaking community as an argument in support of the complete separation from Palestinians by means of a "Great Wall of Israel." The importance of the concept of "border" is reflected in the Russian language. Lebedeva (2000), who investigated semantic features of the noun *border* and its derivatives, points out that it has an essential bearing on our psychological relations with space. The primary semantic components of the word are *ogranichenie* (limitation) and *razgranichenie* (demarcation), yet the variety of other meanings expressed by the lexeme in different combinations is virtually unmatched in other languages (95, 97). In the context of our interviews the most frequent combinations are "go/be abroad" and "cross the border." They show that "border crossing" is still perceived as a crucial event of life by the former Soviets, though today it is used humorously.

The notions of emigration and immigration are also closely associated with border crossing and have retained the stigma of Soviet times. They were even excluded from the bureaucratic language of Soviet authorities. When emigration from the USSR increased exponentially, the Soviet authorities invented a new cliché to replace it: emigrants were referred to as people "leaving for another country for permanent domicile," abbreviated in Russian to *PMZh.* In some sense the words *emigration* and *immigration* are still taboo among Russian speakers in Israel. It is well known that Israeli society as a whole considers the arrival of Jews in Israel repatriation; Zionists see it as a duty, and religious Jews perceive it as a *mitzvah* (commandment). Yet few of our interviewees apply the term *repatriates* to themselves. Hardly any of the informants use the words *emigration, immigration,* and *repatriation* in the interviews, although it is difficult to imagine a more appropriate context for them than a story about immigration. As noted in chapter 1, interviewees prefer to use the neutral

Crossing borders without restrictions was an unfulfilled dream for several generations of the Soviet people. The travel agency Traveling without Borders, which caters to Russian speakers, reminds them that one's dream of seeing the world can finally come true.

verbs of movement—*leave, depart, come, arrive*—that function as euphemisms.

In the shared perception of space, we see a similarity between the cultures of Israel and the Soviet Union in that both countries were forced to experience isolation. In the early stages of its existence the Soviet Union was the only state trying to realize the communist idea. The reiteration of the ideological mantra "The country is encircled by enemies" fostered a siege mentality in several generations of Soviet people. Then, after World War II, the country was again cut off by the Iron Curtain of the Cold War. In Israel too, years of economic boycott and hostile relations with its neighbors have bred the perception of an alien world encroaching on the country.

The fundamental difference in the perception of space in the two cultures stems from the difference in the size of the two countries. Soviet ideology always emphasized the importance of vast territory (see chapter 3). The fact that the USSR occupied a huge part of the earth's land surface was a source of great pride. In Israel, the small dimensions of the country increase the value of every inch of territory in the eyes of its inhabitants. According to Kellerman (1989), "Zionism may be interpreted as a spatial ideology par excellence" (84). This is particularly important for immigrants from the FSU, who suffer from claustrophobia and fear even the most modest territorial concessions when peace with Israel's neighbors is negotiated. The change of territorial dimensions seems to affect the imagination of immigrants irrespective of their age and education.

Vast and Small Spaces: Power and Insecurity

The excerpts quoted below are permeated with explicit and tacit comparisons of the space of the two countries, and the new homeland tends to be at a disadvantage. The antitheses focus on physical and symbolic dimensions, the most frequent being big-small, center-periphery, exposed-protected, and powerful-weak.

Igor K., 59

> Here in Israel . . . it is provincial. And second of all, there is a factor of scale. I am like the pilot from *Exodus:* Where shall I land the plane? Where shall I land? [*Igor alludes to the novel by Leon Uris.*] There is just a narrow strip of, er . . . land along, er . . . the sea.

Irina G., 18

> It [*the Arab-Israeli conflict*] has become much closer to me. I have come to understand what's going on. In the past, it was sort of far from me. And now . . . Rosh Hanikra is very close to Lebanon. And recently I've seen in the paper that everything that's going on in Lebanon is very close to us; it is just a couple

of kilometers away from us. . . . And how things are related . . . Kiryat Shmona . . . it's terribly close to Lebanon. How can people live there when they know they are shot at? And . . . I would have nightmares. (See other passages with this motif in Yelenevskaya and Fialkova 2002, 212.)

In these passages the limits of physical space are seen as a danger, jeopardizing the physical survival of the nation and individuals. Such a perception may be rooted in the collective memory of the Soviet people, which is still alive even in the younger generation. During World War II, and after the nuclear disaster of Chernobyl, the population was evacuated from threatened areas. Yet even in the worst times, people knew that there was always a place to move to and find refuge. The experience of many families proved that escape depended on the promptness of the decision to leave the home place, so salvation was more a question of time than space. In a tiny country like Israel the concept of evacuation does not make sense. When immigrants come to realize this they react emotionally. This is manifested in the choice of lexis—*to be afraid, strange, incredible, terribly close, nightmares*—and in the use of rhetorical questions and exclamations. While Irina explicitly links her feeling of uneasiness to the political conflict, Igor expresses the same attitude implicitly by the allusion to literature. Note instances of the metaphorical use of spatial terms in the quoted excerpts; for example, Irina uses the adjective *close* in the sense of *familiar, clear,* while the adjective *far* connotes *lack of interest, lack of concern.* The closeness of the borders scares Irina and our other subjects. The Russian linguist Iakovleva (1994) gives numerous examples of how the polar concepts *far/near* in various contexts acquire abstract, metaphorical meaning and are handy evaluations (for example, Moscow is far but the boss is near). They are often juxtaposed, and in such cases the use of modifiers such as *very* and *quite* is impossible (45).

The next excerpt shows that the infatuation with vast space still lingers in the immigrants' mind.

Boris P., 50

BORIS: Well, most often I watch Russian TV. So, then, er . . . but not because it's in my mother tongue, but because I think it's like this . . . First, forgive me, but after all, it's the sixth part of [*pause*] the dry land.

INTERVIEWER: Well, well, no more [*laughs*].

BORIS: Well, okay, it doesn't really matter, but it is still the lion's share. Well, and obviously, it will influence the whole world [*pause*] irrespective of the state it is in. And so such a territory, er . . . won't leave the world in peace, and that's why I want to know. . . .

The once celebrated "one-sixth of the dry land" continues to be a marker of power, which is emphasized by metonymy: the noun *territory* stands for *country* or *state.* The collapse of the USSR does not put into question its influence on the world arena. Although the narrator admits that the "old country" has shrunk and its state of affairs is volatile, he is not ready to part with the myth that it is still a superpower. At the same time, he does not idealize Russia and is aware of its potential to be an adversary in international affairs. Boris suspects that Russia "won't leave the world in peace," yet he cannot resist the habit of expressing haughty pride in his motherland. This is one among numerous examples of personal-life narratives "nested" within the progressive narrative of a nation (Taylor and Wetherell 1999, 39), which enables storytellers to feel part of the nation's success and fame.

Our observation that Israel evokes the feeling of claustrophobia in the immigrant community is supported by the emergence of a folklore verse parodying the once-popular children's poet Mikhalkov (1999, 6).

Sofia Y., 48
[*She quotes the quatrain popular before the peace treaty with Jordan was signed*]

A iz nashego okna	From the window of my room
Iordania vidna,	Jordan can be seen in full
A iz vashego okoshka	When in your room we sit,
Tol'ko Siria nemnozhko.	Only Syria is seen a bit.

In the original version, the kids boast about the view of the "main square of the country," Red Square, and make fun of those who are deprived of the privilege.

A iz nashego okna ploshchad' Krasnaia vidna. A iz vashego okoshka Tol'ko ulitsa nemnozhko.	One can see Red Square from our window, while from the small window of your room, one can only see a little bit of a street.

In the original, the essence of the antithesis is a prestigious versus a commonplace location of the house. In the folkloric paraphrase, the issue is the proximity of the borders of the two Arab countries. The local space is reevaluated in proportion to the dimensions of the country's territory. The humorous touch cannot hide the implied menace, and the mood of the quatrain is reminiscent of the popular Soviet folklore genre of children's sadistic verses (Belousov 1998, 545–57).

Metamorphoses of Space in the Unknown Land

Reflections about space illustrate the subjects' attempts to investigate and interpret the unknown. In the beginning, when appraising the unfamiliar space, immigrants tend to go to extremes; they describe it as dreamlike and beautiful, or conversely as alien, hostile, almost under a spell. As we will see in the following excerpts, alienation often stems from an immigrant's inability to communicate in Hebrew in public places and the disorientation caused by the exotic nature and an unfamiliar architectural style.

Vladimir Ia., 61

VLADIMIR: So, well, surely, the first impression was that I found myself in some big apartment, which is clean and in which the air is pleasant. I found myself on Nordau [*a pedestrian mall in Haifa*]. I strolled along Nordau as if it were an apartment. It's a big apartment, and long. I walk, and it is clean and pleasant. And I came from Kiev. It was about minus 25 degrees there. That's why I felt as if it were a clean and warm apartment. And the Sokhnut . . . I stayed in Tal'pion . . .

INTERVIEWER: In the hotel?

VLADIMIR: In the hotel. And it took me three days to get from Tal'pion to the Sokhnut. And why did it take me three days?

> Whoever I ask, nobody knows where the Sokhnut is, that is the Ministry of Absorption, nobody knows. (IFA 22128)

Finding one's way in a modern city replete with signs is not a difficult task. But it is not so for new immigrants. Language incompetence prevents the newcomers from making sense of the space organization of the city. The inability to cope with the simplest speech patterns leads to the feeling that space is enchanted (see Yelenevskaya and Fialkova 2002, 214–15). Vladimir adds to his story an element of drama, created by the quasi-dialogue. He imagines a relatively short street as a "long apartment," apparently an association with the notoriously long corridors of communal apartments. Even six years after immigration Vladimir confused "Talpiot," Hebrew for "fortress, or a magnificent building," with meaningless "Talpion," and the "Ministry of Absorption" with the "Jewish Agency." He had not yet learned that a *sokhnut* can be any agency—an insurance agency, a car rental agency—so passers-by could hardly guess that he was looking for the only agency known to new immigrants from the first day of their life in Israel.

Discovering a new spatial environment is a sensory experience. Sight is the dominant source of spatial information, but hearing, smell, and touch complement it and extend the range of one's knowledge of the environment (Gold 1980, 52). Many report unfamiliar sounds, an unusual position of the young moon, or floral scents as their first impression of Israel. Plants become markers of familiar or unfamiliar space, the most prominent examples being chamomile and palm trees. But the strongest sensory sensation experienced by the immigrants is tactile, the skin's perception of warmth. Again to make sense of the new experience, immigrants look for analogies with the familiar spatial environment. A good example is Vladimir's story, quoted in the previous passage. After severe frosts, the pleasant warm temperature and the cleanliness of the streets breed associations with an apartment. The image is so strong that Vladimir repeats it three times.

In his study of recent migrants' narratives in Sydney, the anthropologist Mar (1988) noted the ubiquity of comparisons of places that sharply dichotomized attributes of *here* and *there:* "Comparisons of place tend to emerge in fragmentary forms in

Unlike in the early 1990s, Israeli towns today have an abundance of Russian signs and graffiti. This one welcomes customers to a nearby restaurant. While the French *Bien venu* is modest and hardly visible, the Russian *Dobro pozhalovat'* is written in huge letters and catches the eye from a distance.

interview situations where perceived qualities of physical spaces of and around the body serve as points of reference or affective markers" (60). The instability of interviewees' spatial world is often manifest in the confusion of deictic markers *here* and *there*. Deixis functions as the "semiotic act of establishing spatio-temporal contrasts between points of view in a situation" (van Baak 1983, 52). We perceive space as organized around us and put ourselves into the center of macro- and microcosm (Gak 2000, 127). In the analyzed narratives we often come across antitheses here/there, and in some instances Israel is referred to as *there* and the FSU as *here*.

Esfir' Ia., 35

> Because I had had only one dream: to go away from THERE. When finally that dream could materialize, I asked myself a crucial question: "What am I exchanging for what?" And a

> week before departure, we decided, that is, I decided for myself, that I don't want to go to America, not ever, that it is a black spot on the map for me. I felt that I shouldn't go there, that there is something inside me that wouldn't let me go there. And I decided I would go to Israel. After all . . . at least I know why I am going to Israel; I can explain it to myself clearly. But I cannot explain to myself why I am going to America. That's why we came here.

Gaiane A., 77

> [*About her son family's first days in Israel*] . . . and they were accepted by a kibbutz. They came there without any personal belongings, because they went away from here, they left the Soviet Union under tragic circumstances.

In both of these excerpts, the narrators put the old and the new countries in opposition. While Esfir' has already domesticated the space of the new country, Gaiane still feels more at home in her old country, which is partially accounted for by her advanced age. *Here* indicates proximity of both space and time. It signifies the speaker's involvement in the events described, and it is linked to the expression of emotions. Note that Esfir' describes America as a "black spot." This is an antithetic paraphrase of the Russian phrase a "white spot," which connotes the unknown—for example, "white spots on a map." By changing *white* to *black* Esfir' adds derogatory connotations to the expression.

As we see, spatial confusion in immigrants' stories is intensified by the confusion of the outer and inner space. We have already noted the destruction of the borders between inner and outer space in Vladimir Ya.'s story, and Ekaterina B. experienced similar metamorphosis. Describing her first days in Israel she said she had mistaken apartment houses for hotels, which in the Soviet Union were signs of luxury. Ekaterina was amazed at the vastness of space in Israel. But while normally the notion of vastness is associated with the outer space, she referred to the inner space, in particular to the planning and furnishing of houses (see Yelenevskaya and Fialkova 2002, 217–18).

Not only the flora but also the fauna of Israel causes emotional reaction in immigrants. Confrontation with unfamiliar insects and reptiles that allegedly invaded their apartments is frequently described in immigrants' stories (see, e.g., Bar-Itzhak 1998, 195–99). It is also presented in the Russian literature of Israel: "The apartment is captured by hostile pests, which make it unlivable: scorpions and cockroaches, malicious cats and other substitutes of the fox, eagle owls, and a hedgehog, which according to the Biblical curse had once inhabited the empty land of Israel" (Vaiskopf 2001, 247). We have recorded two stories about insect and snake invasions in the ethnographic diary and one in an interview.

Maria S., 25

> And then I had a traumatic experience, when I saw a big cockroach for the first time—they call it "dzhuk" here. When I saw it for the first time in my room, I was shocked. It was awful. Here is a colorful scene for you. At midnight I go to bed. At half past twelve, there is a terrible thunder coming from the staircase. Somebody somewhere beats on a *pladelet* [*Hebrew for "metal door"*], and terrible screams reach our apartment, "Switch off your *mazgan* [*Hebrew for "air-conditioner"*] at once! We will sue you!" I couldn't understand who this was addressed to. We didn't have a *mazgan,* yet it was very unpleasant. They didn't let me sleep. And then I see something crawling. I jump up. There was a *hamsin* [*Hebrew for "hot and dry south-easterly wind"*]. All the windows were open. I didn't know that they [*cockroaches*] come during *hamsin,* and one has to cover windows with nets. And so there was a *hamsin.* And something is crawling along the plinth. I am terrified. I switch on the light, and the cockroach is crawling along the plinth. I . . . take out a bicycle pump. How can I get it? I don't know how to crush it. I found out that if you beat them with a slipper they simply don't react. It was such a blow for me. In Moscow I used to communicate with cockroaches very nicely. I dealt with armies of cockroaches. I would go to the kitchen at one in the morning with a plastic bag on my head and would smear them all over the walls. I wore a plastic bag because they dropped on my head. We lived in an old house, and all the tenants tried to exterminate them. So they escaped to our apartment. And we couldn't poison them. Our apartment was crowded with the rabble. And I didn't mind having them around. I could even touch them with my hands. Afterward I

> reconciled myself with the local cockroaches too. When I lived in the dorms in Kiryat Yam, I used to come home at midnight. I would open the door, kill four or five of them, and the rest would run away. In the dorms they used to travel from room to room, just like this. Twenty rooms in the dorms were given to students, and the rest of the building was occupied by Ethiopian families. But at some point the number of cockroaches reached a critical mass, and they were poisoned. Then everything was covered with a layer of cockroaches. And the kitchen was covered with several layers. So on the eve of the psychometric test I see such a cockroach for the first time. I don't know how to fight it. I take a bicycle pump, run to one side of the sofa, but the cockroach rushes to the other side. I overtake it, but it runs back. And thus I am driving it all around, but finally, I am done in. I am worn out. And then I have a great idea of pressing it to the wall with a pile of notebooks, which were under the sofa. For a long time I didn't know if it was alive or not. I pushed the pile over and over again. Then I tried to check whether it was alive or not. I watched it for a long time to be sure it didn't stir. Then I dissected it, and transported it to the garbage can part by part. It was done for the sake of my safety. I wanted to be sure it wouldn't resurrect. It wasn't a pleasant experience. I went back to bed. (IFA 21756)

All the stories that Maria told during her long interview are full of pathos and hyperbole. In this excerpt cockroaches emerge as enemies confronting her wherever she lives. Relatively harmless insects with whom she used to "communicate very nicely" in Moscow, cockroaches have evolved into malicious, almost demonic, creatures defying any "weapon" used against them. Maria seemingly enjoyed depicting the detailed description of the battle and her roles of resourceful fighter and implacable victor. Among other things, the domestication of the new space is marked by the taming of cockroaches; although in the dorms Maria was confronted with the whole armies, their killing turned into a daily routine and the presence of the insects stopped bothering her.

Many of our informants had never traveled outside the Soviet Union before emigration and could only imagine life outside their homeland on the basis of media information, literature, art, and hearsay.

Vladislav V., 29

> And in principle, some of the information about "abroad" was inaccessible to us, because we had never been there. And that's why it was difficult to imagine what it's like. It seemed that there was everything there, so to say, it is not that manna drops from heavens, but there is general well-being.

So Israel was part of "abroad," that proverbial notion which for a "Soviet" encompassed the riches and luxury of the "other world" on Earth. In normative usage *za granitsei* (abroad) is a prepositional phrase, which means to be outside one's own country. The Soviet writers Ilia Ilf and Ievgenii Petrov coined the noun *zagranitsa,* which ironically referred to the rest of the world as opposed to the Soviet Union. The word caught on and has retained an ironic flavor. Ekaterina B., 23, visualized "abroad" as a fairy tale, and for her it is synonymous with paradise. Asia Sh., 56, recalled that before immigration, information about Israel came from letters describing it as "paradise on earth." When the prosperity of Israel was put into question, prospective immigrants denied it the status of real "abroad." Hence a popular saying of the last decades of the Soviet power: *"Kuritsa ne ptitsa, Izrail' ne zagranitsa"* (A chicken is not a bird, and Israel is no "abroad"). Trying to imagine Israel, Ekaterina B. mobilized her fragmentary knowledge of the Bible, folk images of the Land of Plenty, and, like many other narrators, rumors about the abundance of consumer goods outside the FSU. Abundance, especially abundance of food, is a motif typical of folklore of many peoples related to the image of the kingdom of the dead. These images merged with fairyland and paradise. Propp (1986) emphasizes that changes in the real world are reflected in the images of the fictional world of the dead. But the emergence of the new motifs does not affect the survival of the old (287–97). The "self set" tablecloth of traditional Russian folklore yields to supermarkets and health resorts, but both refer to the same archetype. The self-set tablecloth always appeared as if out of thin air, set with all the victuals the heart could desire. An example of this popular belief was observed and analyzed by Moroz in 1996. He found that his informants, inhabitants of northern Russian villages, conceptualized paradise as "life in a resort" (Moroz 2000, 204). Many informants link the first favorable impressions of Israel with the Black Sea resorts. Images of the milky rivers and resorts, however, often clash with fear of the unknown, which is perceived as emptiness, embodied by a desert. The desert is one of the most frequent and powerful spatial symbols found in the interviews.

Landscapes: Topophilia and Topophobia

The symbolic value of landscapes varies across cultures and changes as time goes on. Growing concern about preserving what has been inherited from the past may be one explanation of why landscapes are increasingly being rendered symbolic meaning. People are becoming more aware and appreciative of differences and resist the homogenizing effects of globalization (Dodgshon 1998, 117). New immigrants tend to idealize the landscapes of their pre-immigration past. In evaluating the Israeli landscape, be it nature or cityscape, narrators rely on their own experience or on knowledge drawn from literature and art.

Many narratives show future immigrants' ignorance about Israel. It was not limited to vague ideas about the country's history and culture but extended to the inability to imagine local landscape or Israeli towns. Suffice it to say that some interviewees report that they had to search for Israel on the map or on the globe. Ella V., 69, told us that she could not find Eilat on the map because she could not imagine that Israel extended southward of the Negev Desert (IFA 22113, see Yelenevskaya and Fialkova 2002, 219–20). Although all our informants are literate, and many have university degrees, their knowledge of geography often betrays them and leads to misconceptions and absurdities. Ella, for example, imagined that she would see the ancient Egyptian monument, the pyramid of the pharaoh Cheops, in the Negev. Her husband Moisei V., 74, when planning to settle down in Eilat, tried to calm down his wife by saying, "And what can we do? After all, the Sahara is in Russia, and so what?" (IFA 22115). In his anxiety caused by the drastic change in their lives, Moisei confused the African desert with the Kara Kum Desert in Central Asia. Both of these examples are not just amusing but support the premise that unfamiliar space may be confusing and frightening. Note that for a family from central Russia a desert symbolized the border between life and death. Speaking about the desert, our other informants use the word in the metaphorical rather than the literal sense.

Inna Kh., 52

INTERVIEWER: [*About the choice of the country of immigration*] Did you ever think about going to another country?

INNA: You know, I cannot even explain why. Germany . . . I think, I simply absorbed it with breast milk. . . . Shall I go to the Germans? Never! Just as the mere sound of the German language—you know it's an incredible feeling—it has always caused nausea in me. I wouldn't learn it. It's ridiculous, it's a prejudice. It's not even on the level of the conscious, but of the subconscious. America is a DESERT, in which. . . . There [*in Israel*], I have an acquaintance here and another one there, at least some kind of . . . the country is small and in other towns . . . I can at least pick up the phone and talk. And there [*in America*], well I am . . . done for. "But you speak English!" So what can the language do for me? I still come there as . . . from everything I'd read, I gathered that I'd be a twenty-fifth-rate person there. How can I start there? As God knows who, as God knows what and . . . a DESERT! Indeed, the main thing is that it's a huge country and I am there, and it is a desert.

Anatolii P., 26

And we arrive here, and it is still a wasteland, I mean, in the sense that it is [*pause*] a spiritual wasteland. Because you come here, and you have nothing. Well, there might be an address of a guy in Jerusalem, or just a telephone. . . . In sum, you are in a state . . . of utter confusion and it's very hot, it's August.

Note that while Inna speaks about the desert, Anatolii compares Israel to a wasteland. In Russian, both words have the same root: *pustynia, pustyr'*, and both have morphological and semantic links with *pustota* (emptiness). For our informants it is a metaphor of solitude that does not necessarily apply to Israel. Inna uses it to explain her unwillingness to migrate to America, which for some of our other interviewees still remains the ultimate temptation. The existence of the negative image of the desert, which symbolizes aridity, isolation, and despair, has been reported by psychologists studying dream landscapes. In dream reports the desert emerges as the least appreciated environment by people of different age groups. By contrast, fertile landscapes are symbols of hope and renewal (Stevens 1995, 268).

A topophilic or topophobic[3] perception of nature largely depends on where interviewees lived before immigration. Geographers, ethnographers, and sociologists indicate that perception of nature also depends on the place of origin of an ethnic group (Lebedeva 1993, 82–101). Yet our material does not provide such examples. We find that the scenery of immigrants' birthplace serves as a standard and as a basis for comparison.[4]

Lilia V., 22

INTERVIEWER: Do you think you will still want to go to Lvov, when your mother is no longer there?

LILIA: I think so. Just to come for a couple of days and walk in the city—I would need nothing else. . . . To look, to be caught in the Lvov rain. It never rains here like it does there [*pause*], a drizzle, a nasty rain of the fall. . . . The color of the entire country [*Israel*] is . . . it is a little bit faded.

INTERVIEWER: So what color do you miss?

LILIA: Green. Green is very bright, very intense there [*in Lvov*], particularly the green of the young plants, of the young grass, of the young trees.

Anastasia N., 61

And once we were on a romantic German street, this *Romantische Strasse,* a German highway. . . . And you stop there, or pass those little houses, and you get an impression that they are toys. And so . . . We came there, and there were Alpine meadows there, which I hadn't seen for years, for decades. Even in Khar'kov you won't find such meadows. While in the Urals there were such meadows. After all I grew up in Nizhnii Tagil. And there were simple wildflowers there. And there was a long, long meadow, bright green. And the greenery was so bright. There were coniferous forests and the blue sky, which you can never see here. Well, I don't know, sometimes the sky

> is blue, but very rarely. . . . I couldn't imagine Israel at all, I couldn't understand. My brother wrote to us that it was like . . . in terms of climate, if you wish, it reminds one of the southern coast of the Crimea, or of Sochi [*a resort in the Caucasus*], something like this. Yes, everything was alien. Everything was alien and exactly of the sort I dislike. Say, I always preferred Leningrad to Moscow. In Moscow, now it is already a modern city, but then in the first years, when I was there once, it was not really . . . well, a European city. There were buildings of the sort, uncharacteristic of, say, Leningrad. And so when for the first time we went to France, I went out onto the street and saw that it was almost like in Leningrad. Well, the feeling was as if I had come to Leningrad. . . . And here, there are those horrible roofs, as if they were steamers with white funnels sailing off. Flat roofs, extending to the horizon, and gray houses. Gray houses, roofs, gray houses, roofs. And they were so dirty. Even the houses, which I came to like later, the stone faced, Arab houses. They were dirty then, and gray. Or have I got used to things? A terrible amount of ruins, particularly when we were going across . . . The bus there, where we lived, in the *shchuna* [*Hebrew for "neighborhood"*] where we lived, the bus from the *shuk* [*Hebrew for "market"*] passed an old *shchuna*. . . . Now it has been dismantled, demolished, because apparently the time when it was not allowed to demolish houses abandoned by Arabs had expired. So, the most comfortable place for me was a bus. I said, "This is my home."

Both narrators are nostalgic for the landscape of the old country. Everything is dear to them, even the "nasty" drizzle and the environs of Nizhnii Tagil—a city notorious for its air pollution and overall ecological condition. In many narratives, attractive and repulsive landscapes are associated with certain colors. Surprisingly, Anastasia misses the bright blue sky, a feeling that is difficult to share because the sky in Israel is rarely overcast. Just like Anastasia and Lilia, many other interviewees suffer from the lack of green, and they complain about the abundance of yellow in nature and of gray in the cityscape. The negative perception of both these colors may have roots in the Russian cultural tradition. In the prose by Dostoevskii and Belyi, in the poetry by Blok, and more, yellow is associated with disease, madness, and deteriora-

Domestication of space: This Russian graffiti on a Haifa apartment house reads, "Haifa is my town."

tion. Moreover, derogatory connotations of yellow are reflected in the dead metaphor *zheltyi dom* (yellow house), which denotes a lunatic asylum. Gray for Russian speakers is the color of mediocrity and lack of individuality. Sleuths were often referred to as "people wearing gray hats."

Anastasia associates gray houses with the dirtiness and untidiness of the city. Gray and white—the pale colors signify gloom and monotony for the narrator, and the expressiveness is strengthened by the multiple repetition of the adjective *gray*. Israeli cities are opposed to European towns, and the basis for comparison is Leningrad. Every town resembling it is beautiful. Even the impression of France is determined by its alleged similarity to Leningrad: "it was almost like in Leningrad." In fact, as a symbol of urban beauty, Leningrad is mentioned in many of the interviews. (Another example of the symbolic role of Leningrad for FSU immigrants can be found in Mirsky [2005], quoting an adolescent: "I love Leningrad. I wish Leningrad were in Israel" [28].) Symbolic importance is often attributed to cities, the most notable examples being Paris, Jerusalem, Rome, and New York. These are not necessarily beautiful cities, but they appear to have mediated the city symbol as it emerges both in the minds of their creators and those who experience them (Gold 1980, 127). Traditionally St. Petersburg (in Soviet times, Leningrad) was opposed to Moscow and was perceived as the country's most European city (see Golosov and Shevchenko 2004). It was lovingly referred to as the "Northern Venice" and "the window on Europe." Many books and articles are devoted to the city's image and its role in Russian culture (Lotman 1992b). The city has retained not only the aura of mysticism but also of prestige, and in our material it is constantly opposed to provincial towns, be they in Russia, Central Asia, or the Middle East.

Maria S., 25

> You see, when I started the *mechina* [*Hebrew for "pre-university program"*], I "left" Israel. I sort of lived in the Technion, in the bus, in my room. I didn't see . . . I was no longer in Israel. The euphoria was canceled.

The above excerpts from Anastasia's and Maria's interviews contain double inversion of static and moving objects: the houses with flat roofs are compared to steamers, while the bus is perceived as a substitute for home. The ship and the bus are connected to traveling, hence the change of location. In contrast to a real home they can give only temporary shelter. Analyzing the images of the house and home in the Russian literature of Israel, Vaiskopf (2001) observes a similar perception in the prose and poetry by Dina Rubina, Susanna Chernobrova, Tatiana Akhtman, Svetlana Shenbrunn, and Lev Melamid. The house emerges not as a real house; it only pretends to be one: it resembles a boat, it hangs over the abyss or sits on a tree. It is supplanted by a bus or an elevator (247). The frequency of the images of the house and home in the immigrants' literature and personal narratives, as well as consistency of associations, confirms the significance of the solid and reliable house, without which former Soviets do not feel at home.

Immigration: Temporary Life, Temporary People?

One of the most important features of life in Soviet times was limited mobility. Registration of domicile was an obstacle for people who wished to move from town to town, and even from one apartment to another, if it involved towns and neighborhoods of unequal social value. At the same time, once the state granted an individual or a family the right to housing, it did not as a rule revoke it. As regards citizens' professional life, various regulations discouraged workers from changing jobs. For non-party members the chances for promotion even within the same organization were rather slim, yet jobs were secure, and unemployment and layoffs were unknown in the USSR. A change of profession in the course of a career was rare, and anyone setting out to make such a change was seen as an adventurer. On the one hand, limited mobility was detrimental to people's ability to use initiative; on the other hand, it gave an illusion of the predictability of life and social protection. The feeling of permanency and stability forms slowly, and some of our interviewees complain that they haven't had a chance to experience it in Israel.

Lilia L., 42

> You know, in Israel I have always had a feeling that everything is temporary. And I was watching myself as if everything was not happening to me, but as if I was watching myself as a third person. And all the time I felt everything was unreal, unreal.

Irina B., 70

> What depresses us is that we don't have our own housing. It's really depressing . . . this endless *skhirut* [*Hebrew for "renting"*]. . . . A person left his apartment, in which he may have lived for ten years or something like that. And he came here

> and he has no housing. It's depressing. You may not put a nail into a wall; you may not hang things you want on the wall. And you always feel you are a temporary person here. And this very feeling is depressing. And nothing belongs to you, and you are here only temporarily. . . . You don't have a feeling you have come here to live permanently, because all the time you are here . . . er . . . here and at the same time not here. (. . .) An ideal country, Limonia, is yet to be created. As they say [*laughs*] the country of Limonia doesn't exist on Earth. There are pros and cons everywhere.

The opposition of temporary versus permanent is not limited to the perception of time. The unexplored space is also seen as a temporary environment. For some, it is the loss of reality; for others, the feeling of homelessness. Furthermore, the radical change of space makes some informants feel as if they were tourists, enjoying life but fearing that their stay in this exotic place is nothing but temporary. The utopian country Limonia, mentioned in the above excerpt and appearing in one of the conversations written down in our ethnographic diary, deserves special comment. This image is widely used in contemporary Russian speech and is traced to Stalin's prison camps. The Georgian writer Dzhaba Ioseliani, author of *The Country of Limonia,* a novel about prison camps, explained the title in a newspaper interview: "It is a prison name, something like 'A country of miracles,' akin to Solzhenitsyn's *Gulag*" (Gvindadze 2002). In a review of the novel, the well-known literary critic Anninskii (2001) quotes a song from the prison folklore in which Limonia is depicted as a country of freedom with neither sorrow nor grief and as a country of plenty where people drink milk instead of water. A slightly different twist to the image of legendary Limonia is found in Tanich's song (2003), *And Here in the Prison Camp,* stylized as prison folklore. He opposes the familiar hell of the camps to the unknown, hence to the frightening paradise of free life. In Vysotskii's *The Ballad about Childhood* (1988) Limonia is associated with postwar looting and the failed hopes of the war generation for prosperity. In the center of the song's plot is a huge communal apartment whose interminably long corridors are transformed into the corridors of a prison. Times have changed, and so has the image of Limonia. In a recently popular song by Katin (2003) it is no longer

The KVN tradition not only outlived the USSR, it crossed national borders. Young people continue to play the game in Israel, the United States, and Germany. This poster invites Russian-speaking Israelis to attend the national semifinals.

associated with prison, but it still symbolizes the Land of Plenty, the land where trouble is unknown. And to get to this land one has to walk through a long underground corridor. The popularity of the image accounts for its use in tourism advertising and in the popular culture. For example, the name was used for concert programs by the satirists Zadornov, Kondratiev, and Frantsuzov; performances by the TV star Petrosian; and by a KVN team (KVN, an acronym for "The Club of the Merry and the Quick-Witted" is a contest of humor and political satire). We don't know which of the quoted sources our informants alluded to regarding the absence of Limonia in Israel. What is important is that both of them used the ambiguity of the image.

Our material indicates that besides the loss of stability, immigrants experience a change in the perception of the life cycle. In addition to the traditional division of life into childhood, adolescence, youth, and so on, immigrants draw another demarcation line: life before and life after emigration. Psychologists studying migrants have noted that this mental division of immigrants' lives is a typical phenomenon of Russian migrants and a characteristic feature of a traumatized personality (Makhovskaia 2001, 46–47). Moreover, immigration changes one's subjective perception of one's age. There is a distinction between biological and mental age. Socially constructed categories of age do not necessarily correspond with chronological aging, but they are related to social competence and power (Adam 1990, 98–99; Mills 2000). We observe early maturation in teenagers immigrating to Israel alone, without their families. In contrast, in the families in which parents experience difficulties with learning the new language, children very often assume a patronizing attitude, and the roles in the family reverse. In adults the perception of age is closely connected to the ability to find a job corresponding to one's qualifications, or to learn a profession of comparable social prestige. Naturally, an important element in ensuring one's contentment is financial independence. Conversely, a lack of social competence and inability to "find one's place" in the job market, and in the new life as a whole, makes people feel that either they are aging prematurely or becoming infantile.

Leonid B., 36

> Our life has changed altogether. And it has changed to be suited to local life, to local conditions . . . Of course, it has changed. And completely. . . . The life experience acquired there in the course of over thirty years doesn't work at all. That is, in the first period, we felt like we were little kids. Now we have some local experience, even if it is still modest. And in the beginning, it was weird to feel like a child at the age of thirty. What? How? But absolutely . . . we sort of started from scratch. Neither life experience nor anything, so to say. . . .

The division of life into pre- and post-emigration period sharpens the division into past and present. Notably, our interviewees, even the young ones, seldom spoke about the future. Different authors writing about people from the FSU note their reluctance to evince trust in a better future (see, e.g., Golden 2002 and Ries 1997). After decades of waiting for the "joy of tomorrow,"[5] former Soviets have become skeptical about such promises. People who integrate successfully prefer to concentrate on the present, while those who suffer failures tend to idealize and attempt to re-create the past.

Piotr G., 43

> [*About the first days in Israel*] The impression was that life was over. On the second, on the third day, there was a feeling that that was it. Because then we couldn't think that it would be possible to go back and forth without problems. . . . [*Piotr refers to trips to the FSU, which were virtually impossible for émigrés before Perestroika due to difficulties in obtaining Soviet visas.*] Because the impression is that you have passed into a new dimension. There is an impenetrable wall. And it is as if that other life would be no more, but there is a new life, which is in Nazaret. . . . And then it moved to the background, but the first ten days were the most distressing. I felt I wanted to jump off the roof. I really did, though I don't know whether my wife felt the same. But this was my state of mind.

We would like to remind the reader that Piotr became an immigrant not out of conviction but accidentally (see chapter 2).

Although he didn't have to renounce his citizenship, he still perceived emigration as an irreversible step, one that had cut off his roots. The link between emigration and death opens and closes this excerpt. To render his emotional state, Piotr uses spatial metaphors: impenetrable wall and passing into a new dimension. He implies that the necessity of coping with mundane problems helped him to overcome the frustration. However, it did not prove effective in the long run. His spiritual ties with the homeland remained strong, and six years after emigration, having failed to integrate professionally, Piotr returned to Russia. He said: "The most important thing for me is to be able to work. It makes no difference whatsoever whether it is in America, Israel, or Tumen' [*a town in Siberia, where he worked upon his return to Russia*]; it's irrelevant."

Inna P., 49

> Yes, I feel nostalgic. I [*pause*] often say, "I want to go home." But [*pause*] it is a very strange desire. I want to go home and [*pause*] [*to reconstruct the time*] . . . when my parents were still alive. I want to be back in my paternal home. Yes. Otherwise, there are only graves to return to. I have no one left there.

Yeva F., 40

> [*About nostalgia for her hometown, Odessa*] Do not torture me. I miss the town that I remember. But if I go there, I won't find it. It's no longer there.

Emma R., 56

> It's well known—one has to go to Leningrad. I have already been there [*pause*] three times. Well, it has vanished without a trace, although I couldn't even imagine it would. At first it was simply as if I were insane. I walked along the streets here [*in Israel*] and imagined: here I am leaving my house on Ligovka [*an informal name of an old street in the center of St. Petersburg*] and now I am approaching the Nevskii [*the main street of the old city*]. Now I'll cross over, take MY trolley bus and go to the Petrogradskaia [*a city district*]. It was sheer insanity. Well, and it had been, er, like this until I went there [*St. Petersburg*]. I came there and calmed down completely. I understood that it

> was the wrong place for me. . . . I said to a distant relative, "You know, here [*pause*] I am surrounded by shadows, not by people." She says, "But these are good, kind shadows." I say, "But I prefer to be among those who are alive." The atmosphere is too sad there. I couldn't even go past my house. I passed along the other side of the street like this, I looked away [*shows how she walked*]. No, no, it would be impossible for me to be there now.

In these excerpts the notions of space and time are inseparable. The three women are nostalgic for the home that no longer exists and the life that will never come back. The hometowns, even when they are idealized, come to be associated with the "kingdom of the dead." Boym (2001) proposes to distinguish two types of nostalgia: restorative and reflective. "Restorative nostalgia puts emphasis on *nostos* and proposes to rebuild the lost home and patch up the memory gaps. Reflective nostalgia dwells in *algia,* in longing and loss, the imperfect process of remembering" (41). The two types often coexist. The immigrant community's attempts to reconstruct familiar customs and institutions are aimed at rebuilding life according to the old model. But in personal narratives immigrants explicitly or implicitly admit that the gap between the past and the present cannot be bridged.

Whether immigrant life is perceived as temporary existence, a sort of limbo, or as a deadlock, such a state of affairs cannot go on permanently. People choose one of the three options: to return to the old country, to move on to some other country, or to find an acceptable niche in Israel, which is the case with most of the immigrants.

East and West: Myth and Reality

Encounters and clashes between Western and non-Western civilizations and cultures are a never-ending topic in the political and media discourse. They are also part of everyday talk and contemporary folklore, particularly in countries where the two sides intersect. Discussions about the East and the West emerged in the interviews spontaneously. Initially, we didn't plan to focus on the subject, yet in the very first interviews conducted for the project we found that our subjects often used these concepts as signs of a whole range of social and cultural phenomena important for their understanding of life in the new country. Geographical data have little to do with the symbolic division of the world into East and West.[6] Particularly the Orient, "the land to the East of the West is a realm of stories. Its actuality has always been encapsulated in forms of storytelling as fact, fiction, and fable. It invites the imagination" (Sardar 1999, 1). The East and the West are fictional constructs "embroidered with myths and fantasies" (Shohat and Stam 1994, 13). The polarization of East and West culturally is, according to Huntington (1996), one of the consequences of calling *European* civilization *Western* civilization. He believes that "instead of 'East and West,' it is more appropriate to speak of the 'West and the rest,' which at least implies the existence of many non-Wests" (33).

A significant role in the shaping of the concepts of Occident and Orient belongs to literature and art. This influence is analyzed in books and articles by Kabbani (1986); Loshitzky (2000); Morley and Robins (1995); Said (1995); Sardar (1999); Shohat (1989); and Shohat and Stam (1994). Russian culture is also a rich source of images of the East and West. The Soviet-Jewish intelligentsia always prided itself on knowledge of Russian culture in general and literature in particular. Not by chance, the Russian-language press in Israel today extensively uses allusions to Russian and Soviet literature and folklore. In addition, Russian TV, radio, and newspapers perpetuate Russian cultural stereotypes used by immigrants to interpret local contexts. This is why we preface the analyses of the interviews with a brief excursion into the East-West theme in Russian and Soviet culture as a source of influence on our subjects.

In the tenth and eleventh centuries, in the period of Kievan Rus', Russian princes began to establish political and economic ties with Byzantium, Western Europe, the South and West Slavs, and with peoples of Central Asia and the Caucasus. Russian trade and diplomatic missions, merchants' journeys, and pilgrimages triggered the emergence of an early genre of Russian literature, *khozhdenia* (wanderings). This genre originated as stories of pilgrimages to holy places. Impressions of distant lands are reflected in various folklore genres—for example, folk heroic poetry, *bylinas*. *Khozhdenia* present an intricate combination of travelers' accounts of things seen and experienced with stories heard from fellow travelers and the local people.[7] As a result, many of these pieces abound with descriptions of marvels, priceless treasures, lavish vegetation, and miraculous animals and birds, all of which look like paradise on earth (Lurie 1986, 72). Some of them—for instance, *The Tale of the Indian Tsardom, The Story of Ioann Novgorodski's Ride on the Demon,* and *Afanasii Nikitin's Journey beyond the Three Seas*—circulated widely among the literate population and served as a source of oral stories disseminated by pilgrims. Listeners would give pilgrims shelter and food. To attract bigger audiences, storytellers added colorful details to the narration. The genre of wanderings remained popular until the late nineteenth century. An example of such narratives can be found in a play by Ostrovsky, "The Storm," written in 1859. In the twentieth century it was in the curriculum of Soviet schools. One of the characters, Feklusha, tells tall tales about the Orient to eager listeners, recounting, for instance, that the "infidels" have dogs' heads and live according to crooked laws opposite to "ours" (Ostrovsky 1969, 231). Feklusha's worldview exemplifies ignorance and militant ethnocentricity, mocked by the playwright. What is important for this study is that like many of her contemporaries, she opposes Christian righteousness to Oriental "infidelity."

In Soviet times, despite constant pressure to comply with the official stance on capitalist society, popular attitudes toward the West were extremely contradictory. On the one hand, in everyday talk the average Soviet individual reproduced official stereotypes about the aggressiveness and corrupting influence of the West; on the other hand, Soviet people avidly hunted for any information on life in capitalist society (Shlapentokh 1989, 139–52). As mentioned in chapter 3, young people were extremely interested in everything associated with the West and tried to emulate the lifestyle of their peers in capitalist countries. According to Shlapentokh (1989), the two other groups especially strongly influenced by the West were the *apparatchiks* (Soviet functionaries) and the intelligentsia. Oral stories about other countries were no less popular. They were nourished by emigrants' letters—during the periods of the Thaw and perestroika, Soviet authorities allowed foreign correspondence—and by stories of the few "chosen" citizens sent by the state on business or "trusted" to go on vacation after screening by several committees on different levels of the Communist Party hierarchy. Those traveling to Western counties were scrutinized more thoroughly than others. When travelers shared their personal impressions, they tried to meet listeners' expectations. These often contradicted claims by the Soviet propaganda machine, which always found fault with the Western way of life. By contrast, popular wisdom tended to exaggerate the advantages of the West. Had the storyteller dared criticize the West, or cast doubt on the myth of its overwhelming happiness and prosperity, he or she would have been dismissed as a proponent of the official ideology and therefore untrustworthy. Villas, private cars, and fashionable clothes replaced the mythical components of the old image of "distant lands," such as monsters that were neither human nor animal, or gems found everywhere in abundance. This shift also meant that the riches came to be associated with the consumerism of the West rather than with the Oriental luxury.

Inclined to self-reflection, Russian society has always found food for thought in literature. At various times, Russian literature was attracted to different areas of the Orient. While images of the Caucasus and the Crimea fascinated writers and readers throughout the nineteenth century (Pushkin, Lermontov, Tiutchev, L. Tolstoi[8]), Japan came to light at the beginning of the twentieth century (Bely, Novikov-Priboi), and Central Asia became a subject of interest in the Soviet period (Seifulina, Aitmatov, Tikhonov). Interest in these areas would increase in periods of military conflict and liberation movements. Such was the case with the war in the Caucasus of 1817–64, the Russo-Japanese war of 1904–5, and the struggle of the Basmachi, the anti-Soviet movement in Central Asia in 1917–26. The Orient was also embodied in bitter memories of the Golden Horde, perpetuated in folklore and literature. Yet it would be an oversimplification to think that hostility between Russia and its eastern neighbors dominated attitudes to the Orient.

The East also drew attention through its exoticism and loyalty to its traditions. It was perceived as a counter to the cold rationality of the West.[9] Russian writers were aware of Russia's position straddling East and West. Lotman (1993) points out that Yurii Lermontov conceived the distinctiveness of Russian culture as its antithesis to both the West and the East. According to this typology, Russia was designated as the North and had complex interactions with East and West alike. On the one hand, it opposed both of them; on the other hand, it served as the West for the East and as the East for the West (10). Reflections as to whether Russia was an integral part of one of these two worlds were a frequent motif in literature, in particular at the turn of the twentieth century (see, e.g., works by Merezhkovskii, Bely, Blok, Gumilev, etc.). Neither of the two worlds was accepted wholeheartedly. According to Soloviev, a philosopher of the second half of the nineteenth century, Russia's mission was to serve alternatively as a shield against the unruliness and chaos of the East or as a mediator between Western rationality and readiness for action and Oriental self-reflection and mysticism (Soloviev 1989, 602–5).

Jews were often portrayed in Russian poetry and prose. Compared with the peoples of the Caucasus and Central Asia, their Oriental origin and culture were not central issues in shaping attitudes to them. A study of the images and stereotypes of Jews in Russian and Soviet folklore and literature (Dreizin 1990) does not touch upon the Oriental features of Jews at all. Yet many instances show ties between Jews and the East in the shared consciousness of the Russians. Jews are depicted as "hot-tempered southern types" (Kuprin 1957, 225), interspersing their speech with "peculiar adages and comparisons, characteristically vivid and Oriental" (Korolenko 1954, 402). Their behavior can be guided by intransigence in observing tradition, and in extreme cases they resort to cruelty associated with Oriental ways. Thus in Lermontov's "Ballad," the father of a Jewish girl, who has fallen in love with a Russian, stabs his daughter and her lover with a *kinzhal* (dagger) (Lermontov 1969, 255–56). The choice of weapon is not accidental. Both the object and the word have an Oriental origin. Analyzing Soviet literature, Dreizin (1990) makes an interesting observation about Alexander Solzhenitsyn's description of a character in *One Day in the Life of Ivan Denisovich:* "Cezar is a mixture of all kinds of nations: he is either a Greek, or a Jew, or a Gypsy—one can't know" (Solzhenitsyn 1963, 30).[10] Dreizin (1990) points out that for the Russian reader, the three words—Greek, Jew, and Gypsy—share important connotations: representatives of these ethnicities, Jews and Gypsies in particular, are stereotypically associated with dishonesty, trading, and vagrancy (161–62). What is important for us is that in this example Jews are associated with non-Western peoples: in Russian culture Jews share the same niche as various Oriental others. Yet our informants, with the exception of Mountain Jews, do not identify with the Orient at all. On the contrary, they view their own group as more Occidental than the Russians. Voronel comes to a similar conclusion: "Russian Jews are overwhelmingly pro-Western. It is unequivocally so, and they are so attached to the Western culture that it ousts everything which can be called 'slavophile' from their minds" (see Goldshtein 2002, 26).

Some countries are unequivocally perceived as Occidental, others are unquestionably Oriental, and still others seem to be "borderline" and their placement on the East-West axis is subject to debate and controversy. By virtue of its geography and history, Russia in different periods borrowed from Eastern and Western cultures. For almost three centuries during the Middle Ages, Russia endured incursions of the Golden Horde, nomads who invaded the country from the East and influenced Russian culture. And in the early eighteenth century, Peter I imposed Westernization, which met with acute opposition. The split in society over the benefits of the Western tradition for Russia was also manifested in the nineteenth century in the struggle between "Slavophiles" and "Westernizers." Westernizers believed that Peter I had turned Russia sharply to its logical and historically determined course: participation in European culture. The Slavophiles maintained that his momentous reforms had been contrary to logic and opposed to history (Riasanovsky 1965, 182). An interesting interpretation of the ambivalence related to Europe in the history of Russia has been proposed by Uspenskii (2004). He believes that since the concept of Europe encompasses a wealth of associations linked to its history and traditions, the name *Europe* can be used as a metonymy and as a metaphor. When it functions as a metonymy, we witness cultural expansion: what is typical of the center spreads to the periphery as part of a natural process. When it functions as a metaphor, we can see only cultural orientation to Europe, the process artificial in its nature. Uspenskii maintains that Russia can be viewed as Europe only in the metaphoric sense. Natural expansion of the European tradition did not happen there. Instead we can observe deliberate attempts to become European; in other words, this process is not centrifugal but centripetal. Pushkin's image of the window that Czar Peter I cut into Europe connotes that to do this Peter first had to erect a wall separating Russia from Europe (16–18). In the Soviet period, although concentrating its political and ideological efforts on opposition to the West, the USSR was constantly in competition with it. But was not this challenge in itself an indication of mimicry and the Soviet rulers' admission of a hidden attraction to the West? The argument over the wisdom of joining the community of Western countries sparked controversies in Russia again after the disintegration of the USSR.

Attitudes to Russia from the outside are also divided and ambivalent. Neumann (1999) shows a systematic othering of Russia; for centuries it was marginalized in both space and time and was represented as hovering on the border of European identity (163). The American political scientist Watts, like many of his colleagues, places the USSR among Asian countries and indiscriminately refers to the country as the *USSR* and as *Russia,* disregarding the difference between the two (Watts 1982). By contrast, Milner-Gulland (1999) divides Russia into European and Asian parts. He published his comprehensive study of anthropological and cultural issues of Russian life in the series "The Peoples of Europe" and specified that his analysis was based exclusively on the European part of Russia (3). Such a division seems to be rather artificial, yet it has a long tradition. In the nineteenth century it was common in inquiries in various fields. Milner-Gulland notes the ambivalence of the Russians' cultural orientation: Russian culture was never self-sufficient; on the contrary, it has always required interaction with Europe and to a lesser extent with Asia. But the idea that it is essentially "Scythian," barbarian, spontaneous, and Asiatic is an early twentieth-century affectation (228–29).

Like Russia, Israel is at the crossroads of East and West. Despite its Middle Eastern location it is often perceived as a European country. On the basis of social structure, language, and religion, anthropologists distinguish six cultural regions. One of them is Europe and countries whose cultures are influenced by Europe: the United States, North Africa, and Israel (Lebedeva 1999, 34). Americans place Israel in the Occident because of its cultural, social, and historical links with the United States (Watts 1982, 4). Israeli society is aware of the ambiguity of its collective identity; the division of Jews into Europeans and Orientals is a sensitive issue in domestic politics and everyday life, and the two groups compete for leadership and cultural dominance. The mass immigration from the FSU in the 1990s has reinforced the bias of the society as a whole toward Westernization. As Lustick (1999) notes, in the late 1980s and early 1990s many Israeli Jews favored the entry of Soviet Jews on the grounds that they were "neither Arab nor Oriental" (428). The Soviet Jews themselves viewed the westernization of Israel as one of the primary conditions for their successful professional and social integration in its society. This thesis is emphasized in essays written by immigrant academics of the previous and current waves (see, e.g., Tumerman 1982, 145–58; Voronel 1982, 135; Epstein and Kheimets 2000a). It is constantly discussed in the Russian-language press, and it is reinforced in the passages from the interviews analyzed in this chapter.

Having left a country situated at the crossroads of two civilizations, our informants landed in another conglomerate of cultural traditions: in Israel, European Jews live side by side with Jews from Morocco, Yemen, Iraq, Ethiopia, and other countries, as well as with Arabs, Bedouins, Druzes, and Circassians. As noted earlier, only upon arrival in Israel did immigrants realize how poor their knowledge of the new country was and how misleading Israel's pre-immigration image was. Their expectations followed three major patterns: Israel has close relations with America, so it is not the East; Israel has many features of European countries so it is a "little Europe" in the Middle East; Israel has an Oriental flavor, bright colors, noisy crowds, and an exotic nature. Confrontation with the reality, however, tended to demolish the assumptions about the "Western-ness" of Israel. Following are two examples in which our subjects try to answer the question about Israel's place on the symbolic axis.

Olga G., 72

> We didn't consider Israel the East, you know. First, it is her attitude to America, Israel's attitude, her relations with America. Secondly, it is Israel's closeness to European countries. . . . We didn't know anything at all about Israel. And we thought we had come to the West. But in the end we found ourselves in the East!

Grigorii G., 30

> No, it is not the East. That's for sure! Not really! Rather, it is closer to the West. At least, you know, they try to be like the West. And they want to think about themselves as the West. Yet, of course, there is Oriental influence here too. But it is not the people who bear Oriental influence. It is the atmosphere and the environment that . . . Whether we want it or not, we have to take it into account.

The relativity of the concepts East and West emerge in many interviews and makes immigrants compare Israel to other countries and various republics of the FSU:

Vitalii B., 79

INTERVIEWER: How do you perceive Israel: as the East or the West?

VITALII: I perceive it as the West. . . . Yes, I perceive it as a Western country, because it's really, and [*pause*] and . . . In the past there was this question of how to classify it, as Africa, or as Europe. But if Turkey is Europe, and Greece is Europe, then it is so close to . . . So in effect, Israel is also Europe.

Mariula F., 25

> I didn't know anything. It's damned funny, but I thought that there were only Jews in Israel. And because I knew that all Jews were Caucasians [*Mountain Jews*], I thought that in Israel there were only Caucasians, and nobody else. . . . I was shocked. I say, "Mum, so we'll arrive now, and where shall we live?" Back there [*in Russia*] a woman said, "As soon as you arrive they'll take you to hospital. Whoever is sick, or just, well, I don't know, but they'll distribute all of you among . . . and will treat you. And then they'll take you to the seashore and you'll live in tents." I say, "Good! This sounds like nomadic Gypsies. We'll be in tents near the sea. I had no idea about Ashkenazi, *etiopi* [*Hebrew for "Ethiopians"*]; I didn't know that there were Indians here, and this sort of . . . I couldn't even imagine such a thing. I thought everyone was Caucasian. And when we landed in Israel, in the airport [*inaudible*], I saw Russians, I

> saw the blacks, I saw *etiopi*. I say, "Oh, dear! Are they all Jewish?" And she [*her mother*] says, "Well, I don't know. One has to ask Abram and Yeva [*Mariula hebraizes the name, replacing Adam with Abram; Yeva is Russian for "Eve"*] who is Jewish and who is not. I know that we are."

Although Mariula lived in a large town in the Urals, populated by various ethnicities including Ashkenazi Jews, she identified Jews only with her mother's family, Mountain Jews. An interesting detail is Mariula's allusion to the rumor that new immigrants would be taken to hospital. A possible source of such rumors was distorted information about centers of absorption and expectations that every step of immigrants' life would be regimented. In chapter 2 we mentioned that Mariula identified with Gypsies, which explains why when trying to imagine life in Israel she compared it to a Gypsy camp. Mariula's expectations of a smooth landing facilitated by members of her family who had moved to Israel earlier did not materialize. Violating all the norms of Soviet hospitality in general, and Caucasian in particular, her uncle did not give his sister and his two nieces shelter even for one night, which allowed Mariula to conclude that "people in Israel turn into beasts."

Only a few interviewees said they had associated Israel with the East, but they fantasized about it as an exotic scene from *Arabian Nights*.

Inna F., 26

> I couldn't imagine it at all. I didn't have a clear picture; that is, when I closed my eyes, I would imagine something bright, some bright colors, nothing definite. The only thing was that I imagined it as an Oriental market, as an Oriental bazaar. I saw it as something bright and loud. I didn't imagine it as Europe, and it turned out it isn't.

Such polar expectations of Israel were typical of many immigrants' narratives. What accounted for the controversy, and why was the "placing" of Israel in the "East" or in the "West" such a crucial issue for our informants?

Imagining Israel: A Two-faced Mythological Phantom

As we have already mentioned, in Soviet times traveling abroad was an extraordinary life event, and emigration was perceived as an irreversible step, a true upheaval. Countries of Eastern Europe and developing countries were not considered "abroad"; they were treated as an extension of the USSR. An extreme case was Bulgaria, which in popular parlance was often referred to as "the sixteenth republic of the Soviet Union." In the late 1980s, when mass emigration began, Israel also acquired this status. One of our informants summarizes this scornful attitude.

Anatolii P., 26

> It is neither London nor New York, and what is there to talk about? Yeah . . . That is, I always perceived the West as "abroad," and the East never impressed me. All the Eastern parts were not really abroad for me, but some . . . the Third World. And Israel was like that too.

The notions of East and West acquire an axiological meaning for Anatolii. In his system of values the West is associated with everything he aspires to. Israel is despised as part of the East. The features Anatolii attributes to the West and the East are set in similar oppositions in other interviews.

Many of our informants—for example, Evgenii L., 66; Emma R., 56; Inna R., 49; and others—recount that their first image of Israel was formed by booklets and videos circulated by the Jewish Agency and meetings with the Israeli emissaries sent to the Soviet Union to convince emigrants-to-be to choose Israel as their destination. Maria P., 24, recalls her first encounter with Israelis in Moscow (see Fialkova and Yelenevskaya 2004a, 461–62; IFA 21761): Even though most of them were Soviet-born, she emphasized that they looked and behaved like Westerners. The spirit of freedom, which Israelis emanated, attracted the girl. Maria implied that the ultimate dream of potential immigrants was to go and live in America; if not in America, then in Europe. Like Anatolii, Maria admitted that her pre-immigration image of Israel was detached from reality. But while Anatolii has reconciled himself to the new country and adopted a more tolerant stand—"it's a country with normal people, like everywhere else, only the climate is different"—Maria's enthusiasm has vanished, and from idealization and exaggerated expectations her mood slumps to skepticism and disappointment. It is clear from her interview that Maria no longer considers Israel to be "normal" or "civilized." In the context of her interview these adjectives are used as synonyms of "European." As we have already seen in several excerpts, "Europe" often functions as a generic term, and is close to what Shohat and Stam (1994) call "neo-Europe"—which includes the Americas, Australia, and other countries (1). The term *neo-Europe* reflects the conviction of the public that European cultural unity exists, based on common roots. But despite the name, the apex of the pyramid sometimes shifts from Europe to America, a phenomenon frequently seen in the analyzed interviews.

Our next informant, a retired doctor, is not bothered by the disparity of habits and traditions of European and Oriental Jews. Neither, for her, does the race or place of origin serve as a dividing line between the East and the West. The main criteria are specific types of behavior.

Galit B., 60+

INTERVIEWER: How do you perceive Israel: as East or as West?

GALIT: That's an interesting question. I cannot give a simple answer. It depends a lot on whom you deal with. Now that I live here in Ashkelon, and when I [*pause*] see Israelis, I won't mention their nationality, or rather where they are from . . . I mean those who sit on benches, crack sunflower seeds, and, excuse me, spit on the floor making a mess, I come to understand that I am in the East. And some clothes too, let's say. . . . But when I get to [*pause*] my friends. . . . My husband once met his old school friends, the friends with whom he has been through thick and thin. One of them has already lived here for twenty, er . . . seven years. And when we came there, to Netanya, and I saw the style of behavior of the Israelis there, I realized I was in the West, but not in the East. That's why I think that it depends on the society in which I live, the people I communicate with, and, and this determines how I feel.

Like many other interviewees, Galit views the East not as a different culture but as a place devoid of it. The importance of the notion of culture in the Soviet Union has been discussed by various authors. Boym (1994) asserts that it has become a civic religion that delimits an imagined community of spiritual refinement, a literary aristocracy of sorts (103). Brudny (1998) notes the essential role played by the cultural intelligentsia in the years of perestroika, as reflected by the enormous jump in circulation of quality newspapers and periodicals, as well as by the cultural intelligentsia's heavy representation in the USSR Congress of People's Deputies, the first freely elected Soviet Parliament (14). Another indicator of the significance of the concept of culture is the number of derivatives used in the language: the dictionary of Soviet-Speak has twenty-nine entries illustrating uses of *culture* in various word combinations (Mokienko and Nikitina 1998, 298–302). Interestingly, Galit chose cracking seeds, one of the favorite pastimes of Russian villagers, as the most vivid example of what she dislikes about the East. In Russia the word *derevnia* (village) is often used as a metonymy referring to an uneducated and uncultured person in insults, such as "The village! She can spend hours cracking seeds!" The semiotic function of "seed cracking" has not disappeared after immigration. Lamenting the disruptive influence of English and Hebrew on immigrants' speech, the author of a newspaper article writes about the deterioration of cultural tradition as a whole, manifested in the use of the familiar form of the personal pronoun *you* in conversations with strangers and in seed cracking (Gopman 2003).[11] The village also symbolizes periphery and provinciality, which, as we noted earlier, have derogatory meanings for our informants.

Lilia V., 22

> [*About the first impressions of Israel*] It's a village. The first impression was that it's a village. I was surprised that there were palm trees growing and [*pause*] houses, which looked [*pause*] like boxes. After Lvov I didn't see any architecture here. It was a terrible feeling. And I asked my cousin, "Where are we? Is it a town or a village?"

In Galit B.'s earlier passage, she uses the "East" in the pejorative sense. She doesn't define a positive, Western, model of behavior but implies that it is opposite of what she sees in her neighborhood. She places the West in Netanya, where French is spoken on the streets and used in numerous street signs and shop names. This may have reminded Galit of Europe, although Netanya is not so different from other Israeli towns and has a large community of Oriental Jews. Elsewhere in the interview Galit makes it clear that "Westerners" are her preferred group for communication and friendships. Galit associates the Israeli style of clothing with the East. Yet our interviewees, coming from the Caucasus and Central Asia, see this style as a severe violation of the Oriental code of behavior.

Belka, 22

BELKA: Well, when I came to Israel, when I landed . . I expected to see the people here look quite different: more fair-haired, more curly . . . I thought people would wear some sort of ballroom frocks, although I knew that it was hot here. But everyone was half-naked and wearing ragged jeans.

BELKA'S GRANDMOTHER: And for us it is absurd!

BELKA: It's just that we come from a place where women wear a yashmak and all sorts of kerchiefs, and then when we came to a new country, where girls walked around half-naked and covered only private parts. They walk on the streets, so to say, wearing nothing but bathing suits. It was sort of strange for us.

Like Alexander A. (chapter 3), Belka sees the casual style of clothing as a breaking of social codes. But while Alexander used Western formal clothes as the basis for comparison, Belka's point of reference is the traditional female clothes in Islamic countries. Praise of female modesty characteristic of Oriental cultures and criticism of excessive body exposure attributed to the Western style were expressed by our other young informant, Ekaterina R., 24, who grew up in Central Asia.

Some interviewees—for example, the previously quoted Anatolii P. and Galit B.—link "East" and "West" to specific cities. In the next passage, narrators go further, labeling districts of Haifa as Occidental or Oriental.

Boris P., 50, and Inna P., 49

INTERVIEWER: Do you perceive Israel as a Western or as an Eastern country?

BORIS: Well, [*pause*] it's a conglomerate. Partially it is Western, partially it is Eastern.

INNA: I cannot say outright whether it is Eastern or Western. Well, everything is so mixed. You know, just go to the Carmel [*a prosperous neighborhood of Haïfa*], go there now, go there. Indeed, it's Europe, it's Europe. Everyone there is from . . . it's OUR people, those who walk about there, all of them are OUR people! But go down to the beach, and there are more Moroccans, you know. Go a bit to the side, and you'll see Ethiopians. And, well, er, and here you see Arabs. Well, you know, if you go down by this . . . [*apparently she refers to the cable car that connects the prosperous part of the city situated on top of Mount Carmel with the downtown area of workshops, small stores, and markets*], and there are Arabs there: *tyr-tyr-tyr, dyr-dyr-dyr* [*Inna mockingly imitates Arabic*]. And you don't know the country at all. . . .

BORIS: All of it is the East, which is gradually moving to the West.

Inna and Boris reproduced the well-known cliché used by the Soviet media in the representation of Western towns. Be it New York or Tokyo, London or Paris, each one of them was referred to as a "city of contrasts." These contrasts are explicit in the identification of certain areas as Moroccan, Ethiopian, Arab, and "ours." Narrators implicitly oppose "Western" and "Oriental" neighborhoods as affluent versus poor. For Inna, Westerners are not Israelis with Western European roots or immigrants from America but are "Russians." It is not true that many immigrants from the FSU moved to the expensive area of Haifa identified in this excerpt as the "West." Mostly they live in other neighborhoods, but like many other residents of Haifa they like to spend their leisure time in the shady gardens and promenades of the Carmel area. It would be equally wrong to say that the expensive area of the city is closed to Oriental Jews. Yet in the perception of our informants, those who have made it to Carmel have "shed" their Oriental features. Israeli demographers observe that when choosing a place of residence in Israel, immigrants from the FSU took into account not only availability of housing and employment opportunities but also proximity to relatives and friends. This consideration was particularly important for people from the Caucasus and Central Asia, where in-group solidarity was highly valued in the USSR and is maintained after immigration. The patterns of immigrants' settlement are discussed by Gonen (1998).

The resilience of Soviet ideological clichés and stereotypes is visible not only in the immigrants' interviews. They constantly re-emerge in post-Soviet Russia in literature and in the mass media. For example, in a novel by a best-selling author of detective stories, Boris Akunin (2000), Port Said is described as neither Asia nor Europe. European faces dominate the central streets, but as soon as the carriage turns to an indigenous quarter, you find yourself amid rotting garbage and swarms of flies; there is a stench all around, and grubby Arab urchins beg for small change (26). The similarity in the description of Port Said and Haifa by a writer and oral narrators is based on the common mythical features ascribed in Russian culture to the East and West. Such commonality of images testifies to their semiotic nature.

One of the most pervasive symbols of the East in our sample was the bazaar. Our interviewees made use of three different words referring to the same concept. The Russian nouns *rynok* and *bazaar,* as well as the Hebrew *shuk,* were often used by the narrators as metonymy for the Orient. In modern Russian the meanings of the two words for "market" overlap, but only partially. *Rynok* originated in Middle High German, and it denoted a circle, a square. The word penetrated Russian as a loan word from Polish and Czech, where it meant a city square (Fasmer 1971, 3:530). The common semantic component is "the process of retail trade and a place reserved for it either in the open or in the special buildings or sheds." Among the semantic differences registered in the dictionaries, one is actualized in the analyzed texts. In conversation, *bazaar* is used in the sense of "disorderly conversation, shouting and noise" (Ievgenieva 1981, 55; 1984, 746). This meaning is also recorded in the slang compound noun *bazaar-vokzal* (Schuplov 1998, 93), in which the second component, meaning a "railway station," is also associated with noise and commotion. The word *bazaar* was drawn into Russian from Persian and Turkic languages and became widely used thanks to the popularity of

Arabian Nights (Fasmer 1964, 1:105–6). The words *bazaar* and *rynok* are in some sense interchangeable and have local coloring. In Moscow and St. Petersburg, a market is called *rynok*, in Tashkent and Tiraspol, Moldova, it is referred to as *bazaar*, while in Bishkeck, Kyrgyzstan, *Alamedinskii rynok* and *Tsentral'nyi bazaar* are used. Similarly, both words are used in Kiev: *Bessarabskii rynok*, but *Vladimirskii bazaar*. Interestingly, one of the districts in Kiev is still known to senior citizens as Evbaz, short for *Evreiskii bazaar*, the Jewish bazaar, although the market under this name was dismantled decades ago. The name Evbaz was perpetuated in a popular joke:

> "Which of the Soviet towns has commemorated the Jewish struggle for independence?"
> "Kiev. It was when Evbaz was renamed the Square of Victory." (Shturman and Tiktin 1987, 487)

Note that the joke came into circulation in 1948, the year the State of Israel was created. The humorous effect is created by the disparity between the choice of a new name for the area and the reason for renaming it in reality and in the joke. While the renaming was done to commemorate the Soviet victory in World War II, the joke links it to the victory in the War of Independence.

In the interviews, both *bazaar* and the Hebrew *shuk* were associated with noise and disorder (see immigrants' criticism of Israel as noisy and bazaarlike in Resnik et al. 2001, 437, 440). Dreizin (1990) rightly notes that in contemporary Russian, words referring to trade, property, and possession have a derogatory meaning. They are often used to insult and criticize someone for taking unfair advantage of others, as well as for pettiness and greed. Greed and stinginess are also expressed by the slang verb *zhidit'sia* derived from *zhid* (kike) (5).

As we noted earlier, in Russian folklore and literature Jews were associated with petty trade. After the revolution of 1917, private trade was restricted, except for the short period of the "New Economic Policy" (1921–30). The quota fixed for Jews admitted to institutions of higher learning in czarist Russia was lifted, and there was a strong tendency among Jews to migrate to towns and enter white-collar professions. Even when the quota was de facto reestablished, Jews sought every opportunity to send their children to universities. The descendants of the "small-time traders," urban dwellers, created the autostereotype, which was the antithesis of the old one: a typical Jew came to be a doctor, an engineer, or a teacher. Soviet Jews shared with the other Soviets dislike and contempt for traders. The latter came to be the label for peoples of the Caucasus and Central Asia. In Israel, new immigrants characterize the Oriental other as "bazaar people."

Inna Kh., 52

INNA: [*About the reaction of friends to her emigration*] They were nervous, but nobody said, "Oh, Inna, stop, you are doing something stupid!" It was as if they were afraid of taking responsibility. Anastasia tried to explain to me all the time that it wasn't the West, but the East, that "Mind you, you are going to the East!" And the East, well. . . .

INTERVIEWER: Inna, why do you think that when they tried to discourage you, they used the "East" as an argument "against"?

INNA: Because Anastasia knew that I was not a bazaar person.

Veronika G., 61

INTERVIEWER: Veronika, do you feel that in Israel you are in the East or in the West?

VERONIKA: Depending on where I am. When I get to the *shuk*, with its noise and shouting, I know for sure that I am in the East. Well . . . if I go somewhere, say to the theater, then it is more, so to say, civilized. But I seldom feel myself to be in the West here. And as a matter of fact, to be frank, I don't know what the West is. In Russia it was, it was, it was simply terrible.

Similar to Galit B., Veronika does not hesitate to define the East but is vague about the characteristics of the West. The East is opposed to "civilized" behavior rather than to the West, whose essential features are unclear to her. The concept of the market is no longer linked to street theater and entertainment. For Veronika the theater and the market embody social stratification.

In contrast to the previous informants, who come from the European parts of the FSU, Anna and Boris N. are from Central Asia. Throughout the one-hour interview they reveal a tolerant attitude toward the Orient. Like other interviewees from Central Asia and the Caucasus, they constantly see parallels between their old and new homelands.

Anna N., 59, and Boris N., 59

INTERVIEWER: You came to Israel from Tashkent. And in the Soviet Union, Tashkent and Uzbekistan were perceived as the East. . . . What were your expectations of Israel?

ANNA: When I was here in 1996 [*as a tourist*], I had the impression that Israel was the East [*pause*] but that it was looking to the West. But today I would formulate, I would say this, [*pause*] it is probably neither the East nor the West. Israel is in a class of its own.

BORIS: It is the cultured East; I would call it the cultured East. . . . And you know, I think that this peculiarity of Israel, is mostly due to, well, probably not mostly, but it is due to the aliya that arrived here. It has sort of diluted all this Oriental, all this . . . and at the same time retained some . . . Kherson, Odessa, Leningrad, Moscow—all of them contributed something. . . .

ANNA: No, at the moment I don't feel whether it is the East or the West.

BORIS: No, it is the EAST, after all it is an Oriental town, it is an Oriental town [*Boris refers to Afula, where he lives*].

ANNA: So this is how Boris sees it, but I don't.

BORIS: But doesn't the bazaar tell you that it is an Oriental town? It is particularly visible in the East.

ANNA: Well, you might be right. A bazaar is the East.

BORIS: No, why? The bazaar, you can see the bazaar in the Preobrazhensky market [*Here he uses the word* rynok] in Moscow.

ANNA: But the bazaar is typical of the East. There—there are markets. Preobrazhensky market, you yourself said the "Preobrazhensky market." Here you said the "bazaar," and there you said the "market."

BORIS: A *shuk* is a *shuk* everywhere.

ANNA: A noisy bazaar is the East . . .

Anna and Boris are explicit in opposing the connotations of *bazaar* and *rynok*. The Hebrew *shuk* for them is equivalent to the Oriental bazaar, which has a semiotic nature but is not used in derogatory value judgments. Anna and Boris are convinced that the influx of the Soviet Jews has changed the face of Israel for the better, and this improvement is associated with Westernization. Note that Boris refers to Israel as the "cultured East," implying that the East is uncultured by definition. This excerpt contains another frequently reiterated motif: our informants believe that Israel is striving to move closer to the West (see, e.g., earlier statements by Grigorii G. and Boris P.). Emma R. shares this opinion.

Emma R., 56

INTERVIEWER: Do you perceive Israel as the West or as the East?

EMMA: Well, certainly it's an Oriental country making attempts to acquire a Western face. That's how I see it.

Our informants sincerely believe that as a group, Soviet Jews are instrumental in speeding up the Westernization of Israel by maintaining their language, everyday habits, and above all struggling for high educational and professional standards. Our interviewees' talk resembles the discourse of "Anglo-Saxons" as analyzed by Rapport (1998). His subjects also attributed their discontent with how things were done in Israel to the "Eastern" or "Levantine" mentality. Like ex-Soviets, "Anglo-Saxons" were convinced that they could introduce Western efficiency into the country and serve as a source for emulation in business matters (75).

The East striving to look like the West is a cliché, which is not only typical of the analyzed interviews. The novelist Akunin (2000) writes, "Russia is very much like Japan: it is also the East reaching for the West" (94). Ironically, Soviet immigrants to Israel perceive Russia as the West par excellence, while the view from Russia contradicts such an approach and puts the country in an intermediate position, where it bounces between the East and the West.

The next informant once lived in Central Asia, but only for a short time. As a teenager during World War II he was evacuated from Odessa to Tashkent. His three years there as a war refugee left vivid memories, which he often enlists to make sense of his immigrant experiences. Speaking about Israel, or Uzbekistan, he positions himself as an outsider making judgments about inferior others.

Vladimir K., 73

VLADIMIR: They [*Israelis*] are hot-tempered, easy going, too free-and-easy, you know, they talk loudly, [*inaudible*] conversation. At first it confused me, their greetings, almost . . . Well, in 1942 I came to Uzbekistan. And in 1945 I left. In fact, yes, I worked all the time I lived there. And I worked in a Russian team. And to be sure, the factory, yes, the Russians held the factory firm. There were very few Uzbeks there, and those Uzbeks who worked there, they occupied inferior positions. . . . Yes, these people [*the evacuated Russians*] couldn't go to the army. I am explaining why there were many Russians. Well . . . So we had few contacts with the Uzbeks. But observing them, yes, I did observe them a lot. Yes, I observed them. And I knew that *anasha* [*hemp*] reigned there. I knew that somewhere near the bazaar there was a clandestine smoking room. I even tried it myself a couple of times.

INTERVIEWER: Tell me, please, did you imagine the Eastern nature of Israel as analogous to Uzbekistan?

VLADIMIR: No, I was mature then [*Vladimir refers to his age on immigration*]. I understood that everything would be different. No, certainly not. No. I didn't imagine it as I see it now. The evaluation came later, and it is, if I can say so, I now have a deeper insight into Asian . . . er . . . the insight into the Asian nature of local life. . . . Well, one can see it in the bazaar. Here he stands and trades. It's, well, here the genuine East unfolds in front of you. No, incidentally, "Asiatic" is not an insult. God forbid. . . . Yes, about Asia, I left it almost unexplained.

INTERVIEWER: It's very interesting.

VLADIMIR: Well, it's clothes, it's food, and it's the way they talk. And then I was convinced that drugs should reign here. . . . There is a hangout next to our house; they come here every night. The other day I said in horror, "Who will serve in the army?" Because you can see young people there, blooming peo-

> ple. Blooming young people, really blooming and tall. But they are all sickly; they look as if they were exhausted after siege. Yeah.

Note the disparity between declarative statements on the nature of Asian life and character, and an indirect evaluation emerging from Vladimir's descriptions. He tries to be politically correct, yet deep-rooted prejudices against Oriental people, whether Israelis or Uzbeks, are obvious. He adds a new item to the list of negative stereotypes of the East: drug addiction. People from Russia have always been tolerant of excessive drinking. Until recently, drug abuse was not widespread, although severely stigmatized. For Vladimir the use of drugs by Israelis is a manifestation of the destructive influence of the East. He castigates Oriental Jews as drug addicts. Ironically, some members of the lay public in Israel, encouraged by the mass media, are inclined to blame immigrants from the FSU for the spread of alcoholism, drug addiction, and prostitution (Jones 1996, 146). In both cases, addiction is seen as a threat to the national identity.

This excerpt gives us one additional explanation for the patronizing attitude of the immigrants from the FSU to people living in the Orient. Vladimir mentions that the Uzbeks had low social status. He presents them as an inferior caste, occupied in trade rather than in industry, which was of special significance during the war. He includes himself in the group of superiors, who in this case are Russians. The proportion of natives in responsible positions in the Soviet republics varied over time, but the patronizing attitude of "Big Brother" remained intact after the dissolution of the Soviet Union and is not difficult to discern in many interviews in the sample. The stereotypes of the East and West are bolstered by the mass media. The clash of Occidental and Oriental values is a never-ending topic of the Russian-language press in Israel. As indicated in chapter 3, journalists in Israel and in Russia make analogies between the Israeli-Palestinian and the Russian-Chechen conflicts. Examples from the literature include the following: "Russia and Israel are destined to defend themselves from the onslaught of the Islamic civilization"; Palestinians are called "the Chechens of the Middle East"; and warnings are given that denial of these analogies may lead to crimes against one's own nation (Briman 2001, 11–12; Shaus 2002, 7; Chernov 2002, 9). Fear of displaying weakness has intensified among the immigrants during the years of the Intifada. It is heard in private conversations, it is discussed in the Internet forums, and it is manipulated by some "Russian" politicians. An interview with the leader of the right-wing immigrant party Our Home Is Israel, Avigdor Liberman, was devoted to his criticism of the government's "policy of weakness, compromise decisions and constant hesitation" (Zaichik 2002, 4). The title of the interview, "One Cannot Afford to Be Weak in the East," summarizes Liberman's position on the Israeli-Arab confrontation and reinforces the anti-Oriental stereotypes of the immigrant community.

The public in Russia shows interest in the topic too, and it is also heated by ethnic problems, the focus of which is in the Northern Caucasus. In 2001, NTV International, the Russian TV channel popular in Israel, began screening a series of programs titled "Russia: East-West" and authored by the leader of the Democratic Union Party, Valeria Novodvorskaia. She looked at Russian history through the prism of relations with the East and West. This is how the viewers were introduced to the series: "We will carefully choose the particles of the West from the rubbish of history piled up in front of us. These particles are sitting on it like pearls. We will pick the flies off the steaks, because, clearly, the particles of the West in our history are the steaks, while the dark gravy of the Orient is the flies. We will check whether they can be entirely separated, so that only steaks stay, while the flies buzz off" (program airing 24 June 2001). Besides the gastronomical metaphors, the salient motif of this quotation is the acutely negative attitude to the East. Later in the program, Novodvorskaia illustrated her claims through scenes from popular Soviet movies, thereby attempting to demythologize Russian history by mobilizing Soviet mythology as it appears in the movies. Our informants' views on the East and the West were in many respects similar to Novodvorskaia's position. They repeated maxims from popular books, movies, and TV programs almost word for word, often convinced that these were their own creation. Novodvorskaia's TV series itself made no direct impact on our subjects because program was broadcast after the interviews were conducted. Yet the movies shown in it were familiar to several generations of former Soviets and were an important source of Eurocentric stereotypes.

It would be a simplification to say that all the immigrants constructed their relationship with the East on the basis of negative stereotyping and castigation. Some mobilized colorful images of the East familiar from childhood fairy tales; others identified with the Orient because they had grown up in Eastern parts of the FSU; and still others preferred to emphasize attractive features of the Orient rather than look for flaws. Dana L., 23, for example, opposes the strictness and prohibitions ruling the Russian way of life to Eastern kindness and hospitality. Her peer Vladislav hoped that upon immigration to Israel he would find himself in the West. After ten years in Israel, he is not at all disappointed that it was no more than an illusory dream. Like Dana he emphasizes the warmth and openness of life in the East.

Vladislav V., 29

VLADISLAV: The East and the West are first of all behavior, the way people behave. Well, it's again about culture. . . . There, say, take a dirty street . . . do people throw garbage around? . . .

INTERVIEWER: But you say that you prefer the East to the West. What appeals to you in the East?

VLADISLAV: They are closer, they are. . . . The West, although it seems prosperous, it is sort of, secretive. You see, people harbor a grudge, sort of. And here the people are Orientals and they are more open. And I like this type much better; I don't like secretive people.

As we have already seen, features attributed to the Oriental way of life can annoy or fascinate. Gaiane A. spent most of her life in Uzbekistan. She was open to and appreciative of the Uzbek way of life, and she is equally respectful of her new homeland. Inclined to reflection and analysis, she often draws parallels between life in Uzbekistan, Russia, and Israel. Although by virtue of her upbringing and profession (a linguist, specializing in English studies) she has absorbed Russian and Western cultures, she appreciates many manifestations of the Oriental lifestyle. Although she dislikes tardiness, she readily admits that after the rat race of large Western cities there is an advantage in the unhurriedness and patience typical of the East. The freedom given to children in

Uzbekistan and in Israel doesn't annoy Gaiane, as she perceives it as a sign of goodwill. Like other interviewees from Central Asia and the Caucasus, Gaiane praises the respectful attitude of young people toward the elderly as an important part of the Oriental tradition. Not only the retired people, whose concern about the issue is natural, but also the middle-aged and the young believe that this tradition is valuable and are upset when they notice signs of its deterioration (see Fialkova and Yelenevskaya 2004a, 472).

All the excerpts we have discussed presented the East and the West as two poles, as if giving proof to Kipling's words: "Oh, East is East, and West is West, and never the twain shall meet" (Kipling 1983, 71). Still, we want to conclude this chapter by citing an interviewee ready to make the most of the two traditions, whatever separates them.

Leonid L., 50

> I look upon Israel as a place of my domicile. I don't ponder as to whether it is the East or the West. . . . I don't have a general view of Israel as a unified community of people, as a unified state. No, it seems to me there is no unity here. Everyone lives . . . those who are used to the West live according to the Western standards; those who lived in the East follow the Eastern lifestyle. Yes, it's a mixed country.

5

Lucky Coincidence, Fate, and Miracles in Immigrants' Lives

It has become customary among scholars of miracles to start treatises on the subject by putting the multiplicity of definitions in order and clarifying what they intend to study. Philosophers and theologians are concerned with miracles in the objectively oriented sense of the word—exceptional events incompatible with the known order of nature, events that presuppose the involvement of God or some rational and powerful agent. Stories about such events are also of interest to folklorists, because they are stored in the collective memory and form an important part of traditional folklore. They constitute the genre of the sacred legend (Aarne and Thompson 1964, 254–84; Jason 1975, 42).

As shown earlier, most of our interviewees are secular, so religion carries little weight with them and they do not look for signs of divine intervention when confronted with the extraordinary. But when they cannot find a rational explanation for some events or phenomena, they tend to attribute them to miracles, although in this case the term is used in the subjectively oriented sense and refers to events that astound and cause one to marvel. Some of the narrators refrain from interpretations of the miraculous; others seek to grasp their meaning and decipher the message. But irrespective of whether or not the storytellers are inclined to reflection, they all reveal that the events they describe have had an important impact on their life.

None of the stories analyzed in this chapter can be classified as traditional Jewish or Christian legends, yet they reflect a connection with both traditions. Because life in a new country is

Part of the material in this chapter has been published in Fialkova and Yelenevskaya 2001b.

far less predictable than at home, the unfamiliar often inspires wonder, and some of the interviewees are convinced that their immigrant experiences are outside the normal pattern of events. The narrators dwelled on episodes that astonished them without our prompting. We may conclude that inclusion of these stories in the interviews was not accidental but points to the narrators' hierarchy of values. Apparently they help our interviewees make sense of their immigrant experience. According to Bausinger (1987), "present-day reality, that is, the world of the factual, offers no fairy tales. However, as parts of a fairy tale derive from reality, so are such parts still to be found in reality" (13).

In our sample there are twenty-five stories about prophetic dreams, lucky coincidences, and miracles. Each deals with a single episode presented as miraculous or bizarre. All of them are set in a specific time and refer to real people and places. Because the tellers narrate their own experience, they do not question the truth of these stories but express wonder at the improbable things happening to them. This, according to Oring (1986), is the raison d'être of a legend: the creation of a story that requires the audience to examine their worldview—their sense of the normal, the boundaries of the natural, their conceptions of fate, destiny, and coincidence (126). Importantly, the legends of fate in our sample tell of occurrences that helped resolve the key problems of immigration: finding money for the journey to Israel, finding a home in the new country, and finding a suitable job. Above all, it is the chance meetings of people—reuniting with a family member after decades of separation or finding a life partner—that immigrants view as the miracles of fate.

Miracle and Its Definitions

The similarity in the interpretation of the concept of miracle in Judaism and Christianity appears obvious when various definitions are compared. The *Encyclopedia of Judaism* defines miracles as "extraordinary events which appear to violate the known laws of nature, the cause of which is ascribed to God" (Wigoder 1989, 492). This differs little from a much earlier Christian source, the *Biblical Encyclopedia,* written by the nineteenth-century Russian Orthodox theologian Nikifor: "Miracles are deeds that cannot be performed by man's power or mastery, but by the omnipotent power of God alone" (Nikifor 1990, 789). Like all the other definitions we have found, these two emphasize the divine nature of miracles. Importantly, in both Judaism and Christianity, miracles are often presented as messages, or "signs." As Ashe (1978) remarks, their purpose is to fortify believers with an assurance that God is there, all powerful, and able to rescue them from encompassing misery and doom (28). Extraordinary events may be the result of extraordinary coincidences (Swinburne 1970, 4; Holland 1965, 43). It is often noted that a miracle is an exception with a point: "It has a bearing on human life, and this is so because there is some agency behind it which human beings can relate to themselves" (Ashe 1978, 17). The role of the observer, who sees or infers such an event as miraculous, is not limited to giving a description of an event but its interpretation as well (Larmer 1988, 12, 75). Technological development and changes in the human realm cause changes in views on miracles. Some writers see the miraculous in extrasensory perception (ESP), telepathy, and clairvoyance, which have become popular in recent decades. Although interpretations given to these phenomena violate criteria established in philosophical and theological literature, it is this approach to miracles that is close to contemporary secular folk understanding and is implied in the narratives analyzed in this chapter.

The Wonderful Interplay of Fate and Chance

In contrast to the concept of miracle, which is part of the religious worldview, the concept of fate is rooted in paganism and is tied to mythology. This is why entries interpreting the notion of fate are commonly found in encyclopedias of mythology. (See, e.g., Bell 1982, 83; Karev 1982, 471–74; Kennedy 1998, 133; Tolstaia 1995, 370–71.) The *Encyclopedia of Judaism*, on the other hand, provides no information on fate but gives interpretations of the concepts of predestination, providence, and free will, which treat the issues of God's governing inscriptions and human choice (Wigoder 1989). Neither do we find references to fate in Nustrem's *Bibleiskii slovar'* (Bible Dictionary, 2000), or in Nikifor's *Bibleiskaia entsiklopedia* (Bible Encyclopedia, 1990).

The notion of fate has undergone changes over centuries of history and differs in the collective consciousness of various peoples. Detailed analysis of culture-specific aspects of the concepts of fate and destiny can be found in Wierzbicka's *Semantics, Culture, and Cognition* (1992). Karev (1982) summarizes the common parameters of the notion of fate in folk philosophy: "In the mythology of various nations, fate is linked to the idea of unknown force, which determines various events and orders human life (in a wider sense it determines the life of a society)" (471). In Slavic mythology, fate is perceived as an irrevocable verdict beyond the power of individual will. Attempts to avert predestination or to outsmart fate are doomed to failure (Kovshova 1994, 142; Nikitina 1994, 132–33; Tolstaia 1994, 146). Contrary to fate or destiny in other cultures, the Russian notion of *sud'ba* implies external control that "may come from other people—for example, from social tyranny or political oppression—rather than from other-worldly forces" (Wierzbicka 1992, 69). Judaism does not deny human free will. Some interpret it as a choice between good and evil, hence the numerous Jewish folktales about good deeds, which allow people to escape predestined death. The Jewish oikotypes complementing Aarne and Thompson's system (1964) classify these tales as 934*F, "Charity rescues from death" (Shenhar 1982, 56–65); 934*G, "Rescue of boy fated to die on his wedding night"; and 934B-*A, "Successful escape from death." A selection of such tales is preserved in the IFA.

In spite of the deterministic aspects of the notion of fate it is not divorced from chance. The ancient Greek deity Tiche and the Roman Fortuna personified fate and brought together the predestined and the accidental. Toporov (1994) notes the bipolar structure of the notion of fate. The dichotomies of finite/infinite and determinate/indeterminate permeate the discourse on fate. Moreover, Toporov emphasizes that fate and chance accompany humans throughout their lives and have an anthropological flavor: humans are conscious of the power of destiny and chance over their lives. Everyone has to confront his or her own destiny, and everyone can benefit from his or her own unique chance (38).

The significance of the belief in the freak nature of good luck and the power of chance among our contemporaries is reflected in Russian phraseology, some of which has been borrowed from literature. For example, a jocular rhymed maxim pronounced by one of the characters of Lermontov's novel *The Hero of Our Time*—which runs *"Natura-dura, sud'ba indeika, a zhizn' kopeika"* ("Nature is a fool, fate is nothing but a turkey, and life is only worth a *kopeck*")—caught on and is used in speech (Lermontov 1969b, 318). A similar attitude is expressed in the popular song *Shumel, gorel pozhar moskovskii* (Moscow fire was burning and roaring). A poem written by Sokolov in 1850 and devoted to the Moscow fire of 1812 gained popularity in 1912 during the centenary celebration of the victory over Napoleon (http://slova.ndo.ru/?file=arhiv&liter=17&id=all&page=108). It turned into a folk song, and as often happens the text was modified several times. The best known version ends as follows:

Sud'ba igraet chelovekom Ona izmenchiva vsegda, To vozneset ego vysoko, To brosit v bezdnu bez sleda.	Man is a toy in the hands of Fate, She is forever frivolous and changing. At times she lifts him up, he swallows the bait. But then the cunning one laughs and hurls him to the abyss.

The classic authors of Soviet literature Ilf and Petrov paraphrased the words of the song in their novel *The Golden Calf: Sud'ba igraet chelovekom, a chelovek igraet na trube* (Fate plays with man, and man plays the trumpet). Both the original and the paraphrase are often cited in speech, even though not everyone is aware of their sources. Fatalism and dependence on the power of fate are reflected in numerous phrases and exclamations with the word *sud'ba,* for example:

Sud'bonosnoie reshenie	Fateful decision
Blagodarit' sud'bu	Thank one's lucky stars
Iskushat' sudbu	Tempt fate
Reshaetsia [ego] sud'ba	His fate is being decided upon
Kakimi sud'bami?	What fortunate wind brings you here?
Ne sud'ba!	It is not in the cards!

In addition, contemporary Russian speakers widely use phrases perpetuating the theme of respect for and anticipation of a lucky chance: Lady Luck and His Majesty Lucky Chance. All of these are used in everyday conversations, in media discourse, in movies, and in popular songs. The pervasiveness of these phrases in speech is remarkable because the Soviet era created its own mythology, intended to replace traditional folk beliefs. One of the principal themes of Soviet mythology was power of the human over nature, over circumstances, and over his or her own life. Predestination was no longer tied to divinity, but solely to the founding fathers of Marxism and their writings (Mokienko and Nikitina 1998, 664, 470). While in the Slavic mythology fate is power, and human life is the object of its action, in Soviet mythology man became the master of his own fate. Even the notion of miracle underwent changes. It was no longer associated with divinity but with human actions and human will. It was customary to speak about "miracles of wit," "miracles of art," and even about "miracles of labor heroism."

Narratives presented in this chapter reveal eclecticism in the informants' perception of the notions of fate, destiny, chance, and miracle. They are blurred and interchangeable. Having made the decision to emigrate, the narrators felt they were challenging fate. But having become immigrants, they felt that they were caught in an intricate web of circumstances beyond their control; only happy coincidences would miraculously change this fateful constellation.

Lucky Coincidences in Finding a Job

In our sample there are four narratives about success in the search for the first job in a new country. All the storytellers are women who arrived in Israel at the peak of immigration in the early 1990s. They share some features relevant to their stories. They come from big Soviet cities, are extremely career oriented, and three of them hold doctorates. At the time, the overall job situation in the country gave rise to acute pessimism among immigrants hunting for jobs. Rumors proliferated that there was no chance to find a job without using connections. These were mythologized and affected the newcomers' morale. As follows from the stories, each of the narrators was aware of additional difficulties in their individual cases. Isanna L., 65, and Anastasia N., 61, were close to retirement age, which minimized their employment opportunities. Sofia Y., 48, felt that her value on the job market (teaching

English) had fallen dramatically because of competition with native speakers. Sofia and Anastasia F., 43, perceived finding a job as a matter of life and death: one was single and had no family in Israel, the other was a single mother with a toddler—both could rely only on themselves. It is important to mention that stories about job hunting refer to the very first months of the narrators' life in Israel. This was the period when the lack of Hebrew proficiency, absence of a social network, and general disorientation in the workings of local life increased our informants' anxiety and insecurity. Under the circumstances, possible failure in finding a job was perceived as a sad but feasible outcome, while success was viewed as an extraordinary piece of luck. Here we quote two of these stories, Isanna's in this section and Anastasia N.'s in the next one (see two others in Fialkova and Yelenevskaya 2001b, 307–12).

Isanna L., 65

> One day, in August 1991, four months after arrival in Israel, I went to a job interview. It was not my first one, and I was not particularly hopeful. The interview would be in the hospital called *beit holim* R. [*Hebrew for "hospital"*], and I was to meet the head of the chemical lab, Professor L. After a lot of wandering, after numerous ascents and descents, I entered a unit, which looked more like a shed than [*pause*] a medical lab. I saw plenty of doors, all of them wide open, an elevator, and on my left there was a place where gowns were given out. Next to the elevator there was a chair, which could hardly keep a balance on its [*pause*] worn-out legs. I ventured to sit down on it and prepared to wait for the end of the doctors' meeting. Sometime later Professor L. showed up and invited me to his office. The style of his clothes was "democratic," to say the least. [*Isanna means informal.*] I entered a room which had no window. On the wall at the left there was a blackboard which could be used for explanations and writing formulas. Next to it there was a big bookcase with a lot of books in it. On the right there were shelves with paper folders. I wasn't too nervous because I didn't hope for success. Suddenly . . . hardly had I had time to open my mouth when the professor was called to the room next door to answer a telephone call. While he was away, I studied the room to fill the time. All of a sudden, my

attention was drawn to a couple of reproductions. I thought one of them . . . As I knew the picture, I was pretty sure one was a painting by Kandinsky. When L. returned, the first thing I said to him was, "Is it Kandinsky you have here?" To this he replied, "Do you know who Kandinsky is?" After this, the conversation switched to professional issues. I talked in broken Hebrew, summoning English words for help when needed. He told me to call him [*pause*] in a couple of weeks. When two weeks later I called him, he didn't remember who I was and what I was talking about. And then again—I don't know why—I said, "We spoke about Kandinsky, you remember, don't you?" And contrary to all my expectations he said, "Sure, I remember! Nobody spoke to me about Kandinsky except you." Some more time passed, and I was hired. Having begun working, I learned that Professor L. was a person of great versatility. He is interested in art, he lectures at the National Museum of Israel, and he is interested in modern art, and in particular Russian Modernism. Besides, he is interested in music, but this is not the issue here. So, without knowing anything about his interests and passions, I hit the nail on the head, as they say. As far as I understood the situation, I was hardly a good find for any employer: I was 56 [*pause*], almost 57 then. Nevertheless, he hired me, and sometimes brought me tickets to concerts. Our relationship has become, to some extent, informal. Naturally, it was a professional relationship, but we often discussed art and exhibits, and even now, after I have worked there for eight years, we still do. He still employs me, in spite of my advanced age. Approximately in the same period, one of my relations wrote a verse—to commemorate my birthday or some other occasion—and there were stanzas in it, which read as follows:

V semie davno legenda brodit Kak v neizvedannoi strane Isannin pervyi shag k rabote Byl ot kartiny na stene.	A legend wanders like a creature In Land unknown to us all: Isanna's job was launched by Picture, Kadinsky's picture on the wall.
I eta samaia legenda Dokazyvaet nam vpolne To, chto bagazh intelligenta Ne v bagazhe, a v golove.	This simple legend makes it clear That no knowledge is in vain. The riches of the intelligentsia Are not in trunks but in the brain.

This narrative is structured as a novella. Its action is set in historic time and space. Space is identifiable and is marked by the name of the city. The story emphasizes the narrator's initial pessimism. Although almost a decade has passed, Isanna reproduces the event in minute detail, without hedges or self-correction, which suggests that the described event was a landmark in her immigrant experience. She focuses on the obstacles along her way. Even space is perceived as subversive, and the hospital looks like a labyrinth. Against the background of difficulties the successful outcome has the effect of defeated expectancy, which is emphasized by the words "suddenly," "all of a sudden," "contrary to all my expectations." Isanna's narrative incorporates a humorous verse, which is already a new version of the original story. Note that the author of the verse, also an immigrant of the same period (Yurii Tulchinskii), refers to Isanna's story as a "legend." He does not use the word as a literary term but implies that the event was remarkable, and the story had circulated among friends. While the verse clearly carries a didactic message, emphasizing the importance of broad education for successful integration in the new society, the original story downplays it. The narrator is amused that her knowledge of Russian art came in handy so unexpectedly. This absence of an explicit didactic message is typical of legends. Though heavily disguised, the moral injunctions and adhortations of legends are too amusing or too poignant to be ignored (Nicolaisen 1987, 174).

In the moral of the verse the antithesis of the contents of trunks and knowledge in the brain is not accidental. Some of our subjects, as well as our many friends and acquaintances, told us amusing and sometimes sad stories about the items they had carried from one continent to another. Still infected by the habit of hunting down consumer goods that were in short supply, and afraid that they would not have enough money for the essentials, immigrants of the early 1990s brought huge supplies of soap, toothpaste, stationery, and even toilet paper to Israel. Conversely, pessimistic about their chances of finding jobs in their field, many immigrants left professional books and sometimes even their own scientific publications behind. The absurdity of such a choice became obvious shortly after immigration and gave rise to a great number of litanies as well as humorous stories.

Two years after the interview with Isanna was conducted, we learned that her story had been reproduced, unfortunately without her permission, in memoirs written by a friend of her family and published in her hometown, Kiev. Following is the translation of the relevant passage from Russian:

> An experienced biochemist, Dr. Isanna Likhtenshtein worked for many years at the Strazhesko Institute of Cardiology. . . . In Haifa her road to Calvary began when she traipsed from one medical institution to another. From day to day her hopes grew more fragile. At the end of the 37th or 49th failed job interview Isanna was preparing to leave and turned to say goodbye to her interviewer. And all of a sudden she said, "What an interesting painting by Kandinsky you have here!" After a *pause* the possessor of the office roared, "R-r-e-t-u-r-r-r-n! Sit down! Among my employees—oh yes, you are already my employee—nobody except you and me has the slightest idea that this picture on the wall is by Kandinsky!" It is now over ten years that Isanna has been working successfully at this R&D institute. So here is the Power of Art and here is the role of His Majesty Lucky Chance for you. (Shanin 2002, cliv–clv)

The new version of the story deviates from the original in several respects. The author has no intention of disguising Isanna's identity; on the contrary, he is at pains to supply as many details as possible to make the story sound reliable and the protagonist recognizable. He gives the full name not only of the chemist but also of the institution where she had worked, which is well known in Kiev. After the publication of Shanin's book we asked our informant if she preferred her name to be omitted from the excerpt, but Isanna did not mind the disclosure of her real name. On the other hand, the author of the book is unfamiliar with Israeli realities, so he does not mention either the name of Isanna's boss or the hospital where she is employed. Moreover, he confuses a hospital with an R&D institute, probably because in Kiev, Isanna worked at such an institute; he automatically transfers her to an institution of the same category. As we have heard Isanna tell the story many times, we know these could not have been her mistakes and omissions. The story being part of her standard narrative repertoire, she hardly ever changes it, and the correct names are never omitted. They also appear in the version that we recorded, but at the interviewee's request we deleted them. To increase the dramatic effect of the story, the author of the memoirs resorts to hyperbole regarding the number of unsuccessful interviews. These never came anywhere close to thirty-seven, let alone forty-nine; they barely exceeded fifteen. Shanin also changes the sequence of events. In the original, a brief exchange about Kandinsky was just a prelude to the interview that didn't directly influence its outcome but singled Isanna out as a personality among numerous immigrant job seekers that her future boss interviewed. By contrast, both the author of the verse and the author of the memoirs present Isanna's familiarity with Kandinsky's art as the sole explanation for her success in the job interview. Like the writer of the verse, the memoirist emphasizes the role of art in Isanna's life story. He uses an allusion to a popular Soviet movie, *The Magic Power of Art.* Additionally, he implies that an immigrant's success in finding a job is not due to his or her qualifications but to sheer luck, referred to in popular Russian parlance, as noted, as Lady Luck or His Majesty Lucky Chance.

Lucky Coincidences in Finding a Person

According to a popular belief, a change of place may bring about a change in fortune (see, e.g., Nicolaisen 2001). Many of our subjects see immigration as a fresh start, a change of luck, and a way to get out of a deadlock, be it poverty, family trouble, or loneliness. As noted in chapter 1, the percentage of single and divorced women among the FSU immigrants is quite high. Immigration and acculturation stress triggered a high rate of separation and divorce among new immigrants, thus also increasing the number of unmarried women. The Russian-language press and stories circulating in the community tell many a tale about women coming to Israel with children and leaving men behind in the old country. In this respect immigration at the end of the twentieth century is markedly different from immigration from Eastern Europe a century earlier, when men ventured to explore the new world while women stayed at home. This is reflected in immigrant folklore of the time, as set forth by Rothstein (2000).

With so many single women around, stories about encountering a new love and a new life partner in a new country find eager listeners and are widely circulated in the community, as they breed hope and perpetuate the mythology of good luck. The hope of finding a new love in a new place is a part of Russian folklore. When sleeping away from home, girls say to themselves: *Na novom meste / prisnis' zhenikh neveste* (In a new place, may you see your fiancé in your dreams). The following story told by Svetlana T., a microbiologist, is very long, so we will omit some of the details, such as the exposition of family ties and background information about friends.

Svetlana T., 56

> Well, first, I think nothing happens by accident in life. I am fully convinced of it. There are some regularities in life. But because I believe in Supreme Power, I believe that there is something . . . not a road shown by religion, but the road of faith and belief in the Super Power. I think there is something to lead us along the road of life. And as my friend Tanya said . . . when this story with Senia [*diminutive of the male name Semion*] began . . . she kept saying to me, "Sveta" [*diminutive of Svetlana*], she said it many times, "Sveta, each of us has a Guardian Angel. We should just listen carefully to be sure we do not miss the sound of his wings beating. We should do our best to hear his voice. And you have to decide now, because I think it is just the right thing for you, just the right thing." Well, here is how it was with Senia. Now in retrospect, when we talk about it, it seems. . . . We grew up on neighboring streets, one on Perovskaia Street, and the other on the street right behind the Kazan Cathedral. Our schools were next to each other, and we walked along the same streets. We went to the same shops, the shops of our neighborhood. These were OUR shops. That is, we used to go to the same kiosk and we used to buy newspapers from the same Jew. Even today Senia remembers his name. I don't though. . . . Then it turned out that we have friends in common, school friends and university friends. That is, we were very . . . I am absolutely sure that he often walked along Perovskaia street, and I am sure that I saw him. I am sure I saw him but I just passed by. I saw him, but I paid no attention. And neither did he. The first time we met was when he came in . . . in 1995. He came as a tourist to visit his sister. And he didn't want to come to Israel then. . . . [*She means he didn't want to*

> *emigrate.*] And it was this very rare occasion when I came to visit Tanya, and it all happened as if by mere chance. So I came to visit Tanya. I could so rarely come to visit her, because of my work. . . . [*The narrator told us that she had met her future husband by accident.*] And he looked quite content—a suntanned holiday-maker—but the most important thing for me was that he was a Leningrader. And not just a Leningrader, but he was soon going back there. With my constant longing for Leningrad . . . I simply got glued to him. And I saw that it was a Leningrader who knew the city so well—every little street, every little lane, and he was eager to talk to me about them. I liked him very much, but this whole thing, sort of, had nothing to do with me, nothing at all.

Indeed, Semion went back to his hometown and Svetlana's friend reported that he had asked about her in his letters. Three years after their first encounter Semion did immigrate to Israel. The beginning of his life in the new country was marked by grief—both of his parents passed away shortly after immigration. At that time Svetlana also went through a crisis in her private life. She was on the verge of separating from her partner and took it badly. The two Leningraders met again at a birthday party in the same house where they had met for the first time.

> How many years had passed since that first encounter? Three years. When I saw him again my heart sank. Because, you know, the first time I saw him, he was a happy fellow, quite content with his life. And then I saw someone who was miserable and completely lost, a man in limbo. He was pale, thin, and anxious about his situation . . . and the country was absolutely alien to him. . . . I immediately recalled how I felt in such a situation and I felt so sorry for him, so terribly sorry.

Their further contacts were mostly by phone, because the distance so easily covered in the USSR proved to be a major trip in Israel. As one immigrant wittily remarked, "Israel is a huge country, in which the distance is not measured in kilometers but in shekels." Besides fares being too high for newcomers, there is almost no public transport on the Sabbath, the only day when it is feasible for a secular immigrant to visit his or her friends and family living in other towns. The lack of public transport is not a problem for many Israelis who own cars, but newcomers often feel confined to their homes and deprived of the freedom of movement.

Telephone conversations between our narrator and her new acquaintance proved to be sufficient to establish intimacy and friendship. Svetlana deliberates on the type of this attachment.

> I realized he was in love with me. No, I don't know whether he was in love with me or he was clutching at a straw, you know what I mean. Because he understood that here was someone interested in him and his fate.

Some time passed, and Semion managed to find a reasonable job. He called Svetlana to say that he was faced with a dilemma. To accept the job would mean reconciling himself to their relationship being limited to a telephone friendship. Semion was convinced he would have little opportunity to see Svetlana regularly but felt it would be hard on him, as he could no longer imagine his life without her. The alternative would be to reject the job and move to Svetlana's town. Our narrator was torn apart.

Svetlana is always surrounded by friends in need. Obliged to give up her job due to poor health, she immediately joined a volunteer organization that helps new immigrants, and now she spends a lot of time and effort helping newcomers deal with bureaucracy, write business letters, and so on. When she had to choose between two men, her old boyfriend—a well-to-do veteran Israeli—and Semion, who was still little more than a stranger, she tried to figure out which of the two needed her more. She felt that by choosing Semion, she would have to take responsibility for an extremely shy, lonely, and unsettled person who reminded her of a child. At that time they had met just three times. Tormented and confused, Svetlana nevertheless plunged forward to start a new life with a new man.

> So we came to live together, and it felt as if we had been together all our life. We feel very close to each other. And I think that we were destined to go through all the difficulties and

> hardships of life separately to meet in Israel. Isn't it a miracle? Yes, it is simply a miracle.

The story begins with deliberations about the Guardian Angel, but this does not reflect a religious worldview; rather it is a general philosophical belief that "there is something, somewhere guiding our life." Such a view is widespread in the FSU, and as the Russian sociologist Ryvkina (1996) remarks it is not at all connected to religion (59). The angel has acquired a folk image in the narrative, which is manifested in the wording: "We just have to listen carefully to be sure we do not miss the sound of his wings beating. We should do our best to hear his voice."

An important part of the narrative is the image of the city. The narrator and her new friend are both its children and it brought them together in a distant land. Svetlana keeps talking about Leningrad, which in the early 1990s reverted to its former name, St. Petersburg, which was established by Czar Peter I. The image of this city has a long history in Russian literature and folklore. Two contradictory features always intermingle in this image. On the one hand it is a demonic city whose marshy soil is covered with the bones of its builders. The city is doomed to be destroyed by the pitiless elements. On the other hand, St. Petersburg has the image of a city of unparalleled beauty and spirituality (Lotman 1992b; Sindalovskii 1999; Toporov 1984, 4–29). The demonic image is not present in Svetlana's narrative; she reproduces only the idealized image. The narrator emphasizes that she and her husband failed to meet when they lived in the same city; they met only after fate tested them by separating them in space and time: the two came to Israel at different times, and they lived in different and distant cities in Israel.

The collection of Russian proverbs of the prominent nineteenth-century linguist and folklorist Dal' has a whole section connecting fate, patience, and hope (Dal' 1957, 149–54). Svetlana paraphrases one of them: *Ne uznaesh goria, ne uznaesh i radosti* (If you haven't experienced grief, you will never experience happiness). Again we see an implicit moral: Happiness comes as a reward for patience.

The next narrator, Albert R., immigrated to Israel in 1991. He considers his immigration a success, mostly because he didn't have to give up his vocation. He is a musician and is often invited to play at parties and in old-age homes. He and his saxophone are a familiar sight in the business center of the city where he lives. Passersby often stop to listen to his tunes and to chat with him in Hebrew, Yiddish, or Russian. His repertoire is varied and includes Jewish folk songs and popular Soviet and Western tunes.

Albert R., 72

ALBERT: I had a friend there. He was, er . . . a civil engineer. He liked music. I taught him [*in the USSR*] [*pause*] . . . . By the way, he is here, in Israel, but I cannot find him. He was a great lover of music, and I taught him to play saxophone. He came here [*before Albert emigrated*]. He hadn't seen his mother for about fifteen years. He used to correspond with her secretly, but I don't know how. He came here and dropped in at the restaurant Babushka. And, naturally, there is a band playing there. And he says, "Isn't it great that Albert taught me to play and to listen to music. And my brother was sitting nearby. "Which Albert? What's his family name?" He says, "R——d." "But it's my brother!" And to make it short, that's how they met. He bought drinks for everyone in the restaurant: "I have found my brother!" He [*the friend*] came back [*to the USSR*] and gave me his [*Albert's brother's*] telephone number. I got in touch with him by phone. I first came here to visit him in 1989.

INTERVIEWER: How many years hadn't you seen each other?

ALBERT: Forty-four years. I have a newspaper article somewhere here with a photo of our reunion.

Finding his only brother after nearly half a century of separation was a crucial turning point not only in Albert's life but in the life of his whole family—it triggered the decision to emigrate from the USSR. On the surface, the narrative is almost devoid of emotion; the only indication of joy is that Albert's brother paid for drinks for everyone at the restaurant. The novella has a happy ending: a lucky chance helps the two meet. Their reunion was turned into a public event, attracting the interest of the local newspaper. What is left out of the story is that subsequently the relationship between the brothers soured and they drifted apart. In spite of being near, they remained even farther from each other than when they lived thousands of kilometers apart.

Finding New Friends in the New Country

While dividing narratives about lucky coincidences into groups we realized that some could be placed in at least two different categories. Thus Anastasia N.'s story quoted below tells us not only about finding new friends but also about finding a job. We have already mentioned the importance of friendships for our subjects. In the absence of a social network in the first weeks after immigration, the readiness of veteran Israelis to help mere strangers was taken almost as a miracle.

Alina R., 49

ALINA: I think our immigration is a very special story. I want to tell you what happened to our family, and I hope that next generations will know about it. We were the first to come to Israel [*she refers to her extended family*]—we had neither family nor friends to rely on. . . . We were given the name of a hotel—mind you, we didn't know anything about that hotel, and we didn't know anything at all. We arrived at night and finally found it in Hadar. . . . The room . . . in my whole life I'd never seen anything of the sort. The bed took up all the space in the room, and a shower was right there in the room too, so water from the shower stall streamed across the floor and under the bed. The windows were sealed, and if you moved the blind, you would see the garbage cans of the market. . . . We got up in the morning and headed for the only place where we knew we could receive help, the *Sokhnut* [*the Jewish Agency*]. This we did know. We immigrated on April 6, and the Passover vacation started on April 8. And so in the morning we came to *Sokhnut* and there they told us quite clearly: "This is direct absorption and we have nothing to do with it. If you fail to rent an apartment today, and we don't fill in the necessary papers, you'll have to wait ten days." Ten days! We received 1,000 shekels in the airport and we had $450 that we were allowed to take out from Russia. We had four suitcases with inflatable mattresses in them, so that if there was no place to stay we could at least lie on mattresses. We also brought pillows, bed clothes, plastic plates, and a few personal belongings for the first days. . . . [*Alina's husband managed to rent an apartment before the holiday began, but it was shabby and in a very poor neighborhood.*] It was the eve of the Passover. We came back to the hotel and at the entrance I saw some people lying on the ground. And I say to my husband, "What's the matter? They must be sick!" He came up to look and said that they were drug addicts. I had never seen drug addicts before. And then I saw them right near the hotel and with syringes. We grabbed the children and [*rushed inside*]. We have to wait until tomorrow night. And tomorrow we will stay in. This place is no good for walking. Whatever will be, will be. But I said to my husband, "If I see people like these here in the neighborhood where you rented the apartment, and if the apartment is of the same sort [*as the hotel room*] . . . I will ask my mum to do her best and transfer the money and I'll go back. I won't stay here! I haven't brought the children to live in a place like this and in such circumstances." And while we were in the room, there was a knock at the door. This was a man with a girl. He invited us for a Passover meal. He spoke Russian but in such a way that it was clear he hadn't used it for about twenty years.

INTERVIEWER: Had you met them before?

ALINA: No, they were complete strangers. There was an announcement on the Haifa radio that a large wave of immigrants had arrived and they were still in hotels. So the municipality appealed to the residents to invite immigrants for the Passover. We couldn't understand even half of what he said. We spoke English a bit and Yiddish. . . . When the man left my husband asked me to take the kids and wait downstairs because he wanted to stay alone a bit. No sooner had I closed the door than I heard him crying. I had never heard him cry before. And I hope it was the last time. In the evening the man came to pick us up. He brought his father with him, who had come from Poland in 1956. To provide us with interlocutors he brought his parents. And when we came to their house we saw a different Israel. . . .

Anastasia N., 61

So if we are going to talk about us . . . who helped us and about the lucky chance which is called here *hizdamnut* [*Hebrew for "opportunity," "chance"*], am I right? So it was like this. Naturally, we had no money then, because we received the minimum sum then; as far as I remember, it was 330 shekels per capita, and we were three capita, three persons, one retired and two of pre-retirement age. Well, and the incident which occurred struck terror into us. Because my husband wanted to have a look around and managed to get out through a closed window [*and broke it*] [*laughs*]. . . . We rushed to find out who could . . . and how much it would cost. And we were told that it would cost 50 shekels. And if you take into account that we had only 300 shekels for food and for everything else. . . . So we decided we would do the work ourselves. We went to look at . . . well, you know that people here take out doors, windows, and all sorts of things and leave them next to garbage cans. And we found a big window measuring approximately 2 to 1.5 [*laughs*] meters. So we stopped in front of it and we think, "How shall we take it out? These two meters sort of consist of two parts . . . And there were people strolling there, locals, the former, well, aliya of the seventy . . . of 1972. And they treated us as if they were, so to speak, our patrons. They gave us advice, as it was customary in the [*Soviet*] Union, and, in general, as it is customary among Jews. And one of them says to another one in a managerial tone, "Look, Miron, why don't you help these guys cut the glass out?" And it was necessary to tear off all the stuff, and only then to cut it out. And this guy Miron, a very pleasant person, and in some way resembling my father in appearances and stature. My father was of approximately the same height, and so he says, "*Beseder,* [*Hebrew for "okay"*], so what can I do? We tell him what happened. "Beseder, don't worry, don't get so upset." And we also tell him: "Well, we were told it would cost 50 shekels." He says, "It won't cost you anything." But we don't know anything about him—who is he, what is he? It will cost nothing, but who knows, what if he doesn't charge 50, but I don't know, 25, which is still too bad. . . . It was only our impudence and despair, on the one hand impudence and on the other hand despair, to think that we would be able to cut it out ourselves. Because he, a man who knew what he was doing, he ruined two windows before he succeeded, because it is very difficult to cut such thick glass. And we didn't have anything [*any tools*] at all. Well, nevertheless, he cut it out and put it in for us [*pause*]. Naturally we made tea for him and talked. Then it turned out that one of his relatives was either leaving or coming, yes, he had been visiting and was leaving [*for Russia*] then. And my husband said he wanted to give them letters. You see, we simply didn't know then whether mail functioned properly. So we only sent letters when there was an opportunity to send them with someone. And so there was this opportunity. And he went. My husband is very sociable. So he started chatting there, and met Miron's wife. They were 65, 68, 64, something like this. . . . They invited us . . . right before Rosh ha-Shanah [*Hebrew for "New Year"*], some time in August, I don't remember now. . . . They invited us for Succoth [*pause*] or for something else, I even don't remember now what it was. So we went to their place, and then we invited them, and so we got to know each other. Well, naturally, what did we talk about? We discussed appropriate issues [*She refers to themes that bothered new immigrants*]: How shall we manage? What shall we hope for? [*laughs*] How shall we make a living? And they, Regina in particular . . . she is a very "cozy," very warm person. You know there is this type—you simply want to embrace her [*laughs*]. She used to say, "Nasten'ka [*diminutive and endearing for Anastasia*], don't worry! *Ihiie beseder"* [*Hebrew for "It'll be okay"*]. And we wanted to, we wanted so much to believe them! . . . And Regina said right from the start, "Well, you have to. If you want to see the hospital, my daughter has a friend. She works in the hospital." And I asked her, I say, "Would it be possible for me to go and have a look? I cannot even imagine what they do here and how." I sort of thought that everything should be different but . . . [*pause*] I wanted to see. And, indeed, sometime later she said that there was this friend, and she lives on our street, or a little bit below, and she is ready to show me 'round. She had spoken to the head of the department and he agreed to let me come and observe the work of the department. There was no talk about anything else. And, of course, with my Hebrew. . . . You know when we finished *ulpan* we didn't know anything except the song *"Be kova sheli, iesh shalosh pinot, shalosh pinot be kova sheli"* [*Hebrew for "My hat has three corners, three corners has my hat"*] [*laughs*]. We had a very nice, but a very nothing special sort of teacher. Well so we came here [*to the hospital*], she in-

> troduced me and left. And I started coming. I came here again and again, and finally he decided to employ me. In fact I was the first one, except a Russian woman who had worked here for about twelve years [*pause*] or more by the time I arrived. Yes, that was our lucky chance. (IFA 22140)

These two stories are similar in many details. Note that both narrators give the exact amounts of the money they had and describe the fear of poverty that struck the new immigrants in the first period in Israel. Anastasia is slightly ironic in her account of the events, while Alina was overwhelmed with emotion and with tears in her eyes told the interviewer about her despair, humiliation, and gratitude to the strangers. The direct absorption mentioned in Alina's story replaced the absorption centers. Instead of being sent to a specific place where new immigrants lived, studied Hebrew, and were guided in the first months, the FSU immigrants were free to go to any town and manage their life on their own. In the period when Alina's family arrived, the demand for rental apartments grew exponentially, and consequently the prices rose too. As a result freedom was limited (see Gonen 1998). So many immigrants felt that instead of coming to the "land of prosperity" they dropped to the very bottom of society. After the humiliation of passing through Soviet customs (Alina told the interviewer that she had been stripped of a family relic—a silver spoon passed from generation to generation), the new immigrants were confronted with the indifference of the bureaucratic machine. Had they failed to rent an apartment they would have had to sleep on the street because the money they had was not enough to stay in even the cheapest hotel for ten days.

In both stories, help came from the people who could communicate with the immigrants in Russian and had lived through the hardships of immigration themselves. In Alina's case the change of the family's fortune is directly connected to the Passover. Even though Anastasia does not remember for which holiday—Rosh ha-Shana or Succoth—they were invited, she makes a point of mentioning it in her story. A similar story is found in Mirsky (2005).[1] A frequent motif of Jewish folklore is miraculous help bestowed on the poor on the eve of the Jewish holidays. In traditional stories the poor suffer from their inability to spend a holiday in an appropriate fashion. This is not what bothered our informants. Although unaware of Jewish folktales, our interviewees not only became actors in one but also disseminated them.

Forecasting the Future

Although many immigrants claimed that their decision to immigrate was accidental and not thoroughly thought out, later some of them recalled events that were interpreted as signs that their immigration to Israel was predestined. Most of these stories, like Anastasia Ts.'s narrative below, reflect the mixture of cultural codes and a strong influence of Christian folklore.

Anastasia Ts., 48

> There was just one dilemma—to leave or not to leave? But there was no question as to where to go. It would be Israel. Israel is a Jewish state. The most interesting thing is that . . . when I was in Kiev, there, in Kiev, on a bus, a woman said to me, "When you come to Jerusalem," I thought she was nuts, and she says, "Bow down in front of the Church of the Holy Sepulcher and ask for a blessing for Olga and Maria." I thought the woman was simply nuts. It was at the time when I had no intention to leave. Later, this even came back to memory, and I thought it was my destiny, and I had to go. Jerusalem has always been the center of the earth. I cannot say it is the center of the Jewish state—I don't really understand these things—but I understand that it is the center of the earth, the center of the entire world, the center of the universe. This I understand very well. And because of this I certainly wanted to . . . I wanted. (IFA 22122)

Nina K., 60+

> I want to tell you about an episode that occurred near the synagogue [*in Moscow*] and which often comes back to memory. . . . So I [*pause*] arrived here in June 1991 and what I am going to tell you happened in . . . probably in 1989. I had no intention to emigrate then. . . . Together with a friend I went for the celebration of this holiday, Simkhat Tora. And all of a sudden . . . the crowd was cheerful, everyone was chatting, dancing, and all of a sudden a man comes up to me and starts talking English to

> me. I don't know how he guessed that I knew English, and he began to ask me about our life. Well, er, I said we were okay. . . . Well, I cannot say that my life was bad. It would be wrong. He asked me what I knew about the Jewry, about this thing and other. And I said, "No, in this issue I won't be able to show any erudite knowledge." Then he says, "In fact, I have spent $20,000 to found a library so that you could learn about Jewish life." He turned out to be a member of some American society, don't remember which. The interesting thing is that when we parted, he said, "Next year in Jerusalem." And I screamed, "No, I won't come!" You see, I couldn't foresee my destiny then, I couldn't think I would come here.

Both narrators seek to show that their decision to emigrate was not a fait accompli during the rendered events. Nina strongly opposed the idea, and Anastasia paraphrased Hamlet's existential question to reveal the scope of the dilemma. What she found remarkable was that although she herself had not made a decision yet, the stranger behaved as if it was stamped on her forehead that she would go to Jerusalem. Nina also emphasized that the American had chosen her among all the others in the crowd in the period when few people in the USSR could speak English. Anastasia emphasized the importance of Jerusalem for her, but hers is not the longing for Jerusalem that for centuries has been expressed by Jews in the Diaspora in the phrase "Next Year in Jerusalem." The city symbolizes the center of the world as it is known from Russian and Ukrainian folklore (Tolstaia 1999; Fialkova 1999b). It is not accidental that in FSU immigrants' stories the image of Jerusalem is almost nonexistent. According to Khazan (1999), in twentieth-century Russian/Soviet culture, the decrease in significance of the "Jerusalem text" reflects the general loss of spirituality and relation to the holy. He believes that the Soviet political and ideological taboo on the texts dedicated to Jerusalem may be seen as a radical example of the universal secularization of culture in modern times (25). A parallel image of Jerusalem as the center can be found in the personal narratives of religious Jewish women, who think of Israel as the navel of the world and believe that "God has performed countless miracles so that we can live in Israel" (Sered 1992, 60). In the imagination of the stranger from Anastasia's story, Jerusalem is a place for pilgrimage, for ritual bowing at the Christian holy sites; and if she cannot do it herself, she entrusts Anastasia with the task.

Belief in miracles, which is an important component of the religious worldview, is transformed in the secular mind into belief in prophetic dreams and unexplainable coincidences. Both are part of the immigrant mythology created and transmitted by the urban dwellers irrespective of age, education, or occupation. Contemporary mythologies do not replicate their traditional predecessors. Neither is there similarity between the mythical thinking of religious Jews, who repatriated to Israel for the sake of settling the land of their forefathers, and the folk beliefs of secular and assimilated Soviet Jews. But this does not mean that members of the latter group live without myths of their own.

In spite of the difference of the plots, all the analyzed narratives are devoted to crucial pre-immigration and immigration experiences of the storytellers; furthermore, they share the same didactic value and function as tales with a purpose. They encourage listeners to be optimistic about their future in the new country and serve to support the morale of fellow immigrants in the upheaval of resettlement. Stories are made to sound miraculous; the marvelous element is in the telling rather than in the actual events. Narrators pile up details about adverse circumstances and people who create obstacles to the achievement of their goals. Tension builds in the anticipation of a bad outcome, but then an unexpected turn in the course of events breaks the spell and results in catharsis. The irregularities noted by our informants are minute and probably undetectable to those unfamiliar with the social and cultural background of the Soviet Jews. Even if coincidences can be explained by normal cause-and-effect relations, when they occur in a period of crisis or are linked to serious changes in life, their significance tends to be overwhelming. Ashe (1978) makes a good point concerning such tiny "synchronicities": "The constant tendency in these mini-miracles is to contrive a relationship or correspondence, a happening that is intelligible rather than random, and makes sense" (176). These "mini-miracles" may be meaningful not only to individuals but to whole groups.

The creation of the mythology of success is typical of the upwardly mobile groups in the immigrant community. Generally, there are two different reactions to such stories: some feel

"Success is disseminated here" reads an ad in a Russian newspaper. *Success* has become a magic word for upward mobile immigrants of the 1990s. *Photo courtesy of Janos Makowsky.*

encouraged and see them as incentive to strive harder for success, while others label them as "mere fairy tales" or "fables" that are false. Parallel to the mythology of success, immigration breeds a mythology of fated hopelessness, in which misfortune and unfairness rule. Stories of happy coincidences connected to repatriation to Israel and seen as miracles are integral to the Jewish folk tradition. As stated, repatriation, or aliya, is considered a *mitzvah* (Hebrew for "commandment") and its fulfillment is gratification in itself. Moreover, the act of repatriation can be rewarded by miracles such as a healing, cure of infertility, escape from death, and so on. Such stories are often included in personal narratives of religious Jews. Contrary to their tales, the narratives quoted and analyzed in this chapter do not regard coming to Israel as a mitzvah. This partially explains why secular Soviet Jews are less prepared for the hardships of immigration than their religious compatriots.

The majority of the stories in the sample share the same deep structure. The phenomenon of immigration is viewed as a trying experience. Hardships and pain are seen as an unavoidable part of this experience. Success and accomplishment of goals is viewed not as a reward for faith and virtuous deeds but as a lucky coincidence, a twist of fate. In Aarne and Thompson's classification (1964), lucky coincidences appear under "Jokes and Anecdotes" (1640–74). Our interviewees do not treat coincidences humorously; they see them as messages. But instead of interpreting these events as miracles caused by God, they see them as a sign of fate. The common features of the narratives enable us to introduce a new oicotype.

947C*-*B Feared (troublesome) change of home place proves lucky

I. Hero/heroine cannot leave for a new place or feels badly in a new place because of

- A. Ignorance of a foreign language
- B. Loneliness
- C. Absence of an apartment
- D. Absence of a job (and/or money)
- E. Fear of inability to study
- F. Other complications

II. Hero/heroine is haunted by search for a solution to a problem (sometimes perceived as fatal)

III. Unexpected help comes in the guise of a lucky chance, which

- A. Is brought about by a stranger
- B. Results from mockery
- C. Results from a witty answer
- D. Is triggered by an accident (e.g., a broken window)
- E. Is promoted by a stranger who appears to be a colleague or a friend of a family member
- F. Results from other lucky coincidences

IV. Hero/heroine solves the problem

- A. Marries
- B. Reunites with a family member

C. Finds an apartment
D. Finds a job (and/or money)
E. Fulfills the wish to study
F. Other solutions

Migration is always a challenge to fate, particularly so for Jews from the FSU brought up in a closed society. We agree with Ashe's conception of miracles (1978) in the eyes of their observers: "Behind miracles is the belief that Something Other does exist, does weave irregularities into the pattern; and this belief has a rebellious, defiant flavor. Whatever the Something is, it raises man above his apparent fate" (27). This uncertain "Something" manifested in prophetic dreams and lucky coincidences raises the immigrants' daily experiences to miracles.

6

Language and Immigrants' Identity

The topic of immigration is closely related to language. Immigrants' stories can be viewed as speech portraits in which individual mannerisms intertwine with verbal behavior characteristic of the whole community. Because Russian speakers in Israel are a culturally vibrant group, the interviews enable us to observe the evolution of speech genres and language dynamics that are manifest in neologisms and slang, as well as in the allusions used to illustrate immigrant experiences. Naturally, they also provide material on patterns of code-mixing and code-switching.

Throughout this book we have used elements of ethnolinguistic analysis to interpret our informants' utterances. In Russian studies ethnolinguistics was pioneered by Nikita Tolstoy. The school he created has made a major contribution to the mapping of folk culture as reflected in rites, beliefs, and folk terminology. Although most of our informants are secular urban dwellers, their stories are interspersed with elements of Russian and Soviet mythology, often used unconsciously and embedded in the language use and imagery.

The least researched linguistic topic arising from the interviews is analysis of laymen's talk about language. The subject is studied by folk linguistics and covers a wide range of topics—the investigation of social structure as reflected in speech, folk accounts of homonymy and synonymy, deliberations about language abnormality, and the analysis of attitudes to various speech styles—admiring some and avoiding others as taboo (Niedzielski and Preston 2000, 2). The main goal of this chapter is to examine

Part of the material in this chapter has been published in Yelenevskaya and Fialkova 2003b.

the mobilization of language awareness in our subjects. Reactions to the linguistic change in the life of FSU immigrants will become clearer after a brief introduction to the linguistic situation in Israel.

The Language Policy of Israel

Jews in the Diaspora spoke Yiddish, Ladino, Judeo-Arabic, Tat, and so on, all of which absorbed Hebrew words. Hebrew, "the holy tongue," was used for praying and reading religious literature and poetry. From the end of the nineteenth century to the first formative years of the state of Israel in the mid-twentieth century, the shaping of the new Jewish identity was closely related to linguistic choice. The revitalization of Hebrew and its transformation into a language for daily life was a cornerstone of the Zionist ideology (Spolsky and Shohamy 1999, 65–93). To modernize Hebrew and make it the dominant language of the Jewish population of Israel, the policy of avoidance of all languages brought from the Diaspora was pursued (Olshtain and Kotik 2000, 206). While some of the immigrants of the early waves willingly gave up their mother tongues and switched to Hebrew, others did so under pressure from society and their own children. The "melting pot" philosophy prevailed in Israel until the 1980s, when a change in policy occurred as a reaction to the rapid influx of Soviet Jews that began in 1989. For the first time in Israel's history, the establishment had to officially foster an immigrant language as a channel of information, education, and culture, hoping that it would serve as a vehicle for easier and faster integration (Glinert 1995).

The group of FSU immigrants in Israel is large enough demographically to support the continuous use of the Russian language (Spolsky and Shohamy 1999, 236). The demographic factor is reinforced by institutional support in the form of political parties founded to defend the immigrants' interests and the Russian-language media. Immigrant teachers run an extensive network of evening schools providing instruction in major subjects in Russian. Russian libraries and community centers have been opened in most of the immigrant enclaves, and service industries cater to Russian speakers in various domains.[1] The Russian language had metaphoric significance in the USSR as a source of "wealth and

"If you don't read books, you will soon forget your ABCs." This 1920s-era poster in a shop window reminds immigrants of the dangers of language attrition.

power" (Ries 1997, 30–32), and it has retained this meaning for immigrants, as we shall show later in the analyses. The Russian speech community in Israel reveals the three variables indicative of ethnolinguistic vitality: status, demography, and institutional support (Giles et al. 1977).

As a result of these sociopolitical developments, FSU immigrants of the 1990s constitute the first immigrant group in Israel that openly refused to suppress the culture and language of their country of origin. Although in the last two decades a more tolerant attitude toward multiculturalism and multilingualism has developed in Israel, the new immigrants' obduracy is a source of social and ideological conflict that spills over into the media. Among such examples are protests against the use of Russian in the election campaign (see Press-Service of the IBA12 December

"Don Quixote—Your Books in Your Own Language." Russian book fairs are attended by hundreds of people and offer a wide choice of books for all ages and tastes published in the FSU and in Israel.

2002) and reports about Russian-speaking employees prohibited from speaking Russian among themselves (Sheikhatovich 2002, 23). Government organizations also show concern about the unwillingness of the immigrants to shed their "Russian-ness," instead continuing to live on the basis of their original culture and distancing themselves from the Israelis (Horenczyk 2000, 18).

Linguistic Adjustment and Integration Processes

The role of host-language acquisition as the principal tool for immigrant integration is the second line of linguistic research devoted to FSU immigrants. Because the educational level of the FSU immigrants was high, the jobs they aspired to required a high level of proficiency in the local language as well as in English. But second-language teaching in the FSU was often inadequate, and this has complicated immigrants' professional integration. Studies investigating the dependency of occupational adjustment on language proficiency of former Soviets were undertaken in the United States and Israel (see, e.g., Chiswick 2000; Epstein and Kheimets 2000a; Menahem and Geijst 2000). Another direction in sociolinguistic research on FSU immigration is the issue of language maintenance and language attrition. Ever since the disintegration of the USSR and the increase in migration in the FSU, the interest in this subject has been on the rise among Slavists (Andrews 1993, 1999; Karaulov 1992; Moskovich 1992; Naiditch 2000; Pfandl' 1994; Zemskaia 2001). Studies conducted in Israel report that on average immigrants acquire Hebrew quite fast (see, e.g., Markowitz 1997; Kheimets and Epstein 2001b), but in spite of the growing proficiency in the local language, there is a strong orientation to the maintenance of Russian. Irrespective of the age and social group investigated, Russian scores better than Hebrew for its aesthetic value and as a vehicle of culture (Olshtain and Kotik 2000; Niznik 2003). Russian spoken in Israel abounds in Hebrew borrowings reflecting Israeli realities and seamlessly integrated into the language thanks to a well-developed system of inflections. According to Naiditch (2004), we can observe the emergence of an Israeli version of the Russian language that can be compared to the Australian version of English.

Most linguistic studies investigating FSU immigrants were based on surveys and structured or semistructured interviews; only a few turned to in-depth unstructured interviews, although they are widely used in anthropological and sociological studies of migrants. As Findlay and Li (1997) remark, it is important to focus on migrants as proactive, socially embedded, intentional agents who influence and are influenced by the social worlds in which they are located. The meaning of migration is established over long time spans and when migrants are engaged in an act of reflection about their immigrant experience, they can raise their consciousness to the discursive realm (34–35). Moreover, in postmodern societies, in which information and knowledge rank among the most important commodities, the enhanced role of re-

Although this real-estate agency chose an English name for the sake of prestige, the signs helping customers find the entrance and listing the available services are given in Hebrew and in Russian. As on other signs, the Russian is interspersed with Hebrew borrowings that have entered the immigrants' speech.

flexivity is manifest in the constant reshaping of social practices on the basis of knowledge about those practices (Fairclough 1999, 74).

One of the primary features of language is reflexivity. Speech is permeated by reflexive activity as speakers remark on language, report utterances, describe aspects of speech events, and guide listeners in the proper interpretation of their utterances (Lucy 1993, 11). This reflexive activity intensifies when adults begin to learn a new language, because comparisons between it and the mother tongue are inevitable. If learning occurs simultaneously upon entering a new language community, speakers also become more sensitive to the cultural and social implications that bilingualism involves (James 1999, 105). When immigrants reflect on the roles of their mother tongue and various languages of the old and new homeland they reveal consciously held views and unconscious value systems (Bugarski 1980, 383), which are not easily inferable from surveys and structured interviews. By analyzing these reflections this chapter aims to explore which approach to language—instrumental or symbolic—prevails in immigrants' narratives. It also examines how pre-immigration linguistic experiences affect linguistic adjustment in the new country. And finally it seeks to determine what values immigrants attribute to the languages that constitute the linguistic repertoire of the community, in particular Russian, Hebrew, and Yiddish. With these priorities in mind we aim to show immigrants' motivation in making specific language choices and to analyze when a specific choice serves as a tool or as an obstacle to integration.

Taking Bearings in the Multilingual Society

Reflections on language emerged as an essential part of the subjects' autobiography. For most of them, plunging into a new linguistic environment was a trying experience. Before emigration they were proficient only in their mother tongue, Russian. Even many of those who had lived in Ukraine, Byelorussia, Uzbekistan, or other countries of the FSU did not speak the language of the titular nationality fluently. Only one informant reported that she was Russian-Ukrainian ambilingual,[2] another was stable functional bilingual (Armenian-Russian), and five others reported fluency in Ukrainian, Byelorussian, or Armenian (see Fialkova 2005b about the status of the Byelorussian and Ukrainian languages in Israel). In all Soviet republics, except Russia, secondary schools were divided into two groups: those in which instruction was in the language of the republic, with Russian as a second language; and those in which instruction was in Russian, with the language of the republic as a second language. A considerable percentage of the population, including members of the titular nationalities, preferred their children to study at "Russian" schools, which gave better opportunities for tertiary education and a career. Russian was not only the language of international communication but essentially the secondary, and in some regions the primary, functional language (Grigorian 1996, 42). Although it was euphemistically referred to as the "language of inter-ethnic communication," in practice Russian was the state language of the USSR, the language of politics, science, and culture. Even doctoral theses had to be presented in Russian, thus elevating it to the status of a "cognitively more developed language" (Hawkins 1984, 59). Making the Russian language and culture a unifying force of the country was a major ideological goal. The Sovietization of life was actually a Russification (Hagendoorn et al. 1998, 485). The attitude toward the languages of the republics is vividly expressed in several interviews. Rosa Ch., 27, recalls that she managed to avoid learning Byelorussian at school, together with children of the officers of the Soviet army who moved from town to town and with the students with health problems. Moreover, she claimed that even as a child she was convinced that a "Jewish child could do very well without Byelorussian." Her peer Ekaterina R., 24, admitted that her knowledge of Uzbek was limited to a few words, although she studied it at school. In her case the excuse was gender: "Only Dad spoke it. Dad knows Uzbek and he communicated. And we, as Oriental women we were quiet, and our men were always in the foreground." Such indifference to the languages of the republics, caused by the intuitive knowledge that Russian speakers had better economic and social opportunities in the USSR, had vanished by the late 1980s and early 1990s, in particular after the dissolution of the Soviet Union. Demand for greater autonomy went hand in hand with emphasis on elevating the status of national languages and cultures. And so the Jews, who considered themselves a discriminated minority, realized that what had been an asset was turning into yet another obstacle to having equal rights and opportunities. Growing nationalism was cited as one of the major reasons for emigration in our sample, and linguistic nationalism was seen as part of the threat. Evgenii L., 66, for example, recalled the uncomfortable feeling he experienced as a witness to the discussion about the dominance of Ukrainian shortly before the dissolution of the Soviet Union: "I asked myself: And where am I? And there was no answer to this question. I wasn't there." Evgenii's command of Ukrainian was sufficient to understand the discussion, yet he couldn't imagine himself living in a completely

Ukrainized Ukraine. Evgenii described the beginning of what was later called a "linguistic war," a struggle in which mass media and even diplomats of the newly formed countries and Russia were involved (Savoskul 2001, 79).

Many of our subjects reported taking language classes before emigration. For the first time learning a new language was taken seriously, as it was viewed as an important part of preparation for their new life. Not everybody, though, chose Hebrew. Some of the interviewees, all of them professionals and academics of a mature age, decided to stake their professional future on English. They suspected that they would not be able to master a new language in a short period of time and preferred to focus on the advancement of their career in English, which they had all learned and/or used in research activities before emigration. Among younger people relying on English were those who considered it more important to integrate into international professional networks rather than national. Furthermore, some immigrants didn't exclude the possibility of further re-emigration. As mentioned in chapter 1, five of our subjects have left Israel for the United States and Canada since the interviews were conducted. Zemskaia (2001) observes the tendency to focus on English among FSU immigrants to countries whose languages are not widespread and, consequently, do not have high international status—for example, Finland and the Netherlands (42). Fluent English not only proved to be an asset but also a deterrent to learning Hebrew. One interviewee, Sofia Y., 48, said that upon arrival in Israel she quickly learned that her attempts to get what she needed in governmental offices and public places were much more successful when she spoke fluent English than broken Hebrew. She even used this strategy with the Russian-speaking officials, taking advantage of the prestige of English in Israel. Another informant claimed that she had lost motivation to improve her Hebrew, as she saw it as a threat to her proficiency in English. The subjects who opted for English admit that even today, a decade after immigration, their Hebrew remains weak, yet they can easily get by speaking Russian and English. They consider their proficiency in English a factor that secured their professional success in Israel. This is consistent with conclusions made by Kheimets and Epstein (2001b), who investigated patterns of integration of scientists from the FSU. Gershenson (2003) shows that this pattern is also characteristic

The announcement of a concert of the popular Soviet and Russian satirist Mikhail Zhvanetskii infuriated at least one passerby. Someone wrote across the poster in Hebrew: "Who is this man? What is written here? Are we in Vladivostok or what? Russians, go learn Hebrew!"

of artists. She analyzes the linguistic choices made by the popular drama theater Gesher, which was created by FSU immigrants. While the theater switched from Russian to Hebrew in order to win popularity among the Israeli public, its founder and director, Evgenii Arye, uses Russian to communicate with the actors and English for public relations.

Yet most of the interviewees reported learning Hebrew before emigration. Their stories bring up several issues. The first is the surprise and pessimism that arose when people were confronted with the task of learning to read the Hebrew alphabet.

Some informants compared it to hieroglyphs and opposed it to Latin, not Cyrillic. Both are markers of the culture of the other, but Latin seems more familiar and accessible. In Russian, as well as in Hebrew, the noun *hieroglyph* is not only associated with the Orient but also has the figurative meaning of "illegible, difficult to understand" and is pejorative. Naiditch (1998) observes that "the meaning 'odd,' 'wrong' is present in the Russian expressions *ne po-russki* (not in Russian) and *po-evreiski* (in Jewish, in Jewish manner) (292). Sofia Y., 48, compared her first attempts at writing Hebrew letters to "drawing ears," an association with the graphic features of the Hebrew letters *bet, kaf,* and *pei.* Another informant, Laura M., 55, told us that the Hebrew alphabet had adorned the kitchen of her apartment before immigration.

Laura M., 55

> I hung them [*Hebrew letters*] in the kitchen, where I used to spend most of my time, right in front of my eyes. And in those two years, I didn't learn a single character; that is, I felt it was impossible, simply impossible.

Another theme emerging from the interviews is that Hebrew-teaching was a thriving private business. Note that before perestroika teaching Hebrew was illegal, and some teachers were jailed (Kheimets and Epstein 2001a; Ulanovskii 1982). One interviewee told us about her relative, who fell victim to this policy.

Yulia Kh., 53

> I remember grandmother's brother. . . . Once he was just going along the street, and they took him. [*The use of the verb* take *instead of* arrest *was a traditional Soviet euphemism.*] And until now . . . he just vanished in thin air, we don't even know where his grave is. Because he taught children the Hebrew language. And my grandfather also taught. After he [*grandmother's brother*] disappeared, grandma forbade grandpa to go out, "You'd better stay at home. What shall I do if they arrest you? Shall I have to let in tenants, or what?" And she didn't let him out for a long, long time. For a very long time grandpa didn't go out at all, granny told us all about it.

Because the system of Jewish education was destroyed, there were virtually no professional teachers of Hebrew in the USSR when immigration to Israel resumed in the late 1980s. A few of our interviewees were lucky to have had Israeli teachers, employees of the Jewish Agency, as their language instructors, but the majority reported that their teachers were nonprofessionals. One such teacher, a retired Russian diplomat named Vassilii Ivanovich, had picked up some Hebrew when posted in Israel in the early 1950s. Mentioning his name, our informant laughed heartily. It is a typical Russian name, and the expectation at the time was that only Jews would teach Hebrew. So whenever the teacher was not Jewish, our informants emphasized it in their stories. In addition, the name reminds any former Soviet of the legendary revolutionary figure Vassilii Ivanovich Chapaev, which increases the comic effect (see chapter 7). Another Hebrew teacher was a student of the humanities in the town of Angarsk, Siberia. This young enthusiast of Hebrew decided to learn it for her own self-education. Every three months she would go to Novosibirsk for a crash course run by the Jewish Agency, and then return to her hometown to teach others what she herself had just learned. Some enterprising immigrants having no professional background in pedagogy were convinced that teaching was the best way to activate their fragile Hebrew. Demand proved so high that they did not suffer any shortage of students. Some of the amateur Hebrew teachers were as eager to teach a language as to expose their students to some elements of Jewish culture and history. Their classes were highly praised in the interviews. Stories about Israel, as well as songs and tales in Hebrew, helped the students cope with the feeling of insecurity caused by pre-emigration ignorance about the country. Israel was a real terra incognita, so any information about it, provided by a friendly source instead of hostile Soviet propaganda, was welcome. In addition, language classes integrating facts about the culture were a far cry from traditional foreign-language learning in the FSU, which was often restricted to mere translation of texts with no communication.

Assessment of the first attempts at learning Hebrew varied widely. While some believe that they had learned basic grammar and had accumulated sufficient vocabulary to communicate in the first stage of immigration, others complained that in Israel they had to begin from scratch. Memories of the first months in

Israel, when immigrants had no means of communication with members of the receiving society, still haunted our subjects and were rendered in a highly emotional manner.

Ludmila Z., 44

> It was not a year of Hebrew, but a year of a deaf and mute person. Well, during my second year here I already understood something, but I couldn't communicate, I couldn't speak. I spoke with my hands and legs.

The theme of deafness and muteness in this context is based on Russian verbal imagery. The word *nemets* (Russian for "German") originally meant "alien" and was derived from *nemoi* (Russian for "mute") (Fasmer 1973, 3:62). Inability to express oneself was perceived as a social handicap and emphasized dependency on others.

Discussing language and ethnicity, Fishman (1977) refers to language as the quintessential symbol of ethnicity, the recorder of paternity, the expresser of patrimony, and the carrier of phenomenology (25). Many subjects spoke about the role of Hebrew and Yiddish for Jews. Hebrew emerged as the unsuccessful competitor of Yiddish as a vehicle for tradition and culture and as a primary indicator of Jewish identity.

Tamara Z., 51

TAMARA: I think Jewishness has to unite all the Jews. Culture and all of it, it has to be unified. And I think that if someone is Jewish, he should know Yiddish. And if he doesn't, he is not a Jew.

INTERVIEWER: Do your children know Yiddish?

TAMARA: They don't. My children don't know Yiddish.

Like Tamara, many immigrants admit that they failed to transfer their knowledge of Yiddish to the children, but this has not decreased the symbolic value of the language. Our younger informants—for example, Sofia Sh., 31, and Inna F., 26—said that their in-laws considered their inability to speak or understand Yiddish a sign that they were not "ours." Moisei V., 74, is equally sure that the knowledge of Yiddish is an indispensable part of being Jewish. While talking critically and patronizingly about Jews from Morocco, he singled out his one "Moroccan" acquaintance who could speak Yiddish. When the interviewer, aware that Moroccan Jews were more likely to be proficient in Judaeo-Arabic or French, expressed surprise, Moisei said, "Yes, he spoke Yiddish. After all, he is Jewish." Anderson (1991) cautions, "It is always a mistake to treat languages in the way that certain nationalist ideologues treat them—as *emblems* of nation-ness, like flags, costumes, folk dances, and the rest" (133). Our sample shows that people perpetuate this prejudice. In everyday talk, Yiddish, and less frequently Hebrew, is referred to as the "Jewish language." The symbolic role of the "Jewish language" is manifest when Yiddish is referred to as "such a cultured language" (Ella, 70+) or as a language not suited to expressing malice (see Yelenevskaya and Fialkova 2003b, 41).

The frequently expressed opinion that Yiddish is a more suitable language for Jews than Hebrew is partially rooted in the imperial approach to minority languages nurtured in the USSR.

Inna Kh., 52

> I was lost in Hebrew . . . because the more I progressed the harder it became. . . . And I would say, "Dear, why couldn't they communicate with God [*in Hebrew*] as it was ordained and make Yiddish the language of the European Jews?" And everything would be wonderful. After all, Russian became the language of all the peoples of the USSR. So why couldn't they do the same with Yiddish? After all it's easier to learn.

Even those who don't speak Yiddish have sentimental memories of it, evoking events of childhood, festivities, and songs. Our interviewees gave examples of words inserted into Russian to express emotions. Inna Kh., for example, recalls that her grandmother used to scold her in Yiddish, and her mother taught her Byelorussian husband how to say "I love you" in Yiddish.

Many speak about the secret function of the language and agree that it motivated children to learn it in order to understand what adults were trying to conceal. Yiddish is not the only language mentioned in the sample as a secret means of communication. Tat has the same function for Jews of the Caucasus. Elvira

A., 20, from Dagestan, was taught the language by her mother to enable the girl to use it as a code inaccessible to outer groups.[3] After immigration the need for a secret language didn't disappear, but the privilege of using it passed to the younger generation. Parents report that their children speak Hebrew among themselves when they do not want adults to understand. In peer groups, however, Russian serves as the language of exclusion of the Hebrew-speaking children (Niznik 2003). Thus both native and second languages are used by our informants as a secret code, and the ability to use language in this function is perceived as an advantage over others.

Some of our older interviewees recounted that, desperate for a means of communication with veteran Israelis, they had to "recall" Yiddish, which they hadn't spoken since childhood. Albert R. said, "I didn't speak Yiddish for a whole fifty-year period. Can you imagine that? And all of a sudden they began to speak and I recalled everything." The language that had been neglected turned into a savior.

Asia Sh., 56

> [*About the first friendship with veteran Israelis*] They turned out to be from Rumania. . . . They don't speak Russian, and I don't speak Rumanian. How can we communicate? And Yiddish, it was a true magic wand. . . . I had never spoken Yiddish, never, but the situation was really extreme.

While stories of revived Yiddish are numerous, none of our interviewees had had knowledge of or exposure to Hebrew before preparations for emigration began. Only six subjects (Inna Kh., Anastasia N., Ekaterina S., Yulia Kh., Shimon K., and Laura A.) mentioned that their parents or grandparents had studied Hebrew and had some Jewish education. But even in these families Hebrew was used only in the form of occasional code-mixing. Furthermore, because the use of Yiddish was sporadic, nobody reported recognizing familiar words from Yiddish in the process of learning Hebrew. Yet one of our subjects, Grigorii G., 30, reflecting on his success in learning Hebrew, reported, "I heard a proverb: Jews don't learn Hebrew but recall it." Grigorii regularly reads Hebrew-language papers and watches Israeli TV channels. He often quotes clichés that are part of the Israeli popular discourse, and this "proverb" might be one of them. It may be derived from a folkloric custom of Shalom Zakhar (peace to the male child). On the Friday night following the birth of a son, Ashkenazi Jews gather to eat lentils as a sign of mourning. It was believed that while in the womb, the child was taught the entire Torah, but as he entered the world, an angel struck him on the lips and he had forgotten everything (Wigoder 1989, 681). The possible source of this custom is the Babylonian Talmud (Niddah30b).[4] In spite of the popular wisdom, those of our informants who have some recollections of a "Jewish" language recall Yiddish or Tat, but not Hebrew. Nevertheless, Hebrew also emerges in the interviews as a symbol of what Anderson (1991) refers to as an imagined community.

Maria P., 24

> [*About the decision to emigrate*] It all started when my mother's sister began learning Hebrew. . . . My mother's sister announced, kind of casually, that she was learning our native ancient Jewish language. And at first we couldn't even understand what language she meant, because everyone knows what Yiddish is all about. But what is Hebrew? This was unclear. It was in 1988. These things were still so rare then; that is, there were no announcements about the Jewish Easter then; that is, everything was still underground.

First of all note the oxymoron—Jewish Easter, the usual reference by Russian speakers to Passover. But more important for us here is the belief that one's native language is the language of one's ethnic group. This belief is expressed in the interview of an ethnic Armenian who claims that Armenian is her mother tongue, although she was seven before she began to learn to speak it and still cannot read or write it. We hear the same motif in the stories of Jews from the Caucasus. Some of them can barely speak the Tat language, or understand only oral speech, yet they invariably refer to it as "our language." The lack of correlation between high and low proficiency in a language and its perception as one's mother tongue is a known phenomenon (Fishman 1972, 104–5; Edwards 1985, 110–13).

Linguistic naïveté is found not only among laypersons but also crops up in the work of government offices. The ex-husband of one of our subjects is a Russian speaker although he was adopted as a child by an Azeri and a Ukrainian. He registered as Ukrainian in Israel. This is how the interviewee describes her divorce procedure.

Ekaterina N., 46

> Someone advised him he should say that he is Muslim. . . . And after he claimed he was a Muslim—nobody looked into his passport there [*in court*]—everything was translated into Arabic. I was amused. I say, "What's the use of translating for him into Arabic?" . . . If at all, translate into Turkish! And then they said to me that there are only two languages in Israel, Arabic and Hebrew. And if he is a Muslim, then, yes. But in fact, while he speaks at least a little bit of Hebrew, he doesn't know Arabic at all. Only those words that are a little bit like Turkish. But then, I also know them. Yes, that's how it was. That's how it is here.

Ekaterina's husband's attitude toward ethnicity was purely pragmatic. First, he chose his mother's ethnicity to distance himself from his Azeri father and thus avoid the entry "Muslim" on his identity card. Then, to win time in court he presented himself as Muslim, hoping that it would slow down the divorce procedure. This incident shows again that the notions of ethnicity, nationality, and religion are often confused and used interchangeably. Moreover, belonging to a nationality sometimes presupposes command of the titular language.

An interesting episode illustrating both ideological and instrumental approaches to the notion of the mother tongue is described by Ulanovskii (1982). When in 1977 he was summoned to the KGB to testify against his friend, Anatoly (Nathan) Shcharansky, he demanded that an interpreter from Russian to Hebrew be provided. He claimed that Hebrew was his mother tongue, although he had learned it as an adult. In this way he tried to avoid the deliberate distortion of his answers by the KGB (258–59).

Our material confirms findings of the Russian sociolinguists concerning the actual use of the language and claims made by speakers in multilingual communities about their mother tongue. Whatever the de facto situation, these claims depend on the social and ideological situation and can change over time. The salience of this phenomenon increases in situations of social transitions, be it immigration or disintegration of a multinational state. Grigorian (1996) reports that in 1989–90, bilingual respondents tended to say that their native language was Russian. Since the disintegration of the USSR, the majority have claimed that their mother tongue is the language of their nationality. Thus in Kazan' in 1996 all the Tartars among the four hundred respondents claimed their mother tongue was Tartar, although 35 percent were not proficient in it and didn't use it in communication (44–45).

The issue of "mother tongue" is ideological. In Israel, for example, teaching Hebrew as the mother tongue has always been closely related to the passing on of the national ideology and values and the formation of a national identity, whether to native-born Israelis or to new immigrants. This has affected language-teaching strategies, although today the wisdom of this approach is being reappraised (Spolsky and Shohamy 1999, 65–94). Surprisingly, linguists are not immune to the confusion between the mother tongue and the language of ethnicity. In her studies of the Russian language abroad, Zemskaia (2001), an influential Russian scholar, limits her investigation to ethnic Russians and excludes ethnic Germans or Jews even if their first and home language is Russian (44).

The prestige and functionality of language vary from one speech network to another within the same speech community (Fishman 1972, 98). Every immigrant settling down in a new country consciously or subconsciously chooses one of two strategies in verbal behavior: convergence, a speaker's desire for social integration, or divergence, a speaker's desire to promote social distance (McCann and Higgins 1990; Heinz 2001). Pfandl (1994) introduces a more detailed taxonomy of immigrants' linguistic strategies: assimilative, anti-assimilative, and consciously bilingual behavior. He hypothesizes that the first two strategies, in spite of the seeming polarity of underlying intentions, lead to the same result—a loss of the first language (104, 108). These various linguistic strategies are visible in immigrants' speech and in the writings of émigré authors publishing in Russian (Moskovich 1992, 129).

In our material there are several stories about immigrants' first attempts at convergence with the Hebrew-speaking majority, followed at a later stage by a reverse strategy, divergence. Dana L., a university student, was eager to look and sound like a true Israeli. She changed her first name, took private lessons to get rid of her Russian accent, and adopted a local style in clothes. But when the goal was achieved and people couldn't recognize her as "Russian," she lost interest and drifted back to her Russian-speaking friends. Another student, Rosa Ch., was eager to find Hebrew-speaking friends among her fellow students, but only succeeded in befriending a new immigrant from Brazil whose grandmother was from Russia (see chapter 3). Mature adults also reported that in the beginning they were eager to mix with Israelis. They wanted to understand their new compatriots' way of life and values and enter desirable social circles. In addition, these ties were seen as a means of improving their Hebrew.

Gaiane A., 77

> [*About the integration of the younger generations of her family into Israeli society*] I don't know to what extent they will assimilate. Nadia [*Gaiane's daughter-in-law*] . . . , I remember she comes home and says, "That's it. I understand Hebrew and I don't have to go to their parties any more." . . . "So, now," she implied, "Now I can choose acquaintances according to my taste."

This sounds very calculating, and although other interviewees relating similar experience showed more tact, all these utterances boil down to one thing: After the first period of euphoria, when the receiving society was excited at the mass exodus of the Soviet Jews, and immigrants were moved by the hearty welcome of the old timers, both parties returned to their familiar networks. For immigrants this was also the beginning of separation of the functions of Russian and Hebrew. Hebrew was the language of work and studies, and Russian was the language of home and leisure. Not only the middle-aged and the elderly made this distinction; our young informants showed the same tendency.

Elena A., 21

INTERVIEWER: I understand that you go or you would go to the theater in Russian and that you read Russian literature. So you don't avoid Russian culture, the culture we absorbed there, do you?

ELENA: Sure I don't. And again, certainly, I read books in Russian. It is not that I cannot read a book in Hebrew. It's just that you read fiction to enjoy it; well, if I read a book in Hebrew, I might enjoy it, *aval* [*Hebrew for "but"*] it won't be the same. So I don't have proper understanding of the language yet. No, I don't have the same understanding of the language as I have of Russian, because it is my native language, right? I still read books in Russian. In fact, I prefer to listen to music in Russian. And [*pause*] if I went to the theater, I would choose Russian, that's for sure.

Note that both the student-interviewer and the interviewee raised the favorite topic of the immigrants—Russian culture, of which the language is seen as the core element. The sacral and mythical role of language has been emphasized by various researchers. According to Anderson (1991), "The great classical communities conceived of themselves as cosmically central, through the medium of a sacred language linked to a superterrestrial order of power" (13). Smith (2002) claims that in a secular community, culture inherits the sacrality of religion, and the language retains its role. This is particularly relevant for people who grew up in communist societies. Brudny (1998) maintains that in the absence of a market economy and capital the most important power was symbolic power, and intellectuals were regarded as crucial to the regime because of their role as creators of national symbols and myths (15).

The exaggerated loyalty to the culture and language of the old country may lead to the ghettoization of the community. As we mentioned earlier, this worries Israeli society, and critical voices are heard within the community itself. Shimon K., an eighteen-year-old master's degree student, expresses indignation at "this Russian community" that makes no effort to integrate into Israeli society but has its own associations, hobby groups, and schools. He finds it appalling that people are "deliberately trying to preserve Russian culture here and don't want Israeli culture." But in the same interview Shimon, who is religious, says that although all the members of his family are fluent in Hebrew, they speak Russian at home. He reads fiction in Russian and says

Tickets for Russian drama, ballet, opera, and variety shows are on sale at the booking office called Haifa Seasons. The name is an allusion to the Russian Seasons, performances of the Russian opera and ballet theaters in Paris initiated by S. Diagilev in 1907. Although the quality of shows brought to Israel is not always first-rate, they invariably attract large audiences.

that for him Hebrew is the language of religion. He regrets that his future children are unlikely to speak Russian; he doesn't expect to marry a Russian speaker, as so few of them are religious.

Linguistic Blunders

Aarne and Thompson's classification (1964) of folktale types includes jokes based on language misunderstandings—AT1699. Ben-Amos (1973) singles out a subgenre of immigrants' folklore, dialect stories: "Although in most cases the narrative situation itself is funny, the narrators add comic effect by speaking the new language with the intonation and vocal system of the old language" (124). He observes that such narratives are part of the repertoire of the second generation, who speak the normative language of the receiving society but are exposed to accented speech at home. In Israel, where the variety of immigrants' accents is great, this type of narratives is a favorite of veteran Israelis. Because our informants are first and 1.5 generation immigrants we have no examples of such stories, but humorous reflections about one's own and one's friends' language blunders are frequent in FSU immigrants' discourse. We have included some examples of such stories in this chapter because like other stories quoted in the previous sections they illustrate immigrants' inclination to reflect on language. Unlike the narratives and rhymes cited in chapter 7, many of these stories are self-ironic. All of them are examples of bilingual humor. The comic effect arises from the play with homonyms in the languages in contact, from incorrect use of the foreign language, and from semantic distance of phonetically close lexical units.

Lilia V., 22

> My aunt was going somewhere by taxi, and her Hebrew was still rather poor—she had been in the country for a year then. It was hot so she said, *"Tadlik bevakasha mazgan. Ani isha khama."* [*Hebrew for "Can you switch on the air conditioner? I am a hot woman."*]

In Russian, as well as in English and Hebrew, one meaning of "hot" is sexually excited. The humor of the situation is reinforced by the advanced age of the passenger and by the myth of "Russian" prostitutes flourishing in Israel.

Vitalii B., 79

VITALII: This is what happened to her [*his wife*], it was here, in this apartment, and it was very funny. We had . . . er . . . once, pigeons dirtied the walls. There was a whole flock of birds of passage having a rest here, where this family lives. . . . They came here and flew around throughout a night and dirtied all the walls and windows, everything with, er, ha-ha.

INTERVIEWER: Droppings.

VITALII: Yeah, with red droppings. . . . We thought it was paint, and, er. . . . And above us, you know, there is an architect's office. And so we are leaving the apartment, and we are standing on the stairs, and here is the head of the office. And Natalia thought it was his . . . she thought that they were renovating. Only later we understood that, er. . . . And she begins to ask him. Well, she says that there are pigeons. No, she began to ask, "Do you do renovations?" And he says, "No, we don't renovate apartments." And she is trying hard to explain, "Well you know, we have those pigeons here." But instead of pigeons, she said lice [*Indeed, pigeons in Hebrew is* "yonim" *and lice is* "kinim."]

INTERVIEWER: Oh, no!

VITALII: And he rushed away from her, quickly got to his car, and slammed the door behind him. It was a great scene! [*both laugh*] So now I don't know whether he believes we have no lice or still thinks we do.

Boris P., 50

Well, I called at the bank to cancel a check. I didn't know the word *levatel'* [*Hebrew for "cancel"*]. I say, *"Lizrok otkha"* [*incorrect Hebrew*] [*laughter*]; that is, "throw yourself out."

In fact, Boris makes two mistakes: one is the confusion of the verbs—"cancel" and "throw out"; the second is a mistake typical of Russian speakers: confusion of the pronouns *oto* and *otkha* ("it" and "you").

Sofia Y., 48

In the first weeks of our life in Israel my close friend Masha couldn't walk in town peacefully. She kept wondering how come all those people know her name and address her with a question, *"Ma-a-sha."* The explanation came in the *ulpan* when she learned a simple Hebrew sentence, *"Ma ha-shaa?"* [*Hebrew for "What time is it?"*]

Our ethnographic diary contains an identical narrative that a student told one of the authors about her grandmother.

Leonid L., 50

Well, there is a story with the verb everyone knows, *lehizdaen*. Everyone knows that *lehizdaen* is not only "to arm oneself," "to equip oneself" but has another meaning because *zain* is not

> only a "phallus" but also a "spear," "armor." That is why the verb *lehizdaen* is used in Hebrew only in combination with "patience": "equip yourself with patience". Well, so there is this young lady who worked as a secretary. They called her in the office; she received telephone calls. She believed that to *lehizdaen* can be used in any sense [*apparently he means in any context*], with any object if the preposition *"ba"* is added. And she decided to use it. Somebody calls and wants to leave a message. She says, *"Rak rega, ani ezda'en baiparon."* [*This sentence is ambiguous and can be interpreted as "Just a second, I'll arm myself with a pencil"* or *"Just a second, I'll screw myself with a pencil"*]. And in response she hears, *"Im ein lakh mashehu akher, az tizdaini baiparon.* [*"If you have nothing better, screw yourself with a pencil."*]

Although Russian speakers are pleased to discover parallelism in the imagery of Hebrew and Russian, their ventures in using new idiomatic expressions often end in blunders, some of which become proverbial. When Leonid's interview was over, his wife announced that the story about the secretary was no good for our project because it had already been on the radio; she thought that made it unsuitable for folklorists. Leonid may have been one of many listeners reproducing it in conversations with friends and changing the original wording and details of the plot. This episode proves again that today mass media are among the main channels of folklore dissemination.

Anastasia F., 43

> Once at the market I was dumbfounded when I heard a roaring voice of a seller advertising his goods: *"Grudi, grudi!"* [*Russian for "breasts"*]. He was selling grapes, so I thought that he was either trying to say *"vinograd"* [*Russian for "grapes"*] or the word *"grozdi"* [*Russian for "bunch"*]. I came up to him and said, "Don't shout so loudly *grudi;* it is 'breasts' in Russian." He was startled and then laughed and said, "So I was right. Both are sweet."
>
> Once I fell into a trap set by my Arab students. Politely, they asked me to say in Russian the word *zuby* [*teeth*]. Suspecting mischief, I still pronounced it. The group burst out laughing.

> Of course, they explained to me that in Arabic it is a four-letter word [*to be more precise it is an obscene word for "my penis"*]. Later I learned that Arab students studying in the Soviet Union also amused themselves playing games with this word.

Ludmila Z., 44

> For a short time I worked in a hotel. Once, I finished cleaning all the rooms and saw that I'd lost a key. And I had to tell a Hebrew speaker that I'd lost a key. And I didn't know then the word *lost.* So I went to the Russian girls to ask: "Girls, how shall I say *lost?*" And when they said *yebadetee* [*a homonym of the Russian "fucked"*], I stood looking absolutely blank. And we had a habit of making practical jokes there. So I said, "You must be joking!" And I asked about eight different people before I dared pronounce it. I came up to this guy Meir and said, *"Ani yebadetee mafteah"* [*Hebrew for "I lost a key"*]. And I was waiting for his reaction. I was standing there all tense. And I was silently watching him. Well, he reacted okay, and only then did I understand that they hadn't been making fun of me.

Confusion in these three excerpts stems from the phonetic similarity between words in different languages. Note that the word that Ludmila did not dare pronounce is such a strong taboo that she was convinced it would shock even a speaker of another tongue. The newspaper article "Foul Words," written on the use of Russian obscenities in Israel, describes situations similar to the last two excerpts (Solovei 2003). The author observes that veteran Israelis have learned some of the juiciest curses of the Russian language and widely use them without understanding their meaning (see chapter 3 on *suka bliad'*). Both of us have been confronted by such situations at work. In some cases linguistic naïveté was demonstrated by students and sometimes by colleagues. We both enlightened our interlocutors as to the true meaning of the expressions and the social implications of their use in public. Larisa Fialkova has even lectured on Russian obscene language, its etymology, and gender bias. Russian *mat* (obscene language), is traced to the pagan past, and until recently it functioned as a male code. Its use was contextually regulated, almost ritualized. It could be heard in oral speech, mostly in private conversations, and was popular in graffiti. *Mat* was generously used in various

The restaurant Traktir is a tribute to pre-Soviet Russia. Neither the word itself nor its last letter, mute Ъ, were used in the Soviet period. The drugstore Putin-24 Hours is a tribute to post-Soviet Russia, where president Putin's ratings remain high and stores open around the clock have become part and parcel of urban life.

folklore genres, especially in jokes and *chastushkas.* Only in the last decade has the taboo on using it in public discourse and literature been lifted. Gusejnov (2004) remarks that at the end of the Soviet epoch *mat* invaded the mass media and became a subject of lively discussions in public discourse (145). The perception of *mat* as marginal lexis, however, remains strong (Akhmetova 1997; Iakovenko 2000; Mikhailin 2000; Toporkov 1995). Immigrants' narratives focused on the use of obscene language range from anger to amusement, the latter caused by the destruction of one more taboo and the feeling of superiority imparted by the knowledge of a secret code unavailable to veteran Israelis.

Our aim in this chapter has been to explore the mobilization of language awareness in members of a community brought up as monolinguals and who found themselves in a multilingual society. Our material confirms D. Preston's conclusion (1996) that which details of language nonlinguists are aware of depends more on a variety of sociocultural rather than strictly linguistic facts (72). First it relates to the awareness that language is a status category. In the USSR Russian gave better access to economic resources and power, and the Jewish intelligentsia prided itself on knowing Russian better than many ethnic Russians. The imperial attitude toward speakers of minority languages of the USSR has been transferred to the linguistic situation in Israel, but now Russian, a minority language of Israel, is associated with superior culture to Hebrew, the language of the country's majority.

Like everyone in a bilingual situation, immigrants become aware of the specialization in function and valuation of language (see, e.g., Hymes 1986, 39; Lambert and Taylor 1996). While Russian remains the chosen language of informal communication among adults, Hebrew and/or English are associated with formal settings and public spheres of social interaction. But these borders are not rigid. Hebrew complements Russian in informal communication among the young, and Russian is increasingly used in formal settings—such as business, high-tech industries, and university research groups—consisting of co-ethnics.

Immigrants' narratives demonstrate both instrumental and symbolic approaches to language. While proficiency in Hebrew and English is seen as a vehicle of upward mobility, Russian is assigned symbolic value. All our adult informants perceived it as the language in which they could realize the full potential of their personality, express emotions, and feel at ease. Yiddish and Tat, but not Hebrew, on the other hand, are valued as the heritage languages that link FSU Jews to their historic roots.

Immigrants' memories of the first, "mute" period of life in Israel are charged with emotions. Predominantly monolingual, often unfamiliar with foreign travel, and hence unexposed to cultures outside the Soviet Union, FSU immigrants experienced the loss of ability to understand and be understood as a major component of the culture shock. The level of frustration was particularly high among the intelligentsia. As Hodge and Kress (1979) remark, the socially powerful do not like to be ignorant, and the intellectually powerful do not like to be impotent (100). The loss of the capacity to communicate was regarded by the immigrant intellectuals as a barrier to using their knowledge, intellect, and professional abilities and therefore was seen as an obstacle to attaining a desirable social status. The biographical method proved useful in tracing the evolution of language attitudes among the FSU immigrants. Previously taken for granted, the mother tongue acquired a symbolic value. Forgotten or neglected Yiddish came to be associated with the lost ancestry. Idealization of Hebrew, typical of the initial period of immigration, gave way to its perception as the language of survival. The complex interplay of the symbolic and instrumental approaches is clearly evident.

7

The New Life of Russian and Soviet Folklore in Israel

As stated in the introduction to this book, the interviews we conducted incorporate elements of traditional and contemporary folklore. According to our observations, jokes, proverbs, and jocular rhymes are among the most frequent genres of the immigrants' folklore. This is not accidental; these were also the most popular genres of Soviet urban folklore. We also came across *bylichkas* (demonic legends) and stories about fortune-telling.

Folklore is inseparably connected to worldview. Just as immigrants' self-identification changes under the influence of their new environment, so does their worldview. The Israeli anthropologist Zilberg (1995) introduced the term *contact zone* to describe the humor of FSU immigrants in Israel (9). We believe this concept can be applied to the folklore of the immigrant community as a whole. It is based on the following sources: Russian-Jewish folklore, traditional Russian folklore, and Soviet urban folklore. These three components are measured against immigrants' experiences and observations of Israeli life and are synthesized in the new texts and performances. Mobilization of the traditional folklore of the old country is a familiar phenomenon in immigrants' cultural practices. Because the *shtetl* and its culture were destroyed in the territory of the Soviet Union in the 1930s and 1940s and the Soviet Jews became urbanized, there are no instances of *shtetl* folklore and only few examples of Russian peasant folklore in our sample. As noted in the preceding chapters, Soviet Jews felt an affinity with Russian and Soviet culture, including its traditional forms, so naturally this serves as the point of departure for folklore innovations.

Part of the material in this chapter has been published in Yelenevskaya and Fialkova 2003a.

Returning to immigrants' favorite folklore genres, we shall focus on the role of humor. The top of the list is unequivocally occupied by the *anekdot.* It is important to give a precise definition of this term because, as Ben-Amos (1969) observes, folklorists attempted to construct logical concepts that would have potential cross-cultural applications and to design tools that would serve as the basis for scholarly discourse, providing it with defined terms of reference and analysis. In the process, however, traditional genres were transformed from cultural categories of communication to scientific concepts, without regard for cultural expression and perception (275). The semantic fields of the Russian words *anekdot* and *shutka* do not correspond to the English *anecdote* and *joke.* Jason (1975), who compiled a dictionary of multilingual terminology in ethnopoetics, does not treat the Russian *anekdot* as an autonomous term but only in the combination "*anekdot o znamenitykh liudiakh*" (a short story from the life of a known person), which is consistent with the English *anecdote* (57). She defines *shutka* as a "non-narrative genre, in prose or in verse which is based on a punch line" (55). In Russian encyclopedias of literature *shutka* does not appear as a separate entry and does not have the status of a literary or folklore genre. In dictionaries of the Russian language it is defined as an amusing and witty trick or witticism and a short comic play (Ievgenieva 1984, 4:737; Ozhegov 1983, 801). Contrary to *anekdot, shutka* is proprietary, and the narrator and the author is usually the same person (Levinson 1999, 376). As compared with a narrator of a shutka, a person telling an anekdot never claims authorship. Shmeleva and Shmelev (2002) emphasize that even when narrators tell their own anekdoty, they usually conceal their rights to the text (21). In encyclopedias of literature, *anekdot* is defined as a short (often unpublished) story about an insignificant but characteristic event in the life of a historic figure and as a short jocular oral story with an unexpected and witty end (Surkov 1962, 1:232; Kozhevnikov and Nikolaev 1987, 28) and as "a narrative or micro-drama, which exists in many narrative versions, whose invariant sense and stylistic features remain stable in different social contexts" (Levinson 1999, 377; see also Belousov 2003, 581). Hence, the first meaning of the term *anekdot* coincides with that mentioned by Jason. The second, which is more important in contemporary usage, overlaps with her definition of *shutka,* but only partially.

Surkov, Kozhevnikov, and Nikolaev emphasize the narrative nature of anekdot. The latter two authors also point out that it is the "primary genre of contemporary, particularly urban folklore." Many anekdoty combine the features listed in all the compared definitions. There are numerous selections of short, humorous stories about well-known people that end with a punch line. The most famous series are devoted to Lenin, Chapaev, Stalin, Brezhnev, Gorbachev, Eltsin, Putin, as well as Pushkin, Tolstoy, and others (see, e.g., Morozov and Frolova 1999; Shmeleva and Shmelev 2002, 83–95). Attempts to draw precise borders between different types of humorous narratives sometimes lead to confusion. Summing up this terminological discussion, we conclude that the Russian anekdot is an ethnic genre that combines features of a joke and an anecdote.

The role of the joke in modern society is often discussed by folklorists. Although it stimulates laughter, the joke has a serious origin. It concerns general social problems and is therefore to be evaluated as an indicator of culture and social structure. Alterations of this very structure, of the technical world, morals, and political systems immediately appear in the joke (Röhrich 1990, 129). The social significance of jokes is particularly prominent in totalitarian societies, in which open criticism of the political system is ruled out. That is why for decades political jokes were the most important release for the Soviet people's frustrations. For Soviet Jews jokes were even more important, as joke-telling has always been a means for creating and reinforcing group solidarity. "In the absence of any formal organization aimed at representing Jewish interests, oral humor itself took on the functions normally performed by members of the structured community" (Draitser 1994, 246, see also 248–49). The social role of Soviet Jewish humor becomes quite apparent to the reader of sociological and psychological articles and books devoted to the Soviet Jewry: many authors quote popular Soviet jokes to illustrate various postulates. In some cases researchers quote the entire text, but more frequently only the punch line. Here are some examples: "They won't hit your ID, they'll hit your bloody mug" is found in Remennick 1998 (256, see the full text of the joke in chapter 2); "Jewishness is not a luxury but a means of transportation" in Brym 1994 (21), Lebedeva 2001 (158–59), and Ryvkina 1996 (44). Ryvkina also quotes the following joke, "A man applies for a job.

He is asked, 'What's your nationality?' He answers, 'Well, you got it right'" (43). Gitelman (1997) alludes to the joke referring to the Soviet Jews as "invalids of the fifth category" (22). None of these authors thought it necessary to explain the jokes. The psychologist Rotenberg (2000), in contrast, guides his readers in the interpretation of the joke to bridge the cultural gap: "All the Soviet writers fall into two categories, Jews and Russians. The Jews are Konstantin Paustovskii, Korneyi Chuckovskii, Victor Nekrasov, while the Russian writers are Alexandr Chakovskii, Alexander Dymshits, Tsezar' Solodar'. The first group comprises honest writers known for their ethical behavior, while the second consists of ethnic Jews known for their conformism and loyalty to the Soviet authorities. The gist of the joke is, therefore, that they are expelled from the in-group owing to their behavior" (214).[1]

The significance of jokes in oral communication and immigrants' media is partially explained by the stress-moderating role of humor discovered by Freud (1959) and later described by psychologists and folklorists as an adaptive coping mechanism (see, e.g., Fialkova 2001; Lefcourt and Martin 1986; Nevo and Levine 1994; Obrdlik 1941–1942). Humor, according to Zilberg (1995), contributes to the community's attempts to forge a new collective identity and to respond effectively to the challenges of the new social environment (10).

Familiar Faces, New Places

FSU immigrants exported to Israel protagonists of famous Soviet jokes. Among them are the glorified commander of the Russian civil war, Vassilii Ivanovich Chapaev, with his loyal orderly Pet'ka; the founder of the Soviet state, Lenin; and characters from Russian fairy tales and popular movies. They all retain distinctive features of appearance and characteristic patterns of behavior. Analyzing a series of popular Soviet and post-Soviet jokes, Chirkova (1998) observes that many characters are recognizable not only due to specific features and behavioral patterns but because they are "in charge" of the semantic code appropriate to their personality (33). When placed in a different environment these features highlight either the similarity of the two societies and cultures or conversely their complete difference.

"The Reds are in town!" Israeli politicians not only conduct their election campaigns in Russian to win over the Russian-speaking electorate, they rely on symbols familiar to the former Soviets. This poster, plastered on mailboxes, electric poles, and even garbage containers, called on the residents of Haifa to put an end to the fifty-five-year rule of socialists and toss it into the "garbage dump of history."

The IFA collection of the FSU folklore contains twenty-one jokes about Vassilii Ivanovich Chapaev.[2] They circulated in the Soviet Union and are not linked to immigrants' experiences. In all of them, Chapaev, a legendary commander of the Red Army, emerges as Ivan—the fool of the Soviet power. Our ethnographic diary contains two jokes that link Chapaev to Israel.

> Pet'ka [*diminutive of Piotr*] meets Vassilii Ivanovich. "Vassilii Ivanovich, is it true that you've been to Israel?" "Me? In Israel? *Ma pit'om* [*Hebrew for "No way"*], Pet'ka!"

> Vassilii Ivanovich Chapaev enters the town of Ofakim at the head of the Red cavalrymen. He is welcomed by the cheering crowd of Ethiopians. Vassilii Ivanovich asks, "Listen guys, are there Whites in the town?"

A typical feature of the immigrants' jokes is code-mixing. Even when their protagonists are familiar to all former Soviets, only members of the Russian-speaking community can fully enjoy them. The first of the two jokes subtly shows a shift in the general attitude toward Israel in the FSU. It stopped being a one-way destination. And yet, fear of disclosing one's ties to Israel is not yet completely gone. In the joke Vassilii Ivanovich betrays his lie by using the Hebrew phrase, which was among the first to enter the vocabulary of the Russian speakers in Israel. The second joke manipulates the symbolism of color. In traditional Chapaev jokes, the Whites are monarchists fighting against the Red Army. On Israeli soil, however, the opposition changes and acquires a racial motif: as noted in chapter 3, the FSU immigrants' attitude to Ethiopian Jews is patronizing and slightly contemptuous. They are the black others. In addition, this joke shows that immigrants identify various towns in Israel as towns for "whites" and towns for variously colored others.

The IFA contains seventeen jokes about the Russian female fairy-tale character Baba Iaga, who is always represented as an old and ugly creature.[3] Mockery and critique of traditional narrative genres is a salient feature of contemporary folklore (Jones 1985; Preston 1994; Rörich 1990). These authors observe that the most suitable material for these parodies are the best known fairy tales, such as Snow White, Little Red Riding Hood, and Cinderella, because the characters and the plots are easily recognized. Transferred to a new sociohistoric context, fairy-tale jokes mock the ever-present optimism of the traditional narratives and the purity of romantic love. Many of these jokes foreground the implicit eroticism of the original texts. Another characteristic feature of this genre is the interaction of heroes from different fairy tales and children's stories. Jones, for example, quotes a joke in which Snow White meets Pinocchio. In our sample Baba Iaga appears together with Leshii (a wood goblin character from *bylichkas* [demonic legends]), Little Red Riding Hood, Sleeping Beauty, and so on. Only in two of them do the protagonists appear as immigrants to Israel.

Dana L., 23

Baba Iaga runs into Buratino in Israel, and they ask each other, "How are you doing? How is your absorption going on? Have you settled down?" Buratino says, "I am a student at the University of Haifa. And I am the most intelligent of all there." In reply Baba Iaga says, "That's nothing! I study at the Technion [*the Israel Institute of Technology*] and I am the most beautiful of all there." (IFA 22134)

Buratino is the protagonist of Aleksei Tolstoi's tale the *Golden Key* (Tolstoi 1992). Written in 1936, this Russian adaptation of Pinocchio has been a favorite of several generations of Russian-speaking children and was much better known than the original Italian tale. The joke works through the familiar features of the characters: Buratino is a simpleton and an ignoramus, and Baba Iaga is the symbol of ugliness. Placed into the environment of Israeli universities, these images serve to disparage Israeli students and to point to their alleged inferiority to the immigrants. The appearance of this couple in university jokes goes back to Soviet times. The difference is in the place but not in the gender-related stereotypes. Buratino was the most intelligent in the department of literature, known to be overpopulated by female students, and Baba Iaga was the best-looking girl in the department of mathematics, where male students prevailed. More than a year after the interview with Dana, another Russian-speaking student of the University of Haifa told a new version of the Baba Iaga joke that though it changes one of the characters retains the gender-bias associated with the two universities.

"Where can one find Baba Iaga?"
"At the Technion."
"And where can one find Sleeping Beauty?"
"At the University of Haifa." (From the ethnographic diary)

Another character from Tolstoi's tale entered Soviet folklore, and his image was the source of a phraseological unit that has acquired a proverbial function: to work like Father Carlo.

Yeva F., 40

INTERVIEWER: Yeva, do you remember your first contacts with Israelis?

YEVA: I remember them very well. Probably, because we were

> very lucky. Although, to be frank, whoever I talk to . . . each one of us had his own wizard and his own fairy. Even those who always complain, there is such a type, you know. Well, I am an optimist by nature, so when I was given something, I was grateful, when I got nothing . . . but then why did they have to give me anything at all? That is, I arrived here, and while I hadn't done anything worth even a brass farthing for this country, I was given money already at the airport. In that country [*the Soviet Union*] nobody gave me anything, although I worked for that country like Father Carlo, and, and all the generations of my family regularly paid income tax and everything else one had to pay. And how did we live there? And we didn't expect any favors from Nature, yeah [*both laugh*]. And here "Nature" immediately gave us some money. That is, they told us how much we would get. We would get money, but why would we get it, I couldn't really understand that. But thanks a lot for it, my Dear State!

As a true native of Odessa, Yeva generously intersperses her speech with proverbial expressions. In this excerpt she uses three, all of them serving to compare the state's attitudes toward its citizens in the USSR and Israel. Her amazement that the state of Israel supports new immigrants even though they have made no contribution to the country's well-being is rendered with the help of an idiom expressing worthlessness. The Russian equivalent of the English "not worth a brass farthing," *lomanyi grosh* (a broken penny), is even more hyperbolic. By contrast, Yeva's own and her family's contribution to the prosperity of the Soviet Union is conceptualized as constant hard labor that was not adequately rewarded. The allusion to Tolstoi's "to work like Father Carlo" is a metaphor often used in speech. To show that financial help was unexpected, Yeva paraphrases the maxim by the Soviet biologist Ivan Michurin, "We cannot expect favors from Nature, to take from Nature is our goal." By alluding to the maxim, Yeva implies that her experience in the Soviet Union prepared her for struggling hard with the state. It was this expectation that makes her perceive the first months in Israel as a fairy tale and compare Israelis helping new immigrants to wizards and fairies (see this motif in chapter 5).

"The Festival of our Childhood. A fancy-dress ball around the New Year tree with the stars of Russian TV." New Year performances for children is another new tradition established by the immigrants of the 1990s. Parents enjoy encounters with fairy-tale characters as much as little spectators.

The next narrative has two different sources. One informant told it as a joke; the other claimed she had heard it as a true story on TV.

Sofia Y., 48

> A New Year performance for kids at a *matnas* [*Hebrew for "community center"*]. The Snow Maiden announces that Grandfather Frost is coming. The lights go out, and the drums beat. When the stage lights up again, Grandfather Frost is there, with a big bag full of gifts in his hand. The kids are mesmerized by the miracle, and gaze at him in total silence. All of a sudden a child's voice comes from the audience:

> *"Ima, mi ze?" [Hebrew for "Mom, who is it?"]*
>
> *"Ani yodaat? Ulai Mashiah" [How should I know? It might be the Messiah].*

Immigrants from the FSU remain loyal to their pre-immigration customs and cultural habits. Although observation of Jewish holidays has become part of life for many families, including secular ones, familiar holidays celebrated in the old country have not faded into oblivion. Men still give women flowers on March 8—International Women's Day—and veterans of World War II parade their orders and medals on May 9. Although January 1 is an ordinary workday in Israel, people continue to celebrate the New Year. In her study of the evolution of the images of the New Year fir tree and Grandfather Frost, the Russian folklorist Dushechkina (2001) writes that the tradition is relatively new and emerged in Russia in the 1830s and 1840s (253–62). The two major symbols of the festivity can be traced to two different sources: the fir tree came from Germany and Grandfather Frost, originally called Moroz Ivanovich, is an adaptation of the mythological character popular in Russian villages. In Israel, New Year celebrations are associated with the Christian tradition, and FSU immigrants are reproached for celebrating St. Sylvester's Day. Yet, many immigrants heard the name of the saint only in Israel. Some Israelis perceive New Year celebrations as a sign of immigrants' attachment to Christianity, which is frowned upon by the Jewish population of Israel. Israelis still remember stories told by their grandparents about pogroms that often erupted on January 1 in the countries of Eastern Europe as a result of excessive drinking on the eve of the New Year. Notably, in nineteenth-century Russia, New Year celebrations were criticized by old believers, who were against a custom that involved felling trees. They were also opposed by the Russian Orthodox Church on the grounds that the tradition had come from the West and could erode the meaning of the Nativity. In 1935 the Soviet government decreed that the New Year should be a state holiday, and since then it has been celebrated in the USSR and then in the FSU as a completely secular holiday. Among the toys decorating the fir tree were animals, balls, cones, and sweets. There were no toys representing the scenes of Nativity or Adoration of the Magi. The dolls representing Grandfather Frost and the Snow Maiden were placed beneath the tree. Grandfather Frost, though, looks different from Santa Claus. He is an old man wearing a long red, white, or blue coat, a hat, and felt boots. He has a cane in his hand and carries a bag with gifts for children on his back. Grandfather Frost is believed to walk or travel on a sleigh, but he never flies. Contrary to Santa Claus he never punishes children for misbehavior. His most valued features are kindness and generosity. In the 1990s, immigrant families that did not bring their old toys from the FSU had to reconcile themselves to the foreign-looking Santa Clauses available in Christian Arab stores. The case of the Snow Maiden was even more problematic—she had no counterpart on the toy market. So, ingenious children substituted their Barbie dolls, dressed in white, for the Snow Maiden. Only in 2003 did the Snow Maiden, in her traditional Russian costume but made in China, become available in Israel.

In Soviet tradition the fir tree was crowned by a star, although this was not the symbol of Bethlehem but the Red star of the Kremlin. The New Year was one of the few Soviet holidays unburdened by Soviet symbols, and probably for this reason it was particularly loved by the people. Post-revolutionary emigrants "imported" the image of Grandfather Frost as one of their most cherished memories of childhood (Dushechkina 2001, 258). A similar attachment to the New Year tradition can be observed among the immigrants today. They perform all the familiar rituals: during the festive supper on December 31 people bid farewell to the outgoing year and greet the new one. Because there is nothing to replace the "Central Bells" in Israel, former Soviets raise glasses of champagne when the Kremlin's clock tower strikes twelve. Because of the time-zone difference, the ritual is repeated one hour later, at midnight local time. In the absence of a real fir tree a plastic replacement decorated with toys and computerized garlands is an essential attribute of the festivity. Parents are eager to pass the tradition on to their children, and New Year performances featuring Grandfather Frost, the Snow Maiden, and their entourage enjoy box office success.

Israelis often disapprove of the immigrants' attachment to the culture of the old country, taking it as a sign of "ghettoization." The joke about Messiah mocks the cultural gap separating immigrants from the receiving society. For the Israeli mother who

The Snow Maiden—in her traditional Russian costume but made in China and purchased in a store in the Arab neighborhood of Haifa—is leaning on a pot with a cactus, which is not a conifer but is just as biting.

has brought her child to a Russian performance, an exhilarated response to the Russian folklore personage is akin to the reaction to the appearance of the Messiah, whose expected arrival signifies the beginning of the era of justice and redemption.

We have already discussed eclecticism in our informants' beliefs. Some folk practices traced to paganism and traditionally associated with Christmas and Yuletide remained popular in Soviet times and were mistakenly linked to the New Year. To illustrate, we quote two stories from an interview with Maria Sh. conducted by Einat Levenberg, a University of Haifa student, as part of her course project on fortune-telling and kept in the IFA.

Maria Sh., 27

MARIA: When I asked her about fortune-telling, granny used to say that it was very dangerous, and one shouldn't do it. And she told me a story. On their street, that is, in their house, there

Grandfather Frost and Santa Claus share professional secrets.

lived a girl, that is, she was already an old maid. She remained single; everyone thought that she'd never married because she practiced fortune-telling. She had a scar on her face, a red line, you know. It wasn't really a scar, just a red line that wouldn't go away. And this is the story they used to tell. At Christmas, together with her girlfriends, or . . . well, I even don't know for sure, she decided to tell fortunes in front of a mirror. And a mirror, as we know, is a border between our and the other world; that is, it is some sort of a door and an entrance. And if you open it, you can get there. And on the eve of the New Year, and the New Year is that period when spirits go for walks . . . The All Saints' Day falls in that period. It was that day, or Christmas, well, it is all the same, because spirits walk around then too. And so she told fortunes before the mirror, she told fortunes before the mirror . . . with candles, with the mirror, she recited some charms and spells. One has to sit for a very long time and she did. And all of a sudden in the corridor, in the depths of the mirror, at the end of this corridor a devil emerged. She got scared. When something like this happens you have to turn the mirror with its back towards you. But she was so frightened that she didn't think of it. And the devil came closer and hit her in the face with his tail. And this line remained on her face for good. And she even went nuts, she got a bit crazy after that. And she never married.

EINAT: Terrible! And how . . .

MARIA: [*Interrupts*] And my granny's father, you know, he saw his future wife, he also saw her in the mirror. In fact, he was a communist and didn't believe in fortune-telling. He believed nothing, neither that God existed, nor devil. But he also, when he was still a bachelor and once, at the New Year [*party*], they were all telling fortunes, and so they persuaded him. He says, "Okay, why not? Just for fun I can also do it." And strange as it might seem he saw his future wife in the mirror. Yes, that's how it was. And then he really met her. . . . Then he met her and he immediately realized it was her.

Maria is a university student. She is Jewish and in the course of the interview she said she was a believer, but her religious affiliation remained undisclosed. The repertoire of her stories ranges from Christmas fortune-telling through divination using the Torah to transmigration and existence of the evil spirit known in the Jewish folklore as the Dibbuk. Interpreting the rites linked to fortune-telling, she used concepts from Judaism and Christianity although she was aware that fortune-telling is forbidden in both of these religions.

In chapter 2 we quote an informant who explained that her ignorance of Jewish tradition was due to the prohibition by the Communist Party. As follows from Maria's story about her communist grandfather, upholding the Russian peasant tradition was also banned as the manifestation of an idealistic worldview and a deviation from Marxist-Leninist philosophy. Although fortune-telling was discouraged by the Soviet authorities and by the

Church, it was still practiced, and stories about fortune-telling form a popular genre of contemporary Russian adolescent folklore (Toporkov 1998). In traditional and contemporary folklore, fortune-telling, in particular with the help of a mirror, is considered a taboo and often leads to punishment (Maksimov 1994, 271; Toporkov 1998, 22–23). In this respect, Maria's first story is fully compatible with the rules of the genre of demonic legends. In the second story, which is a family memorate, the narrator emphasizes the clash between the actor's skepticism and the confirmation of the effectiveness of fortune-telling. Normally fieldworkers and researchers separate traditions: Jewish, Christian, and pagan. But the carriers of the folk tradition may blend them into a symbolic unity (Moroz 2001, 10).

Stories about fortune-telling were also told by Ekaterina R., 24, although they were not associated with the New Year. They were also structured like family memorates, in which fortune-telling was punished. Raised by a Jewish father and a Russian mother in Muslim surroundings, Ekaterina looks for unity among the three religions. Yet her interest in monotheism does not diminish her belief in pagan images, which are an integral part of Russian demonic legends.

Ekaterina R., 24

EKATERINA: No *domovoi* [*Russian for "house spirit"*] lives . . . A domovoi may come to live in a house being built. He comes and chooses the house himself. On the other hand, a domovoi may be brought to a house by someone. Say there is a cat in the house. This means a domovoi is there. . . . If a cat, an alley cat, comes into a house and walks around insolently, this means that a domovoi is trying to enter the house and show off. Supposing . . . I go to bed, and my domovoi—I understood it was he—he started mischief. He said to me, "I want to sleep together with you!" I say, "What impudence! You'll sleep on the floor under the bed!"

"I'm cold!"

I say, "I don't care whether you're cold or not." I tell him, "Lie down!" I said, "You will sleep under the bed! But you can sit wherever you want."

INTERVIEWER: Do you ever hear his voice?

EKATERINA: No, I cannot hear him, but I feel him; that is, it is all on the subconscious level. Just fancy that! He started ordering me around. I say, "You dare give me orders?!" I say, "You'll have to calm down!" That is now my domovoi sleeps under my bed. And mind you, it is my bedroom that he chose. Nowhere, but under my bunk. And it is exactly like it used to be in Tashkent! But a domovoi doesn't leave the house. One can ask him, "Are you going to join us?" if one moves to another country . . . If one moves to another town, there is a chance . . . If one moves to another apartment, the domovoi sometimes moves too. When a family moves to another town it sometimes happens, though rarely, that the domovoi chooses to stay, but another country . . . So you have to ask him, "Are you leaving together with us?" If you like the domovoi, if he is friendly . . .

INTERVIEWER: Have you asked your domovoi?

EKATERINA: In Tashkent I didn't ask. It so happened that my little brother had brought a cat home. And I knew that with the cat in the house, there would be a domovoi there as well. . . . I don't know whether he left together with us or not. It might be that the domovoi who had lived there arrived here. He kept looking for us [*in Tashkent*] and finally decided to come over here.

A person unfamiliar with the Slavic folk tradition might think that our informant, talking in earnest about her relationship with a house spirit, is psychologically unstable. Yet Ekaterina's "communications" with her domovoi reflect popular beliefs about one of the most popular Russian supernatural beings of ambivalent character. The domovoi can be male or female, kind or evil, and his or her powers can influence the life of the whole family. Sometimes the spirit is depicted as a little man, but he can disguise himself as a cat, dog, calf, snake, or frog. Sometimes the domovoi is represented as a bear with a human head and feet, and even as a sack full of loaves of bread. Ekaterina says she has never seen her domovoi. This is consistent with the belief that the domovoi can be seen only under specific conditions, for example, at midnight when you look into the mirror, or during full moon if you peer through the spikes of a harrow. Ekaterina's reference to her domovoi's wish to sleep in her bed is not accidental: domovois are believed to have sexual intercourse with women, particularly young widows. It is considered extremely important to invite the domovoi to move together with the family to a new house. When left behind, domovois are believed to be sad and tearful. In revenge they can punish the family and cause misfortune. Special rituals and spells are used to welcome the domovoi to the new house (Levkievskaia 1999, 120–24; Maksimov 1994, 28–39). Ekaterina believes her brother's new cat provided a sign that her old domovoi had joined her in a new disguise and is helping her to settle down in the new environment. When the new country is inhabited by old and well-known spirits it looks much friendlier. In our material the domovoi is mentioned by two other informants, Korina Yu., 67, and Dana L., 23.

Personal Experience Jokes

As noted earlier, jokes are the most widespread genre of contemporary Russian folklore. Immigrants' experiences are sometimes sad but often hilarious. Our material comprises many narratives that are structured as jokes. As a rule, they are told by good storytellers that have a rich repertoire of jokes and stories of personal experience. The ways of the old country, its paradoxes and absurdities, remain one of the favorite themes of the immigrants' folklore. Old memories as well as post-emigration experiences in the FSU serve as an inexhaustible source of these stories. The theater director Piotr G., quoted in chapters 2 and 4, returned to Russia and likes to tell stories about his life in Israel and post-Soviet Russia.

Piotr G., 43

> I get royalties there [*in Russia*] as an author, for some . . . one of my plays has been staged there. And so I had to open an account in the Savings Bank . . . and everything was fine, I received the money, I received it. And all of a sudden they noticed that my ID was without registered domicile, because I have no residence permit. And each time I came to get the money, or some . . . Well, they would study my ID for ten minutes or so, and they wouldn't be able to figure out what sort of document it was. Although it's a regular ID, like everybody else's, except for this stamp . . . well, there is also a color photograph, while in theirs it is black and white. . . . And they tell me, "You are

> a foreign citizen." And I say, "Can't you see what it says here: citizenship—Russian. And it says so in Russian."
>
> "Oh, yes, yes, yes. But where is your residence permit?" I say, "I have no residence permit. I live in Israel. And here I have signed a contract and I work." And once—it's funny—but they tried . . . "Very good, so tell us where you live in Israel?"
>
> I say, "You really need to know, don't you? Okay, then." And I say, "My address is Kfar Saba." And again a five minute . . . [*discussion*]. "What? Where? How? And what's the name of the street where you live?" First I wanted to give them the actual address, but then I thought, "What the hell? What difference does it make to them?" And I said, "Lenin Street." And they wrote it down. Although, it is Weizmann Street, but after all, it's all the same. I said, "Lenin Street." And they say, "That's okay now."

As noted in chapter 4, the *propiska* (registered domicile) was one of the cornerstones of life in the Soviet Union. Without it people were unable to get a job, send children to school, use medical services, and the like. This was an effective means of controlling domestic migration. Although the authorities' grip on individuals was loosened after the dissolution of the Soviet Union, the residence permit is still a relevant category in various bureaucratic procedures. Piotr makes fun of the rigidity of the rules and turns the situation into a farce by claiming his Israeli address is Lenin Street (see note 7 in chapter 3 about a Lenin Street in Germany). In the Soviet period, every town and village would have a street, a square, or an avenue named after Lenin. Although in many Russian towns monuments to Lenin were torn down, and his name disappeared from city maps, in people's minds Lenin's cult remains. There is one more detail of interest here. Piotr makes a parallel between Lenin Street and Weizmann Street, thus implying that there is a certain lack of imagination in the street names of Israeli towns and that the cult of the state's "forefathers" is not a specifically Soviet phenomenon.

The next narrator, Nina Z., is a guide. Her profession constantly enriches her repertoire of stories, and each of them is a brilliantly performed sketch. Despite her great experience in speaking in public, as soon as Nina saw the cassette recorder her enthusiasm dissipated. During the interview she was constantly on guard, and she switched the recorder off whenever the conversation touched upon private issues. Asked by the interviewer about the reason for censorship, she explained that partially it was a lingering habit from Soviet times, but partially it had developed in response to what she called "industrial espionage": Nina is on the alert for tourists with recorders who might be competitors stealing the texts of the tours that she developed. All the stories she did allow us to record were evidently part of her standard repertoire. In this chapter we quote two of them relating guides' experiences.

Nina Z., 46

> My first tour, the very first tour that I conducted a year after my arrival in Israel, impressed me tremendously. . . . The driver was a Moroccan, you know the type: with a thick [*gold*] chain, about two fingers thick and very curly hair. When I showed up for the tour, he asked, "Are you from Russia?" I say, "Yes." He says, "Do you know Masha?" I say, "No, I don't." He says, "What d'you mean you don't know her? After all, she is also from Russia." The next day I brought a map of Russia to show him. He looked at it and said it was ridiculous. It's impossible that this whole thing is just one state. I tell him, "You see, that's why I don't know Masha." And this impressed me a lot. . . . Another story is not about me, but about my colleague who recently accompanied a "New Russian" in a luxurious limo. He strained, the New Russian of about twenty-four, twenty-five, he strained all the convolutions of his brain to perceive the sanctity and the beauty of Jerusalem. The culmination of the tour was the ascent to the summit of the Mount of Olives. According to all the three religions, this is the site of the Messiah's advent; and here there is no difference of opinion, everyone is certain of this. And while standing on the top of the mountain, my colleague said to the New Russian, "Can you see the gold dome of the Mosque of Omar? The Muslim world believes that this is the place from where Mohammed ascended to heaven. And next to us is the bell tower of the Russian Orthodox Monastery of the Ascension. This is the place from where Jesus ascended to heaven according to the Christian world." And the young man, whose mind was probably

> not too weak as long as he managed to become a New Russian, strained his brain once more and said, squinting, "Holy shit! This place you have here is a true Baikonur!

In chapter 3, note 4, we quoted a joke about Moroccan Jews. Perceived as Oriental others, they often appear in jokes translated into Russian from Hebrew and those created by the immigrants. As in Nina's narrative these jokes emphasize naïveté, ignorance, and sometimes hostility to the "Russians." The second story features a "New Russian," a hero of numerous post-Soviet jokes circulating in the FSU and in Israel. A New Russian is a nouveau riche, as ignorant and coarse as he is rich. This series emerged as a reaction to the rapid impoverishment of the majority of the population and to the loss of social prestige by the intelligentsia after the dissolution of the Soviet Union. A characteristic detail is the tourist's age: a prototypical New Russian is young. Although Nina has not met the tourist herself she portrays him as undergoing a mental effort to digest the guide's explanations. The last sentence of the narrative sounds like a punch line. To express his surprise and admiration, the tourist likens Jerusalem to Baikonur, the Soviet space-vehicle launching site.

As shown in chapter 3, the feeling of superiority over veteran Israelis is a pervasive motif in the immigrants' discourse. The veterans' alleged ignorance, be it of geography, science, or music, is fertile ground for various humorous narratives. The same phenomenon can be observed in the humor of the Russian-language press (Zilberg 1995, 12–15). What immigrants overlook is that the decline of their social status restricts their communication to people in nonprofessional occupations. Moreover, their main criterion for judgment is familiarity with Russian and European culture, and their own ignorance of Jewish and Israeli culture is seldom considered a deficiency. In many instances, immigrants ridicule their employers or superiors. "In the workplace, where differences in power and authority are part of the fabric of interaction, humor is one useful strategy for getting a negative or critical message across in an ostensibly acceptable form" (Holmes and Marra 2002, 66). Those immigrants whose Hebrew is not fluent are bereft of this opportunity when they communicate with their colleagues. But as compensation, subversive humor is often used in narratives circulating within the immigrant community.

Anastasia Ts., 48

> When my husband found a job they used to have lunch in the open air. So they were sitting in the sun, chewing on their sandwiches, and listening to music—something by Mozart. The *balabait* [*Hebrew, here meaning "employer"*] came up to them and asked, "This is good music! Who is it?" He [*the husband*] says "It's Mozart." And he [*the employer*] says, "*Ole hadash? Kama zman hu ba-aretz?*" [*Hebrew for "A new immigrant? How long has he been in Israel?"*]. (IFA 22123)

Anastasia told us another story (IFA 22124), a different version of the one just quoted. The only modification is that the role of the ignoramus is transferred to a religious teacher, and the cultural symbol she failed to recognize was Albert Einstein. Parallel to the stories about the ignorance of the Israelis are narratives about members of the receiving society suspecting FSU immigrants of being uncivilized and unable to cope with urban conveniences.[4]

Most of the jokes in the immigrants' repertoire are of the kind that involve disparagement; that is, "one party is disparaged or aggressed against by another party (either another character in the joke or the author)" (Suls 1983, 51). Instances of self-irony are less frequent than aggression, and in most cases they appear in humorous narratives about language mistakes (see chapter 6). Here we quote two informants criticizing the in-group. The first quote is a paraphrase of a popular couplet that sums up the informant's appraisal of the in-group's criticism; the second is a joke.

Inna Kh., 52

> [*The interviewee expresses annoyance with unemployed immigrants and pensioners who criticize Israel while using social benefits*] And here they are, sitting for hours in front of the house, abusing everybody and everything. They always know better! For this alone I was ready to kill them, or just out of spite to stand with an Israeli flag and say, "I am for Avoda!" You know, there [*in the USSR*] they used to say, "If the water reservoir has dried up, then the kikes have drunk it up." And here it is, "If no water runs from the taps, it is an intrigue of the Avoda chaps."

"Esli v krane net vody, znachit vypili zhidy" (If the water reservoir has dried up, then the kikes have drunk it up) originally appeared in a song about anti-Semites. Unfortunately, we failed to find the name of the author, although the original, and the couplet in particular, remain tremendously popular. It appears on numerous Russian Internet sites that attribute it alternatively to Vladimir Vysotskii or Yulii Kim, both poets and performers of their own songs. Its paraphrases reflect the changes in the social and political scene in the FSU and in Israel. Kikes, for example, are replaced in later versions by Armenians or Chechen terrorists (www.kvestnik.org/cgi-bin/newssite4/news_look_inside.cgi?newstime=2001/04/20/17_49_09&newslang=12, 7 January 2005). Instead of the Avoda—the ruling political party of the mid-1990s in Israel—there was an appeal to vote for Liberman in 2002 (*Esli v krane net vody, golosuem za Libermana,* If there is no water in the tap, vote for Liberman). This paraphrase not only reflects the growing tendency of the Russian-speaking community in Israel to support right-wing parties but also alludes to Liberman's tough policy of water distribution when he was the minister of infrastructure in Sharon's government (www.israel-forum.org/showthread.php?s=ab79e185387728f972834c148efecd01&threadid=8209 20 December 2002).

Dmitrii K., 38

> A man with a little dog comes to a restaurant. The waiter serves him, but does not leave him in peace. He hangs around, looks hesitant, and finally ventures to come back to the table. "You might think I have always worked here. You might even think it is my profession! Being a waiter!"
>
> "No, I don't think so."
>
> "Don't think that in the Union I worked as a waiter. As a matter of fact I am an engineer. In the Union I used to work as an engineer at a big industrial enterprise."
>
> "Fine with me."
>
> "And look at the workers over there . . . they are not just porters. Each one of them is a candidate of sciences [*Ph.D.*]. They worked in an important lab. And look at this woman."
>
> "No, I don't think they are porters."

"And can you see this woman? The one who is packing up the goods . . . She used to be the manager of a confectionery factory. Don't think that she . . . "

"Look, you see the doggie over here?"

"Why?"

"So let me tell you that it used to be a bull terrier in the Union." (IFA 22148)

The loss of professional status, temporary for some and permanent for others, was one of the most sensitive issues in the immigrants' discourse of the early 1990s. The quoted joke ridicules immigrants who cling to the memories of their glorious past and hints that some of the claims may be exaggerated.

Jokes, as well as proverbs, are often inserted into macrotexts as markers of familiar situations. They operate with concrete rather than abstract statements. Concrete statements are not only a rich source of information; the real world they refer to has a more transparent and specifiable logic than abstractly stated words and ideas. Introduced into macrotexts and used as signs of certain situations, jokes arouse a transparent schema-based logic. It is the translation of a mental hypothetical into an analogous concrete reality (Honeck 1997, 180).

Jocular Rhymes

Our material contains rhymes that belong to two folklore genres: *chastushki* and sadistic verses. The *chastushka* is a traditional folklore genre mostly composed of four lines, but sometimes of two or six. Sung solo or in chorus, it functions as an immediate response to the diverse events of everyday life. Chastushkas are sometimes performed as a spontaneous dialogue between two groups (often females "talking" to males) and are sometimes followed by a dance, accompanied by a *balalaika* or an accordion. They often violate political, social, and sexual taboos, which accounts for their popularity today (Alexander 1975, 389–92; Bokov 1950; Toporkov 1995). Chastushkas circulate orally, although many have been published in books and anthologies of traditional and contemporary folklore. In recent years several collections have appeared on the Internet. Of special interest is the site "History of Russia Reflected in *Chastushkas*" (www.inftech.ru/chast/chaind06.htm, 8 April 2004).

We quote four versions of a chastushka devoted to emigration to Israel that became popular in the 1970s. Two texts were recorded from a former refusenik, the historian Leonid Praisman, who immigrated to Israel in 1985; one was downloaded from the Internet, and one other was told at a party where all the guests were immigrants of the 1990s. Both performers recited these chastushkas but did not sing them. The Internet site, however, enables cybernauts to read them to the accompaniment of a tune played on a balalaika. A traditional tune and a traditional musical instrument become part of a virtual performance. The webmaster, Misha Smirnov, lives in the United States, but the chastushka that we quote was sent from Israel.

Nadoelo mne v Ryazani Tantsevat' s toboi kadril'. Sdelai, Vania, obrezanie, My poedem v Izrail'.	Boring is to dance quadrille, Vania, make decision! We will move to Izrail' After circumcision. (From the ethnographic diary)[5]
Slyshish, Vania dorogoi, Slyshish nozhik tochitsia, Sdelai Vania obrezanie— Strast' v Izrail' khochetsia	Listen, Vania, my sweetheart Can you hear the sound of a knife being sharpened? Come on, Vania, get yourself circumcised, I am dying to go to Israel. (www.barynya.com/misha/, 8 April 2004)
Vsei derevnei my guliaem, Samogonku piem v razliv. Traktorist Semenov Vania Uiezzhaet v Tel-Aviv.	Villagers are drunk and happy, Vodka flows beyond belief. Tractor-driver, Sen'kin Vania Goes soon to Tel-Aviv.
Proschevai moia Malania, Uiezzhaiu za kordon, Potomu chto po mamane Ia ne Tiut'kin, a Gordon.	Farewell Malania, honey Now I will live abroad: Mama's name has come in handy I'm not Tiut'kin but Yakhot. (recited by Leonid Praisman)

These and numerous other versions were composed during the period when Jews were allowed to emigrate, when their role in Soviet society was reversed: the fifth paragraph, which used to close many doors, suddenly became a benefit. The chastushkas mock the desire of non-Jews or Jews who concealed their roots to leave the Soviet Union. To emphasize the non-Jewishness of the candidates for emigration chastushkas use typical Russian names and surnames (Vania, Tiutkin, and Semenov).[6] The choice of lexis imitates vulgarisms of peasant speech, for example, *proshchevai* (farewell), *mamania* (mother), *strast' khochetsia* (I am dying to), and *guliaiem* (in the sense of celebrating). Even placing the would-be emigrants in a village is a violation of the stereotype of the Soviet Jew; so too is the profession of a tractor driver (the stereotypically non-Jewish profession of a miner is discussed in chapter 2; analysis of this aspect of Jewish stereotypes in traditional Polish folklore can be found in Goldberg-Mulkiewicz 1983). Finally, the drinking scene typically points to the "Russianness" of the actors. Circumcision is not a rite signaling conscious conversion to Judaism but a trick aimed at attaining a goal. In the fourth chastushka, Tiut'kin takes his mother's maiden name. It turns out that he is a Halachic Jew, but the chastushka implies that his Jewishness is phony. This rhyme mirrors a joke quoted in chapter 2 in which "Ivanov on his mother's side" is presented as a phony Russian. Holmes and Marra (2002) observe that subversive humor is essentially distancing humor. "The humor and the distancing effect may be simultaneously expressed by the selection of particular linguistic devices, such as the strategic use of the name of the individual who is the focus of the humor, the choice of pronouns which emphasize in-group versus out-group boundaries, or the use of role play to parody the attitudes or behavior of others" (82).

The feeling of insecurity is familiar to all immigrants. In Israel this is made sharper by the fragility of the political situation and the constant preparedness for war. This might account for the increasing popularity of sadistic verses. We found examples of these verses in the interviews and on the Internet. In 2002 a weekly newspaper supplement *Beseder: dlia tekh komu esche smeshno* (Okay: For Those Who Are Still in the Mood for Laughter) launched a competition for the best sadistic verse from readers under the heading "The Black Box."

Sadistic verses that originate in Israel, like their counterparts that became popular in Moscow and Leningrad in the mid-1970s, hyperbolize and caricature fears of life. They deal with the topics that worry immigrants: personal safety and terrorist attacks, financial problems and bank loans, misunderstandings between the secular and the orthodox, and so on. While some of them parody verses well known in the FSU, others introduce subjects, actors, and social phenomena new to the genre. Sadistic verses evolved from an oral genre to a written form: in the 1990s there were numerous publications in the FSU mass media, and the *Anthology of Black Humor* (in this context "black humor" is a synonym of sadistic humor) has already appeared in two editions (Belousov 1998, 551). Like chastushkas, many sadistic verses have migrated to the Internet. Clearly, this new form of dissemination of folklore is becoming more prominent with the spread of electronic technologies. It confirms Ben-Amos's postulate (1971) that "in reality, oral texts cross into the domain of written literature and the plastic and musical arts; conversely, the oral circulation of songs and tales has been affected by print" (14). A sizable collection of sadistic verses can be found on the popular Israeli site www.souz.co.il. Traditionally, the perpetrators in sadistic verses are "kind" mothers, "generous" grandparents, "naive" children, and other characters generally believed to be good. In the selections posted on the Internet we came across Habbadniks, Israeli soldiers, members of the Kach movement, and even Grandfather Frost.

Ded Moroz v meshochek bombu polozhil
I podarok etot mal'chiku vruchil.
Ne pliasat' mal'chonke, pesniu ne zapet'—
Dazhe shapku bol'she ne na chto nadet' . . .

Grandfather Frost filled his bag with a bomb,
Smiling he handed this gift to a boy.
Kiddy-boy never will waltz or hum rap;
Alas, became useless even his cap . . .

V Iaffo gulial inostrannyi turist.
Tikho podkralsia k nemu terrorist.
Vystrel razdalsia, turista ne stalo.
Metko streliaiut soldaty Zahala.

Along the street of Jaffa strolled an overseas tourist
Quietly sneaked up on him a treacherous terrorist.
A gun fired, the tourist drooped
Zahal boys never miss when they shoot.

Israelis are known to be proud of their army, but in the topsy-turvy world of jocular rhymes, the soldiers of the army (Zahal) are presented as being as dangerous to civilians through incompetence as terrorists are through malice. The subject of terrorism often emerges in sadistic verses. Notably, it was the most prominent topic presented in the previously mentioned newspaper competition.

The next verse hints at two problems common for immigrants (*oleh*). One is the jealousy of some old timers toward upwardly mobile immigrants from the FSU. Indeed, some of the immigrants bought cars and apartments even before finding stable jobs, which often annoyed hardworking taxpayers. The other problem, much to their dismay, is the immigrants' realization that the money given to them by the state of Israel, known as *korzina absorbtsii* (absorption basket), was only a loan in case they wanted to re-emigrate. As a result, the Idud Bank, which regulates the movement of immigrants in and out of the country, was perceived as a punitive organization.

Novyi ole priobrel "Pontiak."
Spichku metnuli emu v benzobak.
Bystro vzorvalis' pary ot benzina.
Net, ne vernet on "Idudu" korzinu.

A new *oleh* bought a posh "Pontiac."
Someone threw a match into its tank
Petrol explosion, the fire was red,
No one will pay to Idud his debt.

The success of members of a minority group, even if it is imagined rather than real, can irritate those who compete for resources. The stereotypes of this success may be the same in different places and periods. In our example a new immigrant, the owner of an expensive car, inspires a desire to destroy the symbol of his success. Analyzing ethnic prejudices in the interview material, Adorno quotes a subject who said, "you never see a Negro driving an ordinary car [*several types of which the subject names*] but only a Cadillac or a Packard" (1950, 616). The actors as well as the car makes vary, but the stereotypes remain.

As mentioned in chapter 4, one of the most acute causes of suffering in the early stage of immigration is the absence of a home. Unaccustomed to renting apartments from private persons, former Soviets were ready to take a mortgage (*mashkanta*) and loans, although this meant heavy financial obligations for a long period of time. This was unusual, and therefore frightening. Moreover, to get the money to buy an apartment one needed several guarantors ready to pay off debts in case of the buyer's bankruptcy. Aggression caused by fear and confusion are ridiculed in the following couplet:

Deti v podvale igrali v mashkantu. Zverski zamucheny desiat' garantov.	Kids in the cellar played the game of *mashkanta*. Cruel was the death of the tortured guarantors.

This rhyme was recorded from Dana L. and parodies one of the better known sadistic verses—*Deti v podvale igrali v Gestapo / Zverski zamuchen santekhnik Potapov* (Kids in the cellar played the game of Gestapo / Cruel was the death of the plumber Potapov). The original is easily recognizable because of the minimal lexical innovation. Any topic associated with Nazism is particularly sensitive in both Israel and the FSU. Memories of the Gestapo's atrocities are alive and have been transferred by World War II survivors to the postwar generations. The parallelism of the original and the paraphrase takes this verse to the limits of what either society is prepared to tolerate.

The following two quatrains deride the clash between the secular immigrants, indifferent to Jewish tradition in general and *kashrut* in particular, and the militant religious sector of the country's population.

Mal'chik s kotletoiu kushal tvorog, Zorkii HABADnik ego podstereg, No ne uznaiut neschastnye dedy, Chto malen'kii vnuk ikh pogib za kotletu.	A lamb chop with white cheese a little boy ate, A vigilant HABBADnik caught him in the act. The grief of the boy's parents never would stop If they learned that their offspring had perished for the chop.
Mal'chik s kotletoiu kushal tvorog, Zorkii HABADnik ego podstereg, B——g da pomiluet greshnuiu dushu Tol'ko koshernoe sleduet kushat'.	A lamb chop with white cheese a little boy ate. A vigilant *HABBADnik* caught him in the act. G——d bless the sucker tempted by sin Only *kashrut* can keep you clean.

Zilberg (1995) notes that ridicule of *kashrut* norms is a frequent theme because it challenges the immigrants' perception of Jewishness (16–17). Like many other sadistic verses, these two exploit incongruence. It is difficult to imagine someone choosing the combination of foods described in the verse, and it is equally unrealistic that a violation of *kashrut* would be punished so severely. Note that the last line of the first verse adds a pathetic note reminiscent of the phrases "*pogib za Rodinu, pogib za revolutsiu*" (he died for his fatherland, he died for the revolution) and the like. A traditionally naive or mischievous character, the "little boy" unexpectedly turns into a fighter for principles. The second verse is pseudo-didactic. It presents the death of the little boy as a deserved punishment. Note that following Jewish tradition, the spelling of the word *bog* (God) omits the vowel so as not to pronounce the name in vain.

Even these few examples show that sadistic verses born in Israel have retained the primary features of their Soviet precursors. The world presented in them is inherently dangerous to humans. A new immigrant has replaced the "little boy," but he is also accident prone and a target for malicious individuals. Punishment even for minor offenses is out of proportion, and the cruelty of death is brought to the point of absurdity. The hyperbolization of evil makes it grotesque and unreal, and therefore funny. By making fun of the things that frighten us, we downgrade them and make them less menacing.

As already noted in this chapter, immigrants' humor is often subversive and aggressive. Ben-Amos (1973) undermines the myth that Jewish humor is predominantly self-disparaging: "Rather, invariably the object of ridicule is a group with which the raconteur dissociates himself. Joke telling is a verbal expression which manifests social differentiation. The fact that Jews tell jokes about each other demonstrates not so much self-hatred as perhaps the internal segmentation of their society" (129).

Tsaddik Stories

Few of our informants are familiar with Jewish legends or Holy Scriptures, therefore references to Jewish lore are rare and mostly relate to clandestine observation of the Jewish tradition in the Soviet period. Only one of our informants, Dana L., told us stories about Rabbi Nakhman from Uman'. Her grandmother lives in this Ukrainian town, and Dana used to spend summers there as a child.

Dana L., 23

> They discovered Tsaddik [*here, a "Hassidic rabbi"*] in Ukraine. This was a holy Jew in the town of Uman'. And it [*the grave*] was discovered on the private land of a Ukrainian, I even remember she was an anti-Semite, and I think she even did business collecting money . . . she arranged it as this sort of a site, you know . . . one could sit there, eat and . . . and the Hassids swarmed there, they came in hordes. And before immigration, we thought that if a Tsaddik is so near, it would be a shame not to go and pray there. And so we came there. And there were slips of paper all over the place. And there were prayers written on them in Russian. My uncle took the text and read [*the prayer*] for all the family, although he is not among those who believe. But, probably, it is engraved in us all, and so he read that whole prayer that would help things to work out for us. He read it all, he prayed and we took pictures of ourselves there. And we came to Israel having obtained the Tsaddik's support.

We conducted two interviews with Dana. This story was recorded during the first session. Dana did not know the name of the rabbi then. She told more stories about him two years later, by which time she knew his name. None of these stories sounded like a traditional Jewish legend: one was about an anti-Semite (in Dana's second story it was a woman) who became rich because the rabbi's grave was on her plot of land and about Hassids' attempts to steal the body. The only "miracle" she attributed to the rabbi's help was that after visiting Uman' her father succeeded in smuggling out old magazines. Dana's belief in the supernatural—be it domovoi, shaman, or Tsaddik—is mixed with skepticism and self-irony, which is characteristic of our informants. Rejecting the essence of a religious outlook, they are always ready to do something that they hope will coax Destiny into being good to them.

Conclusion

In recent years folkloristics has been increasingly interested in what Bausinger (1990) calls "folk culture in a world of technology" and Nekludov, "postfolklore" (http://ruthenia.ru/folklore/postfolk.htm, 9 January 2005). Many researchers in the field observe that the notion of folklore is becoming modified and expanded. Contemporary folkloristics is multidisciplinary and cannot avoid explicating folk heritage in seemingly "nonfolklore" contexts of culture and everyday life, ranging from the various routines of urban life to discourses of literature, science, and social and political journalism (Bogdanov 2002, 3–4). This is why we felt that analyses of our interviews with the FSU immigrants would be incomplete without references to mass media, Russian and Soviet literature, and Internet discussion forums. It also accounts for our frequent use of literature in psychology, sociology, social geography, and so on. Postfolklore, according to Nekludov, is polycentric. It reflects social, professional, clan, and even age stratification of society. Our book also demonstrates the fragmentation of postfolklore, as it is devoted to the lore of several groups: former Soviets, Soviet Jews, and new Israelis. These groups overlap, but only partially—not all ex-Soviets have left the FSU, not all the migrants settled down in Israel, and not all the new Israelis from the FSU are Jews.

The process of immigration always involves intercultural contacts, and consequently the differing assumptions of specific cultural groups are challenged in the process of communication. Knowledge of one another's past, habits, and customs can be an asset for society as a whole because it contributes to more effective negotiation of social meanings and, it is hoped, more effective intercultural communication. The qualitative analyses of personal narratives undertaken in this study provide rich data about the culture-related meanings shared by former Soviets in Israel. They can also influence relations between folkloristics and social studies. While so far folkloristics has benefited from sociological methodology, social studies have seldom used the results of folklore research. The situation is gradually changing, and the attention that social scientists pay to personal narratives and jokes might be the first signs of this change. The interdisciplinary interaction should, however, move further from the application of folkloric data in preparing questionnaires to consultations that folklorists could hold with social workers, psychologists, and other professionals responsible for immigrants' integration.

Many excerpts from the interviews quoted in this book show our informants' contradictory attitudes toward various aspects of life in their old and new homelands. Our goal was to trace the roots of these contradictions in the past and present experiences of our subjects. Leaving for Israel, Soviet Jews dreamed of finding a homogeneous society in which they would feel secure and welcome. Unprepared for the multicultural, multilingual, and multiethnic nature of Israel, FSU immigrants were confronted by a paradox: they came to realize that they had been at home among strangers, and they were strangers among their own people. The discovery of a multitude of physical types, languages, and customs destroyed the image of the Jew as it had evolved in the Soviet Union. To be born a Jew does not always imply a common faith, hence it does not function as a unifying element. According to Durham (1989), "ethnicity is both an identity and an instrument; it is at once a statement of cultural membership and a tool or weapon by which members attempt to negotiate improved standing within a social system" (138). This duality is particularly important in societies in which ethnic belonging is exploited by ideologists. As we have attempted to show throughout this book, the same word may denote different, sometimes conflicting notions. Thus the concept of "Jewishness" is subject to manipulation by policymakers, the mass media, and the lay public: when it is applied to potential immigrants it is generously widened; when it is applied to the newcomers it is deliberately narrowed. Ethnicity used as an instrument was a source of Jewish Soviet folklore; later it nourished the folklore of exodus, and finally it contributed to the emergence of the folklore of immigration, in which Russian-speaking Israelis again portray themselves as a distinctive minority.

The Soviet Union was conceived as a state whose primary aim was the creation of an ideal society. Throughout the years when the population suffered from poverty and undernourishment, in the periods of mass purges and wars that took a heavy toll, Soviet ideologists never tired of promising the nation the ultimate victory of justice, equality, and economic prosperity. Soviet ideology proved successful in rearing several generations of optimists convinced that the "bright future" awaiting them or at least their children justified the hardships of the present. This belief and an overwhelming pride in the Soviet motherland gave way to disillusionment, which was manifested in the surge of jokes that derided the defeat of the system. Among the most severe critics of the Soviet system were those who wanted to emigrate. Extreme pessimism associated with the USSR often caused overoptimistic expectations of life away from it. Confronted with the sobering reality of immigration, our informants resorted to two conflicting strategies: demonization of their country of origin or its idealization. Quite often the two merged within the same interview. For most of our informants there is no stable correlation between ethnic self-identification and attitude toward Israel. Identification of the self as a Jew does not guarantee acceptance of Israel. It often happens that expectations of utopian harmony are defeated and work against the affiliation of the self with the Jewry. But whether Jewish or not, satisfied or disappointed with immigration, all the informants came to realize that living in Israel means sharing a common fate. This is a significant step on the road to revelation; the next one might well show that *they* are much more like *us* than we used to think.

In the first decades of the existence of the state, Israel, following the American example, tried to prevent the fragmentation of society into various cultural groups and pursued a melting-pot policy. But the reality in both countries made policymakers realize that success in building a culturally homogeneous society is a Pyrrhic victory. Immigrants of the 1990s were the first group who actively opposed assimilation policies and showed determination to preserve the culture of the old country. Having gone through assimilation in the USSR, Soviet Jews were not ready to repeat the experience in Israel.

FSU immigrants in Israel are deemed a returning diaspora. The idealized view of this group presupposes mobilization of symbolic ties with Jewry. Indeed, many of our interviewees showed curiosity and interest in the history and tradition of the Jewish people, and Israeli way of life becomes an integral part of their personality. For other immigrants this interest subsides when the Jewish way of life stops being a novelty, and they attempt to recreate the familiar world of the old country in their new homeland. Ben-Rafael (2001) emphasizes the role of electronic technologies and transport for the globalization of diasporas: What is now to be derived from the new traits of modern societies is that at the level of the private individual, the basic experience of this kind of diaspora means nothing less than "dual homeness," that is, the fact of having two homelands—the original and the new (346–47).

The question "Who is whose diaspora?" is sometimes difficult to answer, in particular when we discuss returning diasporas and diasporas of states that no longer exist—for example, Yugoslavia and the USSR. Jews, whose dispersion was the source of the notion of diaspora, are considered by Zionists to be Israel's diaspora regardless of where they live, whether they dream of moving to Israel or whether they are attached to their countries of birth. Sheffer (2003), for example, devised a nomenclature of diasporas and placed all Jews in the group of "historical diasporas," which were created as long ago as the Middle Ages. Sheffer's approach was severely criticized by Tishkov (2003), who claimed that the author's nomenclature did not reflect diasporan dynamics and changing group strategies. Tishkov perceives all former Soviet citizens, irrespective of their ethnicity and their current country of domicile, to be members of the Russian (Soviet) diaspora, and he maintains that immigrants themselves accept this concept (166). On the basis of our material we cannot agree with either opponent in this debate and believe that neither of them embraces all current complexities.

The emergence of a Soviet (Russian) diaspora is based on those very cornerstones of culture that have been the focus of our analyses in this book. Soviet components of identity are not behavioral because the society and the state no longer exist; rather they form the symbolic and mythical background of a person's worldview and mentality, manifested in language and idiom.

They are activated in Internet activities, international competitions of ex-Soviets residing in Russia, near- and far-abroad and joint scientific and cultural projects (see Fialkova 2005b; Fialkova and Yelenevskaya 2005; Yelenevskaya 2004, 2005). The vast majority of ex-Soviets try to reproduce a familiar way of life, including traditions of child rearing and education, leisure activities, cuisine, holidays, and so on.

An important factor to be considered in studies devoted to FSU immigrants is Russians' major attitude change toward émigrés. They are no longer perceived as traitors; for the first time since the 1920s they are deemed a valuable asset and a potential lobby for Russia's interests in their new countries of residence. The new Soviet diaspora is in the making, and Russia wishes to be its organizing force.

In the last decade, contact between immigrant enclaves has been steadily increasing. Immigrant newspapers in one country often reprint articles from the Russian-language press in others. NTV International—whose viewers live in Europe, Israel, North America, and Australia—broadcasts various cultural events, bringing together former Soviets living in all corners of the world. TV commercials of telephone companies attract customers by showing Russian speakers who enjoy discounted rates for calls to their relatives and friends in Israel, the United States, Germany, CIS, and other countries. Several dating services run by ex-Soviets boast large databases containing information about Russian speakers residing in different countries who are eager to meet their former compatriots in order to marry those who are "just like you are" (see Weiskopf 2006). Russia sponsors cultural events in immigrant enclaves and posts information about them on the Internet. Finally, numerous grassroots sites created and maintained as community or personal Web pages appear to attract many Russian-speaking immigrants irrespective of their place of residence. Not all ex-Soviets involved in personal and group interaction with former compatriots consciously belong to the Soviet diaspora. Some of them display interest in maintaining links with the old country, although this does not presuppose loyalty to the Russian Federation, and the discourse of return to the fatherland has only a marginal role.[1] Others are more oriented to the successful integration in the host country, which in their view presupposes complete abandonment of the language and culture of the country of origin. The attempt to distance oneself from the past under societal pressure is, however, a sign of insecurity and social instability and does not always lead to seamless integration.

Folklore plays an important part in the development of a diaspora. Common myths evolve and circulate orally, in immigrants' media and in the virtual reality of the Internet, influencing the beliefs and behavior of the dispersed former Soviets. It will depend on the economic situation as well as the flexibility and goodwill of the receiving societies and of Russia whether attraction to the old country will grow into solid diaspora unity like the Armenian or the Chinese, or whether it will disappear in the second and third generations of immigrants.

The material included in this book targets scholars in various fields: Jewish studies, Slavic studies, oral history, cultural anthropology, and above all immigration studies. Discussions emerging after presentation of our papers at conferences of folklorists, linguists, ethnologists, and anthropologists indicate that this study has both theoretical and applied value. Not only academics but also practitioners in the fields of education, career guidance, and social work feel the relevance of the study to their work. Analyses of the elements of Soviet mythology and the antecedents of the beliefs, habits, and idiosyncrasies of the former Soviets that we undertook should be helpful to professionals working with immigrants from the FSU in Israel as well as in other immigrant-receiving societies. To design effective programs facilitating the integration of immigrants into their new homelands it is important for educators, psychologists, and social workers to be familiar with the cultural background of the immigrants mobilized to build effective survival strategies.

APPENDIX: LIST OF THE INTERVIEWEES

Ada G., 49, married + 2, emigrated in 1991 from Lvov, Ukraine, lives in Haifa, an engineer by training, now a housewife (on welfare due to chronic disease), group 1.

Ada L., 53, divorced + 2, emigrated in 1990 from Minsk, Byelorussia, lives in Upper Nazareth, a teacher, now a housewife (on welfare due to sickness), group 1 or 2.

Albert R., 72, married + 1, emigrated in 1991 from Kishinev, lives in Haifa, a street musician, a pensioner, group 1.

Aleksey F., 70+, married, emigrated in 1993 from Moscow, lives in Haifa, a medical doctor (Ph.D., professor), now a pensioner, group 1.

Alexander A., 43, married + 1, emigrated in 1991 from Moscow, lived in Haifa, in 1997 emigrated to the United States, a programmer (Ph.D.), group 4, Russian.

Alexander Z., 27, married + 1, emigrated in 1991 from Moscow, lives in Haifa, a graduate student, group 4, Latvian (?) Recorded by Hanna Shmulian.

Aleksandra L., 82, a widow, emigrated in 1993 from Moscow, lived in Haifa, in 2000 re-emigrated to Russia, a clerk, now a pensioner, group 1.

Aleksandra N., 50, married + 3, emigrated in 1996 from St. Petersburg, lives in Upper Nazareth, a radio engineer by training, takes odd jobs, group 1 (father Mountain Jew, mother Byelorussian Jew).

Alina R., 49, married, emigrated in 1990 from Vitebsk, Byelorussia, lives in Carmiel, a teacher, group 1 or 2. Recorded in Hebrew by Hanny Minheim, student of the Haifa University.

Alla Ambakumian-Aslanyan, 50+, married + 2, emigrated in 1994 from Erevan, Armenia, lives in Haifa, teacher of piano by training, in Israel performs occasionally and is involved in the family business, the restaurant Ararat, group 4.

Alla K., 65+, married, emigrated in 1992 from Moscow, lives in Ashkelon, a medical doctor, a pensioner, group 4.

Anastasia F., 43, divorced + 1, emigrated in 1991 from Kiev, Ukraine, lives in Haifa, a university lecturer (Ph.D.), group 1.

Anastasia L., 50, married, emigrated in 1990 from Leningrad, lives in Beer Sheva, a civil engineer, retrained and works in occupational therapy, group 1.

Anastasia N., 61, married + 1, emigrated in 1990 from Kharkov, Ukraine, lives in Haifa, a biochemist, group 1.

Anastasia Ts., 48, married + 2, emigrated in 1991 from Kiev, Ukraine, lives in Haifa, a bibliographer, now the owner of a Russian bookstore, group 2 (father Russian).

Anatolii M., 33, divorced, emigrated in 1998 from Jankoi, Crimea, librarian by training, lives in Upper Nazareth, handicapped, group 2 (father Ukrainian).

Anatolii P., 26, single, emigrated in 1990 from Leningrad, lives in Haifa, a sound operator, group 3.

Anna K., 28, married + 2, emigrated in 1994 from Chernovtsy, Ukraine (grew up in Moldavia), lives in Haifa, a seamstress, employed as a cleaning woman, group 1.

Anna N., 59, married + 2, emigrated from Tashkent, Uzbekistan, in 1999, lives in Afula, engineer by training, retired, group 2 (father Russian).

Arkadii T., 57, married + 1, emigrated in 1990 from Kharkov, Ukraine, lives in Haifa, a biochemist by training, works as a home attendant, group 1.

Armen Aslanyan, 30+, married + 2, emigrated in 1994 from Erevan, Armenia, lives in Haifa, a performing musician and a teacher of trumpet, group 3.

Asia Sh., 56, married + 1, emigrated in 1990 from Cheliabinsk, lives in Upper Nazareth, a schoolteacher, group 1.

Belka, 22, single, emigrated in 1995 from Makhachkala, Dagestan, lives in Hedera, a student (dentistry), group 1, a Mountain Jew. Recorded by Laura Abramov.

Bella, 79, a widow + 2, emigrated 1991 from Donetsk, Ukraine, lives in Haifa, nurse by training, now a pensioner, group 1.

Boris B., 24, married, emigrated in 1999 from Kiev, Ukraine, lives in Haifa, a medical doctor, was interviewed a month after immigration, later passed professional exams, found a job and separated from his wife, group 2.

Boris N., 59, married + 2, emigrated in 1999 from Tashkent, Uzbekistan, lives in Afula, engineer by training, retired, group 4, Russian.

Boris P., 50, married + 2, emigrated in 1992 from Cheliabinsk, lives in Haifa, an electrical engineer, works as an electrician, group 1.

Carolina A., 31, divorced + 1, emigrated in 1992 from Makhachkala, Dagestan, a Mountain Jew, lives in Haifa, a medical secretary by training, employment unknown, group 1. Recorded by Laura Abramov.

Dana L., 23, emigrated in 1990 from Rostov-on-Don, Russia, lives in Haifa, she used to spend summers in Uman', Ukraine, a student, group 1.

Diana G., 21, single, emigrated in 1993 from Moscow, lives in Haifa, a student, group unknown.

Dmitrii K., 38, married + 1, emigrated in 1995 from Mariupol, Ukraine, lives in Haifa, a teacher and a coach, employed as a guard, group 1.

Dmitrii L., 26, single, emigrated from Samara in 1999, lives in Haifa, a technician, a student of the pre-academic unit, group 1.

Dmitrii N., 53, married + 3, emigrated in 1996 from Sankt-Petersburg, lives in Upper Nazareth, a radio engineer by training, employed as a worker, group 4, Russian.

Ekaterina B., 23, married, emigrated in 1999 from Kiev, lives in Haifa, an economist by training, a housewife, group 4, Ukrainian. Three years after the interview separated from her husband and returned to Kiev with her Israeli-born son.

Ekaterina N., 46, divorced + 1, emigrated in 1990 from Baku, Azerbaijan, lives in Haifa, a civil engineer by training, works as a cleaning woman, group 1.

Ekaterina R., 24, single, emigrated in 1993 from Tashkent, Uzbekistan, lives in Krayot, a nurse by training, employed as a worker, group 3, Christian (mother Russian).

Ekaterina S., 61, a widow, emigrated in 1994, from Kiev, lived in Baku for 25 years, lives in Upper Nazareth, an engineer by training, a pensioner, group 1.

Elena A., 21, single, emigrated in 1995 from Makhachkala, Dagestan, lives in Haifa, a student, group 1 or 2, knows the Tat language (passively). Recorded by Alina Sanina.

Elena N., 26, married, emigrated in 1999 from Tashkent, Uzbekistan, lives in Afula, a chemical engineer, was interviewed a month after immigration, later found a job in her field and divorced, group 2.

Ella, 70+, married + 1, emigrated in 1992 from Baku, Azerbaijan, lives in Haifa, group 1.

Ella N., 53, divorced + 2, one in the Ukraine, emigrated in 1998 from Sevastopol, Ukraine, economist by training, works as a cleaning woman, group 1.

Ella O., 55, divorced, emigrated in 2000 from Belgorod, lives in Haifa, a nurse by training, works as a home attendant, group 1.

Ella V., 69, married + 2, emigrated in 1991 from Kursk, lives in Ashkelon, a teacher by training, in Israel worked as a cleaning woman, now retired, group 1.

Elvira A., 20, single, emigrated in 1996 from Makhachkala, Dagestan, lives in Haifa-Hedera, a student at the University of Haifa, group 1, a Mountain Jew.

Elvira D. 34, married + 3, emigrated in 1994 from Tbilisi, Georgia, lives in Haifa, a railway engineer by training, at the time of the interview worked as a cleaning woman, now has a job according to her profession, group 4, Armenian.

Emma R., 56, married + 2, emigrated in 1990 from Leningrad, lives in Beer Sheva, an oculist by training, works as an optometrist, group 1.

Esfir' Ia., 35, married + 1, emigrated from Moscow in 1989, lives in Haifa, chemist, group 1.

Evdokia Kh., 11, emigrated to Israel in 1998 from Simferopol, Ukraine, lives in Beer Sheva, group 2.

Evgenia, 70, married + 1, emigrated in 1999, from Severoural'sk, Kazakhstan, lives in Haifa, a medical doctor by training, a pensioner, group unknown.

Evgenii G., 30, married, emigrated in 1990 from Vinnitsa, Ukraine, lives in Kyriat Motskin, a technician, group 1. Recorded by Svetlana Berenshtein.

Evgenii L., 66, married (civil marriage), emigrated in 1990 from Kiev, Ukraine, lives in Jerusalem, an architect and a painter (Ph.D.), works as a researcher, group 1.

Gaiane A., 77, a widow + 1, emigrated in 1991 from Tashkent, Uzbekistan, lives in Eilat, a linguist (Ph. D., professor), now a pensioner, group 4, Armenian.

Galit, 70, no family, no information about the date of immigration, emigrated from Kiev, lives in Haifa, an accountant by training, a pensioner, group unknown.

Galit B., 60+ married, emigrated in 1994 from Kiev, Ukraine, lives in Ashkelon, a medical doctor, now a pensioner, group 1.

Grigorii G., 30, single, emigrated in 1991 from Lvov, Ukraine, lives in Haifa, a copy editor (on welfare, handicapped), group 1.

Igor K. 59, married, emigrated in 1990 from Moscow, lives in Haifa, a researcher (Ph.D.), group 1.

Inna F., 26, married + 1, emigrated in 1991 from Kaluga, Russia, lives in Haifa, a bank clerk, group 3.

Inna Kh., 52, a widow + 2, emigrated in 1998 from Simferopol, Ukraine, lives in Beer Sheva, a philologist by training, at the time of the interview was on welfare, now a teacher, group 2.

Inna P., 49, married + 2, emigrated in 1992 from Cheliabinsk, lives in Haifa, an economist by training, works as a cleaning woman, group 4.

Inna R., 49, married + 3, emigrated in 1990 from Leningrad, lives in Haifa, a medical doctor, group 4, Russian.

Inna R., 20+, single, emigrated in 1998 from Alma-Ata, Kazakhstan, lives in Upper Nazareth, a student, group 3. Recorded by Svetlana Berenshtein.

Iosif P., 15, emigrated in 1991 from Kiev, Ukraine, lives in Haifa, group 1.

Irina B., 23, single, emigrated in 1996 from Russia (the town not indicated), lives in Haifa, a student, group 1 or 2. Recorded by Svetlana Berenshtein.

Irina B., 46, married + 2, emigrated in 1995 from Birobidzhan (the Jewish autonomous region of Russia), lives in Upper Nazareth, an economist by training, takes odd jobs, group 1.

Irina B., approximately 70, married, emigrated in 1999 from Kursk, lives in Ashkelon, a medical doctor, now a pensioner, group 1.

Irina G., 18, single, emigrated in 1991 from Lvov, Ukraine, lives in Haifa, a soldier at the time of the interview, group 1.

Irina I., 25, married + 1, emigrated in 1994 from Tbilisi, Georgia, lives in Haifa, a housewife, group 4, Russian, Christian. Recorded by Marina El-Kaiam.

Isaac Sh., 70+, emigrated in mid 1990s from Dnepropetrovsk, Ukraine, lives in Holon, retired (in the USSR taught political economy), group 1.

Isanna L., 65, married + 1, emigrated from Kiev in 1991, lives in Haifa, a medical doctor and a biochemist (Ph.D.), group 1.

Korina Yu., 67, divorced + 1, emigrated from Baku in 1991, lives in Haifa, used to work as a culture officer in sanatoria, retired, group 2 (father an Uzbek). Recorded in 1996.

Laura M., 55, divorced + 1, emigrated in 1990 from Leningrad, lives in Upper Nazareth, forestry officer, group 1.

Leonid B., approximately 70, a widower, emigrated in 1989 from Kursk, Russia, lives in Upper Nazareth, an economist, now a pensioner, group 1.

Leonid B., 36, married + 3, emigrated in 1999 from Ust'-Ilim, Irkutsk region, Russia, lives in Haifa, an electrical engineer, employed as a worker, group 4, Byelorussian.

Leonid Kh., 22, single, emigrated in 1996 from Simferopol, Ukraine, lives in Beer Sheva, a soldier at the time of the interview, group 2.

Leonid L., 43, married + 2, emigrated in 1990 from Friazino, Moscow region, lived in Yoknam, in 2000 re-emigrated to Canada, a programmer, group 1.

Leonid L., 50, married, emigrated in 1990 from Leningrad, lives in Beer Sheva, a medical doctor (Ph.D.), group 1.

Lilia B., 56, married + 2, emigrated in 1998 from Makhachkala, Dagestan, lives in Haifa, a kindergarten teacher by training, does odd jobs, a Mountain Jew, group 1.

Lilia L., 43, married + 2, emigrated in 1990 from Friazino, Moscow region, lived in Yoknam, in 2000 re-emigrated to Canada, a medical doctor, group 1.

Lilia V., 22, single, emigrated in 1995 from Lvov, Ukraine, lives in Haifa, a student, group 2 (father Ukrainian).

Liubov' V., 60, divorced + 1, emigrated in 1993 from Moscow, lives in Upper Nazareth, a textile engineer by training, in Israel took odd jobs, now retired, group 1.

Ludmila L., 16, emigrated in 1990 from Minsk, Byelorussia, lives in Upper Nazareth, group 2.

Ludmila Z., 44, divorced + 2, emigrated in 1991 from Lubertsy, Moscow region, lives in Upper Nazareth, a technician by training, in Israel works as a home attendant, group 4, Russian.

Lydia A., 21, single, emigrated in 1991 from Moscow, lived in Haifa, in 1997 emigrated to the United States, in 1999 returned to Israel but in

2002 got married and re-emigrated to the United States, a computer operator, group 2.

Mania, 70+, a widow, emigrated in 1996 from Ukraine, lives in Haifa, a pensioner, group unknown.

Maria B., 16, emigrated in 1990 from Leningrad, lives in Haifa, a high school student, group 1.

Maria P., 24, single, emigrated in 1991 from Moscow, lives in Haifa, a student, group 1 or 2. Recorded by Hanna Shmulian.

Maria S., 25, single, emigrated in 1991 from Moscow, lives in Haifa, a student, group 1 or 2. Recorded by Hanna Smulian.

Mariula F., 25, married, emigrated in 1992 from Kurgan, Russia, lives in Haifa, at the time of the interview studied for the matriculation certificate, a Mountain Jew, baptized, group 2 (father Gypsy). Recorded by Laura Abramov.

Mikhail N., 64, married +2, emigrated in 1996 from Donetsk, Ukraine, lives in Ashkelon, a mining engineer by training, now a pensioner, group 1.

Mikhail P., 25, single, emigrated in 1990 from Rechitsa, Byelorussia, lives in Haifa, a student, group 1 or 2. Recorded by Alina Sanina.

Moisei V., 74, married + 2, emigrated in 1991 from Kursk, lives in Ashkelon, an engineer by training, in Israel was employed as a worker and a street cleaner, now a pensioner, group 1.

Natalia Sh., 24, married, emigrated in 1993 from Chernovtsy, lives in Haifa, a chemical engineer by training, works as an operator in a private clinic, group 1.

Natalia Z., 61, a widow + 1, emigrated in 1994 from Moscow, lives in Haifa, a biochemist, a researcher (Ph.D.), group 1.

Nina K., 60+, divorced, emigrated in 1991 from Moscow, lives in Upper Nazareth, an English teacher, now a pensioner, group 1.

Nina Z., 46, married + 1, emigrated in 1990 from Kiev, lives in Jerusalem, graduated from the faculty of Library Sciences in Leningrad and finished courses for guides in Kiev and Jerusalem, in Israel, works as a guide, group 1.

Noubar Aslanyan, 58, married, emigrated in 1994 from Erevan, Armenia, lives in Haifa, a composer, Member of Israel Composers' Union, his native language is Armenian, group 2. Recorded in Hebrew by Christine Barzakhian, in Russian by the authors.

Oleg L., 26, single, emigrated in 1991 from Nizhnii Novgorod, lives in Nesher, a student, group 1 or 2. Recorded by Alina Sanina.

Olga G., 72, married, emigrated in 1992 from Zlatoust, Russia, lives in Ashkelon, a translator, now a pensioner, group 1 (she identifies herself as a Polish Jew because she was born in Lvov and lived there before World War II).

Olga Sh., 50+, married + 1, emigrated in 1990 from Leningrad, lives in Upper Nazareth, an entomologist by training, a housewife, group 1.

Olga Z., 50, married + 1, emigrated in 1991 from Moscow, lives in Upper

Nazareth, an editor by training, took odd jobs, currently a housewife, group 1.

Paulina B., 25, single, emigrated from Karaganda, Kazakhstan, in 1994, lives in Kiryat Haim, a student, group 1 or 2. Recorded by Svetlana Berenshtein.

Piotr A., 19, single, emigrated in 1995 from Erevan, Armenia, lives in Haifa, a waiter at McDonald's, group 3, registered as Armenian Christian. Recorded in Hebrew by Christina Barzahian.

Piotr G., 43, divorced, emigrated in 1991 from a big industrial city in the Urals, Russia (the subject asked not to mention the city's name), lived in Kfar Saba, in 1997 he returned to Russia, a theater director, group 1.

Raisa G., 69, single, emigrated in 1994 from Tver, Russia, lives in Haifa, a linguist and a university teacher, now a pensioner, group 1.

Raisa I., 28, married + 2, emigrated in 1995 from Klaipeda, Lithuania, lives in Migdal HaEmek, a kindergarten teacher, group 1 or 2. Recorded by Svetlana Berenshtein.

Rasul O., 24, single, emigrated in 1992 from Makhachkala, Dagestan, lives in Haifa, a student, a Mountain Jew, group 1. Recorded by Laura Abramov.

Rimma G., 69, single, emigrated in 1994 from Tver, Russia, lives in Haifa, a medical doctor, now a pensioner, group 1.

Rosa Ch., 27, single, emigrated in 1995 from Orsha, Byelorussia, lives in Haifa, a teacher, works as an instructor in an orphanage, M.A. student, group 1.

Semion Sh., 50+, married + 2, emigrated in 1989 from Khmelnitsk, Ukraine, lives in Upper Nazareth, an engineer, an invalid, group 1.

Sergei L., 65, married, emigrated in 1990 from Leningrad, lives in Beer Sheva, an electrical engineer, now a pensioner, group 1.

Shimon K., 18, single, emigrated in 1990 from Perm', Russia, lives in Haifa, M.A. student, religious, orthodox, group 1.

Simona K., 23, single, emigrated in 1990 from Lugansk, Ukraine, lives in Acre, M.A. student, works as a waitress, group 1.

Sofia F., 27, married (civil marriage), emigrated in 1990 from Kiev, lives in Haifa, a clerk, group 1.

Sofia Sh., 31, divorced + 2, emigrated in 1993 from Moscow, lives in a kibbutz in the north of Israel, a translator (no academic degree), group 2 (father Russian).

Sofia Sh., 5, emigrated from Moscow in 1993, lives in Haifa, group 1. Recorded by Hanna Shmulian.

Sofia Y., 48, married, emigrated in 1990 from Leningrad, lives in Haifa, a university teacher (Ph.D.), group 2 (father Ukrainian).

Svetlana T., 56, married + 1, emigrated from in 1991 Leningrad, lives in Nazareth, an entomologist by training, on welfare, group 1.

Tamara D., 11, emigrated in 1991 from Kiev, Ukraine, lives in Haifa, group 1.

Tamara Z., 51, married + 2, emigrated in 1991 from Zhitomir, Ukraine, lives in Haifa, an engineer by training, works as a home attendant, group 1.

Tatiana D., 27, married + 1, emigrated in 1991 from Moscow, lives in Haifa, a housewife, group 1. Recorded by Hanna Shmulian.

Tatiana G., 49, married +2, emigrated in 1990 from Rostov, lives in Shenia (?), a teacher, group 1 or 2. Recorded in Hebrew by Hanny Minheim.

Tatiana Zh., 70, divorced + 1 (son in the United States), emigrated in 1994 from Tver', lives in Haifa, a linguist and a university teacher (Ph.D.), a pensioner, works as a home attendant, group 2 (father Russian).

Veronika G., 61, married, emigrated in 1990 from Kursk, lives in Ashkelon, a medical doctor, now a pensioner, group 1.

Victor P., 22, single, emigrated in 1990 from Leningrad, lives in Haifa, a worker and a night student at a computer course for technicians, group 3.

Victoria, 15, an orphan, emigrated in 1993 from Donbass (town unknown), together with her younger sister, lived in two foster families, both religious, now studies in a religious boarding school, though she is not religious, group 1 or 2. Recorded in Hebrew.

Victoria A., 43, married + 1, emigrated in 1991 from Moscow, lived in Haifa, in 1997 emigrated to the United States, a music teacher, group 1.

Vitalii B. 79, married (civil marriage), emigrated from Leningrad in 1992, lives in Haifa, an engineer, now a pensioner, group 1.

Vladimir B., approximately 70, married, emigrated in 1999 from Kursk, Russia, lives in Ashkelon, an engineer, now a pensioner, group 1.

Vladimir Ia., 61, married + 2, emigrated in 1995 from Kremenchug, Ukraine, lives in Haifa, a technician, does various repairs, group 1.

Vladimir K., 73, married, emigrated in 1992 from Moscow, lived in Tashkent, Uzbekistan, during World War II for three years, lives in Ashkelon, mining engineer, now a pensioner, group 1.

Vladislav V., 29, single, emigrated in 1991 from Kursk, lives in Ashkelon, computer technician, group 1.

Yeva F., 40, married + 2, emigrated in 1991 from Odessa, Ukraine, lives in Haifa, university teacher, group 1.

Yeva T., 70+, married emigrated in 1990 from Kharkov, Ukraine, lives in Haifa, a pensioner, group 1.

Yulia Kh., 53, divorced + 1 (a daughter in Canada), emigrated in 1990 from Makhachkala, Dagestan, lives in Haifa, a teacher, works as a cashier, group 1, a Mountain Jew.

Yulia M., 70, emigrated in 1990 from Leningrad, lives in Ashkelon, a pensioner, group 1.

Yulia N., 63, married + 2, emigrated in 1996 from Donetsk, Ukraine, lives in Ashkelon, a chemist by training, now a pensioner, works part-time as a cleaning woman, group 1.

Yulia P., 58, divorced or widowed, emigrated in 1993 from Moscow, lives in Haifa (no information about education), pensioner, group 1. Recorded by Hanna Shmulian.

Yulia P., 27, married + 2, emigrated in 1999 from Kriazh, Crimea, lives in Haifa, a nurse by training, at the time of the interview studied in the *ulpan*, Christian, Russian, group 4. Recorded by Marina El-Kaiam.

Yulia R., 30, married, emigrated in 1996 from Moscow, lives in Krayot, a cultural historian, M.A. student, group 1.

Yulia Sh., 51, married + 2, emigrated in 1989 from Khmelnitsk, Ukraine, lives in Upper Nazareth, an engineer, group 1.

Yulia T., 50, married + 1, emigrated in 1990 from Kharkov, Ukraine, lives in Haifa, an engineer by training, a kitchen worker in a hospital, group 1.

Yurii Kh., 26, married emigrated in 1999 from Tashkent, Uzbekistan, lives in Afula, an electrical engineer, was interviewed a month after immigration, later found a job as a worker and divorced, Russian, group 4.

Zena B., 53, divorced + 3, emigrated in 1994 from Kiev, Ukraine (most of her life in the Soviet Union lived in Gomel, Byelorussia), lives in Haifa, a bibliographer and editor by training (Ph.D.), employed as a manicurist, group 2 (father Polish).

NOTES

Introduction

1. Social scientists writing about immigration and diaspora use a variety of terms to refer to immigrants from the FSU: former Soviets, Russians, Russian-speaking immigrants, Russian-speaking Israelis, Soviet Jews, Russian Jews, Russian Germans, etc. Moreover, Laitin (1999) uses the term *Russian-speaking nationality* to refer to the Russian-speaking diaspora in the FSU countries other than Russia (322–23). Notably, he does not restrict this group to ethnic Russians. So each of these terms points either to the country of origin, the native language of the immigrants, and ethnicity; or to a combination of several attributes. We use the terms *former Soviets* and *Russian-speaking Israelis* interchangeably. We would also like to point out that throughout the book we refer to our subjects as *Soviet Jews*. Although the USSR ceased to exist, the mentality that characterized Soviet citizens proved to be more pervasive than could be expected. Sociological studies of post-Soviet Russia, investigations into post-Soviet mythology, and our own observations have brought us to the conclusion that the use of this term in discussions about the subjects brought up in the USSR is legitimate (see Dubin 2001; Gudkov 2004; Gusejnov 2000, 2004; Kaganskii 2001; Kosmarskaya 2006; Levinson 2004; Yelenevskaya 2004; Yelenevskaya and Fialkova 2004b).

2. See, for example, studies of Soviet Jews in America: Chiswick 2000, Gitelman 1997, Markowitz 1995; ethnic Germans and/or Jews in Germany: Bodemann 2001, Dietz 2000, Khrustaleva 2001a, and Steinbach 2001; Soviet physicians in Israel, Canada, and the United States: Shuval and Bernstein 1997; adolescent repatriates in Finland: Jasinskaja-Lahti and Liebkind 1999; Soviet repatriates in Greece: Keramida 1999, Kaurinkoski 2003; a comparative study of acculturation attitudes and stress among adolescent repatriates from the FSU in Finland, Israel, and Germany: Jasinskaja-Lahti et al. 2003.

3. The adjective *Rossiiskaia* refers to the entire multiethnic state and the multiethnic diaspora of Russia and is wider in meaning than *Russkaia,* which refers only to ethnic Russians.

4. The persuasive power of this slogan in Hebrew is stronger than in English because it is rhymed: "Mi ole le ole—koah shelanu ole!"

5. A similar example of a misconception in folklore research is mentioned by Brunvand (1968), who indicates that the prominent American folklorist Alexander Krappe, trained in the European philological tradition and Eurocentric in his research, claimed that American folklore did not exist (19).

6. An area along the upper stream of the Lena River.

7. Shtyrkov applies the term *secondary folklorization* to the import of notions that the "bookish" culture evolved about specific features of the peasant tradition in the village. We extend this to the phenomenon of importing scientific and popular-science notions to urban folk culture. In both urban and rural cultures this movement is triggered by the spread and influence of mass media.

Chapter 1

1. Israeli anthropologists Lomsky-Feder and Rapoport (2004) questioned the wisdom of using immigrants' mother tongue in interviewing. They argue that this marginalizes immigrants. As an illustration they quoted their own research assistants. These immigrant students who interviewed their peers from the FSU claimed that in some cases immigrants were reluctant to speak Russian, in particular those who became religious, married Israelis, and lesbians. It is worth mentioning that all three assistants had graduated from Israeli universities and may have suffered from language attrition. Our informants, including students, preferred to speak Russian, though almost all of them could opt for Hebrew because all the interviewers in this project speak Hebrew fluently. We agree with Lomsky-Feder and Rapoport that language self-identification of immigrants may evolve differently. It is good when a subject is given a choice as to which language to speak, but it is hardly acceptable that one's own lack of command of the language of the group being studied is used as a theoretical basis of research.

2. We translated excerpts from the interviews without editing them in order to preserve specific features of oral narration and the individual style of each storyteller. We also preserved instances of code switching. Hebrew, Yiddish, and English insertions in the excerpts are italicized.

3. These data (from the Central Bureau of Statistics for 1990–97 and from the Ministry of Immigrant Absorption and the Department of the CIS of the Jewish Agency for 1998–99) are quoted from Al-Haj and Leshem (2000, 8).

4. The fifth line of the Soviet internal passport indicated the bearer's nationality. It came after the family name, the first name, the patronymic, and the date of birth. The *fifth paragraph* has become a phraseological unit (see explanations of its connotations and examples of usage in chapter 2).

5. We don't concentrate on Mountain Jews as a separate group but perceive them as Soviet Jews. All the Mountain Jews in the sample are Russian speakers who share most of the demographic features with other informants. But whenever specific features of the group, for example different myths and traditions, were discussed by the subjects, we always pointed this out. Since we used the "snowball" technique of information gathering, Buchara Jews did not happen to be among our interviewees.

Detailed anthropological analysis of these groups can be found in Bram 2003; Chlenov 2000; Gitelman 1988; Goluboff 2003.

6. Ability to self-disclose does not depend on personality alone but on the culture as well. In the Soviet period, intimate disclosures could have significant political implications. Goodwin et al. (1999) conducted a cross-national study in the countries of Eastern Europe and found that in the post-Communist time the pattern of disclosure remained the same: people were most willing to reveal information about themselves to romantic partners, followed by disclosure to parents and close friends, and were least open with acquaintances (83).

7. Reka is a Russian-language Israeli radio station broadcasting sixteen hours a day.

8. Note that Yulia uses the word *leave* instead of *emigrate.* See the explanation about this substitute in chapter 4.

Chapter 2

1. Naturally, among the multiple identities assumed by our subjects there are those related to gender, profession, family, and so on, but in this chapter we are mostly concerned with ethnic identity.

2. Al-Haj and Leshem (2000) based their survey on face-to-face structured interviews with 707 subjects. The following are reasons for emigration from the FSU as listed by their subjects (the numbers are given in percentages of the total): concern for the children's future, 36.2; no confidence in the future, 31.7; desire to live in a Jewish state, 24.0; low standards of living in the FSU, 19.2; personal reasons, 19.1; anti-Semitism, 17.2; crime and lack of personal security, 10.9; Chernobyl and environmental pollution, 9.1; parents made the decision, 8.6; anticipation of employment in Israel, 6.2; everyone else has done it, 4.4; fear of pogroms and discrimination, 2.1; bad neighbors, 0.5 (11). Ryvkina's sample (1996) was bigger: she conducted 1,000 structured interviews with FSU Jews. In explaining why they wanted to emigrate from the FSU they indicated six main reasons (the numbers are given in percentage): for the sake of the children's future, 52; don't believe in the improvement of the political situation in Russia, 46; afraid of the political instability, 41; wish to improve the standards of living, 36; afraid of anti-Semitism and insults, 29; wish to reunite with the family, 26 (186). Similar distribution of reasons for emigration from the FSU can be found in Brym and Ryvkina 1994, 78–81.

3. Similarly, push factors dominated Jewish immigrants to Germany, and their categories of reasons for leaving the FSU coincide with those named by our subjects (Dietz 2000, 643).

4. One of the reasons for emigration, the Chernobyl catastrophe, is discussed from the sociological perspective in Remennick 2002a and from the folkloric perspective in Fialkova 2001. Stories of the immigrants from the Chernobyl area, as well as stories related to military conflicts

in the Caucasus, indicate that these people felt more like refugees than repatriates. Here is an example from the interview with the Aslanyans:

NOUBAR: In Armenia I have a large collection of disks and scores . . .

INTERVIEWER: You haven't brought . . .

NOUBAR: No. I had two pianos there. How could I? Everything was blocked: brotherly Azerbaijan above and below is Turkey, the enemy. We were besieged. There was no electricity. There was no gas. Electricity was on for just one hour per day.

ARMEN: Half an hour and even 15 minutes, don't you remember this?

NOUBAR: We slept without taking off our overcoats, Larisa, without taking off our coats! I say to our brothers, "Where were you, brother-Jews, where were you? [*overlapping voices, inaudible*] And it wasn't only Jews [*who did not offer help*]. A civilized nation is dying. . . . America, where are you? Now you are rushing to enter Iraq, you want to make order there. . . . America where were you? We were dying! We were really dying there. My leg is still injured; that is, I still, I sleep wearing socks because we got used to sleeping wearing socks. . . . The temperature at home was two degrees, and minus 20 outside.

INTERVIEWER: So did you actually escape from Armenia?

NOUBAR: Yes, it was an escape. I admit that it was an escape.

INTERVIEWER: You arrived in 1994, didn't you?

NOUBAR: The frost that . . . it was a most difficult year. It was in [*pause*] December. . . . It was scary.

ARMEN: It was similar to the siege of Leningrad.

A similar description of deprivation and fear is given by Elvira D., 34, when she describes Tbilisi of the early 1990s. The siege of Leningrad mentioned by the Aslanyans several times is the archetype of civilian suffering for the Soviets and symbolizes starvation, freezing cold, and stubborn resistance of the besieged. Allusion to the Leningrad siege is also found in the interview with Sergei L., 65, who places it in still another context and compares the alarm signals sounded during the Gulf War, with the Leningrad metronome signaling air raids on the radio.

5. There are stories about unfair treatment during entrance examinations and about anti-Semitic student-enrollment policies at universities and colleges. These types of obstacles were considered among the worst manifestations of state anti-Semitism. According to Voronel (1973), "The existence in the Russian empire of a Pale of Settlement and restrictions in the choice of professions, as well as the traditional intellectualism of Russia's Jews, led them to the firm belief that education was a supreme value, for many, it was the supreme value" (26).

6. Vladimir Wol'fovich Zhirinovsky is a Russian politician, a mem-

ber of the State Duma, who is known for his extremist statements and behavior. At the start of his career he owed his popularity to populist promises and xenophobic slogans. In the press and in everyday talk he is often referred to as the "son of a lawyer." This alludes to his statement (allegedly pronounced publicly) that his mother was Russian and his father was a lawyer. The patronymic "Wol'fovich" can be interpreted by Russian speakers as Jewish. In 2006, Wikipedia.com reported that "after many years of denying his Jewish heritage, Zhirinovsky finally acknowledged his father's Jewish identity in 2003. On a private visit to Israel in June 2006, Zhirinovsky paid his first visit to the grave of his father, Wolf Isakovich Eidelshtein, who is buried in the Tel Aviv suburb of Holon."

7. Just as Jewish parents in the USSR didn't discuss issues of ethnicity with their children to avoid traumatizing them, some non-Jewish immigrants follow the same strategy in Israel. But it doesn't mean that they would like their children to assimilate completely, as is the case with Elvira D., 34: "And you know what? It's scary, well, I wonder, my children [*pause*], they will probably be the children of the planet Earth. I think so. Because, er, well, I guess, they will learn to speak Armenian, but who are they? If you look at it from this point of view. . . . Who are they? Are they Israelis? Just Israelis, and that's it? It doesn't really matter what nationality they are."

Elvira referred to the problems of ethnic and religious identity of her three children several times during the interview, and it is clear that she deliberately avoids discussion even when the children themselves broach the subject. She insists that it is for them to decide who they want to belong to when they grow up. On the one hand Elvira claims that "nationality," which for her includes such cultural dimensions as language and tradition, is unimportant; on the other hand, she is afraid that her children will have no affinity with the Armenian culture. Contrary to many other non-Jewish immigrants, ethnic Armenians can join a well-established Armenian community of Israel. Elvira, like another informant, Piotr A., 19, attended several meetings of the Haifa Armenian club but was disappointed by the difference of "dialects and mentality." Apparently the differences were strong enough for the new immigrants from Armenia to form their own society in Haifa. The Aslanyans, active members of the Armenian immigrants' association, do their best to bridge the gap between the two organizations. Recently, ethnic Ukrainians formed the association Ukraintsi Izrailiu (Ukrainians of Israel), and ethnic Russians have founded the organization Russkaia Obshchina v gosudarstve Izrail' (Russian Community in the State of Israel), which popularizes its activities on the Internet site www.homeru.com/ruscom.html.

8. People whose stories and utterances are quoted from our ethnographic diaries are not included in the list of interviewees. We did not record these stories, so we supply only minimal information about their narrators. We have given some of them pseudonyms so that the reader

may trace the stories of the same person.

9. Compare this to the unrecorded story by Sofia Sh., 31. Her friends re-emigrated to Canada, and their Israeli-born children asked their parents: "So we are no longer Jewish, are we?" In the original the narrator emphasized the use of the pejorative *evreitsy* instead of *evrei* (see the explanation about this form in chapter 3).

10. Our informants, Elvira D. and Noubar Aslanyan, mention that some of their acquaintances from Armenia changed their first and/or family names after immigration to look more Jewish. Thus taking a mother's name was practiced in the USSR to avoid Jewish names and is practiced in Israel to claim them.

11. The hypocrisy of the concept of "brotherly nations" is often derided by Russian speakers. See, for example, the ironic allusion to it in the excerpts from the interviews with Inna Kh. and the Aslanyans (note 5).

12. The use of the term *half Muslim* is evidence of the confusion of ethnicity and religion in our sample. A different situation emerges in the self-perception of some Ethiopian Jews, the so-called Falas Mura, who define themselves as both Jews and Christians, or as Jews who have also been baptized as Christians. Many of them observe rituals and commandments of the two religions simultaneously (Kimmerling 2001, 153).

13. *Argumenty i fakty* 2001: No. 42

14. A slightly different version of this joke appears in our ethnographic diary.

> Why were Jews smarter than anyone in the USSR and why are there so many fools in Israel?
> When they are few, Jews are like manure . . . they fertilize soil when they are few. But when they are many they are just a pile of shit.

15. In the Soviet Union, disabled people were divided into three groups depending on the level of disability.

16. In 1949 the Soviet authorities waged a campaign in the press against the Soviet Jewish intelligentsia, which allegedly worshiped bourgeois Western culture and was alien to Soviet ideals. These articles were not overtly anti-Semitic, but people familiar with the Soviet ideologists' codes could easily understand that "rootless cosmopolitans" were Jews. Destructive articles were followed by the firing of many Jews and the arrest of others. In 1952–53 a new campaign was started, this time against prominent Soviet doctors, mostly Jews. They were accused of deliberately prescribing wrong treatment to their patients, Communist Party leaders. As the campaign was gaining momentum, Jews of other professions came to be persecuted too. The witch hunt stopped with Stalin's death and entered history as the "Doctors Trial."

17. Such an absurdity was not accidental in a country where the shortage of consumer goods was familiar to several generations. Dis-

crimination that made some consumer goods available only to privileged groups was derided in the novel by I. Ilf and Ye. Petrov, *The Golden Calf*, written in 1931: "Special placards informed the citizens of Arbatov of the latest novelty in public catering: Beer Available to Trade-Union Members Only" (Ilf and Petrov 1962, 16). The book became a Soviet classic and many of its maxims and expressions have entered modern Russian phraseology. Late in Brezhnev's rule, veterans of World War II got privileged access to some consumer goods, which gave rise to various rumors and jokes about their excesses in exploiting their rights.

18. A study conducted by Nosenko (2004) gives a more specific differentiation. She claims that people specializing in the humanities and the arts are much more interested in learning about the Jewish tradition and their own cultural roots than those who deal with science and technology (214–15).

Chapter 3

1. A similar situation is observed in Finland and Germany, where Finnish and German repatriates from the FSU are also categorized as "Russians" and become vulnerable to all possible prejudices against Russians in general. In contrast to the attitudes toward ethnic repatriation as such, attitudes toward FSU immigrants are in all three countries predominantly negative, at least among the socially and economically deprived segments of the host communities (Jasinskaja-Lahti et al. 2003, 84).

2. The label "provincial" is one of the worst accusations in the eyes of Soviet Jews and is associated with a lack of enlightenment and social drive, hence lack of prestige. Kaganskaia (2005), for example, points out that in the "mental topography" of FSU Jews the division of the world into the capital and the province is one of the most significant dichotomies. This division determines problematic attitudes of the new immigrants to veteran Israelis. Israel is labeled a province par excellence (14). Concerned about what she considers a decline of Israeli science and culture, Isakova (2003c) also tags the country as a province and elaborates on the links between the status of Israel's politics, economy, science, and culture in the world arena and the readiness of Jews in the Diaspora to identify with Jewry: "To be or not to be Jewish [in a democratic state] is a question of choice. The choice in its turn depends on prestige. Wherever it is prestigious to be Jewish, the number of Jews increases. The CIS is a good example of this: in the Soviet period, when Jewishness was an obstacle to better living, the number of Jews dropped systematically. The minute Jewishness came to be a password for moving to the West, or came to signal prestige in the framework of the reconstructed Jewish community organizations, the number of Jews immediately went up" (15).

3. The FSU immigrants' attitude toward Moroccan Jews is reflected

in pejorative nicknames—for example, *morokosy* and *chernozhopye.* The former is a neologism, a paronym of *eskimosy,* Russian for "Eskimo." The alleged stupidity and naivety of the residents of the Soviet extreme north was the source of numerous Soviet jokes ridiculing Eskimos, known as *Chukchi.* The latter nickname, *chernozhopye* (black asses), equally often refers to Moroccan Jews and to orthodox Jews. There are also jokes ridiculing Moroccan Jews. Vladislav V., 29, quotes one: "Here is a short joke for you. They [*Moroccans*] told it about themselves. 'What is in common between a Moroccan and an artichoke?' 'Ninety percent of both is trash.' And that's all" (IFA 22114).

4. The word "communication" is often used in conversational Russian as a synonym of a "friendly relationship."

5. Unlike English, Russian has retained a generic *he.* The generic form of nouns also remains masculine.

6. Alexander Rosenbaum is a frequent guest performer in Israel, while Andrei Makarevich's voice was used in a commercial for Russian speakers by Tnuva, an Israeli dairy company.

7. Similarly, incredulity mixed with pride sounds in the words of the psychologist Khrustaleva, a participant of the roundtable devoted to the new Russian diaspora. She describes a village built by ethnic German migrants from Kazakhstan near Munich. Their houses resemble those in Kazakhstan, and the streets are named after Pavlik Morozov and Lenin. And neighbors still live across from one another. They have transferred their whole way of living to Germany, and they do not mix with the members of the receiving society (Makhovskaia et al. 2001, 30). Perpetuating the memory of Pavlik Morozov is, indeed, worthy of attention. This young pioneer became famous during collectivization in the 1930s. He wanted to denounce his father, a well-to-do farmer, and was murdered by the villagers. Posthumously he was nominated a "pioneer hero" and was mythologized in Soviet children's literature as a model of revolutionary dedication. In recent decades he has become a symbol of treachery, so the German immigrants' loyalty to Lenin and Pavlik Morozov sounds anachronistic and absurd.

8. While parents were free to choose their child's first name, the Jewish family name was difficult to hide. The negative attitude toward Jewish names—ridiculed in jokes quoted in chapter 2—is also illustrated in the following narrative by Simona K., 23, where an adolescent is ashamed of her being different from the peers: "I had no idea of what is a Jew, who is not a Jew, what is it all about until I was twelve. The only thing that interested me . . . I had a friend and her family name was Sidorova, and mine is Khaimovich [*both names are pseudonyms*]. And I simply couldn't understand why . . . I simply didn't like it that Sidorova, Sidorovoi, her name is declinable and Khaimovich isn't. It's Khaimovich and only Khaimovich, and I hated it. This is the only, well, my Jewishness."

9. The stigmatization of ethnic names can take various forms:

they can be derided in jokes and used as pejorative nicknames denoting a whole group. An extreme case is the institutionalization of the discrimination of names. Under the Communists, members of the Turkish minority in Bulgaria could not use Turkish names but were required to use Bulgarian personal and family names (See Agoston-Nikolova 2001, 111; and Levy 2000, 28). In Israel in the 1950s and 1960s new immigrants were urged to hebraize their names.

10. Elena Tolstaia (2000) uses to great effect Russian speakers' amusement with Hebrew names bearing phonetic similarity with Russian words. In a tale devoted to immigrant life she describes the mood of FSU immigrants during the Gulf War. The protagonist recounts that everyone was annoyed by waiting for missiles to fall and the inability to go on with normal life. Out of boredom her friends decided to have a baby to spite Saddam Hussein. Their acquaintances whiled away the time inventing absurd names to match the absurdity of the idea: "We dreamt: If it were a boy, we'd name him *Gad* Atasov; if it were a girl, we'd name her *Noga* Atasova" (13–14). The Hebrew male name *Gad* is a homophone of the Russian noun meaning "vermin," which is often used as a curse.

11. The division of the two concepts of Historic Fatherland and "just" Fatherland persists in the community. In an article devoted to Bob Dylan, Epshtein (2003) writes: "In the Historic Fatherland Bob did not feel as safe as in his real Fatherland and so returned to the States" (20).

12. An example of how Israeli Arabs perceive the attitudes of Russian-speaking Israelis to Palestinians is an interview with the Israeli-trained journalist of Al-Jazeera, Walid Al-Omari: "'Russian' Israelis try to prove that they are more of Zionists than anybody else and they are more extremist in their attitude toward Palestinians in everything—from border control stations to political parties. Your most extremist parties are those that are headed by 'Russian' leaders" (Martynova 2003c).

13. In the twenty-one interviews conducted by the students before and during Intifada, the theme of relations with Arabs was discussed only in one.

14. FSU immigrants display special respect for World War II veterans and continue to celebrate May 9 as Victory Day. They have founded several small museums to commemorate Jews who fought in the Red Army against the Nazis. In a special issue of *Ha-Aretz* devoted to Russian culture in Israel, the journalist Galili (2004) points out that "Russians" reject the notion that Israel was founded as a result of Holocaust but view it as a result of Soviet victory in the war (62).

15. The situation in Nazareth is reminiscent of that in the German/Polish twin city Guben-Gubin (see Dürrschmidt 2002).

16. In similar terms the labor market in Ashkelon is described by Loval Eliav, an Israeli politician, in a conversation with Sana Hasan: "And I have observed with my own eyes how my countrymen look them over, feeling the arms of children to make sure they are strong,

the way the white plantation-owners once examined the teeth of black slaves. . . . Years ago I brought this to Golda's attention [*Golda Meir*]. I told her we are creating here in Israel, the equivalent of an Uncle Tom's Cabin—a Cousin Muhammad's cabin" (Hasan 1986, 54–55).

17. Shipler describes a similar episode: "A multitude of sad and comical episodes spring from the driving need to attach the Arab or the Jewish label firmly and at first glance. Rabbi Bruce Cohen and another Jew, standing one day at a fast-food stand in Tel-Aviv, were arguing over Bruce's idea for projects to promote Arab-Jewish cooperation. Bruce's companion was skeptical. "You can never trust an Arab," he told the rabbi. "Don't you agree?" he asked the man behind the counter. "Don't you agree that you can never trust an Arab?" "I can't agree," said the man, "because, you see, I am an Arab" (Shipler 1986, 370).

18. The Arabic-speaking Druze are members of an independent sect, an offshoot of Islam, living mainly in Israel, Lebanon, and Syria. In Israel most of them live in villages near Haifa and in the Golan Heights. They are Israeli citizens and serve in the Israeli army.

Chapter 4

1. The attitude toward the celebration of the New Year, the favorite festivity among secular Russian-speaking Israelis, remains controversial. Many veteran Israelis perceive this custom as further proof of the FSU immigrants' non-Jewishness. Reactions to this tradition range from mild disapproval to violent aggression. The newspaper *Vesti* published an interview with the actor Alexey Shtukin, who was severely beaten by a mob of youngsters when he came to pick up his daughter from a disco club on New Year's Eve while still wearing a Grandfather Frost (a Slavic version of Santa Claus) costume after his show. Although the teenagers had gone to the disco club to attend a St. Sylvester's party, they were enraged by the actor's outfit and attacked him, shouting, "Death to Christians!" (Danovich 2006). Still, many veteran Israelis have become more tolerant of New Year's parties held in homes and in restaurants. Moreover, it is an important gesture on the part of competing Israeli politicians to demonstrate appreciation of this tradition to the Russian-speaking electorate. The prime minister and the leader of the opposition consider it necessary to greet the Russian-speaking community on the TV channel Israel Plus, which broadcasts in Russian (see, e.g., Martynova 2005b). Celebration of the New Year is an entirely secular holiday for ex-Soviets and is unrelated to St. Sylvester's Day—the name under which it is celebrated in Israel. Yet many veteran Israelis, those who support and those who condemn the celebration of the New Year, continue mixing up the secular with the Christian tradition (Riman 2005).

A law approving the celebration of Victory Day, the day of the Allies' victory over the Nazis, was adopted in Israel in 2000. But only in 2005, during the celebrations of the sixtieth anniversary of the victory, was the central ceremony attended not only by war veterans but also by the prime minister and members of the government, as well as by members of the diplomatic corps. The politician Yurii Shtern, an immigrant of the 1990s and a member of the public committee responsible for the preparation of the festivities in honor of the sixtieth anniversary, said in a newspaper interview that the goal of transforming a community festival into a countrywide festival had been largely achieved (Galinskii 2005).

2. After the dissolution of the USSR many historic events were reevaluated, and today the Great October Socialist Revolution is referred to as the October coup.

3. We have borrowed both terms from Gold 1980, 117–23.

4. A similar example can be found in Golden 2002. She recounts a story of an Israeli writer who "reminisced about his father who had dreamed that Palestine would be 'lilac colored and sweet-smelling' like the most beautiful park in Baghdad. Arriving in Israel and 'faced with the reality of sand, tents and transit camps' all of a sudden his father's dream was shattered." Note that like our interviewees, the man's spatial images are associated with sensory memories.

5. To "live for the sake of the joy of tomorrow" was the motto of the Soviet educator and writer Anton Makarenko. It was often quoted and alluded to in the media and public speeches.

6. The Russian sociologist Dubin (2001) quotes the results of a poll conducted in 1999 by the Central Institute of the Public Opinion Poll in which Russian citizens were asked to locate the border between East and West. Importantly, 37 percent hesitated in choosing any of the answers. The rest of the responses included the Ural Mountains, the western borders of Poland, the Czech Republic, and Hungary (158) Note the geopolitical component of the questions. One of the suggested options corresponded with the border between capitalist and socialist parts of Europe before the disintegration of the Eastern bloc. The Russian geographer Kaganskii (2001) has little doubt about the existence of a symbolic opposition of "East v. West." As to the different interpretations of the border between East and West, they range in the perceptions of the lay public from the "Great Wall of China to the Dnieper" (531).

7. The fictional nature of travelers' stories was typical of the Western repertoire as well. Sardar (1999) believes that this is a source of biased attitudes toward the East. He is convinced that a major part of the Orientalist canon is provided by the speculations, imagination, and writing in all genres: "Books speaking to books solidified the distorted imagination of knowledgeable ignorance into the concrete foundations of the Western self-consciousness and its informational repertoire" (25).

8. We cite here only the names of authors whose works were well known to the public at large and made a serious impact on the self-awareness of Russian and Soviet society.

9. Respect for the industriousness, discipline, and rationality of the

West always goes hand in hand with contempt for the lack of spontaneity and inability to succumb to emotions and impulses. Among the numerous examples of this, two are striking in the similarity of attributes for which Westerners are ridiculed. In Andrey Bely's novel *Petersburg* and in Evgenii Zamiatin's story "Islanders," the protagonists (Apollon Ableukhov and the vicar Dewly) are derided for organizing their life pedantically according to a schedule that is fixed once and for all (Bely 1959; Zamiatin 1989). Interestingly, one of our interviewees, Belka, 22, complains that in the Soviet Union people coming to see their relatives and friends were always welcome, and nobody expected such visits to be announced in advance. It upsets her that in Israel her compatriots have lost spontaneity, abandoned this habit, and behave "as if scalding water had been poured over them."

10. In an interview with the newspaper *Moskovskie Novosti*, Aleksandr Solzhenitsyn expressly referred to this character as a Jew. Moreover, he complains that his portrayal of Cezar Markovich triggered accusations of anti-Semitism (Loshak 2001, 8).

11. Russian pronominal usage and the distinction between the two forms of the personal pronouns *ty* and *vy* are discussed in detail in Friedrich 1986.

Chapter 5

1. Upon arrival in Haifa an immigrant from Australia could not find shelter because hotel owners refused to accommodate a family with a baby. The narrator was in despair when all of a sudden an old friend who had not been told about the family's arrival appeared on the doorstep. He invited them to join him in Tel-Aviv. The narrator emphasizes that her friend was a rabbi and perceives his unexpected help and hospitality as a sign of God's blessing (Mirsky 2005, 120).

Chapter 6

1. A new term linked to multilingualism has emerged in sociolinguistics in recent years: *linguistic human rights*. This is the right to learn one's mother tongue, including the right to primary education in it, and the right to learn at least one of the state languages of the country of one's domicile (Phillipson and Runnut 1995).

2. Scholars of bilingualism agree that it is a gradient and includes various levels of second-language proficiency, but they use different terms for the same phenomena. Thus Valdés (1997) refers to people "who are two native speakers in one person" as *ambilingual*. Those who "can interact effectively with native speakers of the second language in order to carry out a broad range of communicative activities" are defined as stable functional bilinguals (33, 35). The latter group varies in the degree of proficiency. Hickerson (1980) defines equal proficiency in two

languages as "nativelike" control of two languages, or fully bilingual. However she divides the group of "functional bilinguals" into coordinate and subordinate bilingual speakers (84).

3. Elsewhere in the interview it turns out that Elvira's atheist grandfather scolded his daughter for teaching children to speak Tat, because he identified this language with Jewishness, and the latter with religion and anti-Soviet sentiments:

> So once granddad came to see us and heard that Mom spoke Tat to us. After this he quarreled with mom for a long time. I heard something, I heard some conversation, some part of it. And it was very interesting to me. I started asking him why, that is what the reason is, what is the reason why he is against it. Well. He didn't explain the reason, but he said that there wasn't such a notion as "God," there wasn't such a notion as "Jew," there wasn't such a notion at all. And he said to me that when he was a small boy, when he was at school, so . . . the school where he studied, or his headmaster, or his head teacher explained it to them like this. They even had an anthem, some poem, in which it was prohibited to believe in God. It was, say, in the 1930s, or in 1928, or in 1930, it was before the 1940s. And he read a stanza to me. Something of this sort: "The children of the Komsomol, the children who are pioneers, there is no God, no God, no God." Well. This is what I remember. And he said that Mother was wrong when she spoke Tat, the Jewish language, because there is no God.

When conducting fieldwork among Mariupol Greeks, the anthropologist Kaurinkoski (2003) found that they had also stopped teaching the young generation the Greek language for fear of making their life more complicated.

4. We are grateful to Edna Heichal and Professor Dov Noy for their help in finding the possible antecedent of the saying.

Chapter 7

1. What Rotenberg leaves out of his commentary is that the three writers included in the Jewish group are ethnic Russians. Consequently, Jewishness is associated with moral principles rather than ethnicity.

2. IFA numbers of these jokes are 18698, 18714, 18730, 19447, 20795, 20798, 20799, 20809, 20812, 20835, 20837, 20847, 20850, 20855, 20861, 20862, 20870, 20876, 20880, 20883, and 21322.

3. Fourteen of these jokes (IFA 22560–22574) were recorded by Ella Ribak, a student at the University of Haifa, and two (IFA 22134 and 22135) by Larisa Fialkova.

4. Nina Z., for example, complained that her first landlady suspected that FSU immigrants did not know how to use the bathroom. Similar stories were told by others. Here we quote one by Irina I., 25. Note the aggressive reaction to the veterans' admonition. She alludes to the Russian idiom implying savageness—"they have only recently

climbed down the palm tree"—which shows again the animal metaphor (in this case, monkeys) in describing the other.

> It is difficult to find a job here, to find a position, because the locals' attitude to Russians is very, well . . . I don't even know how to explain . . . Because they consider us some sort of plebeians who don't even know what a socket is. You know, in the *ulpan* they asked us, "Do you know what a socket is? Do you know what electricity is?" Well, although when it was conceived, when it was invented, they were still sitting on a palm tree. Well, the attitude to us is simply terrible. And even now, we still communicate with the Russians. And we say about the locals, *they* and *we* about ourselves, although we live in Israel.

5. This *chastushka* was quoted by Draitser (1994), who translated it with Iosif Brodsky's assistance:

> I am bored with you my darling,
> Dancing in Rjazan'
> Let's do a circumcision
> And off to Israel be gone. (258)

6. In the translation we changed some of the original names but retained their ethnic character.

Conclusion

1. Although immigrants seldom raise the theme of return in informal and formal discourse, sociological surveys show that this feeling is not nonexistent. A recent survey conducted among five hundred Russian-speaking respondents shows that 67 percent are definitely opposed to returning to the CIS, while 31 percent are to a different extent inclined to returning to their country of origin. In the same survey only 5 percent define themselves as Israelis, 16 percent identify with Israelis rather than with repatriates, and 32 percent feel equal affinity with Israelis and repatriates (Zemach 2005).

BIBLIOGRAPHY

Aarne, Antti, and Stith Thompson. 1964. *The Types of the Folktale: A Classification and Bibliography.* Helsinki: Suomalainen Tiedeakatemia.

Adam, Barbara. 1990. *Time and Social Theory.* Cambridge: Polity Press.

Adamowski, Jan. 1999. *Kategoria Przestrzeni w Folklorze. Studium Etnolingvistyczne* [The Category of Space in Folklore: Ethno-Linguistic Study]. Lublin: Wydawnictwo Uniwersytetu Marii Curie-Sklodowskiej.

Adler, Patricia A., and Peter Adler. 1994. Observational Techniques. In *Handbook of Qualitative Research,* edited by Norman K. Denzin and Yvonna S. Lincoln, 377–92. Thousand Oaks, Calif.: Sage.

Adorno, Theodor W. 1950. Prejudice in the Interview Material. In *The Authoritarian Personality,* edited by Theodor W. Adorno, Else Frenkel-Brunswik, Daniel J. Levinson, and R. Nevitt Sanford, 605–53. New York: Harper.

Agoston-Nikolova, Elka. 2001. Hybrid Identities: The Pomac Community of Breznitza (Southwest Bulgaria) in Search of Genealogy. *Fabula* 42, nos. 1–2: 110–16.

Akhmatova, Anna. 1989. Requiem. In A. Akhmatova, *Stikhotvorenia* [Poems], 113–19. Paris: YMCA Press.

Akhmetova, T. V. 1997. *Russkii mat: tolkovyi slovar'* [A Dictionary of Russian Obscene Language]. Moskva: Kolokol Press.

Akunin, Boris. 2000. *Leviaphan: Roman* [Leviathan: A Novel]. Moskva: Zakharov.

Alexander, Alex E. 1975. *Russian Folklore: An Anthology in English Translation.* Belmont, Mass.: Nordland.

Alexandrova, Inna. 2002. *Piatyi punkt* [The Fifth Paragraph]. Moskva: Prava Cheloveka.

Al-Haj, Majid. 1998. Soviet Immigration as Viewed by Jews and Arabs: Divided Attitudes in a Divided Country. In *Immigration to Israel: Sociological Perspectives,* edited by Elazar Leshem and Judith T. Shuval, 211–27. Studies of Israeli Society, vol. 8. New Brunswick: Transaction.

———. 2004. *Immigration and Ethnic Formation in a Deeply Divided Society: The Case of the 1990s Immigrants from the Former Soviet Union in Israel.* Leiden, Boston: Brill.

Al-Haj, Majid, and Elazar Leshem. 2000. *Immigrants from the Former Soviet Union in Israel: Ten Years Later.* University of Haifa.

Allport, Gordon W. 1979. *The Nature of Prejudice.* Reading, Mass.: Addison-Wesley.

Anderson, Benedict. 1991. *Imagined Communities: Reflections on the Origin and Spread of Nationalism.* Rev. ed. London: Verso.

Andrews, D. R. 1993. American Immigrant Russian: Sociocultural Perspectives on Borrowings from English in the Language of the Third Wave. *Language Quarterly* 31, nos. 3–4: 153–76.

———. 1999. *Socio-Cultural Perspectives on Language Change in Diaspora: Soviet Immigrants in the United States.* Impact: Studies in Language and Society, vol. 5. Amsterdam: Benjamin.

Angrosino, Michael V., and de Pérez, Kimberley A. Mays. 2000. Rethinking Observation: From Method to Context. In *Handbook of Qualitative Research,* edited by Norman K. Denzin and Yvonna S. Lincoln, 673–702. Thousand Oaks, Calif.: Sage.

Anninskii, Lev. 2001. Ad Limonii [The Hell of Lemonia]. *Druzhba Narodov* 12 http://magazines.russ.ru/druzhba/2001/12/limon.html.

Arutiunova, N. D. 1998. *Iazyk i mir cheloveka* [The Human Language and His/Her World]. Moskva: Iazyki Russkoi Kul'tury.

Ashe, Geoffrey. 1978. *Miracles.* London: Routledge and Kegan Paul.

Atkinson, Robert. 1998. *The Life Story Interview.* Sage University Papers Series on Qualitative Research Methods, vol. 44. Thousand Oaks, Calif.: Sage.

Azadovskii, Mark. 1974. *A Siberian Tale Teller.* Monograph Series, no. 2. Austin: University of Texas.

Azbel, Mark. 1982. Autobiography of a Jew. In *In Search of Self: The Soviet Jewish Intelligentsia and the Exodus,* edited by David Prital, 58–61. Jerusalem: Mount Scopus.

Bakhtin, Mikhail. 1979a. *Estetika slovesnogo tvorchestva.* [Aesthetics of the Verbal Art]. Moskva: Iskusstvo.

———. 1979b. *Problemy poetiki Dostoevskogo* [Problems of Dostoevsky's Poetics]. 4th ed. Moskva: Sovetskaia Rossia.

Barabash, Yu. 1999. "Litsa basurmanskoi natsional'nosti" u Gogolia i Shevchenko ["Persons of the Muslim Nationality" in Gogol's and Shevchenko's Works]. *Voprosy literatury* 6:204–35.

Bard, Marjorie. 1992. Relating Intrapersonal Storying (Ideonarrating) and Interpersonal Communicating. *Southern Folklore* 49:61–72.

Bar-Itzhak, Haya. 1992. "And We Came to the Land of Our Forefathers": The Folk Legend of Yemenite Jews in Israel. *JFER* 14, nos. 1–2: 44–52.

———. 1998. Les Juifs Polonais Face au "Monstre" Israelien: Recits d'aliyaen Israel. *Cahiers de Litterature Orale* 44:191–206.

Bar-Tal Daniel, and Dikla Antebi. 1992. Siege Mentality in Israel. *International Journal of Intercultural Relations* 16:251–75.

Bauman, Richard. 1971. Differential Identity and the Social Base of Folklore. *Journal of American Folklore* 85:31–41.

Bausinger, Herman. 1987. The Structure of Everyday Narration. *Folklore Forum* 20, nos. 1–2:9–37.

———. 1990. *Folk Culture in a World of Technology.* Bloomington: Indiana University Press.

Beker, Avi. 1991. Superpower Relations and Jewish Identity in the Soviet Union. In *Jewish Culture and Identity in the Soviet Union,* edited by Yaacov Ro'i and Avi Beker, 445–62. New York: New York University Press.

Bekerman, Zvi. 2000. From Russia to Israel and Back: Stories of Selves and Bodies in Migration. In *Language, Identity and Immigration,* edited by Elite Olshtain and Gabriel Horenczyk, 105–21. Jerusalem: Hebrew University and Magnes Press.

Bell, Robert E. 1982. *Dictionary of Classical Mythology: Symbols, Attributes and Associations.* Santa Barbara, Calif.: Clio Press.

Belousov, A. F. 1998. Sadistskie stishki [Sadistic Verses]. In *Russkii shkol'nyi fol'klor: Ot "vyzyvanii" Pikovoi damy do semeinykh rasskazov,* compiled by A. F. Belousov, 545–57. Moskva: Ladomir and "AST."

———. 2003. Sovremennyi anekdot [A Contemporary Joke]. In *Sovremennyi gorodskoi fol'klor,* edited by A. F. Belousov, I. S. Veselova, S. Yu. Nekludov, 581–94. Moskva: Rossiiskii Gosudarstvennyi Gumanitarnyi Universitet.

Belova, Olga. 1996. Evrei glazami slavian [Jews in the Eyes of the Slavs]. *Vestnik Evreiskogo Universiteta v Moskve* 3, no. 13:110–19.

———. 1997. Etnokonfessional'nye stereotipy v slavianskikh narodnykh predstavleniakh [Ethno-Confessional Stereotypes in Slavic Folk Beliefs]. *Slavianovedenie* 1:25–32.

———. 1999a. Obraz evreia v narodnoi demonologii slavian [The Image of the Jew in Slavic Folk Demonology]. *Jewish Culture and Cultural Contacts.* Proceedings of the Sixth Annual International Interdisciplinary Conference on Jewish Studies. Moscow: Sefer, 86–99.

———. 1999b. Inorodtsy [Foreigners]. In *Slavianskie drevnosti: Etnolingvisticheskii slovar'* [Slavic Antiquities: Ethnolinguistic Dictionary in Five Volumes]. Vol. 2. Edited by N. I. Tolstoi, 414–18. Moskva: Mezhdunarodnye otnoshenia.

Bely, Andrey. 1959. *Petersburg.* Translated by John Cournos. New York: Grove Press.

Ben-Amos, Dan. 1969. Analytical Categories and Ethnic Genres. *Genre* 2, no. 3:275–301.

———. 1971. Toward a Definition of Folklore in Context. *Journal of American Folklore* 84:3–15.

———. 1973. The "Myth" of Jewish Humor. *Western Folklore* 32:112–31.

Ben-Rafael, Eliezer. 2001. The Transformation of Diasporas: The Linguistic Dimension. In *Identity, Culture and Globalization,* edited by Eliezer Ben-Rafael and Yitzhak Sternberg, 337–51. Leiden: Brill.

Benski, Tova. 1992–93. Testing Melting-Pot Theories in the Jewish Israeli Context. In *Sociological Papers* 1–2, edited by Ernest Krausz and Gitta Tulea, 1–46. Ramat-Gan: Sociological Institute for Community Studies, Bar-Ilan University.

Berenstein, Yulia. 2000. *Mazon lemahshava—havnaiat zuhut bekerev mehagrim mihever ha-amim dereh shimush bemazon* [Food for Thought: Identity Construction amongst Immigrants from the Former Soviet Union to Israel through Food Practices]. Master's thesis, University of Haifa.

Berry, John W. 1997. Immigration, Acculturation, and Adaptation. *Applied Psychology: An International Review* 46, no. 1:5–68.

Bertaux, Daniel. 1981. From the Life-history Approach to the Transformation of Sociological Practice. In *Biography and Society: The Life History Approach in the Social Sciences,* edited by Daniel Bertaux, 29–46. Beverly Hills, Calif.: Sage.

Bezelianskii, Yurii. 2000. *5-yi punkt, ili kokteil' "Rossia"* [The Fifth Paragraph, or Cocktail "Russia"]. Moskva: Raduga.

Billig, Michael. 1997. From Codes to Utterances: Cultural Studies, Discourse and Psychology. In *Cultural Studies in Question,* edited by Marjorie Ferguson and Peter Golding, 205–26. London: Sage.

Bizman, Aharon, and Yoel Yinon. 2001. Perceived Threat and Israeli Jews' Evaluations of Russian Immigrants: The Moderating Role of Jewish and Israeli Identity. *International Journal of Intercultural Relations* 25, no. 6:691–704.

Blommaert, Jan, and Jef Verschueren. 1998. *Debating Diversity: Analysing the Discourse of Tolerance.* London: Routledge.

Bodemann, Y. Michal. 2001. Ethnicity Cosmopolitanized? The New German Jewry. In *Identity, Culture and Globalization,* edited by Eliezer Ben-Rafael and Yitzhak Sternberg, 353–70. Leiden: Brill.

Bogdanov, Konstantin. 2001. *Povsednevnost' i mifologia: Issledovania po semiotike fol'klornoi deistvitel'nosti* [Daily Life and Mythology: Semiotic Research into Folklore Reality]. Sankt-Peterburg: Iskusstvo-SPB.

———. 2002. *Povsednevnost' i mifologia: Issledovania po semiotike fol'klornoi deistvitel'nosti* [Daily Life and Mythology: Semiotic Research into Folklore Reality]. Moskva: Rossiiskii Gosudarstvennyi Gumanitarnyi Universitet.

Bogoraz, Larisa. 1973. Do I Feel I Belong to the Jewish People? In *I Am a Jew: Essays on Jewish Identity in the Soviet Union,* edited by Aleksander Voronel and Viktor Yakhot, 60–64. Moscow: Academic Committee on Soviet Jewry and Anti-Defamation League of B'nai B'rith.

Bokov, V. 1950. *Russkaia Chastushka* [The Russian Chastushka]. Leningrad: Sovetskii pisatel'.

Boym, Svetlana. 1994. *Common Places: Mythologies of Everyday Life in Russia.* Cambridge, Mass.: Harvard University Press.

———. 2001. *The Future of Nostalgia.* New York: Basic Books.

Bram, Chen. 2003. Hakara, heiader hakara uhakara shguia bekvuzot mikerev olei hever ha-medinot. In *Rav-tarbutiut bemivhan haisraeliut* [Acceptance, Rejection, and Mistaken Perception of Repatriate Groups from CIS], edited by Ohad Nachtomy. Jerusalem: Hebrew University and Magnes Press, 163–91.

Briman, Shimon. 2001. Palestino-Chechenskii konkurs neudachnikov [Palestinian Chechen Contest of Failures]. *Vesti-2* 5 July: 11–12.

Brown, Mary Ellen. 1990. Personal Experience Stories, Autobiography, and Ideology. *Fabula* 31, nos. 3–4:254–61.

Brudny, Yitzhak M. 1998. *Reinventing Russia: Russian Nationalism and the Soviet State (1953–1991).* Cambridge, Mass.: Harvard University Press.

Brunvand, Harold. 1968. *The Study of American Folklore: An Introduction.* New York: Norton.

Brym, Robert J. 1997. Jewish Immigration from the Former USSR: Who? Why? How Many? In *Russian Jews on Three Continents: Migration and Resettlement,* edited by Noah Lewin-Epstein et al., 177–93. London: Frank Cass.

Brym, Robert J., with the assistance of Rozalina Ryvkina. 1994. *The Jews of Moscow, Kiev and Minsk: Identity, Antisemitism, Emigration.* New York: New York University Press.

Bugarski, Ranko. 1980. The Interdisciplinary Relevance of Folk Linguistics. In *Problems in Linguistic Historiography,* edited by Konrad Koerner and Robert H. Robins, 381–93. Amsterdam: John Benjamins.

Bulgakov, M. A. 1989. Beg: Vosem' snov [The Flight: Eight Dreams]. In M. A. Bulgakov, *Piesy 1920–kh godov.* Leningrad: Iskusstvo, 249–95.

Cała, Anita. 1995. *The Image of the Jew in Polish Folk Culture.* Jerusalem: Magnes Press and Hebrew University.

Carney, T. F. 1972. *Content Analysis: A Technique for Systematic Inference from Communications.* London: Batsford.

Caspi, Dan, et al. 2002. The Red, the White, and the Blue. *Gazette: The International Journal for Communication Studies* 64, no. 6:537–56.

Cavaglion, Gabriel, and Revital Sela-Shayovitz. 2005. The Cultural Construction of Contemporary Satanic Legends in Israel. *Folklore* 116, no. 3:255–71.

Chafe, W. L. 1990. Some Things That Narratives Tell Us about the Mind. In *Narrative Thought and Narrative Language,* edited by Bruce K. Britton and A. D. Pellegrini, 79–98. Hillside, N.J.: Lawrence Erlbaum.

Chekhov, Anton. 1986. *Chernyi Monakh* [The Black Monk]. In A. Chekhov, *Sobranie sochinenii.* Vol. 8. Moskva: Nauka, 226–57.

Chen, Shoshana. 2002. Kol' Moskva al madaf ehad [The Whole of Moscow on a Single Shelf]. *Yidi'ot Aharonot,* 3 August: 6–7, 14.

Cherniak, Aron. 2005. "Russkaia ulitsa v evreiskoi strane" [A Russian Street in the Jewish State]. *Evreiskii Kamerton,* 1 December: 14–15.

Chernov, Mikhail. 2002. Politika ravnovesia [The Politics of Equilibrium]. *Magazine* 401:8–9.

Chirkova, O. A. 1998. Poetika komicheskogo v sovremennom narodnom anekdote [Poetics of the Comic in Contemporary Folk Jokes]. *Filologicheskie Nauki* 5–6:30–37.

Chiswick, Barry R. 2000. Soviet Jews in the United States: Language and Labor Market Revisited. In *Language, Identity and Immigration,* edited by Elite Olshtain and Gabriel Horenczyk, 275–300. Jerusalem: Hebrew University and Magnes Press.

Chlenov, Michael. 1997. Jewish Community and Identity in the Former Soviet Union. In *Jews of the Former Soviet Union Yesterday, Today, and Tomorrow.* New York: American Jewish Committee, 11–16. *See also Mikhail Chlenov.*

Chlenov, Mikhail. 2000. Mezhdu Stsilloi deiudizatsii i Kharibdoi sionizma: Gorskie evrei v XX v. [Between the Scylla of Dejudaization and Charibdis of Zionism: The Mountain Jews in the Twentieth Century]. *Diasporas, Independent Academic Journal* 3:174–97. *See also Michael Chlenov.*

Christians, Clifford G. 2000. Ethics and Politics in Qualitative Research. In *A Handbook of Qualitative Research.* 2nd ed. Edited by Norman K. Denzin and Yvonna S. Lincoln, 133–55. Thousand Oaks, Calif.: Sage.

Chukovskii, Kornei. 1990. *Sochinenia v dvukh tomakh, tom 1. Skazki, Ot dvukh do piati, Zhivoi kak zhizn'* [Selected Writings in Two Volumes, Vol. 1: Fairy Tales, From Two to Five, As Lively As Life]. Moskva: Izdatel'stvo Pravda.

Coates, Jennifer. 1996. *Women Talk: Conversation between Women Friends.* Oxford: Blackwell.

Dal', V. 1957. *Poslovitsy russkogo naroda* [The Proverbs of the Russian People]. Moskva: Gosudarstvennoe izdatel'stvo russkoi literatury.

Danovich, Lazar'. 2006. Ded Moroz i otmorozki [Grandfather Frost and Thugs]. *Vesti,* 5 January: 8.

Dégh, Linda. 1984. Uses of Folklore as Expressions of Identity by Hungarians in the Old and New Country. *Journal of Folklore Research* 21, nos. 2–3:187–200.

———. 1994. *American Folklore and the Mass Media.* Bloomington: Indiana University Press.

Dégh, Linda, and Andrew Vázsonyi. 1974. The Memorate and the Proto-Memorate. *Journal of American Folklore* 87, no. 345:225–39.

DellaPergola, Sergio. 1998. The Global Context of Migration to Israel. In *Immigration to Israel: Sociological Perspectives,* edited by Elazar Leshem and Judith T. Shuval, 51–94. Studies of Israeli Society, vol. 8. New Brunswick, N.J.: Transaction.

Denisova, G. 2000. Stereotipy i ikh rol' v formirovanii kommunikativnykh navykov v usloviakh "nerodnogo" dvuiazychia [Stereotypes and Their Role in Forming Communicative Skills among "Non-native" Bilinguals]. *Russia and the West: The Dialogue of Cultures* 8, no. 1:202–15.

Diatlov, Viktor I. 2000. *Sovremennye torgovye men'shinstva: Faktor stabil'nosti ili konflikta?(Kitaitsy i kavkaztsy v Irkutske.)* [Contemporary Commercial Minorities: Is It a Factor of Stability or Conflict? (Chinese and Caucasians in Irkutsk)]. Moskva: Natalis.

Dietz, Barbara. 2000. German and Jewish Migration from the Former Soviet Union to Germany: Background, Trends and Implications. *Journal of Ethnic and Migration Studies* 26, no. 4:635–52.

Dobrovich, Anatolii. 2002. Bolen li terrorist-samoubiitsa? Psikhiatr razvodit rukami [Is a Solitary Suicide Bomber Sick? A Psychiatrist Shrugs His Shoulders in Dismay]. *Okna,* 15 August: 4–6.

Dodgshon, Robert A. 1998. *Society in Time and Space: A Geographical Perspective on Change.* Cambridge: Cambridge University Press.

Dorson, Richard. 1964. Immigrant Folklore. In *American Folklore,* edited by R. Dorson, 135–65. Chicago: University of Chicago Press.

Draitser, Emil. 1994. Sociological Aspects of the Russian-Jewish Jokes of the Exodus. *Humor: International Journal of Humor Research* 7, no. 3:245–67.

Dreizin, Felix. 1990. *The Russian Soul and the Jew: Essays in Literary Ethnocriticism.* Boston: University Press of America.

Dubin, B. V. 2001. Mezhdu Vostokom i Zapadom: Simvolika granitsy v postsovetskoi politicheskoi mifologii [Between East and West: The Symbolism of the Border in the Post-Soviet Political Mythology]. In *Pogranichnye kul'tury mezhdu Vostokom i Zapadom (Rossia i Ispania),* edited by V. E. Bagno, 147–58. Sankt-Peterburg: RAN and Institut Russkoi Literatury (Pushkinskii Dom).

Dundes, Alan. 1965. What Is Folklore? In *The Study of Folklore,* edited by Alan Dundes, 1–3. Berkeley: Prentice Hall.

———. 1984. Defining Identity through Folklore. *Journal of Folklore Research* 21, nos. 2–3:149–52.

Durham, William H. 1989. Conflict, Migration, and Ethnicity: A Summary. In *Conflict, Migration, and the Expression of Ethnicity,* edited by Nancie L. Gonsalez and Carolyn S. McCommon, 138–45. Boulder, Colo.: Westview Press.

Dűrrschmidt, Jörg. 2002. "They're Worse off than Us": The Social Construction of European Space and Boundaries in the German/Polish Twin-City Guben-Gubin. *Identities: Global Studies on Culture and Power* 9:123–50.

Dushechkina, Ie.V. 2001. Ded Moroz: Etapy bol'shogo puti. K 160-letiu literaturnogo obraza. [Grandfather Frost: Landmarks of a Long Journey]. *Novoe Literaturnoe Obozrenie* 47:253–62.

Dymerskaya-Tsigelman, Ludmila. 2000. Evrei byvshego SSSR v Izraile i v SNG: Zametki redaktora k materialam sbornika [Jews of the Former USSR in Israel and the CIS: Editor's Notes on Materials Presented in the Collection of Articles]. *The Jews of the Soviet Union in Transi-*

tion 4, no. 19:17–49.

Edwards, John. 1985. *Language, Society and Identity.* Oxford: Basil Blackwell.

Elbaz, André. 1987. L'autobiographie orale d'immigrants comme genre folklorique: Definition et structure. *Fabula* 28, nos. 3–4:279–92.

Epshtein, Dmitrii. 2003. Zovite menia Tsimmi [Call Me Zimmy]. *Okna,* 24 April: 20–21.

Epstein, Alek, and Nina Kheimets. 2000a. Immigrant Intelligentsia and Its Second Generation: Cultural Segregation as a Road to Social Integration? *Journal of International Migration and Integration* 1, no. 4:461–76.

———. 2000b. Cultural Clash and Educational Diversity: Immigrant Teachers' Effort to Rescue the Education of Immigrant Children in Israel. *International Studies in Sociology of Education* 10, no. 2:191–210.

Eriksen, Thomas Hylland. 1995. *Small Places, Large Issues: An Introduction to Social and Cultural Anthropology.* London: Pluto Press.

Esenin, Sergei. 1962. Chernyi chelovek [The Black Man]. In S. Esenin, *Sobranie sochinenii.* Vol. 3. Moskva: Gosudarstvennoe izdatel'stvo khudozhestvennoi literatury, 209–14.

Eterman, Aleksander. 2002. Evreiskoe demograficheskoe gosudarstvo [The Jewish Demographic State]. *Vesti-2,* July 11: 10–12.

Evplov, V. I. 2000. *Evreiskie anekdoty* [Jewish Jokes]. Rostov-na-Donu: Feniks.

Fainberg, Valentin. 2003. Nastoiaschie russkie imena [Genuine Russian Names]. *Okna,* April 15: 28, 39.

Fairclough, Norman. 1999. Global Capitalism and Critical Awareness of Language. *Language Awareness* 8, no. 2:71–83.

Fasmer, Max. 1964–73. Etimologicheskii slovar' russkogo iazyka, v 4 tomakh [An Etymological Dictionary of the Russian Language in Four Volumes]. Moskva: Progress.

Feagin, Crawford. 2002. Entering the Community: Fieldwork. In *The Handbook of Language Variation and Change,* edited by J. K. Chambers, Peter Trudgill, and Natalie Scilling-Estes, 20–39. Malden, Mass.: Blackwell.

Feder-Bubis, Paula. 1997. Patterns of Professional Commitment in the Stories of Immigrant Physicians from the Former Soviet Union in Israel. In *Immigrant Physicians: Former Soviet Doctors in Israel, Canada and the United States,* edited by Judith T. Shuval and Judith H. Bernstein, 61–80. Westport, Conn.: Praeger.

Feldman, Eliezer. 2003. *"Russkii" Izrail': mezhdu dvukh poliusov* ["Russian" Israel: Between the Two Poles]. Moskva: Market DS.

Fenton, Steve. 1999. *Ethnicity: Racism, Class and Culture.* London: Macmillan.

Fialkova, Larisa. 1997. Suchasni lehendy z Ukraini v Izraili [Contemporary Legends from Ukraine in Israel]. In *Ievreis'ka istoria ta kul'tura v Ukraine.* Materialy konferentsii. Kyiv: Institut Iudaiky, 213–18.

———. 1998a. "Katakombnyi" fol'klor Ukrainy [The Catacomb Folklore of Ukraine]. *Zhivaia Starina* 2:35–37.

———. 1998b. Struktura fantasticheskogo obraza v tvorchestve Remizova [The Structure of the Fantastic Image in Remizov's Writings]. In *Rytual'no-mifolohichnyi pidkhid do interpretatsii tekstu: sbirnik nukovykh prats',* edited by L. O. Kyseliova, P. Iu. Poberiozkina, 68–82. Kyiv: IZMN.

———. 1999a. Russkii iazyk v izrail'skoi torgovle: Iazyk immigrantov v svete sotsiolingvistiki. [The Russian Language in Israeli Commerce: The Immigrants' Language in the Light of Sociolinguistics]. *Rusistika segodnia* 1–2:80–89.

———. 1999b. The Holy Land Toponymy in Ukrainian Folklore. In *Jerusalem in Slavic Culture,* edited by Wolf Moskowich, Oto Luthar, and Samuel Schwarzband, 299–306. Jerusalem and Ljubljana: Center for Slavic Languages and Literatures of the Hebrew University of Jerusalem and Scientific Research Center of the Slovenian Academy of Sciences and Arts.

———. 2001. Chernobyl's Folklore: Vernacular Commentary on Nuclear Disaster. *Journal of Folklore Research* 38, no. 3:181–204.

———. 2005a. Opyt adaptatsii v ustnykh rasskazakh "russkikh" izrail'tianok [Narratives of Experiences of Adaptation Amongst Female "Russian" Immigrants to Israel]. *Diasporas: Independent Academic Journal* 1:19–47.

———. 2005b. Byelorussian and Ukrainian Languages in Israel: Preliminary Remarks. *Jews and Slavs* 15:252–64.

———. 2005c. Emigrants from the FSU and the Russian-language Internet. *Toronto Slavic Quarterly* 12 www.utoronto.ca/tsq/12/fialkova12.shtml.

Fialkova, Larisa, and Maria N. Yelenevskaya. 2001a. Ghosts in the Cyber World: Analysis of the Folklore Sites on the Internet. *Fabula* 42, nos. 1–2:64–89.

———. 2001b. Prophetic Dreams and Lucky Coincidences: Modern Substitutes for Miracles. In *The Concept of Miracle in Slavic and Jewish Cultural Traditions: Collection of Articles.* Akademicheskaia seria, vol. 7. Moskva: Sefer, 290–335.

———. 2001c. Svoi i chuzhye—metamorfozy emigrantskogo soznania: na materiale lichnykh rasskazov [My People and the Others: Metamorphoses of Immigrants' Mentality: Analysis of Personal Narratives]. *Vestnik Evreiskogo Universiteta* 23, no. 5:147–62.

———. 2003. Culture-Specific Meaning in Personal Narratives. *Folklorica: Journal of the Slavic and East-European Folklore Association* 8, no. 1:3–22.

———. 2004a. How to Find the West in the Middle East: Perceptions of East and West amongst "Russian" Jews in Israel. In *Times, Places, Passages: Ethnological Approaches in the New Millennium,* edited by Attila Paládi-Kovács, 453–80. Budapest: Publishing House of the Hungarian Academy of Sciences.

———. 2004b. Motifs of Anti-Semitism in Personal Narratives of the FSU Immigrants. *Jews and Slavs* 13:137–54.

———. 2005. Incipient Soviet Diaspora: Encounters in Cyberspace. *Narodna Umejetnost: Croatian Journal of Ethnology and Folklore Research* 42, no. 1:83–99.

———. 2006a. How to Outsmart the System: Immigrants' Trickster Stories. *Studia Mythologica Slavica* 9:279–96.

———. 2006b. Konflikt zakona i spravedlivosti v emigrantskikh rasskazakh o plutovstve [The Conflict of Law and Justice in Emigrants' Trickster Stories]. In *Pravo v zerkale zhizni:Issledovania po iuridicheskoi antropologii* [Law in the Mirror of Life: Studies in Legal Anthropology], edited by N. Novikova, 368–81. Moskva: Rossiiskaia Akademia Nauk, izdatel'skii dom "Strategia".

Findlay, A. M., and F. L. N. Li. 1997. An Auto-Biographical Approach to Understanding Migration: The Case of Hong-Kong Emigrants. *Area* 29, no. 1:34–44.

Fine, Michelle, et al. 2000. For Whom? Qualitative Research, Representations, and Social Responsibilities. In *A Handbook of Qualitative Research.* 2nd ed. Edited by Norman K. Denzin and Yvonna S. Lincoln, 107–31. Thousand Oaks, Calif.: Sage.

Fishman, Joshua. 1972. *Language and Nationalism.* Rowley, Mass.: Newbury House.

———. 1977. Language and Ethnicity. In *Language, Ethnicity and Intergroup Relations,* edited by Howard Giles, 15–57. London: Academic Press.

Fontana, Andrea, and James H. Frey. 2000. The Interview: From Structured Questions to Negotiated Text. In *Handbook of Qualitative Research.* 2nd ed. Edited by Norman K. Denzin and Yvonna S. Lincoln, 645–72. Thousand Oaks, Calif.: Sage.

Forgas, Joseph P. 1988. Episode Representations in Intercultural Communication. In *Theories in Intercultural Communication,* edited by Young Yun Kim and William B. Gudykunst, 186–212. Newbury Park, Calif.: Sage.

Freud, Sigmund. 1959. Humor. In *Collected Papers of Sigmund Freud.* Vol. 5. Edited by J. Strachey. New York: Basic Books.

Friedrich, Paul. 1986. Social Context and Semantic Feature: The Russian Pronominal Usage. In *Directions in Sociolinguistics,* edited by John J. Gumperz and Dell Hymes, 270–300. Oxford: Blackwell.

Gak, Vladimir G. 2000. Prostranstvo vne prostranstva [*Space Outside Space*]. In *Logichiskii analiz iazyka: Iazyk prostranstv,* edited by N. D. Arutiunova and I. B. Levontina, 127–34. Moskva: Nauka.

Galili, Lily. 2004. Anakhnu nitsakhnu be Shoa [We Won over Holocaust]. *Ha-Aretz,* Succot supplement. 29 September: 62.

Galinskii, Ian. 2005. Ten' pobedy i den' pobedy [The Shadow of Victory and the Victory Day]. *Vesti-2,* 26 May: 19.

Garfinkle, Adam. 1997. *Politics and Society in Modern Israel: Myths and Realities.* Armonk, N.Y.: M. E. Sharpe.

Georges, Robert A., and Michael O. Jones. 1980. *People Studying People: The Human Element in Fieldwork.* Berkeley: University of California Press.

Gershenson, Olga. 2003. The Lure and Threat of Cultural Hybridity. *Journal of International Communication* 9, no. 2:106–22.

Giles, Howard, Richard Y. Bourhis, and Donald M. Taylor. 1977. Towards a Theory of Language in Ethnic Group Relations. In *Language, Ethnicity and Intergroup Relations,* edited by Howard Giles, 307–48. London: Academic Press.

Gitelman, Zvi. 1988. *A Century of Ambivalence: The Jews of Russia and the Soviet Union, 1881 to the Present.* New York: YIVO Institute for Jewish Research.

———. 1991. Ethnic Identity and Ethnic Relations among the Jews of the Non-European USSR. *Ethnic and Racial Studies* 14, no. 1:24–54.

———. 1992. Judaism and Jewishness in the USSR: Ethnicity and Religion. *Nationalities Papers* 20, no. 1:75–85.

———. 1997. "From a Northern Country": Russian and Soviet Jewish Immigration to America and Israel in Historical Perspective. In *Russian Jews on Three Continents: Migration and Resettlement,* edited by Noah Lewin-Epstein et al., 21–44. London: Frank Cass.

Glinert, Lewis H. 1995. Inside the Language Planner's Head: Tactical Responses to a Mass Immigration. *Journal of Multilingual and Multicultural Development* 16, no. 5:351–71.

Goffmannova, Ia. 2000. "Podskazyvanie," "poddakivanie" i drugie vidy strategii preodolenia kommunikativnykh barierov ["Prompting," "Assenting," and Other Means of Overcoming Communicative Barriers]. In *Iazyk kak sredstvo transliatsii kul'tury,* edited by M. B. Eshich, 132–53. Moskva: Nauka.

Golanova, E. I. 1996. Ustnyi publichnyi dialog: zhanr interviu [Oral Public Dialogue: The Genre of the Interview]. In *Russkii iazyk kontsa XX stoletia (1985–1995),* edited by E. A. Zemskaia, 427–52. Moskva: Iazyki Russkoi Kul'tury.

Gold, John R. 1980. *An Introduction to Behavioral Geography.* New York: Oxford University Press.

Goldberg-Mulkiewicz, Olga. 1970. Kavim le dmuto shel' ha-yehudi bayetsira ha- polanit ha-amamit [On the Image of the Jew in Polish Folk Culture]. In *Mehkarei ha-merkaz le heker ha folklor.* Ierushalaim: Hotsaat Sfarim Al Shem Magnes, 149–52.

———. 1983. The Stereotype of the Jew in Polish Folklore. In *Studies in Aggadah and Jewish Folklore,* edited by I. Ben-Ami and J. Dan, 83–94. Jerusalem: Hebrew University and Magnes Press.

Golden, Deborah. 2002. Storytelling the Future: Israelis, Immigrants and the Imagining of Community. *Anthropological Quarterly* 75, no. 1:7–35.

———. 2003. Musar ha-skel leumi: Teurim shel' iotsot Brit ha-Muatsot lesheavar be israel' [A National Cautionary Tale: Russian Women Newcomers to Israel Portrayed]. In *Al gvulot tarbutiim u veinehem: Olim tseirim be Israel'*, edited by R. Eizikovich, 157–83. Tel-Aviv: Hotsat Ramot-universitat Tel-Aviv.

Goldshtein, Alexander. 2002. Uvazhenie drugogo [Respect for the Other]. *Okna*, 24 January: 26–27.

Goldstein, Kenneth S. 1964. *A Guide for Fieldworkers in Folklore.* Hatboro, Pa.: Folklore Associates.

Golosov, Grigorii V., and Iulia Shevchenko. 2004. Nation-Building and Common Values in St. Petersburg. In *Nation-Building and Common Values in Russia,* edited by Pål Kolstø and Helge Blakkisrud, 191–216. Lanham, Md.: Rowman & Littlefield.

Goluboff, Sasha. 2003. *Jewish Russians: Upheavals in a Moscow Synagogue.* Philadelphia: University of Pennsylvania Press.

Gomel, Ilana. 2006. *Atem ve-anahnu: lehiot rusim be-israel* [*The Pilgrim Soul: Being a Russian in Israel.* Translated from English by Yael Inbar.] Or Yehuda: Kinneret, Zmora-Bitan, Dvir.

Gonen, Amiram. 1998. Settlement of the Immigrants: Geographic Patterns. In *Profile of an Immigration Wave: The Absorption Process of Immigrants from the Former Soviet Union, 1990–1995,* edited by Moshe Sicron and Elazar Leshem, 232–69. Jerusalem: Hebrew University and Magnes Press.

Goodwin, Robin, et al. 1999. Glasnost and the Art of Conversation: A Multilevel Analysis of Intimate Disclosure across Three Former Communist Cultures. *Journal of Cross-Cultural Psychology* 30, no. 1:72–90.

Gopman, Viktor. 2003. Akh, chto vy govorite! [You Don't Really Mean It!]. *Okna,* 10 April: 42.

Görög-Karady, Veronika. 1992. Ethnic Sterotypes and Folklore: The Jew in Hungarian Oral Literature. In *Folklore Processed,* edited by Reimund Kvideland, 114–25. Helsinki: Suomalaisen Kirjallisuuden Seura.

Grigorian, E. A. 1996. Dinamika sovremennykh iazykovykh situatsii [The Dynamics of Contemporary Language Situations]. *Russkaia Rech'* 2:41–46.

Gudkov, Lev. 2004. *Negativnaiaia identichnost': Stat'i 1997–2002* [Negative Identity: Essays from 1997 to 2002]. Moskva: Novoe Literaturnoe Obozrenie.

Gudkova, V. V. 1989. Beg: Primechania [The Flight: Commentaries]. In M. A. Bulgakov, *Piesy 1920–kh godov.* Leningrad: Iskusstvo, 550–66.

Gura, A. V. 1997. *Simvolika zhivotnykh v slavianskoi narodnoi traditsi.* [Animal Symbolism in Slavic Folk Tradition]. Moskva: Indrik.

Gusejnov, Gasan. 2000. *Karta nashei Rodiny: Ideologema mezhdu slo-*

vom i telom [The Map of Our Motherland: The Ideologem between the Word and the Body]. Helsinki: Institute for Russian and East-European Studies.

———. 2004. *Sovetskie ideologemy v russkom diskurse 1990–kh* [Soviet Ideologemes in the Russian Discourse of the 1990s]. Moskva: Tri kvadrata.

Gvindadze, Nelly. 2002. Pisatel' Dzhaba Ioseliani [The Writer Dzhaba Ioseliani]. *Vechernii Tbilisi,* 23 March.

Habib, Jack, et al. 1998. Kvutsot be-sikun be-kerev ha-olim [Groups at Risk among the New Immigrants]. In *Profile of an Immigration Wave: The Absorption Process of Immigrants from the Former Soviet Union, 1990–1995,* edited by Moshe Sicron and Elazar Leshem, 409–35. Jerusalem: Hebrew University and Magnes Press.

Hagendoorn, Louk, et al. 1998. Inter-Ethnic Preferences and Ethnic Hierarchies in the Former Soviet Union. *International Journal of Intercultural Relations* 22, no. 4:484–503.

Hall, Stuart. 1996. Introduction: Who Needs "Identity?" In *Questions of Cultural Identity,* edited by Stuart Hall and Paul du Gay, 1–17. London: Sage.

Hasan, Sana. 1986. *Enemy in the Promised Land: An Egyptian Woman's Journey into Israel.* New York: Schocken Books.

Hawkins, Eric. 1984. *Awareness of Language: An Introduction.* Cambridge: Cambridge University Press.

Heilman, Samuel C. 1998. Building Jewish Identity for Tomorrow: Possible or Not? In *Jewish Survival: The Identity Problem at the Close of the Twentieth Century,* edited by Ernest Krausz and Gitta Tulea, 77–86. New Brunswick, N.J.: Transaction.

Heinz, Bettina. 2001. "Fish in the River": Experiences of Bicultural Bilingual Speakers. *Multilingua* 20, no. 1:85–108.

Heschel, Abraham Joshua. 1951. *The Sabbath.* New York: Farrar, Strauss and Giroux.

Hickerson, Nancy Parrot. 1980. *Linguistic Anthropology.* New York: Holt, Rinehart and Winston.

Hodge, Robert, and Gunther Kress. 1979. *Language as Ideology.* London: Routledge.

———. 1988. *Social Semiotics.* Oxford: Polity Press.

Hogg, Michael A., and Dominic Abrams. 1988. *Social Identifications: A Social Psychology of Intergroup Relations and Group Processes.* London: Routledge.

Holland, R. F. 1965. The Miraculous. *American Philosophical Quarterly* 2, no. 1:43–51.

Hollingsworth, Christopher. 2001. *Poetics of the Hive: The Insect Metaphor in Literature.* Iowa City: University of Iowa Press.

Holmes, Janet. 2001. *An Introduction to Sociolinguistics.* 2nd ed. Harlow, England: Longman.

Holmes, Janet, and Meredith Marra. 2002. Over the Edge? Subversive

Humor between Colleagues and Friends. *Humor: International Journal of Humor Research* 15, no. 1:65–87.

Honeck, Richard P. 1997. *A Proverb in Mind: The Cognitive Science of Proverbial Wit and Wisdom*. Mahwah, N.J.: Erlbaum.

Honko, Lauri. 1964. Memorates and the Study of Folk Beliefs. *Journal of the Folklore Institute* 1:5–19.

———. 1986. Folkloristic Studies on Meaning: An Introduction. In *ARV Scandinavian Yearbook of Folklore: 1984,* edited by Bengt R. Johnsson, 35–56. Uppsala: Almqvist and Wiksell.

———. 2001. Do We Need a Folkloristic Code of Ethics? *FF Network* 21:2–7.

Horenczyk, G. 2000. Conflicted Identities: Acculturation Attitudes and Immigrants. In *Language, Identity and Immigration,* edited by E. Olshtain and G. Horenczyk, 13–30. Jerusalem: Hebrew University and Magnes Press.

Horowitz, Tamar, Shmuel Shamai, and Zinaida Ilatov. 2003. *ha-tma'a, dialog ve-ha-azama: vatikim ve-olim be-kazrin* [*Assimilation, Dialogue, and Empowerment: Immigrants and Non-Immigrants in Katzrin*]. Tel-Aviv: University of Tel-Aviv, Ramot.

Huntington, Samuel P. 1996. *The Clash of Civilizations and the Remaking of World Order.* New York: Simon and Schuster.

Hymes, Dell. 1986. Models of the Interaction of Language and Social Life. In *Directions in Sociolinguistics,* edited by John J. Gumperz and Dell Hymes, 35–71. Oxford: Blackwell.

Iakovenko, I. G. 2000. Nenormativnyi anekdot kak modeliruiushchaia sistema: Opyt kul'turologicheskogo analiza [The Unconventional Joke as a Modeling System: An Experiment in Culturological Analysis]. *Novoe Literaturnoe Obozrenie* 43, no. 3:335–46.

Iakovleva, E. S. 1994. *Fragmenty russkoi iazykovoi kartiny mira (Modeli prostranstva, vremeni i vospriatia)* [Fragments of the Russian Language Universe: Models of Space, Time, and Perception]. Moskva: Gnosis.

Ievgenieva, A. P., ed. 1981–84. *Slovar' russkogo iazyka v chetyrekh tomakh* [A Dictionary of the Russian Language in Four Volumes]. 2nd ed. Moskva: Russkii Iazyk.

Ilatov, Zinaida Z., and Shmuel Shamai. 1998. Israeli Students' Attitudes toward Children-Immigrants from Russia. In *Immigration to Israel: Sociological Perspectives,* edited by Elazar Leshem and Judith T. Shuval, 273–85. Studies of Israeli Society, vol. 8. New Brunswick, N.J.: Transaction.

Ilf, Ilya, and Yevgeny Petrov. 1962. *The Golden Calf.* Translated from the Russian by John A. C. Richardson. London: Frederick Muller.

Iontsev, V. A. 2001. Ekonomicheskie i demograficheskie aspekty "vneshnei" migratsii naselenia v Rossii [Economic and Demographic Aspects of the "External" Migration in Russia]. In V. A. Iontsev et al., *Emigratsia i repatriatsia v Rossii.* Moskva: Popechitel'stvo o nuzhdakh Rossiiskikh repatriantov, 293–391.

Iontsev, V. A., et al. 2001. *Emigratsia i repatriatsia v Rossii* [Emigration and Repatriation in Russia]. Moskva: Popechitel'stvo o nuzhdakh Rossiiskikh repatriantov.

Isakova, Anna. 2003a. Po pravu nasledovania [By Right of Legacy]. *Okna,* 6 February: 6–7, 12.

———. 2003b. Litsom k litsu [Face to Face]. *Okna,* 27 February: 22–23, 27.

———. 2003c. Vopros prestizha [A Question of Prestige]. *Okna,* 24 April: 14–15.

———. 2004. Alia ty moia, alia [Aliya, Oh, My Aliya]. *Kontekst,* 29 January: 4–6.

Jakobson, Roman. 1960. Closing Statement: Linguistics and Poetics. In *Style and Language,* edited by Thomas A. Sebeok, 350–77. Cambridge, Mass.: MIT Press.

James, Carl. 1999. Language Awareness: Implications for the Language Curriculum. *Language, Culture and Curriculum* 12, no. 1:94–115.

Jasinskaja-Lahti, Inga, and Karmela Liebkind. 1999. Exploration of Ethnic Identity among Russian-Speaking Adolescents in Finland. *Journal of Cross-Cultural Psychology* 30, no. 4:527–39.

Jasinskaja-Lahti, Inga, et al. 2003. The Interactive Nature of Acculturation: Perceived Discrimination, Acculturation Attitudes and Stress among Young Ethnic Repatriates in Finland, Israel and Germany. *International Journal of Intercultural Relations* 27, no. 1:79–97.

Jason, Heda. 1975. *Ethnopoetics: Multilingual Terminology.* Jerusalem: Israel Ethnographic Society.

Jessel, Levic. 1978. *The Ethnic Process: An Evolutionary Concept of Languages and Peoples.* The Hague: Mouton.

Jeter, Kris, and Rita N. Gerasimova. 1998. "I Sleep, But My Heart Stirs, Restless and Dreams": The Mythology of Russian Jewish Immigrant Couples in Israel. *Journal of Couples Therapy* 7, no. 4:81–96.

Jones, Clive. 1996. *Soviet Jewish Aliyah: Implications for Israel and the Middle East.* London: Frank Cass.

———. 2001. A Political and Identity Deficit? Immigration, Israel, and the Olim from the Former Soviet Union. Paper presented at the conference "Primary Solidarities and Middle East Elite Groups." University of Haifa, Israel.

Jones, Michael Owen. 2000. "Tradition" in Identity Discourses and in Individual's Symbolic Construction of Self. *Western Folklore* 59:115–40.

Jones, Steven Swan. 1985. Joking Transformations of Popular Fairy Tales: A Comparative Analysis of Five Jokes and Their Fairy Tale Sources. *Western Folklore* 44:97–114.

Kabbani, Rana. 1986. *Europe's Myth of Orient: Devise and Rule.* London: Macmillan.

Kaganskaia, Maia. 2005. Daleko ot Moskvy [Far from Moscow]. *Okna,*

15 December: 14, 16.

Kaganskii, Vladimir. 2001. *Kul'turnyi landshaft i Sovetskoe obitaemoe prostranstvo. Sbornik statei* [Cultural Landscape and Soviet Habitable Space]. Moskva: Novoe Literaturnoe obozrenie.

Karaulov, Yu. N. 1992. O iazyke russkogo zarubezhia [About the Language of the Russian Abroad]. *Voprosy iazykoznania* 6:5–19.

Karev, V. M. 1982. Sud'ba [Fate]. In *Mify Narodov Mira* v dvukh tomakh. T. 2, edited by S. A. Tokarev, 471–74. Moskva: Sovetskaia Entsiklopedia.

Katz, Ruth. 2000. Attitudes of New Immigrant and Veteran-Resident Israeli Divorced Mothers toward Single Motherhood. *International Migration* 38, no. 95:83–93.

Kaurinkoski, Kira. 2003. Les grecs de Mariupol (Ukraine). Reflexions sur une identite en diaspora. *La Revue Européenne des Migrations Internationales* 19, no. 1:125–46.

Kellerman, Aharon. 1989. *Time, Space, and Society: Geographical Societal Perspectives.* Dordrecht: Kluwer.

Kenigstein, Moshe. 1999. *Lexicon of the "Russian" Aliyah* [in Russian and Hebrew]. Ariel: n.p.

Kennedy, Mike Dixon. 1998. *Encyclopedia of Greco-Roman Mythology.* Santa Barbara, Calif.: Clio.

Keramida, Fani. 1999. The Way to the Homeland: A "Repatriated" Migrant's Life Story. *Oral History* Spring: 75–89.

Khazan, Vladimir. 1999. The Theme and Image of Jerusalem in Early Soviet Russian Belle Lettres. *Jews in Eastern Europe* 38–39, nos. 1–2:25–43.

Kheifets, Mikhail. 2005. Popytka "ozelenit'" sukhuiu territoriu, ili seminar v Nazarete [Attempts to "Green" Arid Lands, Or a Seminar in Nazareth]. *Vesti-2,* 17 February: 20.

Kheimets, Nina, and Alek Epstein. 2001a. Confronting the Languages of Statehood: Theoretical and Historical Frameworks for the Analysis of Multilingual Identity of the Russian Jewish Intelligentsia in Israel. *Language Problems and Language Planning* 25, no. 2:121–43.

———. 2001b. English as a Central Component of Success in the Professional and Social Integration of Scientists from the Former Soviet Union in Israel. *Language and Society* 30, no. 2:187–215.

Khrustaleva, N. S., ed. 2001a. *Psikhologicheskie Problemy Russkikh emigrantov v Germanii* [Psychological Problems of the Russian Immigrants in Germany]. Sankt-Peterburg: Izdatel'stvo Sankt Peterburgskogo Universiteta.

———. 2001b. Uchastie v kruglom stole o migratsii. [A Participant of a Panel Talk on Migration]. In *Sotsializatsia detei rossiiskikh migrantov: materialy Vtorogo mezhdunarodnogo kruglogo stola po problemam kul'turnoi i psikhologicheskoi sotsializatsii detei rossiiskikh migrantov i bezhentsev,* edited by O. I. Makhovskaia et al, 26–31. Moskva: Institut psikhologii RAN.

Kimmerling, Baruch. 2001. *The Invention and Decline of Israeliness: State, Society, and the Military.* Berkeley: University of California Press.

Kipling, Rudyard. 1983. The Ballad of East and West. In Rudyard Kipling, *Poems. Short Stories,* 71–75. Moscow: Raduga Publishers.

Kirshenblatt-Gimblett, Barbara. 1978. Cultural Shock and Narrative Creativity. In *Folklore in the Modern World,* edited by R. Dorson, 109–22. The Hague: Mouton.

———. 1983. Studying Immigrant and Ethnic Folklore. In *Handbook of American Folklore,* edited by R. Dorson, 39–47. Bloomington: Indiana University Press.

———. 1994. On Difference. *Journal of American Folklore* 107:233–38.

Kogan, Aleksandr. 2004. Parlamentskie strasti po "babe Liube" ["Baba-Liuba" Sparks Passions in the Parliament]. *Novosti Nedeli,* 18 March: 11.

Komarova, Galina Aleksandrovna. 2002. *Russkii Boston* [Russian Boston]. Moskva: Institut Etnologii i Antropologii RAN.

Korolenko, Vladimir. 1954. Bratia Mendel'. [The Mendel Brothers]. In V. G. Korolenko, *Sobranie sochinenii v desiati tomakh.,* tom vtoroi. Moskva: Gosudarstvennoe izdatel'stvo khudozhestvennoi literatury, 399–462.

Kosmarskaya, Natalya. 2006. *"Deti Imperii" v postsovetskoi Tsentral'noi Azii: Adaptivnye praktiki i mental'nye sdvigi (russkie v Kirgizii, 1992–2002)* ["Children of the Empire" in Post-Soviet Central Asia: Mental Shifts and Practices of Adaptation (Russians in Kirghizia, 1992–2002)]. Moskva: Natalis Press.

Kovshova, M. L. 1994. Kontsept sud'by. Fol'klor i frazeololgia. [The Concept of Fate: Folklore and Phraseology] In *Poniatie sud'by v kontekste raznykh kul'tur,* edited by N. D. Arutiunova, 137–42. Moskva: Nauka.

Kozhevnikov, V. M., and P. A Nikolaev. 1987. *Literaturnyi entsiklopedicheskii slovar'* [Encyclopedic Dictionary of Literature]. Moskva: Sovetskaia Entsiklopedia, 28.

Krysin, L. P. 1996. Evfemizmy v sovremennoi russkoi rechi [Euphemisms in Contemporary Russian Speech]. In *Russkii iazyk kontsa XX stoletia (1985–1995),* edited by E. A. Zemskaia, 384–408. Moskva: Iazyki Russkoi Kul'tury.

Kuprin, Aleksandr. 1957. Zhidovka [The Jewess]. In A. I. Kuprin, *Sobranie sochinenii v shesti tomakh,* tom tretii. Moskva: Gosudarstvennoe izdatel'stvo khudozhestvennoi literatury, 213–33.

Kvideland, Reimund. 1990. Storytelling in Modern Society. In *Storytelling in Modern Society,* edited by Lutz Röhrich and Sabine Wienker-Pepho, 15–22. Tübingen: Günter Narr Verlag.

Labov, William. 1972. *Language in the Inner City.* Philadelphia: University of Pennsylvania Press.

Labov, William, and Joshua Waletzky. 1966. Narrative Analysis: Oral

Versions of Personal Experience. In *Essays on the Verbal and Visual Arts*, edited by J. Helm, 12–44. Seattle: University of Washington Press.

Laitin, David D. 1999. Identity in Formation: The Russian-Speaking Nationality in the Post-Soviet Diaspora. In *Migration, Diasporas and Transnationalism*, edited by Steven Vertovec and Robin Cohen. Cheltenham, England: Edward Elgar, 321–56.

Lakoff, George, and Mark Johnson. 1980. *Metaphors We Live By*. Chicago: University of Chicago Press.

Lambert, Wallace E., and Donald M. Taylor. 1996. Language in the Lives of Ethnic Minorities: Cuban American Families in Miami. *Applied Linguistics* 17, no. 4:477–500.

Larmer, Robert A. H. 1988. *Water into Wine? An Investigation of the Concept of Miracle.* Montreal: McGill-Queen's University Press.

Lebedeva, L. B. 2000. Semantika ogranichivaiuschikh slov [The Semantics of Restricting Words]. In *Logicheskii analiz iazyka: Iazyk prostranstv*, edited by N. D. Arutiunova and I. B. Levontina, 93–97. Moskva: Iazyki Russkoi Kul'tury.

Lebedeva, Nadezhda. 1993. *Sotsial'naia psikhologia etnicheskikh migratsii* [Social Psychology of Ethic Migrations]. Moskva: Rossiiskaia Akademia Nauk, Institut Etnologii i Antropologii.

———. 1997. *Novaia russkaia diaspora: sotsial'no-psikhologicheskii analiz* [The New Russian Diaspora: Socio-Psychological Analysis]. Moskva: Institut Etnologii i Antropologii im. M. N. Miklukho-Maklaia.

———. 1999. *Vvedenie v etnicheskuiu i kross-kul'turnuiu psikhologiu* [Ethnic and Cross-Cultural Psychology: An Introduction]. Moskva: Kluch-S.

———. 2001. Russkaia emigratsia v zerkale psikhologii [Russian Emigration in the Mirror of Psychology]. In V. A. Iontsev et al., *Emigratsia i repatriatsia v Rossii.* Moskva: Popechitel'stvo o nuzhdakh rossiiskikh repatriantov, 104–224.

Lefcourt, Herbert M., and Rod A. Martin. 1986. *Humor and Life Stress.* New York: Springer Verlag.

Lemish, Dafna. 2000. The Whore and the Other: Israeli Images of Female Immigrants from the Former USSR. *Gender and Society* 14, no. 2:333–49.

Lemon, Alaina. 1998. "Your Eyes Are Green Like Dollars": Counterfeit Cash, National Substance, and Currency Apartheid in 1990s Russia. *Cultural Anthropology* 13, no. 1:22–55.

Lermontov, M. Iu. 1969a. Ballada [A Ballad]. In M. Yu. Lermontov, *Sobranie sochinenii v chetyrekh tomakh.* Vol 1. Moskva: Izdatel'stvo "Pravda," 255–56.

———. 1969b. Borodino [Borodino]. In M. Yu. Lermontov, *Sobranie sochinenii v chetyrekh tomakh.* Vol 1. Moskva: Izdatel'stvo "Pravda," 264–67.

———. 1969c. Geroi nashego vremeni [A Hero of Our Time]. In M. Yu. Lermontov, *Sobranie sochinenii v chetyrekh tomakh.* Vol 4. Moskva: Izdatel'stvo "Pravda," 196–335.

Leshem, Elazar. 1998. The Israeli Public Attitudes toward the New Immigrants of the 1990s. In *Immigration to Israel: Sociological Perspectives,* edited by Elazar Leshem and Judith T. Shuval, 307–30. Studies of Israeli Society, vol. 8. New Brunswick, N.J.: Transaction.

Leshem, Elazar, and Moshe Lissak. 1999. Development and Consolidation of the Russian Community in Israel. In *Roots and Routes: Ethnicity and Migration in Global Perspective,* edited by Shalva Weil, 135–71. Jerusalem: Hebrew University and Magnes Press.

Leshem, Elazar, and Moshe Sicron. 1998. The Absorption Process of Immigrants from the Former Soviet Union, 1990–1995: Main Findings. In *Profile of an Immigration Wave: The Absorption Process of Immigrants from the Former Soviet Union, 1990–1995,* edited by Moshe Sicron and Elazar Leshem, ix–xxxvii. Jerusalem: Hebrew University and Magnes Press.

Levin, Zalman I. 2001a. *Mentalitet Diaspory: Sistemnyi i Sotsiokul'turnyi Analiz* [The Diaspora Mentality: Systemic and Sociocultural Analysis]. Moskva: Institut Vostokovedenia RAN, Kraft.

———. 2001b. Mentalitet diaspory: Sistemnyi i sotsial'nyi aspekty [The Diaspora Mentality: Systemic and Social Aspects]. In *Natsional'nye diaspory v Rossii i za rubezhom v XIX–XX vv. Sbornik statei,* edited by Yu. A. Poliakov i G. Ya. Tarle, 45–53. Moskva: Institut Rossiiskoi Istorii RAN.

Levinson, Aleksei. 1999. Neskol'ko zamechanii po sotsiologii anekdota v sviazi s novymi knigami ob etnicheskom i politicheskom iumore [Some Remarks on the Sociology of the Joke in Light of New Books on Ethnic and Political Humor]. *Novoe Literaturnoe Obozrenie* 37:369–81.

———. 2004. Instituty i identichnost' [Institutions and Identity] *Opyt sotsiografii: Stat'i.* Moskva: Novoe Literaturnoe Obozrenie, 445–538.

Lévi-Strauss, Claude. 1963. *Structural Anthropology.* New York: Basic Books.

Levkievskaia, E. 1999. Domovoi [The House Spirit]. In *Slavianskie drevnosti, v piati tomakh.* Vol. 2. Edited by N. I. Tolstoy, 120–24. Moskva: Mezhdunarodnye Otnoshenia.

Levy, Jacob T. 2000. *The Multiculturalism of Fear.* Oxford: Oxford University Press.

Lewin-Epstein, Noah, Gila Menahem, and Reuven Barham. 1997. Yes to Immigration but What about Immigrants? Local Attitudes to Immigrant Absorption. In *Russian Jews on Three Continents: Migration and Resettlement,* edited by Noah Lewin-Epstein et al., 471–74. London: Frank Cass.

Lisnianskaia, Dina. 2005. Palestintsy i "russkie" izrail'tiane [Palestinians and "Russian" Israelis]. *Vesti-2,* 10 November: 10.

Lomsky-Feder, Edna, and Tamar Rapoport. 2004. Speaking Their Language? Identity, Home and Power Relations in Interviews with Immigrants. In *The Autobiography Adventure: Theory and Practice,* edited by M. H. Menna Barreto Abraho. Porto Alegre, Brazil: Edipucrs, 329–54.

Loshak, Victor. 2001. Raskalennyi vopros: Interviu s Aleksandrom Solzhenitsynym [A Red-Hot Question: An Interview with Aleksandr Solzhenitsin]. *Globus* 454:8, 10.

Loshitsky, Yosefa. 2000. Orientalist Representations: Palestinians and Arabs in Some Postcolonial Film and Literature. In *Cultural Encounters: Representing "Otherness,"* edited by Elizabeth Hallam and Brian V. Street, 51–71. London: Routledge.

Lotman, Yurii M. 1977. Two Models of Communication. In *Soviet Semiotics: An Anthology,* edited by Daniel P. Lucid, 99–101. Baltimore: Johns Hopkins University Press.

———. 1992a. O dvukh modeliakh kommunikatsii v sisteme kul'tury [Two Models of Communication]. In Yu. M. Lotman, *Izbrannye statii v 3 tomakh. Statii po semiotike i tipologii kul'tury.* Vol. 1. Tallinn: Aleksandra, 76–89.

———. 1992b. Simvolika Peterburga i problemy semiotiki goroda [The Symbolism of St. Petersburg and Problems of City Semiotics]. In Yu. M. Lotman, *Izbrannye statii v 3 tomakh. Statii po istorii russkoi literatury XVIII-pervoi poloviny XIX veka.* Vol. 2. Tallinn: Aleksandra, 9–21.

———. 1993. Problema Vostoka i Zapada v tvorchestve pozdnego Lermontova [The Problem of East and West in Lermontov's Later Writings]. In Yuri Lotman, *Izbrannye stat'i v trekh tomakh.* Vol. 3. Tallinn: Aleksandra, 9–23.

———. 1997. Dom v "Mastere i Margarite" [The Home in "Master and Margarita"]. In Yu. M. Lotman, *O russkoi literature: Stat'i i issledovania* (1958–1993). Sankt-Peterburg: Ikusstvo-SPB, 748–54.

Lotman, Yu. M., and B. A. Uspenskii. 1992. Mif—imia—kul'tura [Myth, Name, and Culture]. In Yu. M. Lotman, *Izbrannye statii v 3 tomakh. Statii po semiotike i tipologii kul'tury.* Vol. 1. Tallinn: Aleksandra, 58–75.

Lucy, John A. 1993. Reflexive Language and the Human Disciplines. In *Reflexive Language: Reported Speech and Metapragmatics,* edited by John A. Lucy, 9–32. Cambridge: Cambridge University Press.

Lurie, Ya. S. 1986. Russkii "chuzhezemets" v Indii XV veka [A Russian "Alien" in India in the Fifteenth Century]. In *Khozhdenie za tri moria Afanasia Nikitina,* edited by Ya. S. Lurie and L. S. Semenov, 61–87. Leningrad: Nauka.

Lustick, Ian. 1999. Israel as a Non-Arab State: The Political Implications of Mass Immigration of Non-Jews. *Middle East Journal* 53, no.

3:417–33.
Mahameed, Hashem, and Yosef Gottman. 1983. Autostereotypes and Heterostereotypes of Jews and Arabs in Different Contact Situations. *Israeli Journal of Psychology and Counseling in Education* 16:90–108.
Makhovskaia, O. I., et al. 2001. *Sotsializatsia detei rossiiskikh migrantov: materialy Vtorogo mezhdunarodnogo kruglogo stola po problemam kul'turnoi i psikhologicheskoi sotsializatsii detei rossiiskikh migrantov i bezhentsev* [Socialization of the Russian Migrants' Children: The Second International Panel Talk Dedicated to the Problems of Cultural and Psychological Socialization of the Children of the Russian Migrants and Refugees]. Moskva: Institut psikhologii RAN.
Maksimov, Sergei. 1994. *Nechistaia, nevedomaia i kriestnaia sila* [An Evil, Mysterious, and Divine Force]. Sankt-Peterburg: Poliset.
Maltz, Daniel M., and Ruth A. Borker. 1982. A Cultural Approach to Male-Female Miscommunication. In *Language and Social Identity,* edited by John J. Gumperz, 195–216. Cambridge: Cambridge University Press.
Maoz, Ifat. 2000. Power Relations in Intergroup Encounters: A Case Study of Jewish-Arab Encounters in Israel. *International Journal of Intercultural Relations* 24:259–77.
Mar, Philip. 1998. Just the Place Is Different: Comparison of Place and Settlement Practices of Some Hong Kong Migrants in Sydney. *The Australian Journal of Anthropology* 9, no. 1:58–73.
Marcus, Eliezer. 1977. *The Confrontation between Jews and Non-Jews in Folktales of the Jews of Islamic Countries.* Parts 1 and 2. Doctoral dissertation, Hebrew University of Jerusalem.
Markowitz, Fran. 1993. *A Community in Spite of Itself: Soviet Jewish Émigrés in New York.* Washington, D.C.: Smithsonian Institution Press.
———. 1995. Emigration, Immigration and Cultural Change: Towards a Transnational Russian-Jewish Community? In *Jews and Jewish Life in Russia and the Soviet Union,* edited by Y. Ro'i, 403–14. London: Frank Cass.
———. 1997. Cultural Change, Border Crossings and Identity Shopping: Jewish Teenagers from the CIS Assess Their Future in Israel. In *Russian Jews on Three Continents: Migration and Resettlement,* edited by Noah Lewin-Epstein et al., 344–63. London: Frank Cass.
Martynova, Victoria. 2002a. "Piataia Grafa" otmenaietsia? Nu i chto? [Has the Fifth Paragraph Been Abolished? So What?]. *Vesti,* 6 June: 13.
———. 2002b. MVD: "Vy sluzhite, a my podozhdem!" [The Ministry of the Interior: "Do Your Army Service Boys, and We'll Wait!"]. *Vesti,* 4 July: 8.
———. 2003a. Teoria nenapravlennogo vzryva [The Theory of the Non-

Targeted Explosion]. *Vesti-2,* 30 January: 9,15.
———. 2003b. Absurd nashego vremeni [An Absurdity of Our Times]. *Vesti-2,* 3 April: 9.
———. 2003c. Voina i mir glazami "Al-Dzhaziry" [War and Peace in Al-Jazeera's Eyes]. *Vesti,* 24 April: 5.
———. 2005a. Dikie, kak Tarzan, ili pochemu araby zheniatsia na "russkikh"? [Wild Like Tarzan, or Why Do Arabs Marry "Russian" Women?] *Novosti Nedeli,* 22 September: 2–3.
———. 2005b. Sil'vestr na "russkoi ulitse": Kak sobiraiutsia vstrechat' novyi god politiki i zhurnalisty [Sivester on the "Russian Street": How Politicians and Journalist Are Going to Celebrate the New Year]. *Novosti Nedeli,* 29 December: 2.
McCann, C. D., and E. T. Higgins. 1990. Social Cognition and Communication. In *Handbook of Language and Social Psychology,* edited by H. Giles and W. P. Robinson, 13–32. Chichester, England: Wiley.
Menahem, Gila, and Idit Geijst. 2000. Language and Occupation among Soviet Immigrants to Israel in the 1990s. In *Language, Identity and Immigration,* edited by E. Olshtain and G. Horenczyk, 301–24. Jerusalem: Hebrew University and Magnes Press.
Mieder, Wolfgang. 1997. *The Politics of Proverbs: From Traditional Wisdom to Proverbial Stereotypes.* Madison: University of Wisconsin Press.
Mikhailin, V. Yu. 2000. Russkii mat kak muzhskoi obstsennyi kod: Problema proiskhozhdenia i evolutsia statusa [Russian Obscene Language as a Male Code: Origin and the Status Evolution]. *Novoe Literaturnoe Obozrenie* 43, no. 3:347–93.
Mikhalkov, Sergei. 1999. *Dlia Detei* [For Children]. Moskva: Rosmen.
Miller, Kim. 1997. All in the Family: Family Folklore, Objectivity and Self-Censorship. *Western Folklore* 56:331–45.
Miller, Robert L. 2000. *Researching Life Stories and Family Histories.* London: Sage.
Mills, Melinda. 2000. Providing Space for Time: The Impact of Temporality on Life Course Research. *Time and Society* 9, no. 1:91–127.
Milner-Gulland, Robin. 1999. *The Russians.* Oxford: Blackwell.
Mirskii, Mark. 2004. Michurintsy ot sionizma [Zionist Followers of Michurin]. *Novosti Nedeli,* 1 April: 5.
———. 2005. Russkaia bolezn' [Russian Disease]. *Novosti Nedeli,* 29 December: 27.
Mirsky, Julia. 2005. *Israelim: sipurei ha-gira* [Israelis: Immigration Stories]. Tel-Aviv: Tsevonim.
Mirsky, Julia, and Leah Prawer. 1999. Immigrating as an Adolescent. In *Children of Perestroika in Israel,* edited by Tamar Horowitz, 72–92. Lanham, Md.: University Press of America.
Mokienko, V. M., and T. G. Nikitina. 1998. *Tolkovyi slovar' iazyka sovdepii* [A Dictionary of Soviet Speak]. Sankt-Peterburg: Folio Press.
———. 2001. *Bol'shoi slovar' russkogo zhargona* [A Large Dictionary of

Russian Slang]. Sankt-Peterburg: Norint.
Morley, David, and Kevin Robins. 1995. *Space of Identity: Global Media, Electronic Landscapes and Cultural Boundaries.* London: Routledge.
Moroz, Andrei. 2000. Predstavlenia o grekhe v sovremennoi traditsionnoi kul'ture Russkogo Severa [Perceptions of Sin in the Contemporary Traditional Culture of Russian North]. In *The Concept of Sin in Slavic and Jewish Cultural Traditions,* edited by Olga Belova. Akademicheskaia seria, vol. 5. Moskva: Sefer, 195–205.
———. 2001. Informant "veriashchii" i "neveriashchii" [A "Believing" and a "Non-Believing" Informant]. *Zhivaia Starina* 1:10–11.
Morozov, I. A., and O. E. Frolova. 1999. Pushkin v anekdote [Pushkin in Jokes]. *Zhivaia Starina* 4, no. 24:21–23.
Moskovich, Wolf. 1992. Zametki o iazyke russkogo zarubezhia [Notes on the Language of the Russians Abroad]. In *Russian Philology and History: In Honor of Professor Victor Levin,* edited by Wolf Moskovich, 126–36. Jerusalem: Hebrew University of Jerusalem.
Moyle, Natalie K. 1989. Spacy Soviets and the Russian Attitude toward Territorial Passage. In *Folk Groups and Folklore Genres: A Reader,* edited by Elliott Oring, 87–97. Logan: Utah State University Press.
Naiditch, Larissa. 1998. Russian and German Ethno-Adjectives and Their Collocations. *Lexicology* 4, no. 2:281–306.
———. 2000. Code-Switching and -Mixing in Russian-Hebrew Bilinguals. In *Languages in Contact: Studies in Slavic and General Linguistics,* edited by D. G. Gilbers et al. Amsterdam: Rodopi, 277–82.
———. 2004. Russian Immigrants of the Last Wave in Israel: Patterns and Characteristics of Language Usage. *Weiner Slawistischer Almanach* 53:291–314.
Nekrasov, Nikolai. 1979. Chernyi den' [A Black Day]. *Sobranie sochinenii v chetyrekh tomakh.* Vol. 3. Moskva: Pravda, 332.
Neumann, Iver B. 1999. *Uses of the Other: "The East" in European Identity Formation.* Minneapolis: University of Minnesota Press.
Nevo, Ofra, and Jacob Levine. 1994. Jewish Humor Strikes Again: The Outburst of Humor in Israel during the Gulf War. *Western Folklore* 50, no. 2:125–45.
Nicolaisen, W. F. H. 1987. Legends as Narrative Response. In *Perspectives on Contemporary Legend.* Vol. 2. Edited by Gillian Bennett, Paul Smith, and J. D. A. Widdowson, 167–78. Sheffield, England: Sheffield Academic Press.
———. 2001. "A Change of Place Is a Change of Fortune": Place Names as Structuring Devices in Chaim Bermant's Novels. *Nomina* 24:5–15.
Niedermüller, Peter. 1988. From the Stories of Life to the Life History: Historic Context, Social Processes and the Biographical Method. In *Life History as Cultural Construction/Performance,* edited by Tamás Hofer and Péter Niedermüller. Proceedings of the Third American-

Hungarian Folklore Conference. Budapest: Ethnographic Institute of the Hungarian Academy of Sciences, 452–73.

Niedzielski, Nancy A., and Dennis R. Preston. 2000. *Folk Linguistics.* Trends in Linguistics: Studies and Monographs, vol. 122. Berlin: de Gruyter.

Nikifor, Archimandrite. 1990. *Bibleiskaia Entsiklopedia* [The Biblical Encyclopedia]. Moskva: Terra.

Nikitina, S. E. 1994. Kontsept sud'by v russkom narodnom soznanii [The Concept of Fate in the Russian Folk Consciousness]. In *Poniatie sud'by v kontekste raznykh kul'tur,* edited by N. D. Arutiunova, 130–36. Moskva: Nauka.

Niznik, Marina. 2003. Between the Two Worlds: The Identity Dilemma of Russian-Born Adolescents in Israel. In *Contemporary Jewries: Convergence and Divergence,* edited by Eliezer Ben-Rafael, Yosef Gorny, and Yaacov Ro'i. Leiden: Brill, 235–55.

Nosenko, Elena. 2000. Faktory formirovania evreiskoi identichnosti u potomkov smeshannykh brakov [Mixed Marriages Offspring: Formation of Jewish Identity]. *Diasporas: Independent Academic Journal* 3:87–114.

———. 2004. *Byt' ili chuvstvovat'? Osnovnye aspekty formirovania evreiskoi samoindentifikatsii u potomkov smeshannykh brakov v sovremennoi Rossii* [To Be or to Feel? The Primary Factors in the Shaping of Jewish Self-Identity among Descendants of Mixed Marriages in Contemporary Russia]. Moskva: Institut Vostokovedenia RAN.

Novodvorskaia, Valeria. 2001. *Rossia: Vostok-Zapad. Versia Valerii Novodvorskoi.* [Russia: East-West. Valeria Novodvorskaya's Version]. NTV International, 24 June.

Noy, Dov. 1984a. Sipurei Ha-Aliya shel' Yehudei Morocco [Stories of the Migration of the Jews of Morocco]. In *Sefer Zeev Vilnai.* Vol. 1. Yerushalayim: Hotsa'at Sefarim Ariel, 408–10.

———. 1984b. Ha-Derekh Ha-Pil'it Le'Erets-Yisrael Be-Aggadot-am shel Yehudei Teiman Be-Yisrael [The Magic Way to the Land of Israel in Folktales of the Yemeni Jews in Israel]. In *Saei Yona: Ehudei Taiman' be-Israel,* edited by Shalom Sari, 17–27. Tel-Aviv: Agudat Eele betamar.

Nustrem, Eric. 2000. *Bibleiskii slovar'* [A Bible Dictionary]. Sankt-Peterburg: Biblia dlia vsekh.

Oakes, Penelope J., S. Alexander Haslam, and Katherine J. Reynolds. 1999. Social Categorization and Social Context: Is Stereotype Change a Matter of Information or of Meaning? In *Social Identity and Social Cognition,* edited by Dominic Abrams and Michael A. Hogg, 55–79. Oxford: Blackwell.

Obrdlik, Antonin J. 1941–42. "Gallows Humor": A Sociological Phenomenon. *American Journal of Sociology* 67:709–16.

Ochs, Elinor, and Lisa Capps. 2001. *Living Narrative: Creating Lives in*

Everyday Storytelling. Cambridge, Mass.: Harvard University Press.

Olshtain, Elite, and Bella Kotik. 2000. The Development of Bilingualism in an Immigrant Community. In *Language, Identity and Immigration,* edited by Elite Olshtain and Gabriel Horenczyk, 201–17. Jerusalem: Hebrew University and Magnes Press.

Oren (Nadel'), Itzhak, and Naftali Prat. 1976–2001. *Kratkaia Evreiskaia entsiklopedia v 11 tomakh* [Short Jewish Encyclopedia in 11 Volumes]. Ierusalim: Obschestvo po issledovaniu evreiskikh obschin i Evreiskii universitet v Ierusalime.

Oring, Elliott. 1986. Folk Narratives. In *Folk Groups and Folklore Genres: An Introduction,* edited by Elliott Oring, 121–45. Logan: Utah State University Press.

———. 1994. The Arts, Artifacts, and Artifices of Identity. *Journal of American Folklore* 107, no. 424:211–33.

Ostrovsky, Alexander. 1969. *Five Plays of Alexander Ostrovsky.* Translated and edited by Eugene K. Bristow. New York: Pegasus.

Ozhegov, S. I. 1983. *Slovar' russkogo iazyka* [A Dictionary of the Russian Language]. 14th ed. Moskva: Russkii Iazyk.

Panchenko, A. A. 2001. Inkvizitory kak antropologi, antropologi kak inkvizitory [Inquisitors As Anthropologists and Anthropologists as Inquisitors]. *Zhivaia Starina* 1:7–9.

Parkes, James. 1963. *Antisemitism.* Chicago: Quadrangle Books.

Patton, Michael Quinn. 1987. *How to Use Qualitative Methods in Evaluation.* Newbury Park, Calif.: Sage.

Pearce, Barnett W., and Kyung-Wha Kang. 1987. Conceptual Migrations: Understanding "Travelers' Tales" for Cross-Cultural Adaptation. In *Cross-Cultural Adaptation: Current Approaches,* edited by Young Yun Kim and William B. Gudykunst, 20–41. Newbury Park, Calif.: Sage.

Pesmen, Dale. 2000. *Russia and Soul: An Exploration.* Ithaca, N.Y.: Cornell University Press.

Pfandl, Heinrich. 1994. Russkoiazychnyi emigrant tretiei i chetvertoi volny: Neskol'ko razmyshlenii [Russian-Language Emigrants of the Third and Fourth Waves: A Few Reflections]. *Russkii Iazyk za Rubezhom* 5–6:101–08.

Phillipson, Robert, and Mart Runnut. 1995. Introduction to *Linguistic Human Rights: Overcoming Linguistic Discrimination,* edited by Tove Skutnabb-Kangas and Robert Phillipson, 1–22. Berlin: Mouton.

Press-Service of the IBA. 2002. Shas ne strashen—on smeshon. [Shas Is Not Frightening, It Is Ridiculous] *Novosti Nedeli,* 12 December: 4.

Preston, Cathy Lynn. 1994. "Cinderella" as a Dirty Joke: Gender, Multivocality and the Polysemic Text. *Western Folklore* 53, no. 1:27–49.

Preston, Dennis. 1996. Whaddayaknow? The Modes of Folk Linguistic Awareness. *Language Awareness* 5, no. 1:40–74.

Prilutskii, Alex. 2003. Ukol v dushu [A Sting in the Soul]. *Novosti Nedeli,*

11 December: 20.

Propp, V. Ia. 1986. *Istoricheskie korni volshebnoi skazki* [The Historical Roots of the Fairy Tale]. Leningrad: Izdatel'stvo Leningradskogo Universiteta.

Punch, Keith F. 1998. Introduction to *Social Research: Quantitative and Qualitative Approaches.* London: Sage.

Rabinowitz, Dan. 1997. *Overlooking Nazareth: The Ethnography of Exclusion in Galilee.* Cambridge: Cambridge University Press.

Rapport, Nigel. 1998. Coming Home from a Dream: A Study of the Immigrant Discourse of "Anglo-Saxons" in Israel. In *Migrants of Identity: Perception of Home in a World of Movement,* edited by Nigel Rapport and Andrew Dawson, 61–83. Oxford: Berg.

Rasmussen, David M. 1974. *Symbol and Interpretation.* The Haguc: Martinus Nijhoff.

Rathzel, Nora. 1995. Images of Heimat and "Auslander." In *Negotiating Identities: Essays on Immigration and Culture in Present-day Europe,* edited by Aleksandra Alund and Raoul Granquist, 45–70. Amsterdam: Rodopi.

Razumova, Irina. 2001. *Potaennoie znanie sovremennoi russkoi sem'i. Byt. Folklor. Istoria* [Intimate Knowledge of the Contemporary Russian Family: Daily Life, Folklore, History]. Moskva: Indrik.

Reider, V. 2005. My uchilis' v Rossii [We Studied in Russia]. Institute for Social and Political Research (ISPR.org), www.intersol.co.il/ispr, 29 November 2005.

Remennick, Larissa. 1998. Identity Quest among Russian Jews of the 1990s: Before and After Immigration. In *Jewish Survival: The Identity Problem at the Close of the Twentieth Century,* edited by Ernest Krausz and Gitta Tulea, 241–58. New Brunswick, N.J.: Transaction.

———. 1999. "Women with a Russian Accent" in Israel: On the Gender Aspects of Immigration. *The European Journal of Women's Studies* 6, no. 4:441–61.

———. 2002a. Immigrants from Chernobyl-Affected Areas in Israel: The Link between Health and Social Adjustment. *Social Science and Medicine* 54:309–17.

———. 2002b. Survival of the Fittest: Russian Immigrant Teachers Speak about Their Professional Adjustment in Israel. *International Migration* 40, no. 1:109–21.

———. 2002c. Transnational Community in the Making: Russian-Jewish Immigrants of the 1990s in Israel. *Journal of Ethnic and Migration Studies* 28, no. 3:515–30.

———. 2004. From Russian to Hebrew via HebRush: Intergenerational Patterns of Language Use among Former Soviet Immigrants in Israel. *Journal of Multilingual and Multicultural Development* 24, no. 5:431–53.

Remizov, A. M. 1978. *Izbrannoie* [Selected Works]. Moskva: Khudozhestvennaia Literatura.

Resnik, Julia, et al. 2001. Absorption of CIS Immigrants into Israeli Schools: A Semipermeable Enclave Model. *Anthropology and Education Quarterly* 32, no. 4:424–46.

Reznitskaia, Anna. 2004. Alia 70–kh. Tochka zrenia izrail'tian [Aliya of the 1970s: Israelis' Point of View]. *Kontekst,* 29 January: 13:35.

Riasanovsky, Nicholas. 1965. *Russia and the West in the Teaching of the Slavophiles: A Study of Romantic Ideology.* Gloucester, Mass.: Peter Smith.

Ricoeur, Paul. 1967. *The Symbolism of Evil.* Translated by Emerson Buchanan. Boston: Beacon Press.

———. 1984. *Time and Narrative.* Translated by Kathleen MchLaughlin and David Pellauer. Chicago: University of Chicago Press.

———. 1992. *Oneself as Another.* Translated by Kathleen Blamey. Chicago: University of Chicago Press.

Ries, Nancy. 1997. *Russian Talk: Culture and Conversation during Perestroika.* Ithaca, N.Y.: Cornell University Press.

Riggins, Stephen H. 1997. The Rhetoric of Othering. In *The Language and Politics of Exclusion: Others in the Discourse,* edited by S. H. Riggins, 1–30. London: Sage.

Riman, Aleksandr. 2005. V lesu rodilas' Khanuka, ili Kak sovmestit' evreiskie obychai s khristianskimi [Hanukka Born in the Forest, or How to Match Jewish and Christian Customs]. *Novosti Nedeli,* 29 December: 22.

Röhrich, Lutz. 1990. Joke and Modern Society. In *Storytelling in Contemporary Society,* edited by Lutz Röhrich and Sabine Wienker-Piepho, 127–36. Tübingen: Günter Narr Verlag.

Rosen, Ilana. 1999. *Ma'ase sheha'a . . . : Ha'Siporet Ha'Amamit shel Yehudei Karpatorus* [There Once Was . . . : The Oral Tradition of the Jews of Carpatho-Russia]. Tel-Aviv: Tel Aviv University, Diaspora Research Institute.

Rosenthal, Gabriele. 1997. National Identity or Multicultural Autobiography: Theoretical Concepts of Biographical Constitution Grounded in Case Reconstructions. In *The Narrative Study of Lives.* Vol. 5. Edited by Amia Lieblich and Ruthellen Josselson, 21–39. Newbury Park, Calif.: Sage.

Rotenberg, Vadim. 2000. On the Self-Definition of Jews from the Former Soviet Union Now Living in Israel. *The Jews of the Soviet Union in Transition* 4, no. 19:213–20.

Rothstein, Robert A. 2000. The Girl He Left Behind: Women in East European Songs of Emigration. *SEEFA Journal* 5, no. 1:25–38.

Ryazanova, Lara. 1996. "Rush Hour": Stylistic Features of a Russian Interview Program. In *Orality, Literacy, and Modern Media,* edited by Dietrich Scheynemann, 146–62. Columbia, Md.: Camden House.

Ryvkina, Rozalina. 1996. *Evrei v postsovetskoi Rossii—kto oni? Sotsiologicheskii analiz problem rossiiskogo evreistva* [Jews in Post-Soviet Russia: Who Are They? A Sociological Analysis of the Russian

Jewry]. Moskva: Izdatel'stvo URSS.

Said, Edward. 1995. *Orientalism: Western Conceptions of the Orient.* London: Penguin.

Salamon, Hagar. 1997–98. Gilgula shel Toda'a Giz'it: Mi-Etiopia La-arets Ha- muvtahat [Passage from Ethiopia to the Promised Land: Racial Consciousness in Transition]. *Mehkarei Yerushalaim Be'Folklor Yehudi (Jerusalem Studies in Jewish Folklore)* 19–20:125–46.

Sardar, Ziauddin. 1999. *Orientalism.* Milton Keynes, England, and Philadelphia: Open University Press.

Sarnov, Benedict. 2002. *Nash Sovetskii novoiaz. Malen'kaia entsiklopedia real'nogo sotsializma* [Our Soviet Newspeak: A Small Encyclopedia of Real Socialism]. Moskva: Materik.

Savoskul, Sergei. 2001. *Russkie novogo zarubezhia: vybor sud'by* [Russians of the New Abroad: The Choice of Destiny]. Moskva: Nauka.

Schely-Newman, Esther. 1995 Tunisian Women in Israel. In *Active Voices: Women in Jewish Culture,* edited by M. Sacks, 157–70. Urbana: University of Illinois Press.

Schuplov, Alexander. 1998. *Zhargon-Entsiklopedia sovremennoi tusovki* [Encyclopedia of Contemporary Get-together]. Moskva: Kolokol-Press.

Scollon, Ron, and Suzanne Wong Scollon. 1995. *Intercultural Communication: A Discourse Approach.* Oxford: Blackwell.

Sered, Susan Starr. 1992. *Women as Ritual Experts: The Religious Lives of Elderly Jewish Women in Jerusalem.* New York: Oxford University Press.

Shanin, Yurii. 2002. *Ne ustavaite slushat' starikov: Vospominania pozhilogo kievlianina. Kniga vtoraia* [Never Tire of Listening to the Old People: Memoires of an Elderly Resident of Kiev]. Bk. 2. Kiev: Optima.

Shaus, Iakov. 2002. Iesli vy ne nakhodite analogii, to analogii naidut vas [If You Fail to Find Analogies, Analogies Will Find You]. *Vesti,* 18 April: 7.

Sheffer, Gabriel. 2003. Diaspory v mirovoi politike [Ethno-National Diasporas in Politics]. *Diasporas: Independent Academic Journal* 1:162–84.

Sheikhatovich, I. 2002. Iazyk moi—vrag moi? [My Language, My Enemy?] *Novosti Nedeli,* 14 November: 23.

Shenhar, Aliza. 1982. *Ha-sipur ha-amami shel' edot israel.* [Folktales of Jewish Communities]. Tel-Aviv: Cherikover, 56–65.

Shipler, David K. 1986. *Arab and Jew: Wounded Spirits in a Promised Land.* New York: Penguin.

Shklovskii, Victor. 1983. Iskusstvo kak priem [The Technique of the Writer's Craft]. In Victor Shklovskii, *O teorii prozy.* Moskva: Sovetskii Pisatel', 9–25.

Shlapentokh, Vladimir. 1989. *Public and Private Life of the Soviet People: Changing Values in Post-Stalin Russia.* New York: Oxford University Press.

Shmeleva, Elena, and Aleksei Shmelev. 2002. *Russkii anekdot: tekst i rechevoi zhanr* [The Russian Joke: A Text and a Speech Genre]. Moskva: Iazyki Slavianskoi Kul'tury.

Shohat, Ella. 1989. *Israeli Cinema: East/West and the Politics of Representation.* Austin: University of Texas Press.

Shohat, Ella, and Robert Stam. 1994. *Unthinking Eurocentrism: Multiculturalism and the Media.* London: Routledge.

Shor, Nissan. 2002. Moadon Sagur [A Private Members' Club]. *Maariv,* 8 March: 70–76.

Shraiman, Shelly. 2001. Goriachie kavkazskie parni v Israile [Quick-Tempered Caucasian Guys in Israel]. *Okna,* 21 June: 20–22.

———. 2002. Krazha Lichnosti-2 [Personality Theft-2]. *Okna,* 31 January: 6–8.

Shturman, Dora, and Sergei Tiktin. 1987. *Sovetskii Soiuz v zerkale politicheskogo anekdota* [The Soviet Union in the Mirror of the Political Joke]. 2nd ed. Ierusalim: Ekspress.

Shtyrkov, Sergei. 1999. Istoricheskie predania i perspektivy izuchenia traditsionnykh narrativnykh praktik [Historic Tales and the Prospects of Studying Traditional Narrative Practices]. In *Mifologia i povsednevnost', vyp. 2: Materialy nauchnoi konferentsii 24–26 fevralia 1999,* edited by K. A. Bogdanov and A. A. Panchenko. Sankt-Peterburg: Aliteia, 25–34.

Shuval, Judith T., and Judith H. Bernstein, eds. 1997. *Immigrant Physicians: Former Soviet Doctors in Israel, Canada and the United States.* Westport, Conn.: Praeger.

Shuval, Judith T., and Elazar Leshem. 1998. The Sociology of Migration in Israel: A Critical View. In *Immigration to Israel: Sociological Perspectives,* edited by Elazar Leshem and Judith T. Shuval, 3–50. Studies of Israeli Society, vol. 8. New Brunswick, N.J.: Transaction.

Silverman, David. 1993. *Interpreting Qualitative Data: Methods for Analysing Talk, Text and Interaction.* London: Sage.

Sindalovskii, Naum. 1999. *Peterburg v fol'klore* [St. Petersburg in Folklore]. Sankt-Peterburg: Zhurnal "Neva," ITD "Letnii Sad."

Sinel'nikov, A. 2004. Evreistvo tol'ko po materi—put' v tupik? [Exclusive Matrilineal Jewishness—A Road to Impass. Any Way Out?] *Diasporas, Independent Academic Journal* 3:100–124.

Smidchens, Guntis. 1990. Ethnic and Immigrant Folklore. In *The Emergence of Folklore in Everyday Life: A Fieldguide and Sourcebook,* edited by G. Shoemaker, 133–44. Bloomington, Ind.: Trickster Press.

Smith, Anthony. 2002. *When Is a Nation?* Guest lecture at the University of Haifa, Israel.

Smith, Eliot. 1999. Effective and Cognitive Implications of a Group Becoming Part of the Self: New Models of Prejudice and of the Self-Concept. In *Social Identity and Social Cognition,* edited by Dominic Abrams and Michael A. Hogg, 183–96. Oxford: Blackwell.

Smith, Hedrick. 1976. *The Russians.* New York: Quadrangle.

Smooha, Sammy. 1988. Jewish and Arab Ethnocentrism in Israel. In *Arab-Jewish Relations in Israel: A Quest in Human Understanding,* edited by John Hofman et al., 175–216. Bristol, Ind.: Wyndham Hall.

———. 1990. Minority Status in an Ethnic Democracy: The Status of the Arab Minority in Israel. *Ethnic and Racial Studies* 13, no. 3:389–413.

Smooha, Sammy, and Vered Kraus. 1985. Ethnicity as a Factor in Status Attainment in Israel. *Research in Social Stratification and Mobility* 4:151–75.

Solganik, Irina. 2001. Pust' nenavidiat—lish by boialis': Eschie raz pro "russkii" uspekh [Let Them Hate Us but Fear: Once More about the "Russian" Success]. *Master M* 10, no. 19:38–39.

Solganik, Irina, and Aleksandr Gol'dshtein. 2002. Batalion Aliia [The Aliya Battalion]. *Okna,* 11 April: 8–12.

Solovei, Anna. 2003. Skvernye slovechki [Foul Words]. *Okna,* 1 May: 29–30.

Soloviev, V. S. 1989. Mir vostoka i zapada [The World of East and West]. In V. S. Soloviev, *Chtenia o bogochelovechestve. Filosofskie Tetradi: Sochinenia v 2 tomakh.* Vol 1. Moskva: Pravda, 602–5.

Solzhenitsyn, Aleksandr. 1963. *Odin den' Ivana Denisovicha* [One Day in the Life of Ivan Denisovich]. Moskva: Sovetskii pisatel'.

Spolsky, Bernard, and Elana Shohamy. 1999. *The Languages of Israel: Policy, Ideology and Practice.* Clevedon, England: Multilingual Matters.

Stahl, Sandra K. D. 1977a. The Personal Narrative as Folklore. *Journal of the Folklore Institute* 14, nos. 1–2:9–30.

———. 1977b. The Oral Personal Narrative and Its Generic Context. *Fabula* 18:18–39.

———. 1989. *Literary Folkloristics and the Personal Narrative.* Bloomington: Indiana University Press.

Steinbach, Anja. 2001. Intergenerational Transmission and Integration of Repatriate Families from the Former Soviet Union in Germany. *Journal of Comparative Family Studies* 32, no. 4:505–15 (Special issue on immigrant and ethnic minority families).

Steinberg, Shoshana, and Dan Bar-On. 2002. An Analysis of the Group Process in Encounters between Jews and Palestinians Using a Typology for Discourse Classification. *International Journal of Intercultural Relations* 26, no. 2:199–214.

Stevens, Anthony. 1995. *Private Myths: Dreams and Dreaming.* Cambridge, Mass.: Harvard University Press.

Suls, Jerry. 1983. Cognitive Processes in Humor Appreciation. In *Handbook of Humor Research* [in Two Volumes]. Vol. 1. edited by Paul E. McGhee and Jeffrey H. Goldstein, 1:39–57. New York: Springer-Verlag.

Suny, Ron. 2001. Making Minorities: The Politics of National Boundaries in the Soviet Experience. In *The Construction of Minorities: Cases for Comparison across Time and around the World,* edited by André Burguière and Raymond Grew, 245–68. Ann Arbor: University of Michigan Press.

Surkov, A. A., ed. 1962. *Kratkaia literaturnaia entsiklopedia v 9 tomakh* [A Short Encyclopedia of Literature in Nine Volumes]. Vol. 1. Moskva: Sovetskaia Entsiklopedia.

Swinburne, Richard. 1970. *The Concept of Miracle.* London: Macmillan.

Sydow, Carl Wilhelm von. 1977. The Categories of Prose Tradition. In C. W. von Sydow, *Selected Papers on Folklore.* New York: Arno, 86–88.

Tajfel, Henri. 1981. *Human Groups and Social Categories: Studies in Social Psychology.* Cambridge: Cambridge University Press.

Tanich, Mikhail. 2003. A zdesia v lagere [And Here in the Prison Camp]. www.lesopoval.ru/text/v_lagere.html.

Tartakovsky, Eugene. 2001. Group Psychodynamics of Witchcraft and Witch-hunting: Immigrant Adolescents from the Former Soviet Union in Israel. *Group Analysis* 34, no. 1:129–42.

Taylor, Stephanie, and Margaret Wetherell. 1999. A Suitable Time and Place: Speakers' Use of "Time" to Do Discursive Work in Narratives of Nation and Personal Life. *Time and Discourse* 8, no. 1:39–58.

Tishkov, Valerii A. 2001a. Istoricheskii fenomen diaspory [The Historic Phenomenon of the Diaspora]. In *Natsional'nye diaspory v Rossii i za rubezhom v XIX–XX vv. Sbornik statei,* edited by Yu. A. Poliakov i G.Ya. Tarle, 9–44. Moskva: Institut Rossiiskoi Istorii RAN.

———. 2001b. *Etnologia i politika. Nauchnaia publitsistika* [Ethnology and Politics: Essays in Social Sciences]. Moskva: Nauka.

———. 2003. Uvlechenie diasporoi: o politicheskikh smyslakh diasporal'nogo diskursa [A Passion for Diaspora: The Political Connotations of Diasporic Discourse]. *Diasporas: Independent Academic Journal* 2:160–83.

Tolstaia, Elena. 2000. Krovavyi vykup kliucha: Goticheskii roman [The Bloody Redemption of the Key: A Gothic Novel]. *Solnechnoie Spletenie* 10–11:4–17.

Tolstaia, S. M. 1994. "Glagoly sud'by" i ikh korreliaty v iazyke kul'tury ["The Verbs of Fate" and Their Correlates in the Language of Culture]. In *Poniatie sud'by v kontekste raznykh kul'tur,* edited by N. D. Arutiunova, 143–47. Moskva: Nauka.

———. 1995. Sud'ba [Fate]. In V. Ia. Petrukhin et al., *Slavianskaia Mifologia: Entsiklopedicheskii Slovar'.* Moscow: Ellis-Lak, 370–71.

———. 1999. Ierusalim v slavianskoi fol'klornoi traditsii [Jerusalem in the Slavic Folklore Tradition]. In *Jerusalem in Slavic Culture,* edited by Wolf Moskowich, Oto Luthar, and Samuel Schwarzband, 51–68. Jerusalem and Ljubljana: Center for Slavic Languages and Literatures of the Hebrew University of Jerusalem and Scientific Research Center of the Slovenian Academy of Sciences and Arts.

Tolstoi, A. N. 1963. Pokhozhdenia Nevzorova, ili Ibikus [Nevzorov's Adventures, or Ibicus]. In A. N. Tolstoi, *Povesti i rasskazy v 2kh tomakh, tom 2 (1922–1944)*. Moskva: Gosudarstvennoe Izdatel'stvo Khudozhestvennoi Literatury, 213–332.

———. 1992. *Zolotoi kliuchik ili prikliuchenia Buratino* [The Golden Key, or Buratino's Adventures]. Moskva: Politizdat.

Tolstoi, N. I. 1995. Granitsa [The Border]. In *Slavianskie Drevnosti: Etnolingvisticheskii slovar' v 5 tomakh*. Vol. 1. Edited by N. I. Tolstoi, 537–40. Moskva: Mezhdunarodnye Otnoshenia.

Toporkov, A., ed. 1995. *Russkii Eroticheskii Fol'klor* [Russian Erotic Folklore]. Moskva: Ladomir.

Toporkov, A. L. 1998. Pikovaia dama v detskom fol'klore [The Queen of Spades in Children's Folklore]. In *Russkii shkol'nyi fol'klor: Ot "vyzyvanii" Pikovoi damy do semeinykh rasskazov*, compiled by A. F. Belousov, 15–55. Moskva: Ladomir, "AST."

Toporov, V. N. 1984. Peterburg i peterburgskii tekst russkoi literatury: Vvedenie v temu [St. Petersburg and the St. Petersburg Text in Russian Literature: Introduction]. In *Semiotika goroda i gorodskoi kul'tury. Peterburg*, edited by Y. M. Lotman. Trudy po znakovym sistemam XVIII. Tartu: Tartuskii Universitet, 4–29.

———. 1994. Sud'ba i sluchai. [Fate and Chance]. In *Poniatie sud'by v kontekste raznykh kul'tur*, edited by N. D. Arutiunova, 38–75. Moskva: Nauka.

Trachtenberg, Joshua. 1966. *The Devil and the Jews: A Medieval Conception of the Jew and Its Relation to Modern Antisemitism*. New York: Harper & Row.

———. 2004. *Jewish Magic and Superstition: A Study in Folk Religion*. Philadelphia: University of Pennsylvania Press.

Trolle, Daria. 2002. Borodatyi anekdot [A Stale Joke]. *Magazine*, 12 December: 29–34.

Tumerman, Lev. 1982. Israel: Europe or Asia? In *In Search of Self: The Soviet Jewish Intelligentsia and the Exodus: A Collection of Articles*, edited by David Prital, 145–58. Jerusalem: Mount Scopus.

Turaeva, Z. Ya. 1979. *Kategoria vremeni. Vremia grammaticheskoie i vremia khudozhestvennoie* [The Category of Time: A Tense in Grammar and Time in Art]. Moskva: Vysshaia Shkola.

Ukkonen, Taina. 2000. Storytelling Personal Experiences. In *ARV Nordic Yearbook of Folklore* 56, edited by Ulrika Wolf-Knuts, 139–49. Uppsala: Royal Gustavus Adolphus Academy.

Ulanovskii, Levy. 1982. Hebrew in the Soviet Union. In *In Search of Self: The Soviet Jewish Intelligentsia and the Exodus: A Collection of Articles*, edited by David Prital, 258–62. Jerusalem: Mount Scopus.

Uspenskii, B. A. 2004. Evropa kak metafora i kak metonimia (primenitel'no k istorii Rossii) [Europe as a Metaphor and Metonymy (as regards

the history of Russia)]. In B. A. Uspenskii, *Istoriko-filologicheskie ocherki*. Moskva: Iazyki Slavianskoi Kul'tury, 9–26.
Vaiskopf, Mikhail. 2001. "My byli kak vo sne": Tema iskhoda v literature russkogo Izrailia ["We Were as if in a Dream": The Motif of Exodus in the Russian Literature of Israel]. *Novoe Literaturnoe Obozrenie* 47:241–52.
Valdés, Guadalupe. 1997. Bilinguals and Bilingualism: Language Policy in an Anti-immigrant Age. *International Journal of the Sociology of Language* 127:25–52.
van Baak, J. J. 1983. *The Place of Space in Narration: A Semiotic Approach to the Problem of Literary Space with an Analysis of the Role of Space in I. E. Babel's* Konarmia. Amsterdam: Rodopi.
van Dijk, Teun A. 1989. Structures and Strategies of Discourse and Prejudice. In *Ethnic Minorities: Social Psychological Perspectives*, edited by Jan Pieter van Oudenhoven and Tineke M. Willemsen, 115–38. Amsterdam: Swets & Zeitlinger.
Vershinin, Lev. 2003. Ot liubvi do nenavisti [From Love to Hatred]. *Okna*, 18 December: 30–32.
Voronel, Aleksandr. 1973. The Social Pre-Conditions of the National Awakening of the Jews in the USSR. In *I Am a Jew: Essays on Jewish Identity in the Soviet Union*, edited by Aleksandr Voronel and Viktor Yakhot. Moscow: Academic Committee on Soviet Jewry and Anti-Defamation League of B'nai B'rith, 25–37.
———. 1982. Aliya of the Jewish Intelligentsia from the USSR. In *In Search of Self: The Soviet Jewish Intelligentsia and the Exodus*, edited by David Prital, 121–35. Jerusalem: Mount Scopus.
Vysotskii, Vladimir. 1988. Ballada o detstve [A Ballad about Childhood]. In V. Vysotskii *Sobranie stikhov i pesen v trekh tomakh*. Vol. 2. New York: Russian Publishers and Apollon Foundation, 273.
Watts, William. 1982. *The United States and Asia: Changing Attitudes and Policies*. Lexington, Mass.: Lexington.
Weiskopf, Inna. 2006. *Hitkatvut ve-hekerut be-internet: sipurim ishiim shel mehagrot mi-brit ha-moazot lesheavar be-israel* [Communicating and Dating in the Internet: Personal Narratives of Female Immigrants from the FSU in Israel]. Master's thesis, University of Haifa.
Wierzbicka, Anna. 1992. *Semantics, Culture, and Cognition: Universal Human Concepts in Culture-specific Configurations*. New York: Oxford University Press.
———. 1997. *Understanding Cultures through Their Key Words: English, Russian, Polish, German, and Japanese*. New York: Oxford University Press.
Wigoder, Geoffrey, ed. 1989. *The Encyclopedia of Judaism*. Jerusalem: Jerusalem Publishing.
Williams, John. E. 1966. Connotations of Racial Concepts and Color Names. *Journal of Personality and Social Psychology* 3:531–40.
Wilson, William A. 1986. Documenting Folklore. In *Folk Groups and*

Folklore Genres: An Introduction, edited by Elliott Oring, 225–54. Logan: Utah State University Press.

———. 2000. A Sense of Place or a Sense of Self: Personal Narratives and the Construction of Personal and Regional Identity. *Southern Folklore* 57, no. 1:3–11.

Wodak, Ruth, et al. 1999. *The Discursive Construction of National Identity.* Edinburgh: Edinburgh University Press.

Wolfson, Nessa. 1981. Tense-Switching in Narrative. *Language and Style* 14:226–31.

Yakhot, Viktor. 1973. Reflections on the Reasons for the Exodus of Jews to Israel. In *I Am a Jew: Essays on Jewish Identity in the Soviet Union*, edited by Aleksander Voronel and Viktor Yakhot. Moscow: Academic Committee on Soviet Jewry and Anti-Defamation League of B'nai B'rith, 38–44.

Yelenevskaya, Maria N. 2000. The Comfort of Familiar Words: Allusions in the Russian-Language Press in Israel. *Russia and the West: The Dialogue of Cultures* 8, no. 2:243–53.

———. 2001. Cultural Codes in Single Ads: A Comparative Study of Hebrew, English, and Russian Newspapers in Israel. Paper presented at the conference "Meaning and Its Meanings in Life and in Various Fields of Knowledge." University of Haifa, Israel.

———. 2004. "Sovstal'gia": Sovetskie klishe v immigrantskom diskurse ["Sovstalgia": Soviet Clichés in Immigrants' Discourse]. *Diasporas, Independent Academic Journal* 4:188–206.

———. 2005. A Cultural Diaspora in the Making: Former Soviets in Israel and in Germany. *Jews and Slavs* 15:265–79.

———. 2007. *At Home with Violence: Israeli Russian-Language Media's Use of Cultural Codes in Interpreting Intifada.* In press.

Yelenevskaya, Maria N., and Larisa Fialkova. 2000. The Image of the *Other* in Immigrants' Folklore. *Russia and the West: The Dialogue of Cultures* 8, no. 2:254–65.

———. 2002. When Time and Space Are No Longer the Same: Stories about Immigration. *Studia Mythologica Slavica* 5:207–30.

———. 2003a. Multiculturalism in Folklore: "Russians" in Israel. *Thirteenth World Congress of Jewish Studies.* www.jewish-studies.org/PDFs/69pdf, 1–17.

———. 2003b. From "Muteness" to Eloquence: Immigrants' Narratives about Languages. *Language Awareness* 12, no. 1:30–48.

———. 2004a. My Poor Cousin, My Feared Enemy: The Image of an Arab in Personal Narratives of Former Soviets in Israel. *Folklore* 115, no. 1:77–98.

———. 2004b. From Anti-Utopia to Utopia: Immigrants' Memories of the Soviet Union. Paper presented at the Thirteenth International Oral History Conference (IOHA), "Memory and Globalization," Rome, 23 June.

———. 2005. *Russkaia ulitsa v evreiskoi strane: Issledovanie fol'klora emigrantov 1990–kh v Izraile.* [A Russian Street in the Jewish State: Research into the Folklore of the Émigrés of the 1990s in Israel]. 2 vols. Moskva: Rossiiskaia Akademia Nauk, Institut Etnologii i Antropologii.

Zaichik, Mark. 2002. Na vostoke nel'zia byt' slabym. Intervius Avigdorom Libermanom [One Cannot Afford to Be Weak in the East: An Interview with Avigdor Liberman]. *Okna,* 27 June: 4–6.

Zamiatin, Evgenii. 1989. Ostrovitiane [The Islanders]. In Evgenii Zamiatin, *Izbrannoe.* Moskva: Pravda, 95–147.

Zemach, Mina. 1980. *Emdot ha-rov ha-yehudi be-yisrael klapei ha-mi'ut ha-aravi* [Attitudes of the Jewish Majority to the Arab Minority in Israel]. Yerushalayim: Mosad van-Leer.

———. 2005. Predvybornyi opros [A Pre-Election Survey]. *Vesti,* 29 December: 5.

Zemskaia, Elena A. 2001. *Iazyk russkogo zarubezhia: Obschie protsessy i rechevye portrety.* [The Language of the Russian Abroad: General Processes and Speech Portraits]. Moskva-Vena: Iazyki Slavianskoi Kul'tury, Weiner Slawistischer Almanach, Sonderband 53.

Zerubavel, Eviatar. 1981. *Hidden Rhythms: Schedules and Calendars in Social Life.* Chicago: University of Chicago Press.

Zilberg, Narspy. 1995. In-group Humor of Immigrants from the Former Soviet Union to Israel. *Israel Social Science Research* 1, no. 10:1–22.

NAME INDEX

SUBJECT INDEX

www.ingramcontent.com/pod-product-compliance
Lightning Source LLC
LaVergne TN
LVHW010355080826
844660LV00016B/980/J

* 9 7 8 0 8 1 4 3 3 1 6 9 9 *